NATIONAL POLITICS AND INTERNATIONAL TECHNOLOGY

NATIONAL POLITICS AND INTERNATIONAL TECHNOLOGY

NUCLEAR REACTOR DEVELOPMENT IN WESTERN EUROPE

HENRY R. NAU

The Johns Hopkins University Press
Baltimore and London

To Micki

The Johns Hopkins University Press, Baltimore, Maryland 21218
The Johns Hopkins University Press Ltd., London

Library of Congress Catalog Card Number 73-19344
ISBN 0-8018-1506-1

Library of Congress Cataloging in Publication data
will be found on the last printed page of this book.

CONTENTS

ACKNOWLEDGMENTS

This study was begun as a doctoral dissertation. As such, it owes more than most studies to the intellectual tutelage and stimulation of many individuals. My thesis adviser, Robert E. Osgood, dean and professor of American Foreign Policy at The Johns Hopkins School of Advanced International Studies, read several versions of the manuscript and provided invaluable insight into the exercise of skilled intellectual inquiry. Professor Robert L. Rothstein of The Johns Hopkins University (Baltimore) also read and criticized the manuscript. His intellectual influence on my graduate training was greater than I think he would feel comfortable recognizing. I am further indebted to Professor Lawrence Scheinman of Cornell University. He not only opened many doors for me during my research activities in Western Europe but patiently read and criticized the entire manuscript during the final revision stage. Others who read parts of this study or contributed in a significant way to the ideas it contains include: David P. Calleo, Isaiah Frank, Francis O. Wilcox, and Charles B. Marshall, all of The Johns Hopkins School of Advanced International Studies; Bruce M. Russett of Yale University; Larry Fabian of The Brookings Institution; and George Eads of The George Washington University. For language skills, which proved particularly valuable in this study, I owe much to Lisa Stevens, professor and director of Language Studies at The Johns Hopkins School of Advanced International Studies. Finally, for the original stimulus to study international relations, which eventually led me to this book, I owe a special debt to Norman J. Padelford, professor of Political Science at the Massachusetts Institute of Technology. His personal warmth and professional guidance during my training as an undergraduate encouraged me to pursue a professional career in this important field. All of these individuals share the credit for whatever merit this study may have. Naturally, I alone take responsibility for its shortcomings.

I have also received research support from many sources. A dissertation and training grant from the Foreign Area Fellowship Program financed the original research and write-up of this study, including eighteen months (1969–70) of field research in Western Europe. I am particularly grateful to Joseph LaPalombara, professor of Political Science at Yale University, and James Gould, former executive associate of the Foreign Area Program, for advice and assistance received under this grant. In Western Europe, I was a visiting fellow at the research institute of the German Society for Foreign Policy in Bonn, Germany (Forschungsinstitut der Deutschen Gesellschaft fuer Auswaertige Politik). From the staff and research associates of this institute, in particular the then director, Wolfgang Wagner, and the editor of *Europa Archiv* (journal of the Society for Foreign Policy), Hermann Volle, I received vital aid and encouragement, especially during the arduous months of initial orientation in a foreign research environment. At the European Communities in Brussels, my job could not have been done without the kind personal and professional support of Madeleine Ledivelec, former head of the Euratom Library (subsequently the Scientific and Technical Library of the combined Communities). I am also grateful to Lucien Bernard, librarian of the U.S. Mission to the European Communities in Brussels, who provided additional library and personal assistance.

I owe my greatest debt in the research of this study to the countless private and public officials in Europe and, to a lesser extent, in the United States who were generous with their time and opinions and gave me lengthy and sometimes multiple interviews. Altogether, I had informal conversations with over one hundred individuals from government agencies, industries, and research centers. I remained in correspondence with a number of these individuals after I left Europe. Many of them read and commented on portions of the manuscript. Some criticized the entire study. I should like to thank each by name, but by mutual agreement we decided that their identities should remain anonymous. I have listed below the institutions they represented[1] and should like to thank them here by expressing the personal hope that this study

[1]Germany: Federal Ministry for Scientific Research, Federal Ministry for Foreign Affairs, North-Rhine Westphalia Ministry for Science and Research, Juelich Research Center, Karlsruhe Research Center, Federal Society of German Industry, German Atomic Forum, Editorial Office of Atomwirtschaft, BBK, AEG, Siemens, Interatom, RWE, and American Embassy in Bonn.
France: CEA, Foreign Ministry, Ministry of Industry, Saclay Research Center, EdF, GAAA, and American Embassy in Paris.
Italy: CNEN, ENEL, Foreign Ministry, CNEN Laboratories (Bologna), CISE, and Euratom Ispra Center.
Belgium: Ministry for Economic Affairs and Energy, Foreign Ministry, Office of the Prime Minister (Science Programming and Policy), CEN Laboratories (Mol), and Belgonucléaire.
Holland: Ministry of Economic Affairs, Foreign Ministry, RCN, TNO, SEP, and Neratoom.
Others: Commission of the European Communities (Directorate-Generals I, II, III, IX, X, XII, XIII, and XV), Member-State Missions to the European Communities, U.S. Mission to the European Communities, UNICE, UNIPEDE, OECD, ENEA, EEC Mission to the OECD, Winfrith Research Center (England), U.S. Department of State (Bureau of International Scientific and Technological Affairs), and National Security Council.
For acronyms, see List of Abbreviations.

serves, in some small measure, to facilitate their work and to advance our common understanding of how men strive to reconcile separate needs and collective aspirations.

I received additional financing for subsequent revisions of the dissertation draft from the 1900 Fund of Williams College and the National Science Foundation grant GS 34902. For the latter assistance, I thank my colleagues at The George Washington University and the co-investigators of this grant—John M. Logsdon, associate professor of Political Science, and Burton M. Sapin, dean of the School of Public and International Affairs. I am also grateful to John Cummins and other students in the Graduate Program in Science, Technology, and Public Policy at George Washington for helpful research assistance. Eileen Sprague and Linda Yelton supplied competent and cheerful stenographical assistance. Silvia Alber-Glanstaetten aided in the translation of Italian sources. Kenneth Arnold of The Johns Hopkins Press offered advice at various stages, and Barbara F. Miller made invaluable editorial contributions.

I would not have completed this study if it were not for my wife, Marion Madej Nau. She was as much a part of this endeavor as I, and she undoubtedly has more reason than I to be grateful that it is now complete. I also express a special word of thanks to my parents, John and Johanna. Toward these three people, I have a particularly grateful mind which, as Milton wrote, "by owing owes not, but still pays, at once indebted and discharg'd."

Henry R. Nau
November 1973

LIST OF ABBREVIATIONS

ACEC	Atelier de Constructions Électriques de Charleroi (Brussels)
AECL	Atomic Energy of Canada Limited
AEG	Allgemeine Elektrizitaetsgesellschaft (Frankfurt/Main)
AGR	Advanced Gas Reactor
AKB	Atomkraftwerk Bayern (Munich)
AKS	Arbeitsgemeinschaft Kernkraft Stuttgart
ALKEM	Alpha-Chemie und Metallurgie (Leopoldshafen, Germany)
APC	Atomic Power Construction
AVR	Arbeitsgemeinschaft Versuchsreaktor (Duesseldorf)
ASEA	Swedish nuclear company
BBC	Brown, Boverie et Cie
BBK	Brown Boveri/Krupp Reaktorbau (Duesseldorf)
Belgian CEA	Belgian Commissariat à l'Énergie Atomique (Brussels)
Belgonucléaire	Société Belge pour l'Industrie Nucléaire (Brussels)
Benelux	Belgium-The Netherlands-Luxembourg
BNDC	British Nuclear Design Corporation Limited
BPD	Bombrini-Parodi-Delfino (Rome)
BR-2	Test reactor in Mol, Belgium
CCNR	Consultative Committee for Nuclear Research
CDU	Christlich-Demokratische Union
CEA	Commissariat à l'Énergie Atomique (Paris)
CEGB	Central Electricity Generating Board (London)
CEM	Compagnie Électro-Mécanique (Paris)
CEN	Centre d'Étude Nucléaire (Brussels)
CERCA	Compagnie pour l'Étude et la Réalisation de Combustibles Atomiques (Bonneuil s/Marne, France)
CERN	Organisation Européenne pour la Recherche Nucléaire (Geneva)
CGE	Compagnie Générale d'Électricité
CIPE	Comitato Interministeriale per la Programmazione Economica
CIRENE	Programma Reattore a Nebbia
CISE	Centro Informazioni Studi Esperienze (Milan)
CNF	Compagnie Nucléaire Française
Comsat	Communication Satellite Corporation
Confindustria	Confederazione Generale dell'Industria Italiana
COREPEC	Consorzio SNAM-Progetti-Italimpianti per la Realizzazione dell'Impianto PEC
CNEN	Comitato Nazionale per l'Energia Nucleare (Rome)
CNRN	Comitato Nazionale per le Ricerche Nucleari
COST	Conférence d'Organisation Scientifique et Technologique

CSU	Christlich-Soziale Union
DEMAG	German nuclear company
DRAGON	High Temperature Reactor at Winfrith, England
ECO	Expérience Critique ORGEL
ECSC	European Coal and Steel Community
EDC	European Defense Community
EdF	Électricité de France (Paris)
EEC	European Economic Community
EFIM	Ente Partecipazioni e Finanziamento Industria Manifatturiera
EL-2,-4	Eau Lourde (reactors)
ELDO	European Launcher Development Organization
ENEA	European Nuclear Energy Agency
ENEL	Ente Nazionale per l'Energia Elettrica (Rome)
ENI	Ente Nazionale Idrocarburi
EPA	European Political Authority
ESRO	European Space Research Organization
ESSOR	Essai ORGEL
Euratom	European Atomic Energy Community
EUREX	Enriched Uranium Extraction (Recupero dell'uranio arricchito)
EURODIF	European Gaseous Diffusion Enrichment Plant Study Group
EURO-HKG	Ad hoc company of European utilities to study high temperature reactors
FDP	Freie Demokratische Partei
filière	Reactor family or string
FR-2	Research reactor at Karlsruhe
GAAA	Groupement Atomique Alsacienne Atlantique (Le Plessis-Robinson, France)
GATT	General Agreement on Trade and Tariffs
GE	General Electric
GENTILLY	Canadian heavy water-moderated reactor
GfK	Gesellschaft fuer Kernforschung (Karlsruhe)
GHH	Gutehoffnungshuette (Oberhausen, Germany)
GIHTR	Groupement Industriel pour les réacteurs à Haute Temperature
GKN	Gemeenschappelijke Kernenergiecentrale Nederland
HALDEN	Reactor Project in Norway under auspices of ENEA
HDR	Heissdampfreaktor (Grosswelzheim)
HFR	High Flux Reactor (Petten, Holland)
HOBEG	Hochtemperaturreaktor Brennelement GmbH
IAEA	International Atomic Energy Agency (Vienna)
IMF	International Monetary Fund
Indatom	Groupement pour l'Industrie Atomique Indatom (Paris)
Intelsat	International Satellite Corporation
Interatom	Internationale Atomreaktorbau (Bensberg/Cologne, Germany)
IRI	Istituto per la Reconstruzione Industriale (Rome)
JCAE	Joint Congressional Committee on Atomic Energy

JNRC	Joint Nuclear Research Center
JRC	Joint Research Center
KEMA	Keuring Van Electrotechnische Materialen Arnhem
KFA	Kernforschungsanlage Juelich
kgs.	Kilograms
KKN	Kernkraftwerk Niederaichbach (ex AKB)
KNK	Kompakte Natriumgekuehlte Kernenergieanlage (Karlsruhe)
KRB	Kernkraftwerk RWE-Bayernwerk (Gundremmingen)
KWU	Kernkraftwerk Union (Erlangen)
MAN	Maschinenfabrik Augsburg-Nuernberg (Nuernberg)
MLF	Multilateral Force
MMN	Métallurgie et Mécanique Nucléaire (Brussels)
MWe	Megawatts electricity
MWth	Megawatts thermal heat
MZFR	Mehrzweckforschungsreaktor
NATO	North Atlantic Treaty Organization
NDC	Nuclear Design Corporation
Neratoom	Dutch nuclear company
NRX	Canadian heavy water-moderated reactor
NUKEM	Nuclear-Chemie und Metallurgie (Wolfgang b/Hanau, Germany)
OECD	Organization for Economic Cooperation and Development (Paris)
OEEC	Organization for European Economic Cooperation
OMRE	Organic-Moderated Reactor Experiment
ORGEL	Organique Eau Lourde
PEC	Prova Elementi Combustibili
PEON	Commission Consultative pour la Production d'Électricité d'Origine Nucléaire
PHENIX	French fast reactor prototype at Marcoule
PREST	Politique de la Recherche Scientifique et Technique
PRO	Programma Reattore Organico
PSB	Projektgellschaft Schneller Bructer
RAPSODIE	Réacteur Rapide Refroidi au Sodium
RAPTUS	Rapido Torio Uranio Sodio
RCN	Reactor Centrum Nederland
R&D	Research and Development
RWE	Rheinisch-Westphaelisches Elektrizitaetswerk (Essen)
SDRs	Special Drawing Rights
SEEN	Société d'Études et d'Entreprises Nucléaires (Paris)
SEFOR	Southwest Experimental Fast Oxide Reactor
SELNI	Società Elettronucleare Italiana
SEMO	Société Belgo-Française d'Énergie Nucléaire Mosane (Tihange, Belgium)
SENA	Société d'Électricité Nucléaire franco-belge des Ardennes (Chooz, France)
SENN	Società Elettronucleare Nazionale
SEP	Samenwerkende Electriciteits-Productiebedrijven (Arnhem, Netherlands)

SERAI	Société d'Étude, de Recherches et d'Applications pour l'Industrie
SFAC	Société des Forges et Ateliers du Creusot (Paris)
SFEC	Société pour la Fabrication des Eléments de Combustible
SGHWR	Steam-Generated Heavy Water Reactor
SICN	Société Industrielle de Combustible Nucléaire (Paris)
SIMEA	Società Italiana Meridionale Energia Atomica
SNAM-Progetti	Società Nazionale Metanodotti-Progetti
SNECMA	Société Nationale d'Étude et de Construction de Moteurs d'Aviation (Paris)
SNR	Schneller Natriumgekuehlter Reaktor
SOCIA	Société pour l'Industrie Atomique
SOGERCA	Société Générale pour l'Entreprise de Réacteurs et de Centrales Atomiques
SPD	Sozialdemokratische Partei Deutschlands
SYNATOM	Syndicat pour l'Étude de Centrales Nucléaires de grande puissance en Belgique
THTR	Thorium Hochtemperatur-Reaktor
TNO	Techniker Nederlandse Organisatie
TNPG	The Nuclear Power Group Limited
UCN	Ultra-Centrifuge Nederland
UKAEA	United Kingdom Atomic Energy Authority
UNICE	Union des Industries de la Communauté Européenne
UNIPEDE	Union Internationale des Producteurs et Distributeurs d'Énergie Électrique (Paris)
URENCO	British/German/French Enrichment Plant Ownership Company
USAEC	United States Atomic Energy Commission
WAK	Wiederaufarbeitungsanlage Karlsruhe
WR-1	Whiteshell reactor-1 (Canada)

INTRODUCTION

This study is an investigation of the relationship between politics and technology in international relations. In contemporary thought, this relationship is often perceived in terms of conflict between the emerging global scope of technology and the persisting nation-state organization of politics. Technology is viewed as an ineluctable force making the territorial unit of the nation-state increasingly obsolete. This thesis was first advanced in the study of military technologies, in particular nuclear weapons and their impact on international relations. Today, the thesis is being tentatively advanced in the study of new civilian technologies (oceans, communications, environment, etc.). At the same time, other strains of contemporary thought have stressed the staying power of the nation-state and observed the extent to which existing international structures have accommodated new technologies to the needs and purposes of national interest. Management of nuclear weapons, it is pointed out, was made possible only by the considerable strengthening and extension of the nation-state, particularly in the case of the two superpowers.

In this book, we will examine how nation-states have also sought to accommodate *civilian* technologies to national aims. The study deliberately emphasizes the impact of national structures of interest on international technological and economic activities. It uses familiar methods of interpreting state behavior in military-strategic areas to interpret state behavior in economic-technical areas. In this sense, the study has little in common with functional approaches to the study of technological and economic relations. These approaches begin with the assumption that there is something basically different about state behavior in technological and economic areas compared with state behavior in military-security areas. The expectation that behavior is different gives rise to a different mode of analysis based more on the functional scope and characteristics of specific problems than the territorial or nation-state distribution of political authority. This study, by contrast, does not assume that analysis in economic and technical areas requires a novel focus. It attempts to see how much state behavior in these areas can be explained in terms of the conventional focus of the territorial nation-state.

Few studies have really tried to find patterns of territorial interest in economic and technological issue areas. American studies, in particular, usually fall into two categories: those which focus on strategic-security issues from a predominantly territorial perspective and those which focus on economic-technical issues from a predominantly functional perspective.[1] This study attempts to bridge this division by applying a territorial (which means in today's context predominantly national) perspective to an economic-technical issue. It seeks to isolate the patterns of reality that accompany national efforts to harness the benefits and control the dangers of civilian technologies.

The national focus is chosen for three reasons. First, it is a level of reality in economic and technical areas that is often neglected, because it is assumed that economic-technical relations evoke a much more diffuse and fragmented structure of decision-making than that characteristic of military-strategic relations. We do not dispute this general proposition but argue that national policy-making is an increasingly important, though not exclusive, level of reality in economic-technical relations, which may be obscured by too much emphasis on pluralism and segmental drift. National economic planning and, more recently, national science policies confirm the existence of a national position in economic and technical issue areas, even though this position may be more visible from outside a particular country than inside it.[2] Second, the over-all scope of this study is too large (involving five and sometimes more countries) to allow for the kind of detailed analysis that might be undertaken at a more fragmented level of inquiry (e.g., looking at the myriad of internal groups and institutions that influence national policy-making). We do not neglect subnational groups but limit our investigation to the most important ones (industries, scientific communities, etc.). Inevitably, we cannot pay as much attention to the complexities of interaction among these groups, as we might have if we were studying only one country's policies in an economic-technical issue area. On the other hand, the latter type of inquiry would slight the over-all national dimension of policy-making which may become visible only in the interaction between two or more countries. Third, we believe that the combination of territorial or national perspective and economic-technical problem area may offer as much insight into the peaceful management of world affairs as the eventual application of functional perspectives to national security problem areas (which was supposed to

[1]This division is, in part, an inevitable consequence of the specialized character of American research. In Atlantic studies, for example, strategic problems are studied by one set of analysts (Kissinger, Schelling, Osgood, etc.), economic problems by another set (Balassa, Cooper, Krause, etc.), and technological problems by still a third set (Gilpin, Skolnikoff, etc.). The division may also be due, however, to an American propensity to restrict the scope of problems to make the problems more manageable or more amenable to solution.

[2]The tendency of foreign observers to see a national policy even where domestic spokesmen persistently deny it is reflected in a comment made by Henry Kissinger in 1968: "I have found it next to impossible to convince Frenchmen that there is no such thing as an American foreign policy . . ." For Frenchmen, at least, such a policy exists. See *The Washington Post*, September 17, 1973.

occur after attitudes had been reshaped through functional approaches to economic and technical problems). Territorial perspectives toward change, we argue, have as many normative advantages as functional perspectives. Less advanced states in particular may find functional approaches considerably biased in favor of the interests and internal decision-making processes of more advanced states. The functional logic of integration, as one analyst notes, is "clearly rooted in Western experience and modes of perception."[3] Even within Western circles, not all states are as pluralistic or dependent on a system of fragmented power as the United States.

The territorial perspective of this study includes the member-states of the European Atomic Energy Community (minus Luxembourg which has only a minor nuclear program) and principal outside partner states, such as the United States and Great Britain (the latter not being a member of the Community during most of the historical period examined in this study). The economic-technical problem area is the development of nuclear power reactors for the production of electricity. This combination of perspective and problem area means that we are primarily interested in national programs and policies of nuclear power development in Europe (hereafter shorthand for Western Europe unless otherwise specified). We are less interested in supranational (i.e., Community) aspects of this development. In this study, Community institutions are treated as additional rather than overarching actors. We are also less interested in the intrinsic features of the economic-technical problem area itself. This is not primarily a study of energy problems in Europe, nor is it a study of the economics of nuclear power development. Still less is it a study of the technical characteristics of nuclear reactor technology. All of these considerations necessarily enter into our investigations, but they do not constitute the central core of our analytical concern. We seek to explain how groups identified primarily along territorial or national lines behave in the common or competitive development of big technologies.

The study is nevertheless relevant to contemporary concern over energy shortages and environmental effects of big technology. Much of this concern is expressed in terms of finite estimates of available resources and ecological tolerances coupled with linear or accelerating projections of the use and abuse of these resources and the environment. This approach frequently assumes that, to meet projected crises, states will eventually cooperate or forfeit the advantages of economic growth and political stability. The evidence of this study illustrates the limitations of this approach. States, and political actors more generally, are not uninvolved in creating crises or helpless in affecting circumstances which dissolve crises. They inject the values which alone enable one to

[3]Ernst B. Haas, *Beyond the Nation-State* (Stanford: Stanford University Press, 1964), p. 118.

say that a crisis exists, since a crisis is presumably a situation which threatens some cherished value. And they interfere with the assumptions on which long-term projections are based—such as the level of consumption of energy or the development of new technologies for which "surprise-free" projections cannot account. More interesting and relevant approaches to contemporary problems ask questions concerning which political actors in a particular international setting argue that a crisis exists and whose interests are advanced or impeded by proposed solutions to the crisis.

As we examine in this study, Western European countries faced an energy crisis already in 1956 (perhaps earlier in the coal sector). This crisis, as is the case with most crises when viewed historically, proved to be short-lived. Yet out of the crisis arose a configuration of institutions and relationships, in particular the establishment of the European Atomic Energy Community (Euratom) and a major program of nuclear power cooperation between Euratom and the United States, which affected the balance of interests between Europe and America for years thereafter. Not surprisingly, European countries today are somewhat hesitant to cooperate to solve new energy problems. Thus far, they have seemed to prefer bilateral arrangements to multilateral programs proposed by the United States; and they have reacted deliberately, despite their much greater dependence on external fuel supplies. They have also been less exercised over the environmental impact of nuclear power plants. (Consequently, as the reader will note, environmental considerations do not figure into the story of nuclear power development in Europe until very recently and, even then, only in muted fashion compared to the protests of ecological groups in the United States.) The point is not that these countries are any less sensitive to their needs or those realities which indeed may be beyond their individual and/or collective control. It is rather that their needs may be different both among themselves within Europe and between themselves and other countries outside Europe. In this study we argue that the politics of *defining* crisis situations may be as interesting as the ecology and technology of *decreeing* crises (that is, by the self-evident projection of present trends). No one should mistake this emphasis as an unrealistic rejection of environmental and technological constraints. Instead it is an attempt to shed light on the equally important cultural and political dimensions of crisis.

Our study of nuclear power in Europe is divided into four parts. Part I (chapter 1) develops in greater analytical and historical detail the conceptual focus of our study. It considers, in theoretical terms, two general perspectives applied to the study of technology and international politics and gives the reasons for our choice of one of these perspectives in this particular study. The reader unfamiliar with the contemporary literature on technology and international politics may wish to skip Part I, reading through the rest of the study and especially Part IV before returning to the examination of theoretical issues. On the other hand, the reader interested in theoretical issues may wish to skip some of the specific details of nuclear power development and concentrate primarily on Parts I, II, and IV. In whatever manner the reader proceeds, however, Part I is critical for understanding the study's methods and concepts and particularly the significance as well as limitations of the study's conclusions.

Part II (chapters 2–4) initiates the analysis of peaceful atomic energy developments in Europe from three broad territorial perspectives—Atlantic, national, and Community or regional. Chapter 2 discusses general technological relations between Europe and the United States and explains the increasing salience of economic and technological issues in Atlantic relations in terms of larger political factors which are central to the perspective adopted in chapter 1. As the Atlantic consensus on postwar strategic and economic policies unraveled, national governments in Europe sought to reintegrate domestic economic and technological activities to support flexible national options in a rapidly changing policy context. This phenomenon is the basis of the examination in chapter 3 of national patterns of development in the nuclear reactor sector. Chapter 4 then traces the impact of these national and Atlantic developments on Community nuclear policies and programs. Under centrifugal pressures of nuclear nationalism, Community action has been increasingly limited to service and minor coordination roles rather than over-all integration of nuclear resources.

Part III (chapters 5–8) constitutes the heart of the analysis and moves to a more specific level of inquiry. This section focuses the broad determinants of national and international behavior discussed in Part II around a series of four case studies of nuclear reactor projects. The focus on specific projects permits a more intimate view of the parameters of international cooperation in big technologies and reflects the level of organization contemplated for future European cooperation in technological areas (after the disappointing experience with institutionalized cooperation through Euratom).

Thanks to the orderliness of the technical world, the four case studies break down into the four main types or families (*filières*) of fission reactors currently being developed for electrical power purposes—proven, heavy water, high temperature gas, and fast reactors. These reactor families are distinguished from one another primarily by the type of moderators they employ (or fail to employ as in the case of fast reactors). Within each family, the reactors are further distinguished by the type of coolant used (gas, organic liquids, sodium, etc.). The reader unfamiliar with the basic technical and economic characteristics of fission reactor families is strongly encouraged to consult the Appendix before reading the case studies. This Appendix gives a brief, simple explanation of nuclear power systems adequate to understand the politics of reactor development.

Also, by some good fortune, the case studies in Part III reflect different features of organization which the Euratom countries used to coordinate their aims and resources in reactor sectors. These different organizational features, in turn, reflect varying patterns of politics in the field of technological cooperation.

For example, chapter 5, which treats the development of so-called first generation or proven reactors (principally light water and gas graphite reactors), highlights the politics of external cooperation between the Euratom Community and the United States. Cooperation with the United States, Europe's preponderant strategic partner in the postwar period, inevitably emphasizes considerations of broad diplomatic and strategic politics (sometimes called high politics) in technological relations. Chapter 6, which examines internal European efforts to develop a common heavy water reactor (ORGEL) through the mechanism of centralized Community laboratories, spotlights issues of a more bureaucratic or institutional character. National interests and traditions are expressed in more technical and administrative terms. Chapter 7, a study of high temperature gas reactor development, focuses in large part on Euratom cooperation with Great Britain. This case study incorporates some of the features of dominant power politics evident in Euratom cooperation with the United States but also elements of cooperative politics among relatively equal strategic and diplomatic powers (Great Britain being on a roughly comparable footing with France and also with Germany except in strategic nuclear areas). Finally, chapter 8, the story of fast reactor development in Europe, looks at the dynamics of internal cooperation in decentralized, national laboratories as opposed to Community laboratories studied in chapter 6. Politics in this setting reveals most vividly the features of Franco-German interactions prior to the entry of Great Britain.

Part IV (chapter 9) draws together the results of the broad and specific inquiries of Parts II and III. In this section, we formulate tentative propositions about the way governmental and nongovernmental (primarily multinational industries) groups behave in sectors of "big technology" development. These propositions emphasize the political motivations and interests characterizing such behavior and illustrate the fruits of the particular perspective adopted in this study and explained in Part I. The propositions also provide insights into wider problems of contemporary European and Atlantic technological relations. They constitute important, though not exclusive, considerations that must be taken into account if nations are to manage satisfactorily the promises as well as the perils of modern civilian technologies.

PART I
THE ROAD MAP

CHAPTER 1

TECHNOLOGY AND INTERNATIONAL POLITICS: INTERDEPENDENCE OR INDEPENDENCE

Under the pressures of economics, science and technology,
mankind is moving steadily toward large-scale cooperation. Despite
periodic reverses, all human history clearly indicates progress in
this direction.

Zbigniew Brzezinski, *Between Two Ages*, p. 296

Politics determines the framework of economic activity and
channels it in directions which tend to serve the political objectives
of dominant political groups and organizations. Throughout
history each successive hegemonic power has organized economic
space in terms of its own interests and purposes.

Robert Gilpin, "The Politics of Transnational Economic
Relations," in Robert O. Keohane and Joseph S. Nye, Jr. (eds.),
Transnational Relations and World Politics, p. 53

The above statements offer differing interpretations of the interaction of technology, economics, and politics in contemporary international relations. The first reflects what we define in this chapter to be a technical perspective, stressing the impact of technological progress on the political and social organization of the international system. The second reflects what we call a political perspective, emphasizing the impact of political structures on the content and direction of technological progress. The two perspectives are not necessarily contradictory; and, in a fundamental sense, each incorporates elements of both parochialism and universalism in the interpretation of contemporary events. Nevertheless, they slice into a multifaceted and complex reality from different angles. In this chapter, we seek to illustrate this difference between perspectives by looking at the point from which each perspective begins, the definitions of politics and technology each employs, and the historical understanding of the interaction between politics and technology each adopts. This discussion clarifies the perspective we adopt in this study of nuclear reactor politics in Western Europe and defines the sense in which we use the terms politics, economics, and technology in this investigation.

The first statement above views technological advance as a constraint on human differences and conflict. Technology is seen as a force moving the world toward large-scale cooperation, breaking down the present system of separate nation-states. According to this view, the requirements of economic and technological advance have outgrown the political framework of the nation-state. National governments no longer have control over important aspects of social and economic life even though at the same time they face increasing demands to channel the forces of technology into more humane and purposeful directions. If governments hope to satisfy these demands, they will be "forced" into novel and more cooperative forms of behavior. Traditional patterns of *international* conduct, such as the balance-of-power and commercial rivalries, will have to give place to new patterns of *transnational* interaction, including the growth of global functional organizations and world-wide corporate and monetary structures.[1] Whereas the aim of traditional patterns was to preserve maximum autonomy for individual governments, contemporary patterns seek to integrate national requirements into a larger framework of transnational cooperation and interdependence. Given the increasing inseparability of domestic and international problems, it is argued that governments have no choice but to pursue domestic as well as foreign policy objectives through international means. Technology has altered the mechanisms of effective action and thereby placed new constraints on the implementation of autonomous objectives of contemporary nation-states.

[1]In this study, international refers principally to external relations among national governments (intergovernmental or interstate relations), but it may also include external relations among nongovernmental groups where the latter are identified primarily along national lines (e.g., Pugwash Conferences). Transnational refers to external relations among nongovernmental groups which do not identify primarily along national lines (e.g., Catholic Church) or between a nongovernmental group of one society and a governmental group of another society where the former does not identify primarily along national lines. The distinction has less to do with the governmental or nongovernmental character of the actor [the basis of the definition of transnational in the pioneer volume by Robert O. Keohane and Joseph S. Nye, Jr. (eds.), *Transnational Relations and World Politics* (Cambridge: Harvard University Press, 1972)] than the fact that at least one of the groups claims to, or actually does, act on primarily nonnational grounds. This distinction, it seems, gets at the heart of the debate about transnationalism, since nongovernmental actors have always played a role in international relations. While their role today is much greater, this may be significant for international relations only if these actors pursue, actually or potentially, interests which are different from or may conflict with the interests of present-day nation-states. Otherwise, transnational actors only reinforce national divisions.

It should be noted that, according to our definition, it is also possible for governmental actors to behave transnationally if they pursue interests other than those of their national employers. Our distinction is analytical (i.e., dependent on interest) rather than institutional (i.e., dependent on the position of an actor). Obviously, of course, position may affect interest.

The second statement stresses the specific group or national interests which organize and pursue the advance of technology to maximize political influence. This view is less concerned with the impact technology has in constraining human behavior than with the activities of those groups whose interests are served by advancing technology. Governmental as well as nongovernmental groups, it is noted, "push" the development of technology in directions consistent with their particular interests. These interests continue to affect the course of technological development whether the specific activities take place within the limits of the territorial nation-state or spill over into the international arena. In fact, the spill-over of domestic activities into the international arena may be less an indication of the "imperatives" of modern technology than a consequence of the political organization of the international system under the aegis of dominant powers. The phenomenon of interdependence is most marked among modernized, Western societies, where, over the past twenty-five years, the hegemonial influence of the United States has been essentially unchallenged. Whether this influence today is waxing or waning is a subject of some dispute. What is important is that, even if direct U.S. dominance is receding, the emergence of new transnational procedures and institutions of economic and technological interdependence may serve to perpetuate the indirect influence of the United States and other dominant Western powers. The spread of these institutions, such as multinational corporations, gives advanced economic and technological countries new opportunities to exploit their industrial and intellectual advantages. The more technically sophisticated global structures become, the greater becomes the influence of the most technically sophisticated members. Effective performance of these structures will require that advanced countries play a disproportionate role. In return, these countries will acquire the opportunity to shape policies and institutions to serve their larger political interests. Visible political control may be replaced by more subtle and intricate procedural and institutional controls. Thus, rather than heralding a new pattern of global behavior, transnationalism may conceal an old pattern of national independence and international imperialism.[2]

[2]Many American analysts prefer the term "asymmetry" to that of "imperialism" to describe imbalances in contemporary international politics. They note the historical ambiguities and theoretical difficulties associated with the latter term. See Introduction and Conclusion in Keohane and Nye (eds.), *Transnational Relations*, pp. xxvi and 386–89; and Zbigniew Brzezinski, *Between Two Ages* (New York: Viking Press, 1970), pp. 32–35. Their objections may be valid in a theoretical sense, but the choice of terms may only confirm the different way in which advanced and less advanced countries view these developments. Whether described as asymmetries or imperialism, the issue at stake is control. To emphasize this issue, relatively weaker countries may continue to prefer the politically relevant term "imperialism" to the academically more precise concept "asymmetries." Even among advanced societies, this tendency is apparent. For European views of American power, see Robert Gilpin, *France in the Age of the Scientific State* (Princeton:

Analysts are quite correct in pointing out that the increasing influence of the nation-state may not be incompatible with the increasing importance of transnational relations.[3] Some even argue that the two phenomena are directly reinforcing.[4] Governmental and transnational actors, it is pointed out, engage in complementary rather than duplicative conflict. The interaction is not zero-sum.[5] If the two actors reinforce one another and grow roughly in tandem, however, there is no reason to assume that transnational activity will acquire greater importance than interstate activity. Yet the most interesting claim of transnational theorists is that "the state-centric paradigm . . . is becoming progressively inadequate as transnational relations take place."[6] This implies that the nation-state is becoming a less important focus of analysis presumably because national governments are losing *relative* influence *vis-à-vis* transnational actors. The uniqueness and essential significance of transnational paradigms depend upon a relative shift of influence between national and transnational actors (either going on now or pending in the near future). Otherwise, we are being asked to divert our attention from what transnationalist theorists acknowledge is still the predominant feature of world politics, namely, that "states have been and remain the most important actors in world affairs,"[7] to less important (though perhaps more novel) features whose significance may be only marginal.

The conclusions that analysts reach suggest that they are taking sides on the question of relative significance of national versus transnational phenomena. Some analysts believe that "changes in the structure of the global economy have resulted in a withering of government control of certain activities presumed to be de jure within the domain of governments."[8] These analysts are primarily interested in the political consequences of *economic* interdependence, and while they recognize that increased conflict as well as cooperation may result from such interdependence, they imply that cooperation is more likely given the

---

Princeton University Press, 1968), pp. 4 ff; and Raymond Vernon, "Rogue Elephant in the Forest: An Appraisal of Transatlantic Relations," *Foreign Affairs*, LI (April 1973), pp. 573–87.

[3]See Conclusion in Keohane and Nye (eds.), *Transnational Relations*, p. 375.

[4]Samuel P. Huntington argues, for example, that the "increase in the number, functions and scope of transnational organizations will increase the demand for access to national territories and hence also increase the value of the one resource almost exclusively under the control of national governments." Transnational organizations, therefore, contribute directly to the growth of influence of governments. See "Transnational Organizations in World Politics," *World Politics*, XXV (April 1973), pp. 333–68.

[5]*Ibid.*, p. 366.

[6]Keohane and Nye (eds.), *Transnational Relations*, p. xxv.

[7]*Ibid.*, p. xxiv.

[8]See Edward L. Morse, "Transnational Economic Processes," in Keohane and Nye (eds.), *Transnational Relations*, p. 23; for an economic analysis of these phenomena, see Richard N. Cooper, *The Economics of Interdependence* (New York: McGraw-Hill, 1968).

economic costs of autonomy or conflict.[9] Other analysts, primarily interested in the political consequences of *technological* interdependence, also believe that global changes "create new constraints on the independence of national action. . . ."[10] They too foresee the "increased need for international cooperation," though not necessarily the growth of political integration.[11] While quite different in focus and method, all of these studies share the bias that modernization increases the pressures for transnational and international cooperation, requiring a modification of past concepts of national independence and sovereignty.

Still other analysts reach different conclusions. They believe technology enhances rather than undermines national autonomy. Empirical research, they point out, does not confirm the popular belief that "modern life, with rapid transportation, mass communications, and literacy, tends to be more international than life in past decades or centuries, and hence more conducive to the growth of international or supranational institutions."[12] Instead, they contend, "the increase in the responsibilities of national government for such matters as social welfare and the regulation of economic life has greatly increased the importance of the nation in the lives of its members."[13] The rise of the nation-state is widespread, affecting advanced as well as less advanced countries and security as well as economic issues.[14] For the large and economically developed countries, revival of the nation-state means greater self-sufficiency and independence; for the others, it means increasing dependence. Interdependence of states, on the other hand, is judged to be "less now than it was earlier."[15] Emphasizing interde-

[9]In another article, Morse argues that a "principal characteristic of foreign policies under modernized conditions is that they approach the pole of cooperation rather than the pole of conflict." The implication is that, as the requirement for cooperation increases (under pressures of modernization), states also become more willing to cooperate, largely because of the economic costs of failing to cooperate. The economic cost of autonomy may be offset by political benefits, however, a point we consider again in the above discussion. For Morse's article, see "The Transformation of Foreign Policies," *World Politics*, XXII (April 1970), pp. 371–92.

[10]Eugene B. Skolnikoff, *The International Imperatives of Technology* (Research Series No. 16; Berkeley: University of California, Institute of International Studies, 1972), p. 95.

[11]*Ibid.*, p. 13; Harold Sprout and Margaret Sprout also argue that "it will require . . . concerted international cooperation of a scope and on a scale only dimly imagined as yet, if the earth is to continue to be a congenial habitat." *Towards a Politics of the Planet Earth* (New York: Van Nostrand Reinhold, 1971), p. 15. The issue, as we discuss later, may be "congenial for whom?"

[12]Karl W. Deutsch *et al.*, *Political Community and the North Atlantic Area* (1st Princeton Paperback; Princeton: Princeton University Press, 1968), p. 22.

[13]*Ibid.*, p. 23.

[14]John H. Herz, "The Territorial State Revisited," in James N. Rosenau (ed.), *International Politics and Foreign Policy* (New York: Free Press, 1969), p. 80. Herz argues that even in security affairs the trend is "away from the coherence and consolidation of the new-style empires that had been founded on nuclear monopolies or nuclear superiorities, toward the assertion, or reassertion, of nationhood and independence."

[15]Kenneth N. Waltz, "The Myth of National Interdependence," in Charles P. Kindleberger (ed.), *The International Corporation: A Symposium* (Cambridge: M.I.T. Press, 1970), p. 207.

pendence and loss of national autonomy, these analysts conclude, conceals the benefits as well as dangers of national inequalities in the administration of world order.[16]

Theorists have tried to reconcile these contrasting conclusions by reexamining empirical methods and definitions.[17] None of these attempts seems satisfactory, however.[18] The essential difference seems to be one of perspective and personal persuasion rather than empirical evidence (which, at this point, is inconclusive). Theorists of interdependence and independence disagree about the basic prerequisites of peace and world order. The former believe that the nation-state and state-centric paradigms of analysis stand in the way of an appreciation of contemporary trends that are creating the opportunity for new patterns of internationalism. The latter believe that the nation-state is the best defense of global stability in a world of cultural diversity and technological revolution.[19] For the first, interdependence offers new opportunities for cooperation; for the second, it offers new opportunities for conflict.[20] This differing judgment about the cooperative or conflictive spin-offs of modernization is critical in the dispute about interde-

[16]*Ibid.*, pp. 222–23.

[17]See, in particular, Edward L. Morse, "The Politics of Interdependence," *International Organization*, XXIII (Spring 1969), pp. 311–26; and "Transnational Economic Processes," pp. 23–47. See also Robert D. Tollison and Thomas D. Willett, "International Integration and the Interdependence of Economic Variables," *International Organization*, XXVII (Spring 1973), pp. 255–71.

[18]Definitions do confuse the matter, and some clarification has been achieved (see particularly the article by Tollison and Willett). But a principal issue having to do with the relationship between internal interdependence (i.e., within a country) and external interdependence remains a matter of argument. Morse contends that, even if external interdependence remains constant, increasing internal interdependence enhances the sensitivity of a society to external influences and hence magnifies external interdependence. This is true, but increasing internal interdependence, presuming that government is a key link in such interdependence, also enhances the capacity of a society to defend or shield itself against external influences and, in some instances, to project its resources and values to create such influences. Interdependence theorists tend to view interdependence as a one-way street with external influences shaping internal responses. The reverse may also be true. Part of the problem stems from defining interdependence in terms of sensitivity. The latter term implies a sympathetic response to transnational phenomena. The response instead may be insensitive, that is, a larger power merely ignoring new contacts with smaller powers; or it may be hostile, a country reacting to new contacts by cutting back over-all contacts. Sensitivity is a term better suited to interpersonal relationships than the much more impersonal relationships among states.

[19]Herz writes: "For the time being, so it appears, it is not internationalism, 'universalism,' or any other supranational model that constitutes the alternative to the territorial, or nation-state, system, but genuine, raw chaos." The "neo-territorial world of nations . . . might salvage one feature of humanity which seems ever more threatened by the ongoing rush of mankind into the technological conformity of a synthetic planetary environment: diversity of life and culture, of traditions and civilizations." See "The Territorial State Revisted," pp. 88 and 89.

[20]Waltz writes: ". . . interdependent states whose relations remain unregulated must experience conflict and will occasionally fall into violence. If regulation is hard to come by, as it is in relations of states, then it would seem to follow that a lessening of interdependence is desirable." See "The Myth of National Interdependence," p. 205.

pendence, for if conflict is expected, we may do well not to emphasize interdependence and transnationalism but to focus instead on national action to restrain these phenomena—for example, curb the influence and activities of multinational corporations.

These basic attitudes toward change inform one's choice of perspective as well as result from it. Recently, studies of international politics have stressed the importance of perspective and the need to make explicit one's conceptual framework and normative presuppositions.[21] This need is especially relevant at a time when international studies (and political studies more generally[22]) are moving away from methodological preoccupations to more value-oriented concerns with world problems. The trend is toward advocacy and constructive proposals for reform. In these circumstances, a tendency may exist to discard old distinctions and dichotomies in an attempt to surmount the obstacles to action and change. While this tendency is salutary, it should not go to the point of undercutting an academic concern for perspective and modesty. Any empirical attempt to *describe* present events in international politics is linked with the normative desire to *prescribe* future events. Description is selective and what we describe depends on what we are interested in explaining. Furthermore, what we seek to explain suggests what we want to predict, and prediction is a means of influencing the future by affecting the conditions of present choices.[23]

This linkage between description, explanation, prediction, and prescription places an obligation on every analyst to preface his investigation with a clarification of basic assumptions. However tentative, these assumptions underlie cognitive and analytical processes and constitute our only way of organizing and giving meaning to a diffuse and fragmented reality.

The following discussion sets out some of the alternative assumptions and analytical choices underlying the controversy about technology's impact on international politics. The discussion has two purposes. First, it seeks to suggest in preliminary form one way of understanding and integrating the divergent results of various studies of technology and international politics. It may sensitize us to the fact that these results are each valid *within the perspective adopted.* Though the process of reality-testing must go on to determine which perspective is more reliable, this

[21]Sprout and Sprout, *Planet Earth*, p. 13; Graham T. Allison, *Essence of Decision* (Boston: Little, Brown, 1971); William D. Coplin, *Introduction to International Politics* (Chicago: Markham, 1971), chap. 1; John Spanier, *Games Nations Play* (New York: Praeger, 1972), chap. 1.

[22]See David Easton, "The New Revolution in Political Science," *American Political Science Review*, LXIII (December 1969), pp. 1051–61.

[23]The normative purpose of prediction is skillfully elucidated in Robert L. Rothstein, *Planning, Prediction and Policy-Making in Foreign Affairs* (Boston: Little, Brown, 1972). As Rothstein notes, the controversy about interdependence is more an argument about where we want to go in the future than a description of where we are at present.

process must be undertaken with considerable caution, particularly in the international arena where consensus on basic concepts is sharply limited and where, for the first time ever, international politics as known and practiced among Western countries may have to accommodate the values and aims of non-Western societies—in particular, China and the Afro-Asian world—as well as growing differences in values among Western societies themselves. Second, the discussion lays out the broader context in which the subsequent investigation of peaceful nuclear technology in Europe takes place. This investigation does not aim to resolve the question of interdependence versus independence. By emphasizing the subjective components of knowledge, we recognize the limits of any single contribution to an ongoing study of contemporary problems by many different analysts of many different persuasions. We seek only to demonstrate the explanatory power of a specific conceptual focus applied to a discrete set of events. At the end of this chapter, we give the reasons (both practical and normative) for our choice of both focus and events. The discussion below suggests the alternatives we faced in this choice.

One primary word of caution is necessary. The following discussion does not purport to establish alternative paradigms for the study of technology and international politics. We deliberately use the terms "perspective" and "approach" to indicate the more modest character of our distinctions. Moreover, we do not argue that analysts should use only one or the other of these perspectives in their respective studies.[24] No study can avoid mixing the perspectives, but no study can avoid emphasizing one, either. A perfectly neutral treatment would yield no conclusions. We recognize all of the dangers of caricature and reductionism in an attempt of this sort. But the risks seem worth taking if we succeed in suggesting what different studies can and cannot do because of limitations induced by perspective.

Two Perspectives—Technical and Political

To minimize jargon, we label the alternative perspectives underlying contemporary interpretations of technology and international politics simply *technical* and *political*.[25] In practice, these perspectives differ

---

[24] Analysts shift perspectives between different studies and also within the same study. Thus, any attempt to give examples from specific studies to illustrate alternative perspectives is bound to distort and do injustice to individual authors. For this reason, references will be kept to a minimum in the following section. Where illustrations remain inescapable, I apologize in advance for possible offenses and take excuse in the hope that this type of discussion adds oversight to general issues which would not be possible in a detailed examination of specific studies.

[25] Choice of terminology is always difficult. As Ernst Haas has noted, "the tyranny of words is only slightly less absolute than that of men." [See *Beyond the Nation-State* (Stanford: Stanford University Press, 1964), p. 3]. The author wrestled with numerous word pairs to describe what follows. None was satisfactory. As we note further above,

primarily in terms of their focus of interest. Theorists adopting a technical perspective are most interested in the political adjustments and accommodations that appear to follow from technological change. Their focus is on where technology is going and then on what political consequences this will have. Political studies, by contrast, emphasize the political antecedents of technological change. Existing technology is regarded as part of a previous and ongoing political process in which some parties identify with and promote certain technologies while others oppose or promote different technologies. These parties contribute to the way in which present technologies are defined and pursued. Technological change is less important, therefore, in terms of where it is going than where it has come from. Analysis seeks to identify the political interests and forces associated with the origins and development of specific technologies. The assumption is that these forces are relevant for understanding existing technological events as well as their subsequent evolution (since the loss or shift of political support could affect development).

In theory, the two perspectives may be said to differ in terms of their emphasis on the means as opposed to the ends of human behavior. Technical studies stress the mechanisms (means) and actual outcomes of behavior, with only secondary, if any, reference to the objectives (ends) or motivational sources of behavior. In international politics, for example, it is noted that states frequently agree on specific actions and policies without necessarily agreeing on the ends or purposes of these actions. Indeed, states may often take common action for different, even divergent, reasons. Thus, to understand international events, it may be unnecessary to sort out the competing goals and interests of states. Whatever these goals, states are unable, given the circumstances of coexistence, to translate these goals into consistent action. Objectives are compromised in the process of implementation. The mechanisms of interaction severely limit choice and "force" participants to take action more consistent with the context than the desired ends of policy.[26]

_____

political and technical are also unsatisfactory since, in a fundamental sense, these perspectives are both political and technical. Nevertheless, the simplicity of the terms avoids other complications, and the terms do capture the principal difference of the two perspectives, namely, designation of independent variables. (See discussion of starting points, pp. 22–24.)

Our distinction between political and technical is quite different from that of other writers, but dichotomies affect all analytical studies. See, for example, the contrast between engineering and ecological perspectives in Sprout and Sprout, *Planet Earth*, pp. 15–20.

[26]In highlighting means over ends, the technical perspective, as here defined, shares common ground with incremental models of public decision-making and bureaucratic-organizational models of foreign policy-making. As originally outlined by Charles E. Lindblom [see "The Science of Muddling Through," *Public Administration Review*, XIX (Spring 1959), pp. 79–88], the incremental model anticipates disagreement on the ends of policy and therefore focuses attention on the "agreement on policy itself, which re-

The political perspective, by contrast, is more concerned with the intentions (ends) than the instrumentalities (means) of action. The outcome of behavior is assumed to bear some correspondence to the motives and interests of the actor.[27] The focus, therefore, is on the actors rather than the action, on the expected rather than actual effects of behavior. While states may agree on common policies for different reasons, the significance and outcomes of these policies will depend, to some extent, on the degree of overlap and compatability of objectives. This is particularly true in situations where objectives differ widely or where policy precedents, which might serve as alternative standards of evaluation (as they must in incremental approaches), are few. The international environment is most frequently such a situation, increasing the relevance of the study of ends.

The distinction here, it should be remembered, is one of emphasis, not either/or. Technical perspectives may focus on mechanisms and performance to determine the most rational goals for future action. At another level, therefore, these perspectives stress objectives, sometimes explicitly, more often implicitly. Objectives emerge, however, from the prior consideration of means, in particular, the projected course of technological events. Since past technological trends have led to an expansion of political and social organization, objectives of technical analyses tend to be comprehensive. In today's context, they are usually global or systemic (the universal element of this perspective). As we shall see, however, the attempt to formulate common goals primarily on the basis of technical means and circumstances may itself be interpreted as a policy of specific interests (the parochial element of this perspective). Those who concentrate on means take attention away from the debate over ends and substitute logical analysis for political compromise. If ends follow from means, the groups possessing the larger share of means (i.e., technical capability) enjoy a privileged position for determining ends. Not surprisingly, therefore, those adopting technical perspectives are frequently groups that are most advanced and stand to

---

mains possible even when agreement on values is not." The model denies the possibility of knowing ends (aims and purposes) apart from means (policies and procedures). Bureaucratic-organizational models (Models II and III in Allison, *Essence of Decision*, especially chaps. 3 and 5) also stress organizational mechanisms over the objectives of action. The processes of bureaucracy and bargaining exert a "strain towards agreement" that encourages the compromise of objectives.

[27]This correspondence need not be a perfect one, as is assumed in rational models of policy-making (Model I in Allison, *Essence of Decision*, chap. 1). Moreover, we are not saying that behavior is always conscious. Motives and interests may be inferred, even if the actor himself is unaware of them. The point is that explanation proceeds by trying to establish these motives or interests rather than explaining behavior primarily in terms of external outcomes.

In the above discussion, terms such as objectives, values, goals, interests, motives, purposes, and intentions are used interchangeably to denote expected (either conscious or inferred) effects of behavior, while terms such as consequences, outcomes, results, and performance are used to denote actual effects of behavior.

gain most from assuming and encouraging the pursuit of technologies they command. By contrast, as we note in chapter 9 in the specific context of technological cooperation, less advanced groups may favor alternatives to the technologies of more dominant partners.

Similarly, analysts with political perspectives do not exclude means in their concentration on ends. Means affect the relative positions of actors and condition their expectations and interests. Yet means, except in a primitive material sense, may not be universal across cultural boundaries; they may acquire *mean-ing* only in the context of specific cultures. Thus, in global affairs, past and present cultures, largely identified today with nation-states, may be more significant than future technological trends (the parochial element of this perspective). In political perspectives, future means are projected through the lens of existing cultures, while in technical perspectives, present means are projected to derive future cultures. The fact that political perspectives start with the present division of cultures (nation-states) does not preclude a future unity of cultures (global or transnational). States know who they are only by knowing others. Specific identity thus always implies some concept of common identity. In this sense, political perspectives assume unity as a reference point for disunity (the universal element of this perspective). Nothing precludes the progressive expansion of the elements of unity. Beyond the unity essential for uniqueness, however, the expansion of common interests may occur only through the overlap or compromise of specific interests or the presumptive insight of superior specific interests.

The technical perspective underlies the thesis that technological progress is altering the mechanisms of international behavior and reducing the significance of national objectives in global politics.[28] For all states, it is argued, even the most powerful, to act politically (i.e., in pursuit of partisan objectives) means to act together. Whatever their separate goals, states will have to deal with one another or reduce their chances of realizing any objectives, including purely internal ones.[29] In fact, the increasing salience of domestic goals of wealth and welfare reinforces the need for common action. These goals, it is argued, are preeminently cooperative ones.[30] They aim at the increase of benefits for all and presuppose the integrated effort of all through specialization and

[28]The literature that most heavily influenced the author's thinking in this matter includes, *inter alia*, Skolnikoff, *International Imperatives*; Sprout and Sprout, *Planet Earth*; Brzezinski, *Between Two Ages*; and articles by Morse and the editors in Keohane and Nye (eds.), *Transnational Relations*. The reader should be aware that these studies treat very different issues and are not comparable in any direct sense. In the above discussion, we are treating issues that go beyond the intentions of any of these specific studies.

[29]As one study puts it: ". . . most states retain control over their policy instruments and are able to pursue their objectives. They are just less able to achieve them." See Conclusion in Keohane and Nye (eds.), *Transnational Relations*, p. 393.

[30]See Morse, "The Transformation of Foreign Policies," pp. 377 and 382.

centralization. What is more, these goals appear to correlate with a certain stage of modernization toward which the different societies of the world are moving, albeit at different rates.[31] The diffusion of the goals of industrial society reduces still further the relevance of differing objectives for understanding behavior. Not only the conditions for action but also a growing consensus on the goals of action shift attention from the purposes of agreement. Goals are either only marginally relevant for the purpose of policy-making or constitute an emerging consensus which may be safely ignored.[32]

The political perspective underlies the thesis that modernization enhances national independence and creates the opportunity for a new imperialism.[33] According to this thesis, the growth of interdependence in a world beset by wide cultural, economic, and political differences sets off a competition among states to control and manipulate the new linkages in the pursuit of parochial purposes. Where differences are as profound as they are in international relations, the weight of procedural and institutional mechanisms of interaction is insufficient to guarantee agreement. Even agreement on the need to act together cannot be taken for granted, since the need to act is a function of priorities and national goals. Indeed, it is argued, the definition of problems to be solved through collective action is itself a political activity. Though governments everywhere have associated themselves with domestic goals of wealth and welfare and seek the "good life" as a priority political objective, they do not agree on what constitutes the good life (as more erudite political philosophers have never been able to do).[34] The attempt

[31] *Ibid.*, pp. 372–74; Sprout and Sprout, *Planet Earth*, pp. 28–29.

[32] In the Conclusion of *Transnational Relations*, Nye and Keohane point out the increasing divorce between specific objectives and specific consequences (i.e., what is intended and what happens) in contemporary international behavior. They observe that transnational organizations "with explicitly political objectives [revolutionary groups, etc.] seem to have declined in importance," while "transnational organizations whose principal goals are social and economic have increased in importance" and "may have very significant political consequences" (pp. 376–77). Coupled with their observation that governments exercise a declining influence over transnational economic and social activities (p. 393), one might conclude that political objectives today (being primary inputs of governments) have less to do with social and economic consequences than social and economic objectives have to do with political consequences. The link between *political* objectives and *political* consequences is considerably weakened, at least in social and economic areas.

[33] Here the principal influences on the author's thinking include Deutsch *et al.*, *Political Community*; Gilpin, *France*; David P. Calleo and Benjamin M. Rowland, *America and the World Political Economy* (Bloomington: Indiana University Press, 1973); Hans J. Morgenthau, *Scientific Man Versus Power Politics* (Phoenix Book; Chicago: University of Chicago Press, 1967), and articles by Gilpin, Evans, and Scheinman in Keohane and Nye (eds.), *Transnational Relations*. Once again, no systematic similarity is imputed to these diverse studies. Our discussion is a take-off from, not a treatment of, this literature.

[34] It is far from obvious, for example, that all states seek maximum *economic* well-being at whatever political or social cost. Wealth and welfare are hardly more commensurable goals than power or security, when one recognizes that welfare must include a sense of security and that wealth is as often a means to other ends (usually less tangible) as an end

to define certain problems as global concerns may only reflect a particular version of the good life of those states who have the desire and capacity to superimpose their own standards on the world community as a whole. After all, it is pointed out, how do we detect a problem if not according to some value preference of what is desirable and what is undesirable? A problem implies that something has turned out other than was desired or expected.[35]

The rhetoric and reality of interdependence thus creates the opportunity for a more subtle and total form of imperialism than was possible in any previous period of history. Highly modernized states, anticipating problems of particular and perhaps unique significance to them, draw up an agenda of global issues which dominate the attention and resources of the world community. In this process, it is noted, these states may not seek to exploit others; they may not even be conscious of the favorable consequences of their action for their own interests. Nevertheless, they benefit from the opportunity to define global problems and global solutions to these problems in terms which facilitate the extension of practices and institutions familiar to them.[36]

Weaker states, by contrast, may not share this enthusiasm for dealing with *world* problems. For them, interdependence heightens the awareness of *national* problems, causing them to resist absorption into the vortex of problems of more advanced societies.[37] National goals are defined and pursued as a necessary defense against a presumed con-

---

in itself. As contemporary analysts point out, even advanced states, like Canada, may "prefer national independence to a higher standard of living." Robert Gilpin, "The Politics of Transnational Economic Relations," in Keohane and Nye (eds.), *Transnational Relations*, p. 52. And economic historians note that ". . . most of the peoples of the world have opted for freedom even in mediocrity as against prosperity in subordination." David Landes, *The Unbound Prometheus* (Cambridge: Cambridge University Press, 1969), p. 12.

[35]Analysts attempt to circumvent this problem in various ways. Some reduce what is desired by all people to the bare minimum: ". . . most people in most countries desire to live long and to be as healthy and fit as possible." Sprout and Sprout, *Planet Earth*, p. 28. This formulation misses all of the more significant issues about which peoples may disagree, and it says nothing about how people, while agreeing on a problem, may disagree on how to resolve it (e.g., state versus private health plans). Others acknowledge that conditions like population and pollution may qualify as problems only on the basis of present Western values, but formulate imperatives on this basis nonetheless. Skolnikoff, *International Imperatives*, p. 77. For a view which sharply challenges prevailing Western assumptions concerning population and pollution problems, see Joao Augusto de Araujo Castro, "Environment and Development: The Case of the Developing Countries," in David A. Kay and Eugene B. Skolnikoff (eds.), *World Eco-Crisis* (Madison: University of Wisconsin Press, 1972), pp. 237–52.

[36]Peter B. Evans notes the consequences of well-meaning attempts by developed states to prescribe development strategies for less developed countries. Such attempts have not only led to the extension of institutions and practices of developed states, which are frequently inappropriate in less developed economies; they have also diverted local resources from potentially significant indigenous contributions to development strategies. See "National Autonomy and Economic Development," in Keohane and Nye (eds.), *Transnational Relations*, pp. 335–39.

[37]Herz, "The Territorial State Revisited," pp. 78–80.

sensus about international problems—a consensus which may not exist as yet but may be shaped only through a deliberate reconciliation of opposing aims. There is no presumption of inevitable conflict, it is argued, only the recognition that conflict is also possible and perhaps more dangerous when differences of objectives are concealed in procedural packages that complement dominant interests. Conflict, in fact, may be made less likely by virtue of becoming more visible. If the interdependence focus suggests that states *must* deal with one another, the independence focus suggests that one way states have dealt with one another historically is to decide *not* to deal with one another (to wit, the early American policy of nonentanglement). States, especially new or less cohesive states, may need time and space to consolidate and deepen their sense of self and place. The need may be greater in technological times than ever before. This is not to say, of course, that the need can be successfully fulfilled. Autonomy, analysts note, is a function of total circumstances. But part of these circumstances is the degree to which states display the will and determination to achieve autonomy. While autonomy may be dysfunctional in an economic sense, it may be desirable in a political sense, both from a global and national point of view. For, in times of rapid change, when objectives are in flux and frequent conflict, the decision to minimize contact between states has often contributed as much to peace as the willingness to cooperate.

Different Starting Points

A major reason for different opinions and perspectives, as John Spanier notes, "is that often we are arguing from different starting points, but, because these are usually left implicit, we argue, so to speak, past one another."[38] Technical and political studies adopt different starting points in their analysis of the relationship between technology and international politics. The technical approach starts with a particular technological (or economic) phenomenon and explores the consequences of this phenomenon for existing political structures and attitudes. New developments such as the discovery of nuclear weapons, the spread of multinational corporations, the evolution of interlocking financial and monetary mechanisms, and the emergence of numerous "global" technologies (environmental alteration, space and ocean technologies, genetic technology, etc.) are taken as the starting points of investigations to determine the implications of these events for present political assumptions and institutions. Events themselves raise new problems which require some response or adjustment on the part of political authorities. There is little interest in the political sources of these events. Political factors are regarded primarily as consequences rather than catalysts of technological change. This approach treats tech-

---

[38]Spanier, *Games Nations Play*, p. 8.

nical or economic phenomena as independent variables and political responses as dependent variables.[39]

The political approach reverses this equation. Rather than starting with technical or economic innovations, this approach begins with an investigation of the political factors that existed prior to the emergence of these innovations. It is not only a matter of considering the present political context in which innovations appear but also examining past situations which permitted the technology to emerge in the particular form it did. Why are some technologies regarded as global and others not?[40] What political motivations or configurations contributed to the definition and direction of a particular new technology? What were the political groups and interests that identified a particular problem and pursued a solution through the advancement of technology? The technological event is seen, in some sense, as a response to pre-existent political developments, just as, in the technical approach, political factors are viewed, in some sense, as a response to technological developments. In the political perspective, political forces constitute the independent variables and technological phenomena constitute the dependent variables.[41]

There are unavoidable causal implications in these two choices of starting points. By working forward from the technological event to the political consequences, analysts using the technical approach aver, in some measure however qualified, that technological realities constrain and shape political choice. By working backward from the technological event to prior political choices, analysts using the political approach aver, also despite qualifications, that political choices condition and shape the direction of technology. Admittedly, today's analysts are too sophisticated to adhere to models of singular causality. The reservations of a particular study are frequently as important as the principal inferences. Moreover, most analysts in the social sciences would prefer to

[39]Careful analysts designate these variables explicitly. See, for example, Skolnikoff, *International Imperatives*, pp. 1-11, 93, 151, and 175.

[40]The argument is made that some technologies are global *by nature*. Yet, as a recent study of international organizations concludes, ". . . it is doubtful whether any specific tasks are in themselves essential to the international system . . . the politically relevant questions concern *the propensity of states* to organize the performance of tasks internationally, rather than the inherent nature of the tasks themselves" (emphasis added). See Robert W. Cox and Harold K. Jacobson *et al.*, *The Anatomy of Influence* (New Haven: Yale University Press, 1973), p. 422. For a more explicit formulation of this point of view, see John Gerard Ruggie, "Collective Goods and Future International Collaboration," *American Political Science Review*, LXVI (September 1972), pp. 874-93. The international character of modern technology, in other words, is as much a function of who wants to do what to whom (e.g., who wants to communicate with whom) as it is of the technology itself.

[41]For example, Gilpin argues in his essay, "The Politics of Transnational Economic Relations," pp. 53-54, that economic and technological factors depend upon specific political configurations. As political circumstances change, transnational economic processes also change. For a similar point of view, see Andrew Shonfield, *Modern Capitalism* (New York: Oxford University Press, 1965), pp. 32-33.

speak of correlation rather than causation. Nevertheless, the choice of analytical starting point affects the explanation of events; and technical studies err on the side of involuntary or accidental change,[42] just as political studies err on the side of voluntaristic change.[43] This becomes clearer once we look at how these studies define politics and technology and view the historical relationship of these two forces.

Defining Politics and Technology

In technical studies, technological events tend to be abstracted or "disembodied" from their social and political context.[44] The result is to define technology in nonpartisan terms as "new tools" which "create opportunities to achieve new goals or do things in new ways."[45] Ostensibly, the emphasis is on the opportunities rather than the limitations created by technology. Politics is the process by which men seize these opportunities and apply technology to the consciously chosen ends of societies. "Science thereby intensifies rather than diminishes the relevance of values."[46] Curiously, however, the continued and improved application of technology (which is necessary if only to remedy problems created by the past use of technology) exerts pressure to shift the locus of political decision-making to higher levels of society. In domestic politics, as one study argues, ". . . a major effect of an active science and technology and of a commitment to knowledge as an instrument of social action is a progressive enhancement of the range and influence of the public sector of society in general, and of public decision-making in particular."[47] In international politics, similar pressures force the locus of decision-making from the national to the international arena, since "an increasing number of issues will have to be settled finally in an international forum."[48]

[42]Two examples suffice: Keohane and Nye, in the Introduction of *Transnational Relations*, p. xiii, argue that "governments have generally not been able to control their environments successfully for long periods of time whenever those environments have changed rapidly as a result of large scale social forces or advancing technology. . . . they have had to adjust to changes rather than to shape the forces of history." Similarly, Skolnikoff, in *International Imperatives*, p. 153, concludes that "governments will have only marginal power to alter the course of technology over the next two decades . . . ."

[43]See, for example, the statement by Gilpin quoted at the beginning of this chapter.

[44]Skolnikoff, in *International Imperatives*, following his conscious treatment of technological trends as independent variables, refers explicitly to the "disembodied" implications of technology (p. 93).

[45]Emmanuel G. Mesthene, *Technological Change* (New York: New American Library, 1970), p. viii. The literature on technology and domestic society also reflects a tendency toward technical and political orientations. See in contrast to Mesthene's essay, the essay by John McDermott, "Technology—The Opiate of the Intellectuals," in Albert H. Teich (ed.), *Technology and Man's Future* (New York: St. Martin's Press, 1972), pp. 151–78. On defining technology primarily in terms of opportunity, see also Sprout and Sprout, *Planet Earth*, pp. 218–19.

[46]Brzezinski, *Between Two Ages*, p. 10.

[47]See Mesthene, *Technological Change*, p. 64.

[48]Skolnikoff, *International Imperatives*, p. 95.

Now, strictly speaking, a technology which exerts such a unidimensional influence on the locus of decision-making cannot be described as a "tool." If the location of political decision-making is itself a political issue (*and it is*), a technology that forces centralization enhances the choice and flexibility of some groups, namely those with easy access to the new centers of decision-making, and reduces the choice of others.[49] The advance of technology, therefore, is part of a social phenomenon which reflects the interests of those groups which are most capable of exploiting the shift of power to higher levels of decision-making (federal as opposed to state or international as opposed to national). *Laissez-innover* becomes "the premium ideology . . . of the social classes which find in the free exploitation of their technology the most likely guarantee of their power, status, and wealth."[50] Organizing society to promote and absorb an ever increasing stream of innovation and change places in the hands of these social groups the power to anticipate and define problems and thereby the power to establish their own standards of what is desirable and undesirable as the standards of the entire society.

In political studies, therefore, it is argued that technology cannot be abstracted from its social context. Technology creates its own politics, a politics of technocratic elite control, justified in terms of advanced know-how.[51] From this point of view, the "technological imperative" is no imperative at all but an argument in favor of the development of *certain kinds* of technology, namely those kinds which require centralized forms of political control.[52] A broader understanding of politics would not confine itself to the narrow process of adaptation to the scope of technology; it would embrace the idea of countervailing currents. If technology is indeed a "tool," it should create opportunities for decentralization and self-sufficiency as readily as for centralization and interdependence. What decides the direction in which technology is applied, therefore, is the dialectical process of political competition. Instead of a cumulative process of adaptation to technology, politics reflects the swing back and forth of different group interests using technology to resolve issues of authority and relative influence. This understanding of politics implies a certain capacity to abstract choice from its context (much as the technical definition of politics implies a capacity to abstract technology from

[49]McDermott argues that technological rationality is no less related to group or class interests today than market rationality was in the nineteenth century. See "Technology," pp. 170–71.

[50]*Ibid.*, p. 170.

[51]McDermott argues that "technology should be considered as an institutional system" which does not obscure "systematic and decisive social changes, especially the political and cultural tendencies, that follow the widespread application of advanced technological systems." *Ibid.*, p. 171. In his conclusions, Skolnikoff notes the elitism involved in focusing too heavily on technological advancement. *International Imperatives*, pp. 181–82.

[52]Until recently, for example, much less effort has been devoted to the development of technological tools (computers, etc.) for use and control at state and local as opposed to federal levels of government.

its context). It suggests that individuals and groups can, under appropriate circumstances, break out of the cumulative constraints of incremental change. This possibility may be greater in rapidly changing than normal times, since uncertainty widens the scope for human and social intervention. Thus, present global circumstances may be more conducive to innovative political choice than to adaptive political response.[53]

Understanding Change

These different conceptions of politics and technology are rooted in different perceptions of the past. As Robert Nisbet points out, any attempt to understand change requires an act of faith.[54] Technical and political perspectives incorporate different beliefs about the past. There is no way to verify the truth of these beliefs. The best we can do is declare what the beliefs are and acknowledge their impact on our conclusions.[55]

Technical studies organize the past according to "the long-term multifold trend," the chief characteristics of which are the cumulative growth of knowledge, the acceleration (and recently institutionalization) of technological change, the centralization and concentration of economic and political power, and the spread of secular and manipulative rationality applied to social as well as material problems.[56] The multifold trend is becoming increasingly universal. No systematic attempt is made to specify the relationships among these trends, but there is a sense that "a focus on technological advances and innovations directs attention to changes in every other sector of our milieu" and "provides a productive point, possibly the most productive point of entry, from which to explore the whole range of conditions and trends that are shaping our world."[57] Possibly the most significant underlying trend is the cumulative growth of knowledge which, it is argued, constitutes a "transnational stock" upon which every nation depends for growth and moderni-

---

[53]Albert O. Hirschman finds this concept of politics useful in the study of economic development, especially as an antidote to notions of cumulative political adaptation to growth. Hirschman's approach of "possibilism" draws attention to the novel and unexpected ways in which political responses counteract rather than complement economic changes and produce periodic alternations between centralization and decentralization, economic contact and political insulation. See *A Bias for Hope* (New Haven: Yale University Press, 1971), Introduction.

[54]See his book, *Social Change and History* (New York: Oxford University Press, 1969). "To believe that the vast, plural and infinitely particular history of mankind can somehow be worked into ordered frameworks of either cyclical or linear development . . . calls plainly for a gigantic act of faith" (p. 223).

[55]As one analyst writes: "How do we know whose interpretation of history is correct?" Rothstein, *Planning*, p. 86.

[56]Herman Kahn and B. Bruce-Briggs, *Things to Come* (New York: Macmillan, 1972), pp. 7–30.

[57]Sprout and Sprout, *Planet Earth*, p. 205. The focus on technology is, for practical reasons, unavoidable since trend analysis is most successful in predicting technological events. See Rothstein, *Planning*, p. 172.

zation.[58] In some sense, therefore, knowledge promotes modernization; modernization breeds economic interdependence; and economic interdependence translates, with a time lag, into political interdependence.[59] Political consensus is viewed as a result rather than a requisite of economic interaction.

Advocates of the technical approach point out that during the latter part of the eighteenth century, new technologies associated with the industrial revolution created new links among states and promoted the growth of commerce. These technologies were primarily responsible for the development of imperialism.[60] The advent of nuclear technology after World War II prompted a readjustment of imperial relations. The traditional use of force, essential to the old style imperialism, declined in value; and economic and commercial exchanges acquired greater significance. Today these exchanges create the requirement for new political arrangements, predominantly cooperative and egalitarian ones. International organizations may embody these new realities. Such organizations, it is argued, "will grow in size, responsibility, and authority—probably also in number. They will be much more significant actors in international affairs [in the future] than they are at present."[61] Attitudes will adjust to permit this expansion of international responsibility, if only "as a result of an international crisis growing out of the effects of technology."[62]

The technical view of change assumes that each stage of technological advance represents "something new under the sun."[63] As technology becomes more and more pervasive, contemporary society becomes qual-

[58]Simon Kuznets, *Modern Economic Growth* (New Haven: Yale University Press, 1966), pp. 286–87. Kuznets argues that "tested additions to knowledge . . . are invariant to personal traits or talents and to institutional vagaries and hence are fully transmissable on a worldwide scale, in ways which, say, handicraft techniques in traditional agriculture and industry were not, because they were based on personal knowledge of conditions specific to a given country and could be effectively transmitted only through master-apprentice relations."

[59]The relationship is expressed in proportional rather than causal terms. "The higher the level of economic development of the actors involved, the greater will be the impact of a rise in the level of economic interdependence among the actors on the level of political interdependence among them." See Oran R. Young, "Interdependencies in World Politics," *International Journal*, XXIV (Autumn 1969), p. 732.

[60]Thus, one writer concludes that, though nineteenth-century imperialism was capitalistic, "a socialist or any other kind of society would have developed an outward thrust under the same technical conditions." Eugene Staley, *World Economy in Transition* (New York: Council on Foreign Relations, 1939), pp. 53–54. Contemporary analysts argue only that the technical revolution *enabled* Western states to expand their power over the rest of the planet. Highlighting technical rather than ideological sources of imperialism, however, leaves the impression that the capability to do something is sufficient to explain the choice to do it. See Morse, "Transnational Economic Processes," p. 25.

[61]Skolnikoff, *International Imperatives*, p. 154.

[62]*Ibid.*, p. 183.

[63]Marion J. Levy, Jr., *Modernization and the Structure of Societies* (Princeton: Princeton University Press, 1966), I, p. 14. See also Brzezinski, *Between Two Ages*, p. 195; Sprout and Sprout, *Planet Earth*, p. 3; and Mesthene, *Technological Change*, pp. 24–26.

itatively different from past societies. Obviously, the most advanced societies are on the leading edge of this evolution. It is their knowledge and experience that hold out the prospect of a new social order. While they may assume the role of leadership with some reluctance, they cannot avoid it.[64] Knowledge about a situation, in some sense, necessitates action concerning the situation. The awareness of a problem and the availability of the means to deal with the problem intensifies the sense of obligation to act on the problem.[65] Knowledge is a guide to action on the same footing as ethics. Actual choice becomes obvious choice, and history acquires an ex post facto quality that absolves social groups of primary responsibility for what has happened.[66]

Similarly, obligations associated with awareness constrain choices in the future. Being more enlightened, the leading states have the opportunity to serve their less advanced counterparts. In particular, they have an obligation to educate, to act as "social innovator, exploiting science in the service of man but without dogmatically prescribing the destiny of man."[67] There is less chance today than before that they will misuse this opportunity because, as one study notes in the case of the United States, the ongoing technical revolution "simultaneously maximizes America's potential as it unmasks its obsolescence."[68] Technological advance makes historical concerns with spheres of influence and dominance increasingly irrelevant. Subjective contests over status and prestige will be supplanted by substantive consideration of "human issues."[69] The "old-style" consensus politics, which encouraged compromise over content, is giving way to conscience politics, which equates expertise with

[64]Thus, the U.S. becomes the *ambivalent* disseminator of new values and techniques. It cannot retreat even if it wishes. "This country's commitment to international affairs on a global scale has been decided by history." Brzezinski, *Between Two Ages*, chap. 2 and p. 306.

[65]*Ibid.*, pp. 60 and 204.

[66]Thus, the tendency to view imperialism as an outgrowth of technical conditions (note 60). For a discussion and critique of the way technical models dilute moral responsibility, see Stephen D. Krasner, "Are Bureaucracies Important (or Allison Wonderland)?" *Foreign Policy*, No. 7 (Summer 1972), pp. 159–79. Krasner argues that ". . . the behavior of states is still determined by values although foreign policy may reflect satisfactory rather than optimal outcomes. . . . Before the niceties of bureaucratic implementation are investigated, it is necessary to know what objectives are being sought. Objectives are ultimately a reflection of values, of beliefs concerning what man and society ought to be."

[67]Brzezinski, *Between Two Ages*, p. 256.

[68]*Ibid.*, p. 198. The suggestion is that dominance becomes benign. The point may be similar to Klaus Knorr's distinction between hegemonial and patronal leadership. The former is based primarily on coercive power, the latter on noncoercive or persuasive influence. The distinction is valid and useful, but it also obscures the fact that persuasive influence may often be a more manipulative and decisive tool of power than physical instruments of force. See *Power and Wealth* (New York: Basic Books, 1973), chap. 1.

[69]Brzezinski, *Between Two Ages*, pp. 270–73. The focus on substantive problems rather than subjective perspectives is a distinguishing feature of technical perspectives, as for example, the interest in functions in Skolnikoff, *International Imperatives*. The difficulty in system-level approaches is that the problems (or functions) appear obvious when, in fact, these problems themselves may be subject to alternative definitions depending on subsystem perspective.

enlightenment. Politics flows out of the cornucopia of knowledge. A greater public *consciousness* of the international implications of technology will lead governments to move toward the required forms of institutional adaptation.[70]

In political studies, the past is organized in terms of recurrent patterns. Change is central to this belief as well, but change is no longer a function of cumulative technical or intellectual trends. It is a function of the interaction of human aspirations. Throughout history individual groups and societies have competed with one another to define the terms of their interrelationships.[71] Periodically, dominant groups emerged which sought to consolidate and extend their vision of the "proper" social order to wider areas. The development of technology was less the source than the servant of these imperialist ambitions.

The rise of the middle class in the nineteenth century was the outgrowth of a new conception of the social order, a conception rooted in the aspirations of the French Revolution.[72] To realize these aspirations, the middle class eschewed the coercive practices of politics and power identified with the old aristocratic order. For these practices, they substituted the principles of economic growth and laissez-faire capitalism. They promoted the new technologies to broaden their base of influence and advocated the virtues of decentralized decision-making to neutralize the power of the mercantilist state. Through the doctrine of the harmony of interests, they declared an end to the historical struggle for power. At the same moment, however, they consolidated their own power and "developed a system of indirect domination which replaced the military method of open violence with the invisible chains of economic dependence and which hid the very existence of power relations behind a network of seemingly equalitarian legal rules."[73]

The rise of the professional elite in the twentieth century may reflect recurrent themes of the rise of the middle class.[74] At the end of the nineteenth century, the liberal order split off into two directions, fascist and socialist. After a titanic struggle involving two world wars, the socialist order prevailed.[75] Today, in modernized societies everywhere, tech-

---

[70]Skolnikoff, *International Imperatives*, pp. 176–77.

[71]Thus, as Stanley Hoffmann argues, reality in the international system "is in considerable part the product of a conflict of wills, of a contest of active perceptions competing for the privilege of defining reality." See "Perceptions, Reality, and Franco-American Conflict," in John C. Farrell and Asa P. Smith (eds.), *Image and Reality in World Politics* (New York: Columbia University Press, 1967), p. 58.

[72]Edward H. Carr, *The Twenty Years' Crisis, 1919–1939* (New York: Harper Torchbook, 1964), chap. 3.

[73]Morgenthau, *Scientific Man*, p. 45.

[74]The concept of the professional classes is clumsy, to be sure. It has, nevertheless, been used in the growing literature on technology and society (see McDermott, "Technology," pp. 170–78) and serves our purpose here of a general contrast with the middle classes of the nineteenth century, another amorphous but nonetheless useful concept.

[75]We are speaking here of socialism less in the Marxist sense of common ownership of production than the Western reformist sense of a community of common tasks. These tasks

nocratic elites are at work implementing the design of a more responsible and responsive social order. These elite, it is argued, "exhibit no generalized drive for power such as characterized, say, the landed gentry of pre-industrial Europe or the capitalist entrepreneur of the last century."[76] Their only claim to commanding positions of influence rests in their expertise, their capacity to apply specific technical knowledge to specific technical problems. They substitute the disinterested pursuit of knowledge for the selfish acquisition of gain and the intellectual rule of laissez-innover for the economic rule of laissez-faire. They promote the new social technologies (organizational and managerial techniques in contrast to the mechanical and chemical innovations of the capitalist elite) and stress the centralizing tendencies of technological change to curtail the power of the old capitalist order. They contend that the blurring of distinctions between private and public power (and institutions) lays to rest the traditional antagonism between business and government. A pluralistic style of interdependence marks the end of the era of ideology and imperialism. Concurrently, however, the technocratic elite propagate a new ideology of social performance (effectiveness) and problem-solving. This ideology calls for the progressive centralization of resources and control to attack problems threatening the social order. It "congenially resonates the sentiments of any modern elite in bureaucratized societies who view social problems in terms of technological paradigms, as a kind of engineering task."[77] Advocating change, the ideology is in effect repressive, replacing partisan social contest with planned social containment.

Historically, then, dominant groups have developed technology to serve their social aspirations. Eventually, these groups felt their own principles of social improvement deserved wider application.[78] To extend these principles, they advocated policies of widening contacts and communications. Great Britain in the nineteenth century was the foremost advocate of universal economic liberalism. The United States in the twentieth century is the foremost advocate of universal technological (intellectual) liberalism.[79]

---

are largely social in nature as opposed to economic (capitalism), revolutionary (Marxism), or romantic (fascism). For the classic formulation of Western socialism in these terms, see Karl Polanyi, *The Great Transformation* (New York: Gerrar and Rinehart, 1944).

[76]McDermott, "Technology," p. 156.

[77]Alvin W. Gouldner, *The Coming Crisis of Western Sociology* (New York: Basic Books, 1970), pp. 51–52. In this highly provocative book, Gouldner attacks what he views as a "repressive technocratic current in sociology and the other social sciences, as well as in the general society." He warns against the tendency to abstract social problems from their context, noting that "social science is a *part* of the social world as well as a *conception* of it" and that scientific method "is not simply a logic but also a morality." See pp. 13 and 26.

[78]In one sense, as Edward H. Carr observes, this indulgence may be justified since the dominant group may be so superior that "its well-being necessarily carries with it some measure of well-being for other members of the community, and its collapse would entail the collapse of the community as a whole." *The Twenty Years' Crisis*, p. 80.

[79]This has been called by one writer, "free trade in know-how." See John Diebold,

The extension of aspirations need not be, as earlier theories of realism stressed, the consequence of a lust for power. The projection of ideas may represent instead the very best of the Western conception of man, the desire to ameliorate the human condition. The promulgation of universal (in today's context, global) solutions to social problems is the outgrowth of an arrogance of purpose, not an arrogance of power. The satisfaction of *convincing* others of the rightness of one's own ideas is more heady than the task of *compelling* them to accept these ideas. Education may be a more sensitive and, in the last analysis, more powerful tool of dominance than coercion.

Ideas, however, like power, inevitably encounter countervailing forces. A political perspective recognizes the limits of universal applications of social theories. The advocacy of structures facilitating more open and frequent contacts is always, in part, the advocacy of the skills of those who have the interest and the capability to multiply such contacts.[80] For who was in a better position to trade in the nineteenth century than the British merchant, or who is in a better position to innovate today than the American scientist or engineer. The advocacy of global machinery to manage new technologies may be in the interest of those who will produce most of the hardware and exercise most of the influence in global arrangements. Indeed, global institutions created by dominant powers may often serve to perpetuate the influence of these powers far beyond the point where this influence is justified by real power. This possibility alone, however, suggests that these institutions may not be in the *over-all* interest of weaker participants. The latter may avoid adverse political consequences including the loss of what modest national autonomy they have only by a disciplined detachment from global involvements.[81] Paradoxically, the global solutions they might favor would tend to go far beyond what stronger participants would be willing to accept. Weaker states may insist that global resources be redistributed rather than simply regulated to permit exploitation by those who are already in the best position to undertake such exploitation.[82] Short of significant international transfers, weaker states may prefer a more difficult but also a more contained process of self-development.

"Business, Government and Science: The Need for a Fresh Look," *Foreign Affairs*, LI (April 1973), pp. 555–72.

[80]The point is noted in the Introduction and Conclusion of Keohane and Nye (eds.), *Transnational Relations*: ". . . among unequal states transnational relations may merely put additional means of leverage into the hands of the more powerful states, located at the center of the transnational networks, to the disadvantage of those which are already weak" (p. xx; see also pp. xxiii and 389). The editors go on to argue, however, that transnationalism today is associated with a decline in the dominance of great powers, in particular the U.S. (p. 391).

[81]A point also recognized by Keohane and Nye, *ibid.*, p. 396, and especially the article in this volume by Peter B. Evans.

[82]In U.N. discussions on an international seabed agreement, for example, less developed countries are advocating a central authority that not only regulates seabed exploitation but itself participates in such exploitation. *The Washington Post*, March 3, 1973.

Analysts adopting a political perspective regard the notion that global community is inevitable and that even the above choices represent a kind of global solution (i.e., states must consider the global implications of alternative courses of action) as trivial, since global community in some sense has always existed (even no community or war is a form of community). The real issue is what *kind* of global community will exist, and it seems too early to conclude that the kind emerging under the pressures of modern technology is one in which the locus of decision-making inexorably shifts from the national to the international level. It is just as possible that global community will emerge with national units very much intact, perhaps even stronger than ever. This type of community, it is argued, may be far more representative and democratic than technocratic visions of world unity.

Political studies of change do not stress, as technical studies do, the universal character of knowledge. In some sense, knowledge is regarded as always specific to particular cultures. Knowing involves a selection of what *ought* to be known from what *can* be known.[83] There may be no limit to knowledge, but there is a limit to *meaningful* knowledge. Thus the direction in which knowledge and technology develop depends on values and is not obvious from past choices. Linking actual with obvious choice is a luxury of hindsight. Different societies sense different problems which call for the development of different kinds of knowledge and technology.[84] To be sure, future options are limited by what is already known. But the evolution of future technologies is not inevitable or only a matter of time. It is also a matter of political and social choices which affect funding and the priority and sequence of fields to be explored.[85] In these choices, which are as much social as substantive, most knowledgeable groups may have no greater expertise than other groups.

A Political Approach

The present study applies elements of both political and technical orientations to the analysis of nuclear reactor developments in Western Europe. Nevertheless, the predominant orientation is political. Our argument, in the main, is not that this approach is superior or alone sufficient. We argue only that a choice of orientation is imperative in all studies and that this choice conditions conclusions in a significant way. Conclusions, naturally, may still be questioned in terms of the internal

[83]Morgenthau, *Scientific Man*, p. 166.

[84]Henry Kissinger, "Domestic Structure and Foreign Policy," in Rosenau (ed.), *International Politics*, p. 261.

[85]In the long run, perhaps, knowledge in all fields will be advanced. But when and in what form this knowledge emerges is of critical social and political importance. Nuclear weapons may have been developed eventually without the occurrence of World War II. But the fact that they were developed in wartime and took the form of symbolizing America's emergence as a world power made a considerable difference in postwar international relations.

consistency and logic of the evidence presented. They may also be questioned in terms of the justification of the original orientation on which they are based. But they may not be evaluated independent of this orientation. Assumptions governing analytical starting points may be decisive contributors to the controversies in contemporary literature on technology and international politics.[86]

Four considerations influenced the choice of political orientation: the nature of the subject matter investigated, the current political conditions in Western Europe, the practical utility of an analytical approach which emphasizes leadership, and the normative advantages of a direct focus on national (human) purpose.

Any study of the peaceful uses of atomic energy is likely to highlight political factors promoting technological development. Because of its security implications, the development of civilian nuclear power was, at the outset, and, in considerable part, still remains a primary activity of governments.[87] The commercialization of nuclear power is gradually al-

[86]Two examples may illustrate this point. An early subject of interest in this literature concerned the impact of nuclear technology on international politics. Some analysts argued that nuclear weapons made the concept of war obsolete, while others argued that nuclear war remained a rational option. The different conclusions were, in part, the result of different starting points. The "war is obsolete" school started with the existence of nuclear technology and reasoned that the consequences of using this technology were such as to make war unprofitable and to encourage the formation of larger, political units or arrangements to eliminate armaments and other preparations for war. The "war is an option" school began by examining the political roots or sources (as opposed to consequences) of nuclear weaponry and highlighted the fact that this weaponry was developed out of the commitment to wage war. The technology was a product of political conflict, and its consequences had to be assessed in light of new or continuing sources of conflict. The use of this technology was not inevitable but neither was it highly improbable. Avoidance would depend on the continuous and contrived control of political incentives to use nuclear force.

A second controversy concerned the disclosure in the mid-1960s of a wide disparity in resources devoted to R&D in the U.S. and Western Europe. A decisive American advantage alarmed many Europeans and give rise to the technology gap dispute. Some analysts argued that the political dispute was an outgrowth of some highly impressionistic and, in some instances, inaccurate R&D statistics (i.e., a new soft technology). Regarding these statistics as the occasion for the dispute, they interpreted political attitudes as a response, in most instances an uninformed response, to new developments in transnational technological relations. When the statistics were refined and understanding enhanced, political tempers cooled. The entire episode was viewed as a continuous process of political adaptation to unprecedented technological developments.

Other analysts argued that the technological dispute was the result rather than the cause of political differences. They started with an investigation of political motivations leading European states to regard the initial data as if it were accurate and to escalate an otherwise minor statistical issue into a major Atlantic dispute. They found that growing strategic and commercial differences between the U.S. and Western Europe contributed to the collection and use of R&D statistics as a way of expressing European dissatisfaction with the direction of U.S. policies. When political circumstances shifted in the late 1960s, U.S.-European differences narrowed, and the R&D issue disappeared. In this interpretation, the entire episode is viewed as a discontinuous process of political manipulation of technological phenomena to express conflicts of interest. This interpretation is developed in greater detail in chap. 2.

[87]See Lawrence Scheinman, "Security and a Transnational System: The Case of Nuclear Energy," in Keohane and Nye (eds.), *Transnational Relations*, pp. 276–99.

tering the character of government involvement but only under conditions worked out and supervised by intergovernmental agreement (nonproliferation treaty, etc.). In one critical area of commercial nuclear power, the enrichment of uranium, government involvement remains paramount.

Thus, given the continued direct and indirect role of government and the fact that past habits, procedures, and institutions heavily influence present trends, it did not seem inappropriate to examine the subject matter of this study from a predominantly political point of view, centering on the objectives and interests of governmental actors. Governments unquestionably sought to deal consciously with the development of atomic energy. They may not have successfully harnessed this technology to national ends (though our study provides some evidence to the contrary), but if they act *as if* they *can* control new technologies, this assumption becomes important for interpreting their behavior. And few governments appear to have accepted the "loss of control" argument propounded by students of interdependence.

The political focus does not exclude consideration of nongovernmental and nonnational actors. The orientation is analytical, not institutional. We are also concerned with the interests and objectives of Community (Euratom) actors, domestic nuclear industries and utilities, national research communities, and transnational groupings. By examining the aims of different actors, we can determine the extent to which these aims converge or diverge, thereby establishing a basis for evaluating whether the behavior of transnational actors is modifying or only reinforcing the present international system. Interdependent behavior has been defined as "the outcome of specified actions taken by two or more parties . . . when such actions are mutually contingent."[88] This formulation, in line with a technical orientation, stresses the outcome over the objective of action. Now, in a causal sense, the outcome of action may indeed be independent of the objective, but the outcome may not be *evaluated* independent of the objective (either the objective of the parties involved or of an outside observer).[89] Thus, in the case of

---

[88]See Edward L. Morse, "Crisis Diplomacy, Interdependence, and the Politics of International Economic Relations," *World Politics*, Supplement XXIV (Spring 1972), p. 133.

[89]For example, though contemporary circumstances may make the action of one state contingent on the action of another state, independent of their respective objectives, such action will have an outcome that relates in some manner to the objectives of these states. To evaluate this outcome, states as well as analysts of state behavior must make reference to these objectives. Assuming that states attempt to evaluate the outcomes of action prior to such action, these objectives could also influence the probability of interdependent behavior, since a state faced with a choice between interdependent action with an unfavorable outcome and no action with a less unfavorable outcome may choose no action. It is not safe to assume that these calculations will always favor interdependent action. Calculations of gains and losses from alternative courses of action depend critically on the structure of objectives (and underlying values) in each particular circumstance.

transnational phenomena, it is just as pertinent to ask what the objectives of transnational actors are as to describe the outcomes of their behavior. In fact, as we indicate in note 1 of this chapter, the significance (i.e., evaluation) of the outcomes of their behavior depends critically on whether or not they pursue markedly different objectives from those of their respective governments. If they do not, their behavior, regardless of organizational scope or substantive content, may only reinforce the nation-state system. The focus of this study on objectives of transnational actors helps us to make this important determination.

Nevertheless, it may be questioned whether an approach which arraigns government actors alongside nongovernmental ones (with the implicit advantage of size and salience of governmental actors) is appropriate in sectors involving new technologies—environment, oceans, etc.—in contrast to sectors involving old technologies where government influence was admittedly paramount—nuclear energy, space, aviation, etc. In the new sectors, it is argued, the policy process is highly pluralized; governmental actors play a much reduced role and no longer dominate initiatives. Indeed, the new technologies have been politicized largely by private as opposed to public initiatives. Nevertheless, at some point, the high visibility and cost of modern technology guarantee governmental involvement. Much of the early maneuvering of private actors aims at trying to influence this involvement.[90] Thus, an orientation which regards national policy as the focal point of initiatives aimed at controlling new technologies (rather than one which directs primary attention, perhaps prematurely, to international policy-making) may not be inappropriate at all for investigating the politics of new technologies. This observation holds true even without considering the security implications of these new technologies and hence the obvious interest and potential involvement of governments. Altering the environment, exploiting the oceans, etc., have military as well as civilian uses.

Current political conditions in Western Europe were a second consideration favoring a political orientation. Earlier studies of European politics are focused more on the methods and procedures than objectives of agreement. Community method was a more central focus of analysis than what type of community.[91] These studies have become less applicable as European and Atlantic politics has entered a new phase of flux and re-evaluation. The waning of the bipolar conflict and the full recovery of economic and political confidence in Europe have oc-

---

[90]This seems to have been the case, for example, in the development of U.S. policy on ocean resources. See Ann L. Hollick, "Seabeds Make Strange Politics," *Foreign Policy*, No. 9 (Winter 1972–73), pp. 148–70.

[91]See, for example, Leon N. Lindberg, *The Political Dynamics of European Economic Integration* (Stanford: Stanford University Press, 1963). For a contrasting study emphasizing community types rather than community methods, see David P. Calleo, *Europe's Future* (New York: Norton, 1967).

casioned a review of the premises underlying Western policies in the past. This review has shifted attention away from Community back to national institutions. "The centre of gravity in all the key sectors of industrial development and economic strategy is shifting from the Community institutions in Brussels and Luxembourg to the member governments."[92] Because of this shift, future students of Community politics are urged "to adopt new perspectives which will be more appropriate to the kind of politics that seems to be emerging."[93] The present study does not ignore Community institutions but treats them as additional actors on the same level (relatively) as national institutions rather than as overarching actors dominating national politics.

More explicit interest in national policies and purposes follows from the obvious requirement for new leadership initiatives in Europe. Recent reports draw. attention to the bureaucratic drift and political malaise of European affairs.[94] Political institutions do not suffer from a lack of knowledge about what to do as much as from a lack of will to do it. In these circumstances, technical studies, in which the emphasis is on the common substance of problems, may be less relevant than political studies, in which the emphasis is on the partisan manipulation of problems. This is no argument against knowledge. More knowledge about a subject is always better than less. It is an argument against postponing indefinitely innovative action while more knowledge is accumulated. Reliable or verifiable knowledge is elusive enough as a basis of social science theory, let alone a basis of action in social science practice. Moreover, at some point, the accumulation of knowledge may actually reduce choice and protract inaction. Choice is a function of indeterminacy, and the time for most innovative action may come when conditions are least defined and thus allow for maximum interpretation.[95]

A political orientation isolates the interests and incentives that spark leadership initiatives. Leadership is seldom a function of information alone or even primarily; it depends upon the material and intellectual satisfaction one expects to derive from the burdens and risks of initiative. It also depends upon the capacity to synthesize or telescope issues which goes beyond a mere understanding of the substantive matters involved and includes a sense of timing and intuition.

The emphasis on subjective aspects of leadership may seem out of place in an increasingly interdependent world. Human incentives and

[92]David L. Coombes, *Politics and Bureaucracy in the European Community* (Beverly Hills: Sage Publications, 1970), p. 307.

[93]See Leon N. Lindberg and Stuart A. Scheingold, *Europe's Would-Be Polity* (Englewood Cliffs: Prentice-Hall, 1970), p. 281.

[94]See, *inter alia*, John Newhouse, "Western Europe: Stuck Fast"; and Edward L. Morse, "Western Europe: Why the Malaise?" in *Foreign Affairs*, LI (January 1973), pp. 353–67 and 367–80 respectively.

[95]For perceptive comments on this point, see Kissinger, "Domestic Structure," p. 262, and Hirschman, *A Bias for Hope*, pp. 28–29.

ideas, we are told by some analysts, are rapidly fading fantasies.[96] More interesting sources of change are "unintended" consequences and involuntary adjustments. Yet most studies of interdependence recognize indirectly the continued importance of voluntary change when they advance their paradigms of interdependence in the hope of affecting the perceptions and hence the behavior of foreign policy elites.[97] The desire to affect the way statesmen think about international politics implies that what national policy-makers believe about international politics may actually influence what international politics becomes.[98] National ideas and purposes, in other words, may shape international realities to a greater extent than the repeated emphasis on technological imperatives allows.

Finally, a direct focus on national purposes in the field of international technology has normative advantages which are often overlooked in the desire to circumvent or dilute predominantly nation-state oriented analyses. Technical studies, as we have noted, tend to minimize human responsibility for political action (e.g., imperialism was a product of technological circumstances). Not only is man forever struggling to keep pace with autonomous technological change (and may therefore be forgiven for periodic lapses) but the momentum of technology itself is on man's side, diminishing the requirement for human contributions. It becomes too easy to assume that what *must* be done will be done, irrespective of human initiatives. National governments are called upon to act more responsibly at the same moment they are losing the power and capability to act effectively. With far less power to act, international organizations may be in no better, perhaps worse, position to accomplish what national institutions have been unable or, more precisely, unwilling to accomplish.

The loss of control argument obscures the enormous power of contemporary national governments, especially in foreign policy. By suggesting that power is being diffused, this argument becomes a smoke screen for those who already hold power and may even continue to accumulate it. State-centric approaches may spotlight the power of great powers, but they also spotlight the responsibility. By minimizing the former, interdependence models undermine the basis for the latter. For responsibility is a function of power, the capacity to act. And the nation-state is still the most powerful unit of action in international affairs. De-

[96]For an extreme view, see B. F. Skinner, *Beyond Freedom and Dignity* (New York: Vintage, 1972).

[97]Keohane and Nye (eds.), *Transnational Relations*, pp. xx and 398.

[98]As one writer puts it: ". . . the only way in which transnational developments will exert a beneficial effect and will not simply provide new occasions for conflict is if we (especially our practitioners) jettison some of our most enduring 'eternal verities' about international politics." The implication is that we can change international politics by changing our ideas about it. See Rothstein, *Planning*, pp. 9 and 78.

emphasizing this unit in favor of new transnational actors not only detracts from the opportunity to stress responsible national action but also obfuscates the possibility of irresponsible national action. For economic power can be as oppressive and inequitable as military power. In fact, power may be most evident where it is least visible (e.g., the power of the military-industrial complex), and accountability may be most difficult in a world of invisible economic, as opposed to overt military, relations.

Accordingly, this study resists a tendency to assume that economic politics may be significantly different from military or strategic politics. If economic politics is nonviolent, it is nonetheless partisan. And partisan economic politics always plays itself out against a background of potentially violent strategic politics. Presumably, the difference between these two types of politics is the kinds of goals pursued—wealth and welfare, on the one side, power and security, on the other. Welfare economies produce the products of a peaceful society (appliances, houses, cars, etc.), while power economies produce the products of war (armaments, ammunition, etc.). The products are indeed different, but it is not clear that the technology is all that different.[99] The distinction, therefore, is one of objectives; and the issue cannot be dismissed prematurely by arguing that modernized governments everywhere seek, as their priority political objective, the "good life." As modernized societies become more complex, demand more management, develop larger service (tertiary) sectors, and create more leisure, the opportunities for noneconomic factors to influence economic development may increase. Economic growth in the future may be more culturally-specific than in the past. In this event, attention to political and cultural differences may be increasingly important in determining the international limits of economic rationality.

To summarize, our political orientation leads to the following definitions. Politics is the process of partisan adjustment of interests and objectives (not the cumulative adaptation to technological requirements). It is relations among social units aimed at defining the terms of authority and organization between these units. Politics is, therefore, pre-eminently a relational or contextual phenomenon which takes into account the fact that social units inevitably measure their goals and their capacity to implement these goals, at least in part, in terms of the goals and capacity of others. Technology is the application of knowledge to practical tasks defined and accomplished in a political context where

---

[99]The technology is industrial rather than civilian or military. Producing a civilian jet aircraft, computer, or rocket booster for communications satellites is only marginally different from producing a military bomber, command and control equipment, or an intercontinental ballistic missile. See Kahn and Bruce-Briggs, *Things to Come*, pp. 186–204.

influence is a persisting issue (gains are not necessarily zero-sum but may be unequal). Economics is the process of maximizing material wealth within uneven political and social structures which determine the distribution of wealth and make relevant the question "whose wealth?" The use of these terms becomes clearer in the following chapter.[100]

[100]The author's conception of these terms was most heavily influenced by, among others, Jacques Ellul, *The Technological Society*, trans. Konrad Kellen (New York: Knopf, 1964) and *The Political Illusion*, trans. Konrad Kellen (New York: Knopf, 1967); Bertrand de Jouvenel, *The Pure Theory of Politics* (New Haven: Yale University Press, 1963); and Paul Diesing, *Reason in Society* (Urbana: University of Illinois Press, 1962).

PART II
THE HIGH ROAD

CHAPTER 2

ATLANTIC DIMENSIONS OF EUROPEAN TECHNOLOGY

Interpretations of the technology gap dispute between the United States and Western Europe give evidence of the tendency to assume that economic politics differs from strategic politics.[1] Reaching its peak in the period from 1966 to 1968, this dispute concerned the wide disparity in R&D expenditures invested in the United States compared to Western Europe. The larger American investments, especially in advanced technological areas, were thought to contribute to the greater success of American enterprises abroad. Most interpretations of this dispute viewed the rise of R&D and technological issues in international trade and investment relations as a novel phenomenon.[2] These interpretations were focused on the economic questions of how to measure a technology gap—R&D expenditures, numbers of scientists and engineers engaged in R&D, patent and license statistics, etc.—and how to evaluate these measures in relation to other variables affecting technological performance—market, management, and motivational factors.[3]

---

[1]The material in this chapter was the subject of two earlier articles by the author. See "Die politische Bedeutung der Diskussion ueber die technologische Luecke," *Europa Archiv*, XXV (September 10, 1970), pp. 654–64; and "A Political Interpretation of the Technology Gap Dispute," *Orbis*, XV (Summer 1971), pp. 507–27.

[2]See, *inter alia*, T. F. Schaerf, "The Technological Gap: Issues, Policies and Trade-offs," *Orbis*, XII (Fall 1968), pp. 852–72; Richard Nelson, *The Technology Gap: Analysis and Appraisal* (Rand publication P-3694-1; Santa Monica: Rand Corporation, December 1967); and John Diebold, "Is the Gap Technological?" *Foreign Affairs*, XLCI (January 1968), pp. 276–91. For a similar interpretation by a European economist, see Achille Albonetti, "The Technological Gap: Proposals and Documents," *Lo Spettatore Internazionale* (English edition), II, No. 2 and No. 3 (1967), pp. 139–70 and 263–90.

[3]It is necessary to point out that many of these economic questions in connection with the technology gap were indeed unique and unprecedented. Until around 1960, economic analysis treated technology as a neutral factor, accounting for growth largely as a product of increases of physical and human investment capital. As a result, international disparities in output per worker were explained solely in terms of differences in resource endowments. This approach, as Richard Nelson noted, left "no real room . . . for a meaningful concept of a technological gap." See *The Technology Gap*, Section I. On the role of technology in economic growth, see W. H. Gruber, *Factors in the Development and Utilization of Technology*, A paper prepared for the Conference on Transatlantic Technological Collaboration, Deauville, France, May 25–28, 1967.

The effect of these studies was to suggest that economic issues in international politics are more concrete and empirical than strategic issues and could be resolved by means of expert analysis aimed at securing additional information and hence greater understanding of these issues. In economic areas, in other words, political issues may be primarily the outgrowth of insufficient technical information. The argument in these studies is that, with the appropriate application of expertise, economic issues can be defused and the cooperative rather than conflictive nature of economic politics disclosed. One study argues, for example, that "by raising the technological issue, Western Europe sought greater participation in a single economic system and its technology" (meaning the postwar Atlantic system).[4] Thus, far from reflecting competitive, political motives (characteristic of strategic issues), the technology gap dispute reflected the desire for greater and continued cooperation between the United States and its European allies.

Economic interpretations of the technology gap dispute erred by abstracting technical issues from their political (i.e., relational) context (a tendency, as we noted in chapter 1, of all technical approaches). Few attempts were made to relate the R&D dispute to previous strategic issues and Atlantic politics. Analysts drew a sharp distinction between commercial and strategic technology without acknowledging that the dividing line between military and civilian uses of advanced technology is often a tenuous and shifting one. Determining this line is more a matter of political interests and perceptions than a task of technical or economic definition. Technical advances may arise outside the context of political choice; but if they achieve significance for national policymaking, they must filter at some point through the lens of official scrutiny where they are evaluated in relation to political and social interests and goals. In some instances, technical developments may actually derive from explicit political choices. Thus, a comprehensive interpretation of the technology gap dispute must take into consideration the context as well as the content of Atlantic politics in the 1960s.

This chapter supplies a broader interpretation of technology issues and sets the framework for understanding Europe's effort to overcome technological disparities *vis-à-vis* the United States by pooling research resources of individual countries. It argues that the technology gap controversy represented a stage in the gradual breakdown of the postwar strategic consensus among Western allies. This consensus dealt with basic policies toward the communist world and reflected the predominantly bipolar configuration of postwar international politics. It was this strategic unity that allowed for the separation of strategic and economic issues within the Western world. As long as the Atlantic partners agreed on the primary objectives to be served by Western re-

---

[4]Schaerf, "The Technological Gap," p. 872.

sources, these partners raised few obstacles to the harmonization and integration of economic policies. Indeed, the integration of economic and technological capabilities was the cornerstone of Western strategy endorsing the Common Market and calling for the liberalization of economic relations under GATT and the OEEC (after 1961 the OECD). Agreement on the objectives of integration facilitated the mechanics of integration, leaving functional issues to be resolved on a pragmatic, operational basis by policy-makers in relevant ministries and representatives of particular interest groups. The much heralded pattern of decentralized, pluralistic politics (emphasized, in particular, by studies of the Common Market) was a manifestation of mutual agreement on the urgency to maximize Western strength in defense of Western values.[5]

The strategic consensus underlying functional internationalism in the West began to unravel in the 1960s, and with it the economic and industrial harmony of Atlantic relations unraveled as well. The French challenge to Western strategy called into question the purposes of integration, first at the military and subsequently at the industrial and technological levels. The challenge was precipitated by and helped to accelerate the polycentric evolution of the international system. The blurring of strategic alignments provoked a reassessment of national policies in economic and technological areas. Once the strategic objectives of Atlantic cooperation fell into dispute, each government took a new look at the allocation of resources to functional programs. The tentacles of high-level political concern reached out to recapture policy issues previously delegated to ministries and domestic interest groups. The fluid, fast-changing, and multifaceted ambience of détente politics placed a high premium on reintegration of national policy-making and contributed to the politicization of economic issues which, in earlier circumstances, had been dealt with largely free of high-level involvements.[6]

Through the effort to repossess national resources committed to alliance projects in an earlier era of general consensus, strategic disagree-

[5]The formation of the Common Market would be difficult to understand in the absence of overriding strategic imperatives. The grouping of the six countries was anything but a natural one, either economically or politically. For a century, French ties with Great Britain and, through Great Britain, with the U.S. were more important than ties with Germany. German ties, on the other hand, were stronger with Eastern Europe and Russia than with France. Traditionally, Italy sought to avoid excessive dependence on its more advanced northern neighbors. It required an unprecedented combination of strategic dependence and economic weakness to bring these countries together. Even then, the Common Market did not erase traditional differences; détente has witnessed a reassertion of older patterns, especially in Franco-German relations.

[6]As Richard N. Cooper argues, the intrusion of trade issues into high-level foreign policy concerns "was successfully suppressed during the past 25 years by the postwar agreements, notably the Bretten Woods Agreement and the General Agreement on Tariffs and Trade, governing economic relations among countries; they enabled trade to be relegated to a low level issue." Recent disputes, however, over agricultural, trade, and monetary arrangements have eroded these agreements, allowing "a greater intrusion of foreign trade issues into general foreign relations." See "Trade Policy is Foreign Policy," *Foreign Policy*, No. 9 (Winter 1972–73), pp. 18–36.

ment eventually filtered down to industrial and technological levels. The R&D dispute signaled this intrusion of high-level concern into previously technical and operational issues. The following discussion, therefore, begins with a brief look at the initial dispute over strategic technology and suggests the elements of continuity between this dispute and the R&D controversy over commercial technology. It then probes the politics of the R&D dispute itself. Finally, it argues that the basic issues raised in the R&D dispute continue to permeate Atlantic relations today. Recent trade, monetary, and energy disputes reflect, in contrast to earlier policies of integration and partnership, a growing competition between the United States and Western Europe. The reassertion of national interests and policies does not necessarily imply a disintegration of alliance or Common Market alignments or a return to mercantilist commercial aims. It does suggest, however, a markedly different milieu for bargaining and compromise among Western and now also Eastern countries. A timely recognition of the "new nationalism," which raises again central issues of leadership and priorities, may help avoid unnecessary conflict.[7] In either event, economic and technological issues can no longer be treated independent of larger strategic and diplomatic questions. This fact has implications for Atlantic relations in areas of technological cooperation (to which we return in the concluding chapter of this study) and European efforts to strengthen internal cooperation in fields of civilian research (which is the subject of the main analysis of this study in the nuclear reactor sector).[8]

The Background of the R&D Dispute

Early interpretations of the R&D dispute were based on the question "What is the technology gap?" and developed economic evidence (trade and capital flows, patent statistics, innovation patterns, etc.) to determine whether such a gap existed and, if so, in what specific industrial

[7]The concept of "new nationalism" figures prominently in Theodore Geiger's analysis of transatlantic relations. See *The Fortunes of the West* (Bloomington: Indiana University Press, 1973), especially chap. 6.

[8]A more technical interpretation of the "new nationalism" in Atlantic affairs would stress Europe's economic recovery and advanced state of economic integration as the principal forces bringing political disputes to the surface of recent U.S.-European relations. The results of a spill-over process, these disputes reflect a healthy desire to maintain general consensus and advance future Western cooperation, rather than a breakdown of this consensus. There is much to be said for this interpretation, but it is not clear that relative shifts of economic power automatically precipitate political disputes unless prior differences exist as to the goals toward which this economic power will be applied. In our interpretation above, we ask *why* Europe decided to apply its new economic strength in growing political competition with the U.S., not *how* economic changes in Europe intrinsically entail certain inescapable political consequences. Europe's economic recovery should have had little effect on Western political relationships (except to add more resources to implement common objectives) if broad American and European objectives had remained harmonious, as they were, for the most part, in the 1950s.

sectors.[9] No study asked "Why does the technology gap exist?" What reasons did the Europeans have in 1966–67 for raising the issue and why did the United States seek to redefine the issue as formulated by Europeans? These questions may be understood only in light of the background of Atlantic relations in the mid-1960s.

The technology gap issue moved into the political limelight with the publication in November 1965 of an OECD report showing that R&D expenditures were four times greater in the United States than in Western Europe.[10] In effect, however, this issue was the basis of an earlier dispute within NATO concerning the control of nuclear weapons policy. Soviet development of intercontinental ballistic missiles in the late 1950s altered the strategic situation by giving the Soviet Union the capability to pose a direct threat to the American mainland. This new development raised doubts in European minds that the United States would continue to defend Western Europe under the same conditions as before.[11] Aware of Europe's technological inferiority in providing for its own defense, European statesmen saw the need to secure a more direct and significant role in the decision-making process controlling the American nuclear arsenal. If differences of interest should develop, Europe would then have some control over American strategic technology which alone safeguarded European security.

The subsequent debate over how to meet this new strategic contingency gave rise to a number of proposals for sharing nuclear control, the most relevant one being the Multilateral Nuclear Force. In this debate, France sought a direct role in the formulation of U.S. strategic policy and tried to secure German cooperation to challenge America's nuclear monopoly. The United States, on the other hand, sidestepped the issue of European participation in the *formulation* of American policy and proposed instead a larger European role in the *implementation* of American policy (the effect of the Multilateral Force proposal).

---

[9]This was the central question posed by the OECD in a series of studies on technology gaps. These studies broadly confirmed the existence of a technological gap between the U.S. and Western Europe in both capability and performance but concluded that the disparity had produced as yet "no demonstrable effect on the rate of economic growth of member countries" (p. 23). See summary report of OECD studies, *Gaps in Technology: General Report* (Paris: OECD, 1968).

[10]C. Freeman and A. Young, *The Research and Development Effort in Western Europe, North America and the Soviet Union* (Paris: OECD, 1965).

[11]France was the first to articulate these doubts, but other European countries shared them as well. See Henry Kissinger, *The Troubled Partnership* (New York: McGraw-Hill, 1965). When speaking of Europeans here and elsewhere in this chapter, we do not intend to overlook significant differences among European countries on questions of relations with the U.S. Where essential, these differences will be specified. The collective term nevertheless facilitates a summary discussion of past events in U.S.-European relations and also draws attention to the important minimum set of interests which European countries do share *vis-à-vis* the U.S. as a result of common geographic, strategic, and historical ties.

A compromise was never found. The situation eased after 1966 when France withdrew from NATO's military command, and NATO members established the Nuclear Defense Planning Committee. The latter gave European members a greater voice in *contingency* planning for the use of nuclear weapons, but the sole authority to employ such weapons in *actual* situations remained in the hands of the U.S. president.

From a broad political point of view, it can be said that some aspects of this earlier strategic quarrel filtered over into the later debate on R&D expenditures, management capabilities, etc. Admittedly, on the surface, the two debates seemed unrelated, the first dealing with *military* technology and the second with *civilian* technology. Yet the focus of the second debate on economic issues should not conceal the fact that this dispute really dealt with industrial technology and spotlighted, in particular, advanced industrial sectors, including electronics, aviation, and nuclear power, where the distinction between military and civilian technology is at best tenuous. As will be argued below, Europeans used the language of the technology dispute—R&D expenditures, size of U.S. firms in Europe, etc.—to express concern about the more fundamental political issue of disproportionate American control of key industrial resources in Europe. They raised the question whether U.S. strategic superiority was not rooted in this broader industrial superiority and whether Europe's backwardness in advanced industrial technologies did not constitute a dangerous mortgage on Europe's future political and economic independence.

Given this thread between the earlier strategic controversy and the more recent technology debate (insofar as they both concerned the issue of control of advanced technology—in the one case, military technology only; in the other, more general industrial technology), why did the debate shift in 1965–66 from the military to the economic arena? The answer lies in the progressive relaxation of East-West relations following the Cuban missile crisis. The Cold War tensions of the 1950s kept interest and energies in the Atlantic Alliance riveted on military problems. As these tensions subsided, attention shifted to economic questions. The establishment of the Common Market in 1958 unleashed a massive outflow of American capital to Europe. Moreover, the trade liberalization movement, begun under the auspices of GATT and the OEEC, moved into high gear in the mid-1960s with the Kennedy Round negotiations. As tariff barriers to trade progressively receded, competition sharpened and non-tariff factors such as technology necessarily assumed a greater importance in Atlantic economic discussions.[12]

While Atlantic economic and technological ties were becoming physically more intimate, however, political ties were becoming more and

[12]Richard N. Cooper, *The Economics of Interdependence* (New York: McGraw-Hill, 1968), pp. 76–77.

more strained. The onset of détente disclosed differences in U.S. and European economic interests with respect to trade with the East and advancing economic integration in Western Europe, especially in the agricultural sector. The significant role of American industries in a number of key European markets became more conspicuous as U.S. strategic export controls prevented these companies in some instances from contributing to the domestic and foreign political goals of European host governments[13] and as the strength of American firms in some sectors presented additional problems for European integration.[14] This interference in Europe's economic life was doubly annoying since economic options were the principal instruments of leverage for European countries in their relations with the East as well as with the United States.

Europeans also sensed a widening wedge in global interests between the United States and European countries. In the early 1960s, France and, more reluctantly, Great Britain were in the process of disengaging themselves militarily from non-European areas: France from Algeria and Great Britain from the Far East. At the same time, the United States was extending its military presence into the vacuum left by these countries. The exploding Vietnam situation in 1965 made it clear that Europe's alliance ties with the United States were troublesome not only to the extent that Europe could not be completely sure of U.S. support in all types of crisis situations in Europe (the main concern in the earlier strategic debate), but also to the extent that the United States might involve its allies in political and even military conflicts outside Europe where European countries had just reduced their interests and commitments. A number of European countries thus felt a need for greater political and psychological distance from U.S. aims and policy. The technology issue served, in a measure, to meet this need, acting as a

[13]U.S. strategic export controls have been relaxed in recent years but are still considerably tighter than those of European governments. These controls are particularly stringent and annoying to Europeans in the case of the so-called enemy countries—China, Cuba, North Korea, and North Vietnam. Initiatives by the Nixon Administration have opened up trade opportunities with China, but the export of strategic goods to communist countries remains controversial. In 1971 the U.S. vetoed the sale of British computers to the Soviet Union. *The Washington Post*, May 24, 1971.

[14]It became apparent to many Europeans in this period that the principal beneficiaries of the Common Market were American, not European, firms. The former established centralized headquarters to rationalize their operations on a European-wide basis, while European firms continued to suffer from national divisions. Though Europe could only blame itself for this situation, the success of American firms, particularly in the key technological sectors, added to European frustrations and raised doubts about a united Europe which could not support its own basic industries in the sectors most vital for political independence. Growing U.S. involvement in Europe actually led some Europeans to question the basic concept of the Common Market. See results of extensive interviews in Europe by Jay H. Cerf, *European Investment Climate—1967*, A report to the Board of Directors of the Chamber of Commerce of the United States, Washington, D.C., November 2, 1967.

source of contention in relations with the United States and sharpening distinctions between U.S. and European views.[15]

The R&D Gap and European Interests

This glance at the larger context in which the technology dispute arose throws in relief the political interests at stake in this dispute. By the middle of the 1960s, certain European states, above all France but later Great Britain, Italy, and even West Germany, were "ripe" for an issue to demarcate growing political differences with the United States. Without this background of smoldering discontent, it is difficult to explain the fascination which European governments showed in the 1965 OECD statistics on R&D.[16] In themselves, these statistics were innocuous. They indicated a sizeable lag in European R&D efforts compared to the United States. But they contained no inherent cause for political quarrel with the United States. On the contrary, rough figures showing the same American lead in R&D expenditures had been public since 1963 in a preliminary OECD report.[17] At that time, these figures had scarcely raised an eyebrow in Western Europe. The use of similar, if somewhat more detailed, figures by European officials in 1966 to accuse the U.S. government of having caused the technology gap through its massive support of R&D in American private industry can only be explained in terms of the diverging political perceptions of American and European statesmen in the latter half of the 1960s.

The European reaction to the R&D figures did not develop overnight but evolved through a series of stages in which European officials became increasingly aware of the close tie between modern technological developments and political goals. In 1957 technology was of such remote interest in Europe that it was not even mentioned in the Common Market Treaty. To be sure, the establishment of Euratom involved a technological mission, but the early eclipse of the nuclear community by Common Market events demonstrated that there was little awareness at the time of the broad scope and significance of technology and R&D.[18]

[15]European governments, of course, retained their peculiar schizophrenia about U.S. activities outside Europe. At the same time they sought to distance themselves from U.S. policies in the Far East, they complained about decline of U.S. interest in Europe.

[16]Failing to relate this background to the R&D issue, one American official expressed bewilderment that "a relatively unheralded OECD report . . . caught the public fancy . . . snowballing to the point where the topic is now formally before NATO and the EEC Council." See Ambassador J. Robert Schaetzel, U.S. Representative to the European Communities, *Technology, Europe and the United States,* An address before the American and Common Market Club, Brussels, February 15, 1967 (obtained from Public Affairs Office, U.S. Mission to the European Communities).

[17]C. Freeman, R. Poignant, and I. Svennilson, *Science, Economic Growth and Government Policy* (Paris: OECD, 1963).

[18]For a discussion of early technological issues in connection with the Marshall Plan and the European Agency for Productivity, see Albonetti, "The Technological Gap," pp. 139–70.

The first awakening came after Sputnik and the massive program in the United States to transform the scientific and educational foundations of American society. A publication by the OEEC in 1959 warned that "the full implications of the scientific revolution have not yet sunk into the consciousness of large sections of the population of western European countries. . . . " and concluded that "too much emphasis cannot be placed on the importance of scientific efforts for the future of the European economy."[19] Another study published in 1963 by the OECD urged that governments assume a more affirmative role in the promotion and development of technological instruments to serve the needs of society.[20] These early reports established the framework in which European officials came to perceive technological issues in the context of governmental responsibilities. Thus, when the R&D dispute arose in Atlantic relations, the first impulse of the European states was to view this issue as a problem between governments and not, as the United States insisted, a problem to be resolved between the private sectors of the Atlantic countries.[21]

A second important stage in this evolution of European perceptions came after 1962 through the growing concern, especially in France, over the penetration of American capital into the Common Market.[22] In the winter of 1962, France invoked protectionist measures to stanch the inflow of American capital into France, and in 1965 French representatives introduced proposals in the Common Market urging a common

[19]Dana Wilgress, *Cooperation in Scientific and Technical Research* (Paris: OEEC, 1960).

[20]OECD Advisory Group on Science Policy, *Science and the Policies of Governments* (Paris: OECD, 1963).

[21]The French government, for example, began already in 1960 to collect statistics on R&D to demonstrate and dramatize Europe's technological lag. The work which culminated in the 1965 OECD report also began in this period. These activities suggest that it is a mistake to regard the emergence of new technologies (in the case of R&D statistics, a soft technology) as autonomous and free of vested interests and political motivation. These technologies are always generated in a political context and frequently with conscious political intent. See chap. 1.

[22]U.S. investments in Europe are not insignificant. Unlike European investments in the U.S., which are largely portfolio assets, American investments are direct assets concentrated in key growth sectors and come under the control of a relatively few, large American companies. Direct investment statistics are still scanty, but roughly the following picture emerges. American investments account for only 2–3 percent of total fixed capital assets in European countries but range up to 6–7 percent of fixed assets in the manufacturing sector (hitting 10 percent in the Benelux countries and 16 percent in Great Britain). In key growth industries, U.S. firms control 25–30 percent of the automobile market, 60–70 percent of the aircraft and tractor markets, 65 percent of the computer market, and 30 percent of the telephone market. Three American firms alone—Esso (now Exxon), General Motors, and Ford—account for 40 percent of total American direct investments in France, Germany, and Great Britain. Only twenty firms control 66 percent of total American investments in Western Europe. Christopher Layton, *Trans-Atlantic Investments* (2d ed.; Paris: Atlantic Institute, 1968), chap. 1 and Appendix. See also Jack N. Behrman, *Some Patterns in the Rise of the Multinational Enterprise* (Research paper 18; Chapel Hill: University of North Carolina Graduate School of Business Administration, March 1969), chap. 2.

policy to deal with U.S. investments. As long as these attacks were aimed against U.S. investments directly, however, de Gaulle won little sympathy from the countries with liberal industrial policies, such as Germany and the Benelux states. These countries, and even France itself (liberalizing its policy once again in 1966), could not afford to overlook the economic benefits of American investments. Moreover, a country like Germany could not ignore the political significance of this American economic engagement, especially at a time when U.S. military attention was turning more and more to the Far East. On the surface at least, the investment issue appeared to be a private sector question and hence no *casus belli* for attacking U.S. government policy, even though de Gaulle in his press conference of February 1965 accused the U.S. government of exploiting the international monetary system to extract forced loans from countries holding dollar reserves, thus permitting American corporations to finance their acquisitions abroad.[23]

All of this is not to say that France's Common Market partners were not concerned about rising American capital and market control in key European industrial sectors. Even in Germany and the Benelux countries, grumbling was increasing.[24] Recognizing the reluctance of these countries to challenge American investments head-on, France moved its campaign for a common policy to the level of research as well as investment. Already in 1964 France gained the support of its Common Market partners for an investigation of the requirements of a common science policy in Europe.[25] The Committee on Medium-Term Economic Policy established by the EEC in April 1964 set up a study group (called the Maréchal group after the name of its chairman) to discuss ways to advance European technology and meet American competition. However, the work of this group remained too obscure to evoke much interest; and the investment issue remained too delicate to precipitate common action. To protest the American capital invasion Europe needed a political issue with more public appeal and governmental relevance than research but with less risk than foreign investments.

[23] *Major Addresses, Statements and Press Conferences of General Charles de Gaulle, May 17, 1964–May 16, 1967* (New York: French Embassy, Press and Information Division, 1967), p. 80. De Gaulle's charge was not unfounded and lies at the base of European dissatisfaction today over U.S. monetary and economic policies. (See further discussion above.) But the financial advantage which the dollar reserve system gave U.S. firms was not enough to explain the greater technological dynamism of these firms once they were located in Europe.

[24] See observations on this point by Rainer Hellmann, *Amerika auf dem Europamarkt* (Baden-Baden: Nomos, 1966).

[25] That French interests in this proposal were larger than mere science issues is suggested by Robert Gilpin's observation: "What the French have in mind in calling for a European science policy is not merely cooperation in science and technology but eventually a common policy toward American economic policies and—especially—investments." *France in the Age of the Scientific State* (Princeton: Princeton University Press, 1968), p. 416.

The R&D statistics contained in the 1965 OECD report fulfilled both of these requirements. On the one hand, these statistics provided an explanation for the presence and dynamism of American investments in Europe without directly attacking these investments. The much higher outlays for R&D in the United States resulted in the development of more new products and processes by American firms, and these innovations in turn opened up greater sales and investment opportunities for U.S. firms abroad. At the same time, the statistics showed that this phenomenon was not entirely or even principally a private sector matter. The U.S. government's policy of federal R&D contracts were clearly implicated in the U.S. industrial advantage, since more than two-thirds of all R&D outlays in the United States came from the federal government and over one-half of these government funds flowed into the laboratories of American private industries. Thus, in one flash, the R&D gap illuminated the source of European industrial problems and offered a pretext for challenging U.S. economic influence in Europe at the level of intergovernmental (as opposed to private sector) relations.

Almost immediately R&D became a *cause célèbre* in Europe. At the second OECD Conference of Science Ministers in January 1966 (the first conference having been held in 1963), the R&D report was the principal topic of discussion and alarm. Representatives from countries such as Belgium, which had scrupulously avoided the polemics of the investment issue, charged that one cause of the technology gap was the tendency of American companies to undertake exclusively manufacturing activities in Europe, depriving local countries of the benefits of American research activities (which remained concentrated in the United States), while absorbing ever larger segments of the European sales market.[26] At the NATO meetings in the fall of 1966, the Italian government proposed remedial U.S. action in the form of a technological Marshall Plan to assist Europe in overcoming its technological backwardness *vis-à-vis* the United States.[27] Italy also became aroused, along with Germany, over the potentially discriminatory features of the nonproliferation treaty which threatened to add to Europe's industrial disadvantage. British Prime Minister Wilson warned that Europe faced the prospect of "industrial helotry" unless it reduced its dependence on American technology.[28]

The issue crested in 1967 with the publication of Jean-Jacques Servan-Schreiber's best-seller, *Le Défi Américain*.[29] This book polemicized the U.S. economic invasion of Europe and aroused a popular interest in technology comparable to the Sputnik aftermath in the United States.

[26] *Le Monde*, January 15, 1966.
[27] *NATO Letter*, XV (January 1967), p. 29; and (July/August 1967), pp. 26–27.
[28] *The Economist*, November 19, 1966, pp. 778–79; and January 21, 1967, pp. 197–98.
[29] Servan-Schreiber's book appeared in English under the title, *The American Challenge*, trans. Ronald Steel (New York: Atheneum, 1968).

Technology and National Sovereignty

Before going into the American reaction to this European outcry, let us look more closely at the political justification for European concern over increasing American control of important European industries. The question of control of economic resources within a nation is less politically charged than that between nations. While the American south may complain about industrial concentration in the northeast and far west, it has not suggested that this issue be solved by imposing capital restrictions on investments flowing into these regions. The resources, whether controlled by the southern states or their wealthier coastal counterparts, serve the common economic and political goals of the American government. Between nations this common framework of political and economic goals is frequently missing. Given the existence or potential of diverging goals, the issue of who controls economic resources and can therefore employ them for one set of goals or the other becomes critical.

As long as a rather strong consensus of military and political goals tied the Atlantic Community together in the Cold War period, the issue of control of key resources remained dormant. Except during specific incidents such as the Suez crisis, few Europeans expressed concern over the fact that Europe's security rested with the president of the United States or that American industry staked out sizeable investments in Europe (a development that began even before the establishment of the Common Market). When interests began to diverge, however, initially in the strategic controversy of the late 1950s, the issue of control, in this case with respect to nuclear weapons, became a topic of sharp debate.

The technology controversy reflected the extension of this debate to the control of key industrial resources, important for military but also, and perhaps in the first instance, for economic and sociotechnological purposes. Europeans discovered that just as control over their security resided in the decision-making centers of the American White House, control over their economic and industrial performance in leading sectors of advanced technology increasingly resided in the decision-making centers of American global corporations. The multinational firm with headquarters based in the United States constituted a new form of international economic control, involving a high degree of centralization in the organization of foreign subsidiaries and affecting the most important decisions of these subsidiaries—new investments, R&D activities, etc. After all, to gain this advantage of centralized control was one of the motivations for establishing the global corporation in the first place.[30]

[30]At the time, the degree of centralized control exercised by parent companies was not known in any precise way. One of the few studies of this issue then available found that, for at least one-fourth of twenty-four American subsidiaries in France, "local management enjoyed little autonomy on many issues of vital concern to France." Allan W. John-

Thus, European apprehensions derived from the possibility (whether real or potential) that U.S. parent firms, subject to American legislation and American business, social, and cultural perspectives, might take decisions resulting in subsidiary behavior in Europe contrary to the best interests of host governments. These governments were exercising one of their most fundamental political rights, if not obligations, by asking whether or not sufficient local control of important resources existed to insure that these resources would be applied to domestic goals and objectives, particularly at a time when these goals were, if anything, diverging rather than converging with those of the United States. At stake was a potential loss of national sovereignty. As a Canadian government study of U.S. investments in Canada pointed out at the time,[31]

. . . Foreign control means the potential shift outside the country of some types of decision-making. The extent to which decision-making within the country is eroded varies with circumstances, and basically depends on the power of the foreign firm and its government relative to the government of the host country.

This relationship between the control of economic resources and political decision-making is what was regularly overlooked in economic interpretations of the technology gap. Economics takes as its starting point the maximization of the production of goods and services, assuming that the political consensus on goals toward which these resources will be applied already exists. Politics, on the other hand, is concerned with the prior question of arriving at this political consensus. When this consensus cannot be reached or when a prevailing consensus begins to fracture, the question of the *distribution* of resources, not in the sense of allocation within a system of fixed goals (with which economics is concerned) but in the sense of a resource struggle to determine these goals, becomes just as important, if not more important than the question of the *maximization* of resources.[32]

---

stone, *United States Direct Investment in France* (Cambridge: M.I.T. Press, 1965), p. 72. In recent years, exhaustive studies by Raymond Vernon and associates have shed more light on this matter. Vernon finds that the degree of centralized control of multinational firms varies with organizational structures (geographic versus product) and the amount of experience of foreign subsidiaries. Vernon concludes, however, that "the evidence should not be interpreted to mean . . . that the subsidiaries of US enterprises are free to conduct their own business strategies. . . . discipline and coordination are maintained much more by common training and conditioning than by a stream of commands from the center." See *Sovereignty at Bay* (New York: Basic Books, 1971), chap. 4.

[31]Canada, Privy Council Office, Task Force on the Structure of Canadian Industry, Melville H. Watkins, chairman, *Foreign Ownership and the Structure of Canadian Industry* (Ottawa: Privy Council Office, January 1968). While the problem of American investments is more acute in Canada than in Europe, the fundamental issues are the same.

[32]The failure of economic analysis to relate resource issues to political goals is stressed by Robert L. Heilbroner, "On the limited 'relevance' of economics," *The Public Interest*, No. 21 (Fall 1970), pp. 80–93.

The Management and Market Gaps and American Interests

The American response to the European R&D argument was designed, consciously or not, to circumvent these political implications of European concern. In the period 1966–67, Americans were preoccupied with their growing engagement in Asia. They were in no position to afford a political row with their European allies. Already U.S. strategic policies of nonproliferation and rapprochement with the Soviet Union in the arms control field were encountering skepticism in Europe. No one wanted to add to these troubles by acknowledging that U.S. policy was responsible for the American capital invasion of Europe or that the U.S. government was somehow obligated to do something about Europe's technological backwardness.[33]

Thus, American officials sought to exculpate U.S. policy from any complicity in causing the technology gap, especially the charge that federal R&D contracts were the basis of the American industrial advantage. They needed arguments to show that Europe's technological lag was really Europe's own fault and that the United States could do little more than advise Europe, on the basis of the American experience, on means to strengthen European technology.[34]

The American counterarguments downplayed R&D as the most significant factor in stimulating industrial growth. Instead, management and market factors were stressed. In a speech in February 1967, Secretary of Defense Robert McNamara renamed the gap a management gap.[35] He attributed the American advantage to more advanced managerial techniques and skills in U.S. industries, which, in turn, derived from the broader and more specialized educational system in the United States as well as the more flexible social and cultural attitudes of American industry. The political thrust of this argument was to divert attention away from U.S. R&D policy as the main cause of the technology gap and to indict in its place European policies for failing to modernize European educational structures and break up outdated social and cultural patterns in European industrial markets.

The U.S. stress on market factors coincided with the development of a sophisticated economic thesis by American economists.[36] This thesis

[33]This obligation was implied in the Italian proposals for a U.S. technological Marshall Plan for Europe. For a discussion and analysis of these proposals, see Albonetti, "The Technological Gap," pp. 139–70.

[34]For the arguments of various U.S. government officials at the time, see then Secretary of Commerce Alexander B. Trowbridge, "The Facts About the Gap," *Atlantic Quarterly*, V (Fall 1967), pp. 392–401; and statements by then Vice-President Hubert Humphrey and others, in U.S., Department of Commerce, National Bureau of Standards, *Technology and World Trade: Proceedings of a Symposium, November 16–17, 1966* (National Bureau of Standards miscellaneous publication 284; Washington, D.C.: Government Printing Office, 1967).

[35]*Vital Speeches of the Day*, April 1, 1967, pp. 357–61.

[36]Raymond Vernon has done most to develop this thesis. See, in particular, "International Investment and International Trade in the Product Cycle," *Quarterly Journal of Economics*, LXXX (May 1966), pp. 190–207.

contends that technological leads and lags are the natural consequences of different market features in individual countries. In a country such as the United States with a large-scale market, high wage costs and high incomes, industry might be expected to concentrate on technological developments in capital-intensive, high-income elastic products. Since these products tend to be the most developed technologically, U.S. industry would necessarily enjoy an advantage in pioneer technologies. By contrast, in Europe where markets are fragmented and wages and incomes lower, European industry might be expected to focus on technological development in more conventional, labor-intensive product areas.[37]

Without going into the strengths and weaknesses of this thesis,[38] suffice it to note here that this argument appealed to U.S. politicians because of its emphasis on private sector rather than public policy factors for explaining technological disparities. U.S. government policy could not be held responsible for advantages American companies derived from natural market features.

The management and market gap arguments thus sidestepped European political complaints about advancing American economic control in Europe. To be sure, these arguments reflected valid economic considerations and added perspective to the European fixation with R&D activities. But they were concerned with debatable theoretical issues concerning the causes of technological and economic growth rather than with constructive proposals to close the industrial and power gap which, Europeans felt, was the more significant reality underlying the R&D statistics.[39] A statement by the European Communities' Interexecutive

[37]Another economic explanation of technological disparities between the U.S. and Western Europe may be formulated in terms of the general theory of "collective" or "public" goods. A "public" good is one which is equally available to all members of a group and may be consumed by one member without subtracting from the supply available to other members. According to this theory, the military and space technologies developed by the U.S. qualify as "public" goods available to the European members of the Atlantic Alliance in the form of U.S. nuclear deterrence and the commercial products of U.S. industries in Europe. In these circumstances, the European countries would have no interest in duplicating U.S. technologies but would focus instead on R&D activities promising "private" benefits for specific national purposes. The difficulty with this thesis is that U.S. technologies are not pure "public" goods but also offer private returns (e.g., national prestige) which Europeans can acquire only through independent development of these technologies. Moreover, it is debatable whether technological goods flow as freely across national borders as the "public goods thesis" assumes. See Bruce M. Russett and John D. Sullivan, "Collective Goods and International Organization," *International Organization,* XXV (Autumn 1971), pp. 845–65.

[38]From a political point of view, the thesis obviously erred in equating conventional and pioneer technologies. Even from an economic point of view, as Andrew Shonfield observes, "there are some strong reasons for supposing that in a period of accelerated technological change the advantages of 'forwardness' may be very great indeed." *Modern Capitalism* (New York: Oxford University Press, 1965), p. 59.

[39]For example, the economic debate on the relative importance of R&D, management, and market factors for productivity growth remains inconclusive. A study cited by W. Eric Gustafson in "Research and Development, New Products and Productivity Change," *American Economic Review,* LII (May 1962), p. 178, concludes that "beyond reasonable

Group on Science and Technical Research in 1967 stressed the secondary importance of R&D compared to the broader structural gap dividing the Atlantic partners:[40]

> Whether exact figures confirm or reduce the R&D gap in individual sectors is unimportant. The only significant fact here is that on an overall basis Europe is behind and is obligated to make up this lag.
>
> Moreover, this lag is not solely the result of a temporary aberration which can be overcome by the assimilation of certain techniques. Europe faces today not only the problem of assimilating new techniques but above all the task of altering its structures in order to keep pace with the steadily increasing advance of science and technology.

Thus, what Americans tended to regard as technical adjustments involving the improvement of Europe's management and market capabilities, Europeans sensed as profound political issues going to the heart of the European unification process and the transformation of postwar Atlantic relationships.

The Blurring of the Technological Dispute

Eager to avoid political action, the United States sought to prolong the technical discussions long enough to permit political passions to subside and diplomatic events to shift interest to other subjects. President Johnson set up an expert committee under the chairmanship of his science adviser, Donald Hornig, to clarify or, as administration officials expressed it, to demythologize the gap. Hornig's trip to Europe in 1967 appeared to accomplish this objective.[41] Moreover, by 1968, the technology dispute had been superceded by other diplomatic events. (See below.) Content to let a sleeping dog lie, the White House never released the Hornig Committee report and passed the word to the OECD, after the latter's series of studies on the R&D controversy, that the term "technology gap" should be avoided in subsequent publications.[42]

Just as the broader political context in the mid-1960s created the technology dispute, diplomatic events after 1968 softened the significance of this dispute. These events reflected three contemporary trends

---

doubt causality runs from R&D to productivity and finally to profitability." Studies by Edward F. Denison (assisted by Jean-Pierre Poulier), *Why Growth Rates Differ* (Washington, D.C.: Brookings Institution, 1967) stress managerial and organizational improvements as principal promoters of growth. And work by Jacob Schmookler, *Invention and Economic Growth* (Cambridge: Harvard University Press, 1966) concludes that productivity growth is primarily a product of market growth.

[40]Commissions of the EEC, ECSC and Euratom, *Memorandum Ueber die Probleme, die der wissenschaftliche und technische Fortschritt in der Europaeischen Gemeinschaft aufwirft* (EUR/1711/2/67d) (Brussels: EEC, March 20, 1967), p. 9.

[41]Upon his return Hornig expressed satisfaction that the technology gap had been robbed of its "mystical importance." *New York Times*, July 21, 1967.

[42]Interview with OECD official, Paris, December 1, 1969.

in relations among industrialized, principally Western, countries—polycentrism, protectionism, and parochialism.

Polycentrism in Atlantic relations dates back to Gaullist policies in the early 1960s but has become a practical reality only in recent years with the withdrawal of U.S. troops from Vietnam and the Vietnam-induced retrenchment of American global activities under the Nixon Doctrine.[43] Today, as the rhetoric and, to a lesser extent, the reality of U.S. dominance in the world and in Europe recedes, allied partners in Europe feel less need to lean against U.S. interests in order to assert their own interests, as de Gaulle did by withdrawing from NATO's military command. Not surprisingly, the softening of the U.S. profile has been accompanied by a noticable warming of French attitudes toward NATO, occasioned partly by the Czech invasion of 1968 and partly by domestic preoccupations following French riots in 1968.[44] The diluted American profile was undoubtedly a factor in France's re-evaluation of Britain as an American "Trojan horse" in the Common Market. The concrete onset of polycentrism has also affected German policies, shifting interest from an exclusive preoccupation with postwar ties with the West, especially the United States, to a concerted attempt to re-establish prewar ties with the East. In short, polycentrism has reduced the confinement felt by European countries; and, insofar as one political motivation behind the technology dispute in 1966 was the need in Europe to resist a rigid association with U.S. policies around the world, this motivation has been dissipated by the reassessment of American commitments.

Swelling protectionist sentiments in Atlantic trade relations have also placed the technology dispute in a somewhat altered perspective. Noting the quickening tempo at which American technology is being diffused abroad, American business and labor leaders argue today that the American lead has been shortened, if not eliminated, in certain sectors where European and Japanese producers have made recent inroads into American markets (textiles, automobiles, electronic equipment, etc.).[45] Once

---

[43]On the development of polycentrism in Atlantic relations, see Stanley Hoffmann, *Gulliver's Troubles* (New York: McGraw-Hill, 1968).

[44]For an assessment of recent shifts in French nuclear policy, see Wilfrid L. Kohl, *French Nuclear Diplomacy* (Princeton: Princeton University Press, 1971).

[45]The evidence supporting the claim that the U.S. technological lead has shortened is controversial and rests, for the most part, on studies by Michael Boretsky, senior policy analyst in the U.S. Department of Commerce. For a discussion of Boretsky's views and those of his critics, see Philip M. Boffey, "Technology and World Trade: Is there Cause for Alarm?" *Science*, CLXXII (April 2, 1971), pp. 34–41; and Deborah Shapley, "Technology and the Trade Crisis: Salvation through a New Policy?" *Science*, CLXXIX (March 2, 1973), pp. 881–83. As other economists have observed, the argument rests on the assumption that American innovations, especially in capital equipment, diffuse more rapidly today than ever before, giving low-wage countries such as Japan, Taiwan, and Western Europe a competitive advantage. See William Diebold, Jr., *The United States and the Industrial World* (New York: Praeger, 1972), p. 160.

unsympathetic to European complaints about American expansion in European markets, these leaders now call for protectionist measures to curtail foreign expansion in American markets. The interest in external measures to adjust trade and balance-of-payments accounts (import quotas, export tax rebates, exchange rate adjustments, etc.) represents a general shift away from the focus on internal measures of adjustment, such as technological development, which accompanied the emphasis in the mid-1960s on the reduction of external barriers to trade. At that time, states recognized that, if they could no longer rely on external instruments to affect trade performance, they would have to start thinking in terms of improving the technological efficiency of trading industries. Now, in a climate of protectionist sentiment accenting immediate and fast-acting measures to correct trade imbalances, they prefer once again external actions to avoid more painful and slower-acting internal adjustment. Technological development remains a part of the problem but ceases to be an important part of the solution.

In this focus on external policies to adjust foreign economic accounts, monetary issues became the new center of controversy in Atlantic economic relations. This phase began in 1968 with the imposition by the U.S. government of mandatory controls on American capital exports abroad. Though enacted for other reasons, this policy should have contributed to a slowing down of American investments in Europe. Instead, American companies continued to invest and merely changed the source of finance, borrowing in the dollar market in Europe rather than obtaining funds from parent sources in the United States. The result was a severe disruption of European money markets and a series of exchange rate adjustments by European governments, including separate floating rates in Britain and Italy and a common float among the remaining the Common Market members. Provoked by the unilateral actions of the Nixon Administration in August 1971, which suspended dollar convertibility and curbed U.S. imports, European governments grew increasingly united in an indictment of U.S. inflationary policies at home and U.S. balance-of-payments deficits abroad as the underlying cause of world monetary instabilities.

This monetary debate, while ostensibly different from the earlier technology dispute, nevertheless expresses many of the same European concerns about U.S. economic (and political) hegemony that formed the basis of Europe's interest in R&D several years before.[46] In some respects, the money debate may be more central to international economic relations than trade or technological issues. Europe is more con-

---

[46]On the monetary problem, see, *inter alia*, Diebold, *The United States*, pp. 215–57; C. Fred Bergsten, *Reforming the Dollar: An International Monetary Policy for the United States* (Council Papers on International Affairs; New York: Council on Foreign Relations, 1972); and for a more political analysis, David P. Calleo, *The Atlantic Fantasy* (Baltimore: The Johns Hopkins Press, 1970), chap. 6.

scious of the fact that the dollar reserve system, by allowing the United States consistently to spend more than it earns abroad, bestows a measure of economic flexibility which underwrites American political and industrial activities in foreign countries. With the enlarged Common Market accounting for more than 23 percent of total world exports (compared to 16 percent for the United States),[47] European countries seek a greater measure of control over the rate at which international liquidity expands. They may achieve this by securing a proportionate European influence over the issuance of SDRs (Special Drawing Rights, the new IMF paper gold which may replace the dollar as the key international currency), and/or by establishing a common European currency which, in the absence of international agreement, may rival the dollar in an emerging multiple currency reserve system. The United States, on the other hand, seeks to preserve its leadership role and link monetary issues to strategic and defense expenditures abroad. If Europeans object to American deficits increasing dollar reserves, they must be prepared to assume some of the military responsibilities which exert such a drain on American resources.

After 1971, the drift toward more flexible exchange rates, including in 1973–74 the floating of the dollar and the French franc, took some of the urgency out of the monetary debate. Trade and monetary issues became redefined in the context of a new dispute, the energy crisis. The Arab oil embargo and the quadrupling of world oil prices in the last quarter of 1973 set off a scramble among oil-consuming states to safeguard energy imports. Barter agreements exchanging manufactured exports and technology for oil supplies threatened to undermine the fabric of the postwar liberal trading system. In addition, anticipated balance-of-payments deficits in oil-importing countries and the accumulation of vast foreign exchange reserves in oil-producing countries (both developments the result of higher oil prices) threatened to destroy the international monetary system. Through proposals for energy cooperation among industrialized states (Canada, Western Europe, and Japan), the United States sought to establish an integrated framework to facilitate resolution of the entire range of issues dividing Western countries (trade, monetary, technological, etc.). France, however, sought to compartmentalize issues (e.g., through bilateral deals to satisfy energy needs alone) and rejected the reassertion of broad-scope American leadership. Characteristically, France's Common Market partners took a more ambivalent stance, wanting neither to gang up on the United States nor to alienate France.

Finally, a new parochialism in Western societies, focusing on domestic social and economic ills, has drawn off interest and support for technological pursuits. Sharp cuts in U.S. space and military research ex-

---

[47]The figures exclude trade among Common Market countries themselves. See Geiger, *Fortunes of the West*, p. 173.

penditures have necessitated a painful readjustment in the American scientific community.[48] Rather than the booming enterprise of five years ago, fueled by massive government outlays, American science today is searching for new priorities and leadership. Faced with similar domestic pressures, a number of European governments have also cut back science programs.[49]

The Future of Atlantic Technological Relations

Because technological disputes have fallen out of the limelight, one is tempted to conclude that the issue is passé. There is little doubt that the specific interest in R&D has been superceded by a plethora of other concerns involving strategic negotiations between the superpowers, security and force reduction issues in central Europe, and trade and monetary conflicts. The R&D dispute has not been resolved, however, as much as it has been absorbed into the larger context of contemporary relations.[50] The isolation of this dispute in the mid-1960s was characteristic of the compartmentalized treatment of postwar Atlantic relations. The dispute served the purpose of raising some differences with the United States at a time when most European countries were unprepared to follow up the broader implications of these differences. Countries like Germany and Italy were only beginning to extricate themselves from two decades of dependence on American leadership and resources. They were reluctant to modify the familiar and comfortable formulas of European reliance on American initiatives, especially in security areas. In recent years, these countries have shown a greater boldness in confronting the ramifications of Europe's enhanced economic status. They have begun to perceive and relate industrial and technological issues to larger issues of national significance. Formerly separated, research activities are now viewed more and more as instruments of national policy; and, as one analyst observes, " 'science policy,' an increasingly popular field of government activity, is likely to add to the national bias of policy toward foreign investment."[51] The trend, in short, is toward a

---

[48]Layoffs of scientists and engineers have caused many Europeans, who were part of the original brain drain to the U.S., to return to Europe and an increasing number of American scientists to move abroad. Since 1967 science expenditures in the U.S. have been falling. The 1972 budget contained the first increase in five years, but many observers felt this was scarcely enough to offset the inflation of research costs in the interim. *New York Times*, January 30, 1971.

[49]After the riots in 1968, for example, the French government cut back sharply on atomic energy expenditures. The reordering of national science priorities has been one of the developments adversely affecting European cooperative projects such as Euratom and the space organizations. See chaps. 3 and 4 of this study.

[50]As Raymond Vernon notes, there may be a "dusty sound" to the phrase "technology gap" today. "Yet if the concept was justified five or six years ago, it is still justified today. Nothing very fundamental has changed in the technological relationships between the United States and Europe." See "Rogue Elephant in the Forest: An Appraisal of Transatlantic Relations," *Foreign Affairs*, LI (April 1973), p. 578.

[51]Diebold, *The United States*, p. 195.

more holistic approach to national activities, complicating functional cooperation within the Atlantic Community as well as the European Community.

The new approach is evident first in the greater watchfulness with which the individual European countries follow U.S. industrial activities in Europe. Parochialism centers attention on domestic problems and makes European governments more sensitive to economic and social disruptions caused by foreign investment. The requirement for planning in complex, modern societies places a premium on the effective control of local resources. Diplomatic innovations also emphasize independent economic resources. Germany, for example, saw the full implications of the technological issue only when the nonproliferation treaty threatened to impose external constraints on German industrial performance. Today, a very important shift may be taking place in the attitudes of German private industries, heretofore closely allied with American private firms. In the important electronics, nuclear power, and aviation sectors, German industrialists, with official support, have shown an increasing tendency of late to align with European as opposed to traditional American partners.[52]

The new sense of independence in Europe is also evident at the Community level. In Luxembourg in October 1967 the Science Ministers of the Common Market countries adopted a resolution calling upon the Maréchal group to investigate the prospects of European cooperation in seven new fields of advanced technology—data processing, telecommunications, transportation, oceanography, metallurgy, meteorology, and toxicology (air and water pollution). In 1968 European members of the space organizations, ELDO and ESRO, adopted a united position challenging U.S. dominance in the control and management of Intelsat, the international satellite corporation. This challenge resulted in May 1971 in the conclusion of a new agreement reducing the American voting strength on Intelsat's board of governors to less than 50 percent and gradually transferring the management of Intelsat from the U.S. quasi-public firm, Comsat, to an international office of director general.[53] In the electronics sector, the Commission of the European Communities took a definite stand for the first time ever in October 1969 on a question of U.S. investments.[54] In face of the planned expansion of Westinghouse in the Common Market, the Commission urged European manufacturers to find a common European alternative to this prospect, warning in a separate report that, without cooperation among European firms, Europe would have to abandon all hope of competing with Ameri-

---

[52]For details, see, in particular, chaps. 5 and 8 of this study.

[53]Jonathan· F. Galloway, *The Politics and Technology of Satellite Communications* (Lexington, Mass.: Lexington Books, 1972).

[54]The position was taken in reply to a question in the European Parliament. *International Herald Tribune*, October 17, 1969.

can rivals in this key industrial sector.[55] The Commission's nuclear "white paper" of October 1968 and a Community report on the aviation sector sounded similar warnings for these important industries.[56]

None of this is to say that the European countries are on the verge of overcoming their internal differences and pooling their technological resources to meet "the American challenge." The new nationalism impedes internal coordination as well as external ties. As we discuss in subsequent chapters, the Euratom experience, as well as more recent attempts to initiate new programs of cooperation in other sectors (Luxembourg resolution), does not give much reason to expect significant European progress in this area in the near future. British entry into the Common Market may not significantly alter these prospects.[57] The problem is much more complex. As long as science and industry in Europe continue to draw their principal financial and psychological backing from national governments responsive to national goals and national taxpayers, the chances of any significant coordination of Europe's technological resources remain remote. This is especially true in the absence of any coordination of defense industries, which are closely allied to the civilian technologies under question. For all of its laudable recommendations concerning industrial research cooperation, the Commission's memorandum of 1970 on Community industrial policy (Colonna Memorandum) reflected the basic impasse by devoting all of three short paragraphs to the defense sector.[58] The participation of Great Britain, with its cautious attitude toward defense and foreign policy cooperation, is not likely to change much in this regard. Moreover, in the first years after entry, British industry will be pressed to show visible national gains from Common Market participation. These circumstances are not likely to encourage British initiatives to dilute the significance of national boundaries by means of transnational industrial realignments.

European cooperation in science and technology is further complicated by the opening up of opportunities for cooperation with Eastern countries, especially the Soviet Union. In recent years, all of the major European countries have concluded significant industrial and technological exchanges with communist countries.[59] Statesmen anticipate

[55]Commission of the European Communities, *L'industrie éléctronique des pays de la communauté et les investissements américains* (No. 8240/1/IV/1969/5) (Brussels, 1969).

[56]Commission of the European Communities, "Survey of the Nuclear Policy of the European Communities," *Bulletin of the European Communities*, supplement (September/October 1968). For extracts of the Commission's study of the aerospace industries, see *Research and Technology* (bulletin published by the Press and Information Services of the Commission of the European Communities, Brussels), No. 90 (March 16, 1971).

[57]Though some studies have speculated to the contrary—see, e.g., Christopher Layton, *European Advanced Technology* (London: George Allen and Unwin, 1969).

[58]Commission of the European Communities, *Die Industriepolitik der Gemeinschaft* (No. 4984/1/1970/5) (Brussels, 1970), pp. 172–73.

[59]Such exchanges have included the nuclear sector which we examine in greater detail in the body of this study.

further exchanges as a direct and indirect consequence of negotiations at the European security conference, which convened in 1973 and will continue into 1974. European fear of superpower condominium, stimulated by the SALT negotiations, may replace the earlier confinement of Cold War alignments and motivate pan-European (i.e., excluding the Soviet Union) efforts at technological cooperation. It is doubtful, however, that the Soviet Union will permit its Eastern European neighbors to get ahead of it in the race to obtain Western technology. For the near future, at least, polycentric tendencies will be greater in Western than Eastern Europe, reducing incentives for cooperation within Western Europe while complicating attempts at cooperation with Eastern Europe.

The discussion in this chapter suggests that national politics, far from becoming an increasingly inappropriate perspective for studying technological relations among modernized societies,[60] may be a more relevant focus than integration or interdependence. Rather than losing control to a sprawling and pluralistic form of bureaucratic politics, governments seem to be reasserting control over activities formerly delegated to lower levels of authority. To describe this trend is not to pass judgment on whether governments will succeed in re-establishing national supremacy over technological and institutional fragmentation. The forces of interdependence may be too great. If the trend is ignored, however, confusion and misunderstanding may be heightened. The rest of this study seeks to illuminate the dynamics of national politics in technological relations. It proceeds on the assumption that national variables may be more critical for understanding international technology than global economic or scientific variables. The next chapter examines how such national factors affected orientations and institutions in the nuclear reactor sector and determined, in great part, the outcome of collective efforts to develop reactor projects through Euratom.

---

[60]This is suggested, for example, when analysts argue that the state-centric model "is . . . more useful now than it is likely to be in the future." Robert O. Keohane and Joseph S. Nye, Jr. (eds.), *Transnational Relations and World Politics* (Cambridge: Harvard University Press, 1972), p. xxv.

CHAPTER 3

NATIONAL DIMENSIONS
OF EUROPEAN REACTOR PROGRAMS

A key phase in the development of international issues is the process of defining the problem around which states conflict or cooperate. National institutions and values play a prominent role in this phase. As one analyst notes, "the definition of what constitutes a problem and what criteria are relevant in 'solving' it reflects to a considerable extent the domestic notions of what is just, the pressures produced by the decision-making process, and the experience which forms the leaders in their rise to eminence."[1] These domestic inputs are strongest when the problems are least concrete (security compared to economic issues) or when the international environment is most relaxed (détente compared to confrontation).

In the case of security issues, domestic factors are generally assumed to contribute to conflict. Security can only be defined in terms of the values and experiences of different countries; and if these values and experiences differ widely, statesmen may be unable to communicate with one another, let alone define and settle mutual problems. In the case of civilian technological and industrial relations, domestic imputs are generally assumed to contribute to cooperation. Here the problems, it is argued, tend to define themselves. Technical and economic criteria are the same in all countries, and domestic scientific and industrial groups behave more often according to the universal prerequisites of scientific investigation than the parochial dictates of national interests.

The assumption that domestic factors contribute to cooperation in technological relations may be correct in remote areas of basic scientific research. But increasingly science is being pursued with an eye toward eventual application. One of the consequences of this closer integration of science and technology has been the gradual politicization of scientific activities. As one study relates, "the last ten years have seen the crystallization of something we have learned to call national science

---

[1] Henry Kissinger, "Domestic Structure and Foreign Policy," in James N. Rosenau (ed.), *International Politics and Foreign Policy* (New York: Free Press, 1969), pp. 261–62.

policy, that is, the deliberate attempt by government to utilize its scientific resources, its manpower and its laboratories towards the nation's interest."[2] Consequently, international scientific activities today, not to mention derivative technological activities, may be less free of political intrusions than ever before.[3] The current trend toward reintegration of state activities and national aims (which we noted in the previous chapter) places new emphasis on national as opposed to universal attributes of science. National political, economic, and social differences, therefore, become important for understanding the ways in which societies perceive, define, and evaluate scientific and technological undertakings.

The present chapter explores these differences as they affected the national development of civilian nuclear power in Europe from 1945 to 1970. (Developments after 1970 are treated in the case studies, chapters 5-8, and the conclusions, chapter 9.) It examines comparatively three major dimensions of each national program—political, economic and industrial, and scientific and technological. Political differences go a long way toward explaining the difficulties of cooperation in nuclear programs. In each country, nuclear power enjoyed a somewhat different political significance, giving rise to unique institutions and relationships within a society which complicated associations across societies. Economic and industrial factors, at times, ameliorated but also exacerbated these differences. Indeed, one is impressed in general with the extent to which economic and industrial structures mirrored political preferences and objectives. Even the attitudes of scientific groups did not escape the effects of dissimilar sets of national priorities.

Political Dimensions

Countries may approach the development of major technological programs in several ways. They may take an overt political approach and subordinate these programs to direct governmental control; they may de-emphasize political ambitions by adopting a more technical or industrial orientation; they may assume no coherent orientation at all; or they may combine these alternatives in various ways. Of the Euratom countries, France took the most conscious political stance toward reactor programs. As a result, the nuclear agency established in France (CEA) was a strong, politically coherent administrative body which exercised considerable autonomy in domestic and foreign policy areas

---

[2]Hilary Rose and Steven Rose, *Science and Society* (London: Allen Lane, 1969), p. 131.

[3]*Ibid.*, pp. 180–81. As the authors of this study write: ". . . the sense in which the scientist was above national boundaries . . . could not survive the growing integration of science into the total structure of individual societies. . . . Thus to argue that science is by its nature universalistic increasingly falls into the fallacy of confusing an *is* with an *ought*." See also Diane Crane, "Transnational Networks in Basic Science," in Robert O. Keohane and Joseph S. Nye, Jr. (eds.), *Transnational Relations and World Politics* (Cambridge: Harvard University Press, 1972), pp. 244–45.

of reactor development. By contrast, Germany took a more industrial orientation toward nuclear power (for political reasons, as we note below). The government arm of nuclear policy was administratively weak but technically strong and adroit at facilitating informal liaisons between public and private resources. Institutional strength in Germany was in the private industrial sector. Italy was prevented by internal political quarrels from adopting any coherent attitude toward reactor programs. A fluctuating political scene crippled government initiatives and isolated industrial groups from required public support and stimulation. Institutional fratricide canceled out Italian technical capabilities. Finally, Belgium and Holland combined political and industrial orientations. Committed politically to the uniting of Europe, these countries pursued specialized nuclear programs which exhibited predominantly technical and industrial features. The tendency toward technical specialization assumed and thereby advanced the political goal of European integration.

France

France's political approach to nuclear policy was part of a broader French approach to science and technology in general. Under de Gaulle, but also before then, France grasped the substantive and symbolic significance of modern science for national life. Science was recognized as a crucial ingredient of military power, economic growth, and public welfare. It was felt that, unless France reformed her traditional institutions to integrate science into the larger purposes of national policy, she ran the risk of becoming a political appendage of the scientific superpowers. For France, therefore, "the goal [was] to make science an instrument of French economic, military, and political objectives."[4] The profoundly political character of this effort was suggested by de Gaulle when he observed that the modernization of France must be accomplished "without France ceasing to be France."[5]

French policy reflected the postwar desire to restore national self-confidence to the French state. World War II and the humiliation of Vichy did not discredit nationalism in France as much as it confirmed the need to revitalize the national spirit to serve as a bulwark against future recurrences of national passivity in the face of aggression. In the 1950s, foreign policy developments reinforced the political requirement to cultivate French nationalism. France was excluded from Anglo-American collaboration in the exchange of nuclear information. After

---

[4]For a lucid analysis of how France sought to accomplish this goal, see Robert Gilpin, *France in the Age of the Scientific State* (Princeton: Princeton University Press, 1968). Quote in text comes from p. 7.

[5]See de Gaulle's press conference of February 5, 1962, in *Major Addresses, Statements and Press Conferences of General Charles de Gaulle, May 19, 1958–January 31, 1964* (New York: French Embassy, Press and Information Division, 1964), p. 158.

1958 developments in NATO convinced de Gaulle that France was being excluded from alliance policy as well. With Britain abstaining from continental politics and Germany muzzled by formal and informal political constraints, France emerged as the only country with sufficient national purpose and grievance to articulate and defend "European" interests in relations with the United States. Foreign policy circumstances, therefore, encouraged national formulations of French interests and a comprehensive approach to military, economic, and technological programs.

The integrated approach characterized French nuclear programs from the outset.[6] In October 1945, de Gaulle, then president of the Provisional Government of France, issued an ordinance establishing the French Atomic Energy Commission (CEA). The Commission was charged with the conduct of "scientific and technical research looking toward the utilization of atomic energy in the various fields of science, industry and national defense."[7] Though it is probable at the time, as Lawrence Scheinman points out,[8] that the long-term commercial significance of atomic energy was uppermost in the minds of French officials, the inclusion of defense-related applications of nuclear energy in the CEA mandate anticipated the total approach that France adopted in the nuclear sector. Whether France decided to develop a military program or stay exclusively with civilian applications, the choice would reflect over-all national considerations.

The organization of the CEA mirrored the high-level importance of nuclear issues. Rather than being attached to a ministry (the traditional practice with public institutions in France), the CEA was placed under the direct authority of the prime minister. Internally, the organization was given a dyarchic structure. Scientific affairs were entrusted to a high commissioner (a scientist), while administrative responsibilities fell to the administrator-general (an engineer-administrator usually of the French polytechnician tradition). These two officials, together with the prime minister (or his representative) and three other individuals (in the early years, all scientists), sat on the Atomic Energy Committee, the executive organ responsible for the over-all direction of CEA policy. This unique organizational setup combined scientific and administrative autonomy with high-level political control and was considered at the time uniquely suited for the development of advanced technological programs with crucial significance for national power.

---

[6]The following discussion draws heavily on Lawrence Scheinman's account of *Atomic Energy Policy in France under the Fourth Republic* (Princeton: Princeton University Press, 1965). See also Bertrand Goldschmidt, *The Atomic Adventure*, trans. Peter Beer (New York: Pergamon Press, 1964).

[7]La Documentation Française, "Le Développement Nucléaire Français Depuis 1945," *Notes et Études Documentaires*, No. 3246 (Paris: La Documentation Française, December 18, 1965), p. 6.

[8]Scheinman, *Atomic Energy Policy*, p. 7.

At the beginning, scientific considerations dictated the evolution of the CEA. In the formative years from 1946 to 1951, a nucleus of French scientists, instrumental in the establishment of the CEA, dominated the decision-making process and focused activities on the development of physical and manpower resources to support a long-term program in nuclear research.[9] By 1950 research centers existed at Chatillon and Saclay, and some 250 scientists and engineers had been recruited and trained.

The influence of French scientists declined rapidly after 1951. In that year, Frédéric Joliot-Curie, the most prominent political and scientific member of the French research community, was dismissed from his post as first high commissioner of the CEA because of his communist party affiliations.[10] His successor, Francis Perrin, represented more of the administrative-public servant tradition in French politics and became identified with a cadre of French officials in the CEA who emphasized the military and economic uses of atomic energy over its purely scientific applications. A reorganization of the CEA in 1951 gave this group additional influence by adding representatives from industry and government to the Atomic Energy Committee and reducing the relative strength of scientists.[11]

The shift of influence was clearly visible in the first nuclear five-year plan announced in 1951. The plan provided for the construction of two atomic piles at Marcoule for ostensible commercial uses, but several choices reflected military considerations as well. The decision to base civilian power developments on the natural uranium reactor probably had less to do with a desire for strategic independence from the United States than the simple fact that fuel for the development of enriched uranium reactors was available only in the United States and was not being exported at the time under U.S. strategic embargoes. The decision to use the first reactors to produce fissionable materials (chiefly plutonium) rather than electrical power, however, betrayed a long-term military interest. Fissionable materials could be used to fuel subsequent civilian reactors, but they could also be used to make atomic bombs. As Scheinman argues, the only proven use of plutonium at the time was in the manufacture of nuclear weapons.[12] The decision to collect such material, therefore, prepared the way for future military as well as civilian options.

The strategic character of French nuclear policy became fully evident in the late 1950s and set the framework for the struggle in the 1960s

[9]The scientists held the majority (4 to 2) on the Atomic Energy Committee. *Ibid.*, pp. 28 and 36.

[10]Goldschmidt, *The Atomic Adventure*, pp. 64–65.

[11]Scheinman, *Atomic Energy Policy*, pp. 49–54.

[12]*Ibid.*, pp. 82 and 88. The fact that the CEA set up a special section to prevent misuse of information from the plutonium program likewise indicated military intent.

between political and economic priorities in French programs. In 1955 the CEA undertook, in collaboration with the Ministry of National Defense, the construction of a third nuclear reactor at Marcoule with specific military applications and established the Bureau d'Études Générales (BEG) as the cover organization of a secretly planned atomic weapons unit.[13] These developments strongly influenced the Euratom Treaty debate in the French Parliament in 1956. As we note in the next chapter, drafters of the Euratom Treaty sought to proscribe military development of atomic energy in Europe. The French government under Guy Mollet originally supported this proposal, but domestic proponents of a French weapons program compelled the government to reverse its position. Except for this reversal, the Euratom Treaty may have been turned down by the French Assembly as was the EDC proposal in 1954.[14]

The Euratom Treaty debate, together with the Suez crisis in the fall of 1956, crystallized French sentiment in favor of a military weapons program. Though the official decision to make a bomb was not taken until April 1958, just six weeks before General de Gaulle took office, this decision, as Scheinman writes, "was more a formality than a shift in atomic policy."[15] In 1957, France included funds in the second five-year plan for the construction of a uranium enrichment plant at Pierrelatte, a facility essential to an independent weapons program. The second five-year plan also confirmed the choice of natural uranium reactors as the basis of the French civilian program. Since graphite moderation resulted in more efficient plutonium production (and the civilian reactors had the dual purpose of producing plutonium and electrical power), graphite replaced heavy water (which had been used in the first research reactors) as the moderating substance of subsequent reactors. Thus, the combination of natural uranium, graphite moderation, and gas cooling, which became the technical trademark of French civilian reactors, was not uninfluenced by military considerations. By the time the Euratom Treaty came into force and de Gaulle assumed power, the political-military aspect of French nuclear policy was paramount.

De Gaulle added a psychological dimension to the military aspect of French programs. Under the Fifth Republic, technological programs became the expression of the country's independence in its widest sense.[16] Not only was atomic energy vital for defense and space endeavors, it was important as a catalyst for social and economic modernization.

---

[13]*Ibid.*, pp. 116–22. The Ministry of National Defense also ordered at this time the construction of an atomic submarine with a natural uranium reactor engine. In 1959 this program switched to the development of a light water reactor engine.

[14]*Ibid.*, p. 164.

[15]*Ibid.*, p. 183.

[16]Gilpin, *France*, pp. 3–16 and 188–217.

Most of all, technological independence was necessary to preserve a nation's capacity to express its unique genius. National pride and self-confidence, the basis of independent action, depended on the demonstration of achievement in fields of new technology. This symbolic significance of civilian nuclear technology programs caused the CEA to maintain resolutely its commitment to a French reactor system (gas graphite technique), long after economic considerations dictated otherwise.

Germany

The development of nuclear policy in Germany reflected neither the military concerns nor the political-psychological emphasis of French policy. This fact had less to do with conscious choice than the conditions of Germany's existence after the war as a defeated power. In contrast to the situation in France, nationalism in Germany was totally discredited. Not only was the nation divided, but the allied powers systematically uprooted the nationalistic structures of fascist society, disaggregating power on a state and local basis. Federal powers were reduced to a minimum. As a result, reconstruction in Germany proceeded on a piecemeal rather than on a comprehensive basis. Instead of being connected with central aims of national life, technical and economic activities were compartmentalized. Officials deliberately downplayed the political and military significance of these activities. The aim was to justify scientific and technical undertakings on their own terms.

Since the military uses of atomic power were most visible and the industrial uses still quite remote, this task in the field of nuclear policy was a particularly delicate one. Remarks by the first German minister of Atomic Questions, Franz Joseph Strauss, at the inaugural meeting of the German Atomic Commission in 1956 suggested the fine line German programs would have to follow:[17]

> For us it is not a matter of military or political power. Nor is it a matter of prestige. But it is indeed a matter of asserting and securing the place of the German people among the industrial nations, a place which we have regained again with so much effort.

It would be wrong to conclude, however, that Germany's industrial orientation to nuclear power was nonpolitical. The restoration of domestic confidence in government demanded a businesslike approach to postwar reconstruction. Moreover, the de-emphasis of political factors in

---

[17]*Bulletin des Presse- und Informationsamtes der Bundesregierung* (bulletin published by the Press and Information Office of the Federal Republic of Germany, Bonn), January 28, 1956. The remoteness of industrial applications of nuclear energy and German awareness of the political sensitivity of the nuclear issue influenced the composition of the German representation at the Geneva conference on peaceful uses of nuclear energy in 1955. Four of the five German representatives were foreign office people. *Frankfurter Allgemeine*, February 11, 1956.

connection with nuclear energy promoted three foreign policy objectives of the new German government. First, in light of continuing allied suspicions of German intentions, it was the best (and perhaps only) strategy for restoring German influence in Western circles. It also helped to maintain Western unity on the one issue of paramount political importance to Germany—reunification. By restricting issues to technical and industrial considerations, Germany was able to parry France's attempt to divide the Western alliance and force Germany to choose between Paris and Washington on major political issues, including reunification. Finally, the industrial emphasis defused possible Eastern and, in particular, Soviet reactions to a revival of German activities in the nuclear field.

Thus, in contrast to France, domestic and foreign policy considerations in Germany called for a cautious and fragmented approach to nuclear policies. In content, this approach was industrial and economic; in context, it was no less political than that of France.

Not surprisingly, therefore, the nuclear effort in Germany began in the private and local sector and only gradually acquired a national or public character as the economic costs of nuclear developments mounted and Germany resumed a more normal political role in Western politics. Under pressure from the state government in North Rhine-Westphalia, the postwar allied ban on German research in nuclear reactors and enriched uranium was relaxed in the early 1950s, and the Paris Accords in May 1955 formally lifted these restrictions in return for a German pledge not to manufacture nuclear weapons. In that same month, a group of representatives from twenty electronic and chemical firms set up a study group to examine the new opportunities offered by nuclear research.[18] The German government followed this initiative in October by establishing a new Ministry for Atomic Questions (Bundesministerium fuer Atomfragen).[19] This Ministry assumed responsibility for establishing over-all guidelines in the nuclear field and delineating spheres of competence between private, state, and federal authorities through the drafting of an atomic law (*Atomgesetz*). To assist and advise the Ministry, a German Atomic Commission (Deutsche Atomkomission) was created, composed of outstanding personalities from the scientific, industrial, and government fields.[20] While only an advisory organ, this Commission, by virtue of its expertise, played a leading role in the subsequent development of the German nuclear program. Alto-

---

[18]This group included most of the major firms (Siemens, AEG, etc.) which later played an important role in German development. *Frankfurter Rundschau*, June 4, 1955.

[19]This Ministry went through a series of name changes after 1955, becoming in 1957 the Bundesministerium fuer Atomkernenergie und Wasserwirtschaft; in 1962, the Bundesministerium fuer Wissenschaftliche Forschung; and in 1969, the Bundesministerium fuer Bildung und Wissenschaft. In this study, unless otherwise specified, we use the general designation, Science Ministry.

[20]*Bulletin des Presse- und Informationsamtes der Bundesregierung*, January 28, 1956.

gether, the relatively informal and circumscribed authority of the Atomic Ministry stood in sharp contrast to the administrative power of the French CEA. As one German official later described it, the German formula in the nuclear field was "very small bureaucracy, very large expert groups."[21]

The desire to avoid guilt by association made German officials wary of either imitating or becoming too dependent on the French and British programs, which stressed military applications (the French program especially after 1956). Instead, association with the U.S. program seemed more natural, both because the United States was the principal advocate of industrial uses of atomic energy through the Atoms for Peace Plan and because the United States, as the major Western ally, was the safest partner for Germany in terms of minimizing foreign suspicions, at least in the West. These political considerations contributed to the ironic fact that, at a time when institutional cooperation was being discussed between Germany and France in the context of Euratom, hardly any contact existed between the French and German nuclear programs.[22] In part, this circumstance may be explained by differences in scientific and industrial preferences, e.g., a German preference for American technology and German suspicions of French *dirigisme* in economic policy. But in light of subsequent developments, the overriding consideration seems to have been political.[23] Throughout the next decade, German industrial and scientific groups demonstrated more enthusiasm for cooperation with U.S. partners than French partners. This behavior of private groups coincided with official public policy to resist French attempts to pry Germany away from strategic dependence on the United States. It seems unlikely that the two devel-

[21]J. Pretsch, "Europaeische Zusammenarbeit in der Kernforschung," *Atomwirtschaft*, XI (August/September, 1966), p. 421. The political weakness of the Atomic Ministry contributed to the delay in drafting an *Atomgesetz*, which did not receive parliamentary approval until 1960. In this debate, the SPD championed state control of nuclear developments, especially ownership of nuclear materials; while the CDU/CSU and FDP supported loose government supervision combined with private industrial initiatives.

[22]The first contact was made in June 1956 by Jules Guéron, then a director in the CEA program who later became research director in Euratom. Guéron's visit to Germany was followed by an official visit of Francis Perrin, High Commissioner of the CEA. See Jules Guéron, "Une geographie cordiale de l'Europe atomique," *Les Problèmes de l'Europe*, No. 42 (4th Quarter, 1968), pp. 29–30. Little resulted from these exchanges, as much because of French preoccupation with the domestic debate over a military nuclear program as because of German determination to keep at arms length from these military developments. By contrast, as early as the fall of 1955, German and British officials exchanged visits (*Frankfurter Rundschau*, October 7, 1955), and German industries opened talks with American firms about nuclear assistance (*Koelner Stadt-Anzeiger*, November 25, 1955).

[23]Andrew Shonfield notes, for example, that German business suspicions of French planning were not based primarily on economic or technical grounds but on a political view, namely "that planning, like Bismarck's alliances, implied a horse and a rider . . ." and German business was determined not to be the horse. See *Modern Capitalism* (New York: Oxford University Press, 1965), pp. 245–46.

opments were unrelated. Private groups operate within a political context, and government directives need not be explicit or even always articulated to be understood and observed by nongovernmental actors.

Germany's industrial orientation persisted in the 1960s but with increasingly political overtones. The fact that Germany developed a non-military rationale for the advancement of nuclear energy did not diminish the political significance of civilian developments. In fact, the exclusion of military uses accentuated this significance. In foreign policy, competence in civilian programs assumed the important role that competence in military programs traditionally played. In domestic policy, civilian technological programs became the sole basis of the development of local technological and economic resources. At the end of the decade, two prominent scientists in Germany's nuclear program forcefully affirmed this heightened political character of civilian programs:[24]

It is no longer military power which proceeds parallel with political power. Rather, we believe that political power is acquired today to a large extent from the pursuit of civilian technological projects. The capacity to act politically derives from this pursuit.

A recognition of the salient political nature of nuclear programs caused the German government to assume an increasing financial and managerial role in nuclear affairs.[25] Though federal financing was minor in 1956 in the establishment of research centers at Karlsruhe and Juelich, funds for these centers increased steadily thereafter until, by 1970, national contributions covered more than 90 percent of the costs. Federal participation in program management also accelerated after 1957. In that year, the German Atomic Commission sponsored the drafting of a first unofficial nuclear five-year plan, the so-called Eltville 500 MWe program. When the private sector showed little interest in this program, government officials sought Euratom funds and threatened direct federal funding to stimulate private initiatives. By the end of 1962, these pressures produced the first major advances in German nuclear development. RWE, the largest German electrical utility, and Bayernwerk announced the construction of the first demonstration-size light water reactor at Gundremmingen. Also, in 1962, certain scientific groups in Germany began to advocate openly the advantages of centralized coordination and planning of "big science" projects.

For some time, the coherent approach of the French program had been the object of admiration in German circles,[26] and the USAEC's

[24]W. Haefele and J. Seetzen, "Innovationen durch ziviltechnologische Grossprojekte in den siebziger Jahren" (unpublished manuscript obtained from authors, April 1969).

[25]Gerhard Stoltenberg, *Staat und Wissenschaft* (Stuttgart: Seewald, 1969), pp. 25–62.

[26]See, e.g., the review of the 1962 CEA annual report in Deutscher Forschungsdienst, (The German Research Service) *Sonderbericht Kernenergie*, October 3, 1963.

Report to the American President on Civilian Nuclear Power in December 1962 spotlighted the crucial role of central planning and forecasting in the development of advanced technology. The advanced reactor programs in Germany (fast and high temperature gas reactors) became the focus of this new interest in long-term planning and financing. Under strong urging from the scientists associated with these programs, the federal government announced at the end of 1962 a second five-year plan (1963–67) which foresaw a total expenditure ($625 million) some two and a half times larger than the Eltville program. While still relatively modest compared to the French and British programs, this sum established the principle of federal leadership. From this point on, the proportion of nuclear research funded by state authorities diminished steadily; and private industries came around to accepting the idea of federal (as well as Euratom) assistance without regarding this assistance as a breach of the free market system.[27]

The political importance of German civilian nuclear programs crystallized publicly in the debate over the nonproliferation treaty (much as the military character of the French program crystallized in the earlier Euratom Treaty debate in the French Assembly). The threat of discrimination between nuclear and nonnuclear states in the inspection provisions of this treaty prompted government officials to exercise a vigorous role in trying to preserve the Euratom inspection system (which treated all members as equals, unlike the proposed IAEA system which would apply only to nonnuclear states) and to secure long-term supplies of fissionable fuels for German nuclear manufacturers and consumers. In 1967, the German Atomic Commission announced the third five-year nuclear plan, the first official nuclear program (the two previous plans being unofficial) which called for federal expenditures exceeding $1 billion and placed new emphasis on the development of nuclear fuel facilities.[28] German authorities initiated a Euratom study of a common European enrichment plant and began bilateral talks with the Dutch and British to construct a separate plant if the Euratom proposals failed.

The nonproliferation debate thus accelerated the transition in Western diplomacy from alliance politics dealing with strategic issues to industrial politics dealing with economic issues. This transition was bound to emphasize the political weight of German industrial programs, especially in the nuclear sector. In the area of industrial politics, Germany could afford to assert more openly its national interests.

---

[27]A book published in Germany in 1963 by Niels Grosse entitled *Oekonomik der Kernenergie* documented this change in thinking about government-industry relations in advanced technological programs. See Deutscher Forschungsdienst, *Sonderbericht Kernenergie*, September 5, 1963.

[28]Germany, Federal Ministry for Scientific Research, *3. Atomprogramm der Bundesrepublik Deutschland 1968–72* (Bonn: Federal Ministry for Scientific Research, n.d.).

Italy

If the French and German nuclear programs became increasingly conscious of the over-all national significance of civilian nuclear power, the Italian program became the target of an internecine struggle between liberal and interventionist economic groups within Italy.[29] Groups on the Right, including the core of the Christian Democratic Party and smaller liberal parties, favored reliance on private development of nuclear power and close alignment with the United States on alliance matters. Groups on the Left, including the Socialists and reform-minded Christian Democrats, advocated nationalization of power production and a more neutral position on alliance issues. The struggle between these two forces sharply muted Italian participation in the foreign policy debate dividing France and Germany (i.e., dependence on the United States versus European independence under French leadership) and severely crippled the exploitation of nuclear programs for consistent internal purposes.

As in Germany, private industries took the first steps toward the development of nuclear research in Italy. In 1946 a number of companies, including Edison and Montecatini, established the CISE laboratory in Milan to foster research in the industrial uses of atomic energy. By 1951, CISE scientists had completed most of the experiments necessary to build a research reactor. Government support was needed, and in 1952 the Ministry of Industry set up the CNRN, a technical advisory organ of the government, to coordinate nuclear research. In contrast to the French CEA, CNRN did not enjoy a separate legal identity and dealt only with fundamental as opposed to industrial or military applications of nuclear energy. The weakness of the structure and the vagueness of CNRN's program provoked criticisms from CISE scientists who had not been adequately consulted in the establishment of this committee.[30]

Early tensions between CNRN and CISE reflected the incipient struggle between private and public forces for control of the Italian energy sector. CNRN, fearful of criticism from the Left, distrusted the private financial backing of CISE. As a result, CNRN was reluctant to support CISE's proposal for the construction of an all-Italian reactor.[31] Instead, Francesco Giordani, president of CNRN (and subsequently one

[29]For a detailed discussion of this struggle, see F. Roy Willis, *Italy Chooses Europe* (New York: Oxford University Press, 1971).

[30]Mario Silvestri, *Il costo della menzogna: Italia nucleare 1945–1968* (Torino: Giulio Einaudi, 1968). The author of this book is a CISE scientist who, as the title of the book suggests, is sharply critical of government policies in the nuclear field. While his account must be read with an understanding of the political contest between supporters of industrial versus governmental control of Italy's nuclear program, it is an invaluable (not to mention, amusing) source of information about key events in Italian nuclear development.

[31]*Ibid.*, p. 123.

of Euratom's three wise men—see chapter 4) visited the United States in 1955 and purchased a 5 MWe American heavy water reactor. CISE undertook the installation of this reactor at Ispra, but frictions with CNRN soon led to the takeover of construction by CNRN together with two state-controlled industrial groups, ENI and IRI. In 1959 CNRN decided to turn over the research reactor and the entire Ispra center to Euratom. This decision aroused considerable opposition in CISE and private industrial circles and probably reflected a government attempt to dispose of a research center where private industrial interests were becoming entrenched.[32]

The internal dispute complicated the drafting of nuclear legislation. Not until 1960 was an abbreviated statute passed creating a new organization, CNEN, to replace the CNRN. CNEN was given a legal status within the Ministry of Industry (but not autonomy from ministerial control, as in the case of the CEA) and broader responsibilities in training and certain operational areas of nuclear development.[33] The relationship between the new committee and industry as well as other government agencies was left vague, however. CNEN had no authority for direct interventions in the industrial field, and the Ministry of Foreign Affairs exercised responsibility for external relations in the nuclear field. "In effect," as one study notes, "existing departments had already carved out from the total atomic-energy field that portion which was relevant to their own major concerns," leaving CNEN "with a residue of regulatory and operational tasks associated with research on and development of atomic energy."[34] In sum, CNEN was "an extremely modest counterpart to the atomic energy authorities of other countries. . . ."[35]

In 1962, the internal struggle between liberal and interventionist groups reached its apex. The coalition of Socialists and Christian Democrats which came to power in that year nationalized the electrical utility sector. Parliament established the state-owned electrical utility, ENEL, which took over responsibility for all electricity production in Italy, including the conventional and nuclear operations of private com-

---

[32]The circumstances behind the government's decision to dispose of Ispra are unclear, but it can be assumed, as further discussion above reveals, that government officials preferred to locate Italy's chief nuclear establishment near Rome rather than in the north where industrial forces were dominant. Construction of the Cassacia center, which subsequently replaced Ispra, began in 1958 outside Rome.

[33]General direction of CNEN rested with the Interministerial Committee for Economic Planning (CIPE), while administrative responsibility fell to a Steering Committee whose President was the Minister of Industry. The Secretary-General exercised daily responsibility for CNEN activities. Italy, National Committee for Nuclear Energy, *Programs and Activities* (Rome: National Committee for Nuclear Energy, 1970), pp. 8–14.

[34]John E. Hodgetts, *Administering the Atom for Peace* (New York: Atherton Press, 1964), p. 22.

[35]*Ibid.*, p. 64.

panies such as Edisonvolta.[36] Also under the jurisdiction of the Ministry of Industry, ENEL represented another agency competing with CNEN for operational responsibility in the development of nuclear power.

Nationalization did not end the contest for jurisdiction over nuclear power. In 1963 a political scandal erupted involving the secretary-general of CNEN, Felice Ippolito. A leading figure in Italy's early nuclear activities, Ippolito was charged with illegally holding two government positions simultaneously and spending money unwisely in the development of Italian nuclear programs.[37] In addition to his CNEN post, he was a member of the administrative council of ENEL. The scandal symbolized, in part, the unresolved issue of relative responsibilities of CNEN and ENEL in Italian nuclear affairs. The controversy severely impeded technical programs and occasioned a parliamentary review of nuclear policies.[38] Not until 1967–68 did CNEN and ENEL agree on administrative arrangements for Italy's two principal reactor programs, CIRENE and PEC. And even then a severely disillusioned industrial sector showed little enthusiasm for rapid development of nuclear power.

Belgium and the Netherlands

If Italy had the resources but lacked institutional strength for a coherent nuclear program, Belgium and the Netherlands possessed institutional strength but lacked resources. Generally dependent on foreign trade and technology, these countries developed relatively small nuclear programs, which were significant only as a part of a broader international division of labor in nuclear affairs.

Belgium got an early start in the nuclear field on the strength of vast uranium resources discovered in the Belgian Congo before World War II. During the war, the Belgian government in exile granted exclusive rights to the Congo uranium to the United States and Great Britain. In return, Belgium received privileged access to allied information in the nuclear sector. The McMahon Act in 1949 dissolved these arrangements, though the United States continued to compensate Belgium for uranium supplies through grants for the construction of nuclear research facilities in Belgium. On the strength of these grants, Belgium began its own nuclear effort.[39]

---

[36]In actual fact, ENEL controls 74 percent of electricity production, exceptions being made in the case of private companies producing power for their own use. See *Atomo e Industria*, March 1, 1963.

[37]*Atomo e Industria*, September 1, 1963. See also Silvestri, *Il costa della menzogna*, pp. 323–26.

[38]*Atomo e Industria*, August 1, 1964.

[39]With the revision of the McMahon Act in 1954, Belgium concluded a new agreement with the U.S. guaranteeing the U.S. 90 percent of the Congo uranium through

In 1950 the Belgian government established an Atomic Energy Commission (hereafter Belgian CEA) to encourage and coordinate all Belgian nuclear activities.[40] In 1952 this Commission launched Belgium's program in applied nuclear research, establishing, with U.S. assistance, the Centre d'Étude pour les Applications de l'Énergie Nucléaire. Reorganized in 1957, this center became known as CEN. In laboratories constructed at Mol (northern Belgium), CEN assumed responsibility for all technological research associated with the use of nuclear energy. Like the Belgian CEA, CEN came under the direction of the Ministry of Economic Affairs and Energy.

Belgium's nuclear programs were specialized and, compared to Italy and ultimately France, marked by a consistency of objectives. With technology imported from the United States, CEN launched in 1959 an informal three-year plan, calling for specialization in the study of fuel activities, especially plutonium recycling, and development of several research and material testing reactors.[41] Until 1965, American light water technology was the main focus of research. After that, fast reactors consumed an increasingly larger share of research resources.[42] As this program matured, integration with the German program (see chapter 8) replaced the earlier association with U.S. technology. The five-year plan of 1968–72, except for the growth of the fast reactor effort, continued many of the same programs (e.g., plutonium recycling) begun in 1959. Throughout, Belgium pursued limited objectives within an international framework.

The Netherlands did not begin applied nuclear research until 1955.[43] In that year, government, industrial, and utility groups established RCN to develop technical knowledge and experience in the peaceful uses of nuclear power and to give this information to Dutch industries. A foundation, not a government agency, RCN maintains close relations with Dutch industries and the TNO laboratories organized by the government before the war to carry out research projects for public and private concerns.[44] Government officials sit on the Board of Governors

---

1957 and 75 percent through 1960. In return, Belgium once again acquired equal access with Canada and Great Britain to U.S. civilian nuclear information.

[40]For a sketch of this early history, see Reginald LaMarch and Aime Vaes, "Nuclear Energy in Belgium," *Euratom Bulletin*, V (June 1966), pp. 36–43.

[41]Belgium, Ministry of Economic Affairs and Energy, Atomic Energy Commission, *L'Énergie Nucléaire en Belgique, Bilan des Activités au Cours de la Periode 1960–1962* (Brussels: Imprimerie et Publicité du Marais, 1963).

[42]Belgium, Ministry of Economic Affairs and Energy, Atomic Energy Commission, *L'Énergie Nucléaire en Belgique, Bilan des Activités au Cours de la Periode 1963–1967* (Brussels: Imprimerie et Publicité du Marais, 1968).

[43]Edward Hoekstra, "Nuclear Energy in the Netherlands," *Euratom Bulletin*, IV (September 1965), pp. 66–73; see also the Netherlands, Ministry of Economic Affairs, Interdepartmental Committee on Nuclear Research, *Nuclear Energy in the Netherlands* (The Hague: Ministry of Economic Affairs, n.d.).

[44]See English summaries of RCN annual reports. RCN, *Summary of Activities* (The Hague: RCN, 1962–69).

of RCN, and RCN receives financial support from the Ministry of Economic Affairs, the government branch responsible for nuclear as well as over-all energy affairs. The fact that nuclear responsibility rests with the Ministry of Economic Affairs (also true in Belgium) rather than the Ministry of Education and Science illustrates the primary association of nuclear development with industrial and economic objectives.[45]

The Dutch program has depended heavily on Euratom. This fact has made the Dutch nuclear enterprise less stable than that of Belgium. On the other hand, the Dutch program is also smaller.

Economic and Industrial Dimensions

The individual national programs developed under different economic and industrial conditions as well as contrasting political guidelines. The Euratom countries differ in terms of their over-all energy requirements and dependence on external fuel supplies. In each country, the relationship among the oil, coal, natural gas, and nuclear power sectors varies, and the institutional arrangements in the electricity sector range from fragmented, private structures to centralized, state-owned utility companies. The various industrial structures and traditions also affect patterns of contracting and manufacture in the nuclear reactor and fuel sectors. While these elements often act as independent variables in the choice of nuclear programs, the evidence suggests they also conform to traditional and contemporary political priorities of the individual states. Politics may influence economics in advanced technological programs as often as economics influences politics.

France

The slow development of commercial interest in nuclear power in France contributed, in part, to the largely governmental and military character of the early French program. Despite France's heavy dependence on energy imports, nuclear power did not attract immediate interest as a new source of cheap energy. This was owing, in part, to the stabilization of energy import requirements in the early 1950s, relieving some of the urgency of the immediate postwar years when imports jumped dramatically.[46] It was also owing to the steady drop in the cost of conventional fuels. A third factor was the existence of a state monopoly in the electricity sector minimizing the type of competition

---

[45] A series of advisory councils dealing with nuclear energy coordinates Dutch activities at the interministerial level. The Ministry of Science and Education also contributes support to nuclear activities. See the Netherlands, Ministry of Foreign Affairs, *The Kingdom of the Netherlands: Facts and Figures* ("Education and Science in the Netherlands," No. 32; The Hague, 1970–71), pp. 77–87.

[46] The increase in energy imports after the war was reflected in the enlarged role of oil in power production. In 1929 coal supplied 92 percent of France's energy needs, in 1954 only 68 percent. Oil from the Middle East filled the gap.

which stimulated an early interest in nuclear power in the United States. The EdF, established in 1946, has had a legal monopoly of production, transmission, and distribution of electrical energy in France.[47]

Initially, EdF officials regarded the costs of nuclear power to be too uncertain to warrant a large immediate investment. To explore further the commercial exploitation of nuclear systems, however, EdF participated in the establishment of an advisory body to the CEA which brought together representatives of industry, CEA, and EdF (known as the PEON group). In the summer of 1955, this group approved the construction of a series of power reactors at Chinon totaling 800 MWe of installed capacity by 1965. Like the Marcoule reactors, the Chinon plants employed gas graphite techniques, which served the dual purpose of plutonium production for military programs and power production for civilian uses. At the time, EdF expressed no preference between gas graphite and American light water techniques. To keep abreast of light water developments, EdF decided in 1960 to collaborate with Belgium in the construction of an American-type reactor plant at Chooz, France (the SENA plant—see chapter 5).

In this early phase, French industries played a supportive role in the civilian program as suppliers of reactor materials and components. They exerted little influence in determining the over-all direction of French policy. During the construction of the Marcoule reactors, the CEA organized the participation of the nuclear construction industry around the formula of "industrial architect" (*architecte industriel*). Under this formula, the CEA assigned to industry the supervision of the technical and design studies associated with reactor projects but retained for itself the rights of general contractor (*maître d'oeuvre*) with attendant responsibility for the over-all financial and administrative control of the project.[48] The CEA exercised a similar control in the production and servicing of nuclear fuels. While retaining general responsibility for development and production of fuels, it assigned to industry various operational tasks. In practice, this resulted in the establishment of firms jointly run by the CEA and private companies, but in which the CEA retained over-all authority.[49] The EdF assigned even fewer respon-

[47]In practice, the EdF monopoly allows private firms to produce power for their own use. Altogether, in 1967, EdF activities accounted for 69 percent of total electricity production and 80 percent of total distribution. See *Entreprise*, April 6, 1968, p. 63.

[48]See La Documentation Française, "Le Développement Nucléaire Français," pp. 24–25.

[49]These companies operate the CEA processing, refining, and preparation plants at Le Bouchet (PEC) and Malvesi (Saint-Gobain), the fuel fabrication plants (SICN, SFEC, and CERCA), the reprocessing installations at Marcoule and La Hague, and the isotope separation plant at Pierrelatte. For a listing of these plants and their characteristics, see Euratom, Directorate-General for Industry and Economy, *First Target Programme for the European Atomic Energy Community* (EUR 2773e) (Brussels: Euratom, March 1966), chap. B3.

sibilities to industry. In the case of the Chinon reactors, the EdF acted as its own industrial architect, restricting industrial participation to outside suppliers.

The net result of these practices was a relatively scattered French nuclear industry. To be sure, French firms grouped together into design consortia for the purpose of carrying out industrial architect functions (Indatom and GAAA being two of the earliest of these consortia). But these design consortia, while acquiring considerable technical experience and expertise from CEA contracts, did not integrate manufacturing activities. They did not face, therefore, the critical investment choices associated with over-all financial and economic responsibility which might have stimulated concentration. By contrast, German industries in the mid-1960s were rationalizing and consolidating manufacturing activities. They anticipated the requirements of scale and financial capacity necessary to produce economically competitive nuclear power stations.

The first commercial sale of a light water reactor in the United States in 1964 generated initial pressures for a reorientation of French reactor and industrial policies. The CEA during this period was sponsoring a vigorous campaign to export gas graphite reactors, and in 1964 the PEON group announced intentions in the next five-year plan to expand dramatically domestic construction of gas graphite plants. Both of these activities met with considerable skepticism in EdF and French industry. EdF entertained doubts about the CEA's increasingly political stance on civilian reactor techniques as symbols of national prestige and purpose.[50] French industry, aware of the emerging superiority of light water systems, sought wider responsibilities to match competitive developments in Germany and the United States.

In the early years of the Fifth Plan (1966-70), therefore, groups in the EdF and French industry increasingly urged the CEA to extend French reactor efforts to the development of American light water systems, especially after the EdF's largest experimental gas graphite station, EdF-3, suffered a technical setback in 1966. Industrial circles took steps to facilitate a possible change-over from gas graphite to light water technology. Mergers in 1966 reduced the number of large design groups from five to three (GAAA, Alsthom, and SOCIA, the latter formed from companies previously associated with Indatom and SEEN),[51] and EdF assigned, for the first time, the role of industrial architect to industry in the construction of a reactor sold to Spain in 1966 and in the planning of the large Fessenheim reactors scheduled for construction under the Fifth Plan.[52] Some French firms (e.g.,

[50] Le Monde, January 7, 1965. Also interview with EdF official, Paris, April 1, 1970.

[51] Entreprise, March 10, 1966, p. 35.

[52] Le Monde, May 10, 1966.

Alsthom) also initiated contacts in this period with American firms concerning the licensing of light water technology.

Still mesmerized by the desire for independence, the CEA resisted these pressures. As problems developed with gas graphite reactors, the CEA took a greater interest in alternative models other than the American type, such as natural uranium heavy water reactors or enriched uranium reactors of the British advanced gas reactor design.[53] The few who advocated increased work with light water reactors favored the development of an independent French light water *filière* based on the experience of the CEA's submarine propulsion program (which featured a land-based light water reactor prototype).[54] This alternative would preserve the continued hegemony of the CEA over French reactor developments, while the desire of French industry to use foreign licenses for development of light water technology would mean reduced CEA influence.

After a review of French policy, top-level political decisions in December 1967 reaffirmed the policy of reliance on gas graphite technology but approved the construction of a second light water station in cooperation with Belgium (SEMO plant at Tihange).[55] Financial cutbacks necessitated by the French riots in 1968, however, forced cancellation of plans for the construction of new gas graphite plants under the Fifth Plan and resulted in the release of numerous scientists and technicians at CEA laboratories. Meanwhile, planning for the light water station at Tihange went ahead on schedule. Observing the direction of events, French industries placed themselves in a position to develop American-type reactors. The key electrical company, CGE, broke from the SOCIA group and joined GAAA and Alsthom in setting up the new consortium, SOGERCA.[56] Utilizing Alsthom licenses with GE, this group possessed the capability of developing boiling light water systems; while SOCIA, together with Westinghouse licensees, Framatome and Jeumont Schneider, possessed the technology for the pressurized light water reactor.

Policy announcements by the new French president, Pompidou, in November 1969 reversed the twenty-year-old policy of gas graphite development.[57] Declaring the abandonment of this technique, Pompidou ordered the immediate preparation of tenders for a 600 MWe light water reactor and indicated that the Sixth Modernization Plan scheduled to begin in 1971 would call for the construction of only three reactors, the types to be determined by the progress of the first light water

[53]Maurice Schumann, then French minister of Scientific Research and Atomic and Space Questions, was a reported advocate of cooperation with Great Britain on the advanced gas reactor. The EdF was completely uninterested. *Le Monde*, December 21, 1967.

[54]*Le Monde*, September 14, 1967.

[55]*Le Monde*, December 6, 1967.

[56]*Entreprise*, March 9, 1968.

[57]*Le Monde*, November 15, 1969.

plant and French studies on the heavy water reactor family. Pompidou also announced the establishment of a study group to review and redefine the role of the CEA in future nuclear developments.[58]

Thus, as the decade ended, France set about to free its civilian program from constraints imposed at the start of the decade by military considerations. Economic analysis would suggest that the financial burden of independent programs proved to be too great. But this perspective should not obscure the political changes which accompanied and facilitated the increased importance of economics. In the nuclear sector, the greater salience of economic considerations reflected the maturation of the French military program, which is now an accepted and stable part of French foreign policy. In addition, détente reduced the necessity and significance of independent programs as levers in alliance politics. France no longer faces the same imperative to resist American hegemony. To some extent, civilian programs can be safely decoupled from military priorities. This has not made civilian programs less political. On the contrary, some of the attention that previously focused on strategic questions now fastens on economic relations. French nuclear policy today is as heavily influenced by competitive political and economic concerns *vis-à-vis* Germany as it was earlier by competitive designs *vis-à-vis* the United States.

Germany

In Germany, economic and industrial considerations reinforced political constraints affecting nuclear power developments. In contrast to France (and Great Britain), Germany did not suffer from a shortage of domestic energy supplies. Blessed with the rich coal deposits of the Ruhr, Germany still recorded in 1955 a net export of energy supplies.[59] Atomic Minister Strauss made it clear that Germany had plenty of time to catch up in nuclear research before nuclear power became a necessary and important source of domestic energy production.[60]

Without government leadership in either military or civilian applications, the decentralized, private character of German industry added to the deliberate start-up of nuclear power initiatives. Industrial circles, supported by the Economic Ministry under Ludwig Erhard, opposed central planning (*dirigisme*) in the nuclear sector and advocated the "normalization" of this sector, that is, the integration of nuclear activities into the market economy. (*soziale Markwirtschaft*) much like any other commercial undertaking. Centralization was not unknown in German industrial history, but the fascist experience had discredited policies

[58]For the report of this group, see *Le Monde*, April 26–27, 1970.

[59]This situation changed by the end of the decade, but the political importance of the coal sector and resulting government subsidies to this sector worked against an early interest in nuclear power.

[60]*Bremer Nachrichten*, June 2, 1956.

of corporate concentration.[61] For the moment, German industry sought to avoid the appearance of premature commercial nationalism.[62] In the nuclear area, private initiatives focused, for the most part, on study programs and the establishment of preliminary contacts and license arrangements with U.S. companies.[63]

The Eltville program expressed the largely industrial and cautious bias of German initiatives. Unlike the French (and British) programs announced in 1955, which concentrated on one reactor type and the series construction of nuclear plants, Eltville encouraged a variety of reactor designs (light water, gas graphite, high temperature, organic, and heavy water reactors) and emphasized quality and experimentation rather than quantity and series construction. Despite the technical flavor, however, the program featured three reactor concepts of unique German design—the AVR high temperature gas reactor (chapter 7), a light water design with nuclear superheating, and the KKN heavy water reactor (chapter 6). These scientific choices manifested a clear concern for the national integrity and competitive place of German programs.

This concern was very much behind the gradual increase of federal influence in German nuclear programs. Industry and utilities complained that initial programs failed to offer sufficient public incentives to spark private undertakings.[64] In Germany, unlike France, the electricity market was highly decentralized with over 350 individual companies operating power facilities.[65] Consortia arrangements were re-

---

[61]See Shonfield, *Modern Capitalism*, p. 244.

[62]This was especially true in the energy sector where the coal industry had been "decartelized" as a precondition for the establishment of the Coal and Steel Community. See William Diebold, Jr., *The Schuman Plan* (New York: Praeger, 1959).

[63]Siemens extended its long-standing license arrangements with Westinghouse to cover aspects of the nuclear field and also maintained loose contacts with Britain's English Electric for studies on gas graphite reactors; AEG collaborated with GE; DEMAG established a joint subsidiary, Interatom, with Atomics International of North American Aviation; and Gutehoffnungshuette began collaboration with General Atomic. The choice of American partners was dictated, in part, as we noted earlier in this chapter, by political circumstances. In addition, traditional ties (e.g., Siemens), a general belief in the greater potential of American technology, and the vigorous promotional activities of American nuclear firms in Europe facilitated these contacts. See, e.g., *Westfaelische Rundschau* (Dortmund), December 5, 1957; and *Hannoversche Presse*, December 28, 1957. The only major firm to associate with a non-American partner was Krupp, which established ties with the British company, Atomic Power Construction, for the sale of advanced gas reactors.

[64]See, e.g., comments by Siemens representative, *Mannheimer Morgan*, November 19, 1958, and AEG representative, *Frankfurter Allgemeine*, May 1, 1961.

[65]Only 3 percent of these companies are predominantly private enterprises. The rest are public enterprises (42 percent) financed by federal, state, and local authorities or mixed-type enterprises (55 percent) in which public authorities hold the majority interest. The largest company is RWE, which produces about 30 percent of the total electricity supply. Altogether, the twelve largest producers account for 65 percent of total production, while ninety-four companies account for 99 percent. See Deutscher Forschungsdienst, *Sonderbericht Kernenergie*, December 19, 1968.

quired to experiment in nuclear power, but the availability of cheap conventional fuels militated against consolidation. In addition, the largest German utilities operated their own coal mines and faced internal obstacles in developing a direct competitor to coal-fueled power plants.[66]

Thus, industrial and market pressures forced German authorities to assume a more active role. The type of government-industry relations that evolved, however, was quite different from that in France. In both manufacturing and fuel activities, federal contracts gave primary responsibility for technical and managerial control to industry. As soon as programs reached the commercial stage, the German Science Ministry, unlike the CEA, eagerly reduced its participation, announcing in 1965, for example, that financing and further development of first-generation reactors (principally light water systems) would be left thereafter primarily to industry. After this point, federal research programs concentrated on longer-term projects including advanced reactors and the development of nuclear fuel facilities.[67]

Federal interest remained and intensified on larger questions of industrial concentration and the protection of commercial interests. Even before the nonproliferation issue surfaced, federal authorities acted to encourage industrial participation in public reactor projects. An informal network of associations between scientists, industrialists, and public officials (coordinated, in part, through the German Atomic Commission) gave government efforts a low profile. But federal influence was unmistakable in promoting industrial partnerships both at home and with foreign firms. International associations, in particular, became important as a way of protecting German nuclear programs from potential discrimination of the nonproliferation treaty against individual nonnuclear countries.

Thus, the consolidation of German industries, culminating in 1969 in the establishment by Siemens and AEG of a joint nuclear subsidiary, KWU, did not reflect exclusively economic exigencies. Industrial consolidation was also a way of expressing German national interests in an increasingly economic, as opposed to strategic, world context.

[66]*Der Spiegel*, January 1, 1958. The Economic Ministry under the influence of coal interests frequently opposed budget appropriations for the Atomic Ministry. *Stuttgarter Zeitung*, June 14, 1960.

[67]Private firms also exercised primary responsibility in the fuel sector. NUKEM, a joint subsidiary of Degussa, RWE, and others, dominates operations through subsidiaries with Siemens (Reaktor-Brennelemente-Gesellschaft), the UKAEA (Nukleardienst), and Dow Chemical (ALKEM), producing fuel for pressurized light water, gas, and fast reactors. NUKEM is also involved with Farbwerke Hoechst and Gelsenkirchener Bergwerks in the reprocessing of fuels (the WAK facility in Karlsruhe) and with Holland and Great Britain in the tripartite project for enrichment of uranium. AEG operates a joint subsidiary with GE (Kernreaktorteile Gesellschaft), producing fuel for boiling light water reactors. Private firms also carry on uranium prospecting activities, both in Germany and abroad.

Italy

Unlike Germany, Italy was a country with severe energy shortages, even more severe than France. In 1955, Italy, with few indigenous conventional fuel deposits and with hydroelectric resources practically exhausted, imported more than 60 percent of its total energy supplies (mostly oil from the Near East). The shortage was greatest in the south, but the industrial capacity to absorb new energy supplies was most advanced in the north. The question of nuclear power got caught in this ,regional disequilibrium. Industrial groups advocated the installation of nuclear stations in the north, but government groups (including CNRN), responsive to political pressures, favored locations in the south. Political forces prevailed, and the first two Italian reactor projects involving state-controlled industries (SENN and SIMEA) were located in the south. Edisonvolta, the largest private utility company at the time, constructed a third reactor (SELNI) without government support in the north.

The state-controlled character of industrial structures in Italy (unlike the situation in Germany) contributed to the eventual nationalization of nuclear activities.[68] Once electrical utility companies were nationalized in 1962 under ENEL, the two largest state-owned companies, ENI and IRI, acquired increasing influence over nuclear activities.[69] In 1968, CIPE, the Interministerial Committee for Economic Planning responsible for nuclear activities, established guidelines for ENI and IRI activities in the nuclear field.[70] The ENI group (principal members, SNAM-Progetti and AGIP-Nucleare) was given primary responsibility for nuclear fuel activities (mining and refining of ores, reprocessing, and the study of uranium enrichment techniques), while the IRI group (principal members, Ansaldo Meccanico Nucleare and Italimpianti) assumed chief responsibility for reactor construction. A third state group, EFIM (principal member, Breda), remained the chief supplier of steam generators, heat exchangers, and other conventional

[68]The three state-controlled companies in nuclear-related sectors—IRI, ENI, and EFIM—are actually public holding companies, with financial holding companies under them and manufacturing companies under the latter. The structure is one of a pyramid with IRI, ENI, and EFIM at the apex, production firms at the base, and finance corporations in between. The result is a high concentration of industry with over 300 firms coming under the wing of state holding companies. See OECD, *Reviews of National Science Policy—Italy* (Paris: OECD, 1969), p. 83.

[69]Confindustria, the national association of private industries, strongly opposed this development, making the choice between private or public control of nuclear activities more of an all or nothing decision in Italy than in other Euratom countries. The public/private schism may be characteristic of Italian industrial politics in general. As Shonfield notes, there is a widespread suspicion in private circles that government officials use public office to advance private aims, and a feeling in government that private interests constitute a conspiracy operating outside and against public controls. *Modern Capitalism*, pp. 194–96.

[70]*Atomo e Industria*, September 1, 1968.

parts. A similar role was assigned to private firms—Fiat, Montedison (merger in 1966 of Montecatini and Edison), and BPD—which henceforth served as subcontractors.

Despite the CIPE guidelines, respective competences in the nuclear sector remained unclear. CNEN lacked authority to participate directly in industrial programs, industry had little interest in government programs, and ENEL was under no urgency to develop nuclear power. The discovery of large oil deposits in North Africa relieved Italy of its acute dependence on Middle East oil, and natural gas deposits in the Po Valley added a new domestic source of energy supplies. Curiously, Italy had no immediate economic need or political incentive to develop nuclear power.

Belgium and the Netherlands

The Netherlands relies more heavily on energy imports than even Italy, while Belgium faces a relatively relaxed energy situation, as in Germany. Dutch electricity producers, mostly provincial and municipal companies, established the KEMA laboratories in 1955 to explore preliminary reactor designs with RCN. SEP, a national association of electricity producers, also formulated plans for construction of a nuclear station at Dodewaard. The discovery of vast natural gas reserves in the North Sea, together with the high costs of nuclear power, delayed action on this project until 1965.[71] By contrast, Belgium, in cooperation with France, built its first nuclear plant in 1960 and ordered a second one in 1968. Both of these plants were operated by SYNATOM, a group of private utilities which produce 94 percent of Belgium's electricity.

The sway of private enterprise is perhaps even greater in Belgium than in Germany. Paradoxically, this situation facilitates public-private cooperation, since there is no issue about relative competences. In addition, the government does not face the same requirement of a larger country like Germany to promote technology for prestige reasons. The lead can be left to industry. CEN (the government-sonsored nuclear research center) cooperates primarily with Belgonucléaire (a nuclear design group formed by private industries) on a number of projects at Mol and with the Belgian firm, MMN, engaged in fuel fabrication for light water and fast reactors.[72] ACEC is the principal nuclear construc-

---

[71]G. H. Rietveld, *The Construction of the First Nuclear Energy Plant in the Netherlands* (pamphlet obtained from the Ministry of Economic Affairs, The Hague).

[72]Cooperation is helped by the fact that Belgonucléaire, as a design corporation, benefits from the use of CEN equipment and acts as intermediary between CEN and the manufacturing industries. The industrial group acting as industrial architect in France performs much the same function; the difference lies in the fact that control resides on the government side in the case of France (i.e., the CEA) and on the industrial side in the case of Belgium. (CEN has no direct authority in the industrial field.)

tion firm in Belgium, having participated in the construction of both Belgian nuclear stations under license from Westinghouse.

The principal nuclear industry in the Netherlands is Neratoom, established in 1959 as a nuclear design agency for several engineering firms involved primarily in the ship construction business.[73] Neratoom is most active in the study of sodium technology for the fast reactor program. The same companies sponsoring Neratoom set up a new company in 1968, the UCN, to represent the Netherlands in the tripartite uranium enrichment project with Germany and Great Britain.

Scientific and Technological Dimensions

France

The dependence of French science on politics and the relatively low influence of French scientists on government policy are traditional characteristics of the organization of science in France. This political impotence is the result of the historical separation of French science from the educational, industrial, and governmental institutions of French society.[74] The early influence of French scientists in the establishment and administration of the CEA represented something of a departure from this historical model. Not only did the CEA constitute "a novel and unique administrative structure" in terms of its relative financial and political autonomy of French ministerial structures, but it permitted "for the first time since the [French] Revolution natural scientists *as natural scientists* . . . to hold significant offices in an agency which itself was in a strategic position."[75] It also contributed to the basic transformation of French scientific institutions and traditional methods of research. At nuclear centers like Saclay, "limited scientific resources were consolidated in a complex of modern laboratories. In place of individualistic professors there were now teams of researchers and supporting technicians."[76]

The organization of the CEA did not fundamentally alter the dependence of French nuclear science on politics, however. Historically separated from other sources of support in the society, French scientists developed a tradition of service to the state.[77] This tradition continued in the CEA. The early scientific leaders of the CEA, especially Frédéric Joliot-Curie and several outstanding scientists who spent the

[73]"Nuclear Energy in the Netherlands," *Atoomenergie en haar Toepassingen*, XI, special issue (February 1969).

[74]See Gilpin, *France*, pp. 77–123.

[75]*Ibid.*, p. 166.

[76]*Ibid.*, p. 169.

[77]Members of the French Academy of Sciences were originally appointed and supported by the king. The centralization of the university system under Napoleon reinforced the state character of French education and science. *Ibid.*, pp. 92–94.

war years as members of the Anglo-Canadian team working on the atomic bomb (Pierre Auger, Jules Guéron, Lew Kowarski, and Bertrand Goldschmidt) were strongly influenced by the social and welfare implications of science. Most of these men shared political sympathies with parties of the Left, and Joliot-Curie was a prominent member of the French resistance to fascist occupation.[78] The socialist leanings of French scientists made them suspicious of private industry. As Lawrence Scheinman notes,[79]

French scientists generally, and a substantial number of the Commissariat [CEA] scientists in particular, inclined toward a "statist" economic philosophy. Consequently, these men were concerned lest private industry control or exercise a dominant influence over the development of atomic energy. Even though many of these scientists were not militantly statist, they still desired to keep the CEA small and to either minimize industrial contacts or to exercise close surveillance over such relationships as might develop.

Thus, the historical and political experiences of French science produced a preference for centralized organization and control of nuclear research. Participation by key French scientists in the allied bomb effort confirmed the advantages of coordinated project research, involving specialized teams and hierarchical integration.[80] This preference became important in the attitudes of French scientists toward Euratom research institutions. Many French scientists opposed the shift of French policy in the 1950s toward military applications. Some top CEA scientists left the French program in 1958 and joined the Euratom team. Jules Guéron became the director of Research and Training Programs in Euratom. He brought with him the conviction that nuclear research required centralized coordination and could not be left to the competitive and inconstant policies of private industry. This attitude clashed sharply with the traditional experiences and preferences of German scientists.

Germany

In contrast to France, German science experienced an early integration with teaching and industrial institutions of German society. The rise of German science in the latter part of the nineteenth century is largely attributed to the marriage of research and teaching in the German university community. As Joseph Ben-David notes, "The laboratories of some German universities became the centers and sometimes virtually the seats of world-wide scientific communities in their respective fields. . . . Research started to become a regular career, and scientists in a number of fields started to develop into much more closely

[78]*Ibid.*, pp. 157–59.
[79]Scheinman, *Atomic Energy Policy*, pp. 34–35.
[80]*Ibid.*, p. 24.

knit networks than ever before."[81] The concentration of resources and talents permitted the coordinated exploration of specific problem areas. It was not long before industries recognized the potential of this form of organization for the exploitation of science. Industrial sponsors became important supporters and beneficiaries of university research. Institutes of technology sprang up which were located at and operated by universities but built and maintained by industry.[82] Outside the university system, technical schools became respected centers of training in engineering and technology, producing a stream of technical specialists who found a ready welcome in German industries.

The university-based system of German science and technology contrasted sharply with the state-based system in France. As Gilpin writes, "the university, in effect, became the seat of government for the developing scientific enterprise. Unlike the centralized French university system the nineteenth-century German universities were creatures of the individual states; they enjoyed a considerable degree of institutional autonomy and had a long tradition of intense rivalry."[83] For a time, the decentralized character of German science served the advancement of scientific and industrial programs. By the turn of the century, however, the fragmentation of the university system began to impede the effective coordination of major technological undertakings. The state intervened in 1911 with the creation of the Kaiser-Wilhelm Institutes (now Max Planck Institutes), but these institutes continued the tradition of "one-man institutes, centered around distinguished directors, in what has generally become known as the 'German-style' of research, which places enormous research power in the hands of professors, with an autocratic tradition of control. . . ."[84] Massive efforts during the Nazi period to overcome the centrifugal effects of this system bore some fruit. But even during the war, German science, especially in the nuclear field, never experienced the close integration with national purposes that allied science did.[85]

The postwar development of nuclear programs in Germany, therefore, faced traditional obstacles in the scientific community. The past strength of German capabilities in the nuclear field was undisputed. This strength was primarily theoretical,[86] however, and the postwar hiatus of ten years, during which nuclear research was banned, left Ger-

---

[81]Joseph Ben-David, *The Scientist's Role in Society* (Englewood Cliffs: Prentice-Hall, 1971), pp. 124–25.

[82]OECD, *Reviews of National Science Policy—United Kingdom and Germany* (Paris: OECD, 1967).

[83]Gilpin, *France*, p. 113.

[84]Rose and Rose, *Science and Society*, p. 146.

[85]For a fascinating account of nuclear energy research in Germany during the war, see David Irving, *The Virus House: The German Atomic Bomb Project* (New York: Simon and Schuster, 1968).

[86]*Ibid.*, pp. 299 and 302.

many far behind in the development of modern research organization and methods. Older established scientists cherished the privileges of the traditional system and sought to organize nuclear programs around specific objectives which could be pursued within relatively small institutes. Defensive about their role in the Nazi period, these scientists had little in common with their socialist-leaning French colleagues.

On the other hand, a younger group of German scientists saw the need to conduct scientific planning and research on a more integrated basis. They sought to avoid competition between nuclear centers (which nevertheless occurred to some extent between Karlsruhe and Juelich) and break down the separation and rivalry of various institutes and departments within individual research centers. These scientists were particularly influential in easing the federal government into a more active role in nuclear research, especially in the advanced programs such as high temperature and fast reactors.

While younger German scientists thought more like French colleagues, such as Guéron, they drew more heavily from American than French models of the organization of science and industry. This was a consequence of the peculiar constraints of the German industrial situation. German scientists did not distrust the private sector, as did many French scientists; they realized that their own success depended on encouraging eventual industrial sponsorship of reactor development programs. German industries would not accept the results of government-sponsored programs without careful scrutiny. They would have to be convinced of the value of the programs through early involvement in the information and decisions growing out of these programs. Thus, the German nuclear community never saw eye to eye with French scientists on the need for close industrial supervision. It was not a matter of German scientists being less interested in the national implications of commercial nuclear power; it was simply a matter of their awareness that German industry was strong and could best advance German ideas in international technological competition.

Italy

Nuclear science in Italy suffered from the general ideological conflict in domestic politics between liberal and interventionist parties. Liberal-minded scientists, principally located with CISE and private industry, advocated the long-run *independent* development of Italian nuclear technology.[87] They believed, like some German counterparts (those who emphasized unique German innovations), that the intricacies of reactor development could only be learned through experience from the ground up. They resented the heavy reliance of government scientists on ideas and advice from the USAEC as well as American

[87]Silvestri, *Il costo della menzogna*, chap. 3.

industry. Government scientists, on the other hand, sought rapid advances through immediate import of foreign technology. The traditional antagonism between public and private sectors in Italy made cooperation between these two groups all the more difficult. There was little collaboration between government and industrial scientists of the type characterizing associations in Germany.

Belgium and the Netherlands

The situation in Belgium and Holland more closely paralleled that in Germany. Coordination between government and industrial scientists was smooth. In Belgium, this fact may have resulted, at least in part, from the strong engineering tradition of Belgian science.[88] The focus on applied technology created a common orientation toward goal-directed research in both government and industrial circles. The tendency of the science community to isolate itself and develop autonomous, academic orientations through the pursuit of basic science (a real problem in France and, to a lesser extent, in Germany) did not materialize in these circumstances.

*   *   *

The foregoing discussion throws in relief several key differences among the Euratom countries which become important for understanding the problems of reactor cooperation. First, the national administrative bodies dealing with nuclear power differ in terms of their negotiating roles and capabilities. The administrative strength of the CEA repeatedly discouraged interest in the other countries in dealing with civilian nuclear problems at a formal, governmental level. The more backward the country's nuclear technology and therefore the more necessary that the country have a strong agency representing its interests, the more likely it was that this country (e.g., Italy) had a weak or uncoordinated administration. The fact that nuclear affairs in three countries (Italy, Belgium, and the Netherlands) were the responsibility of Economic or Industrial Ministries, in another (Germany) a separate Science Ministry, and in still another (France) an independent agency under the direct authority of the prime minister, made matters even more difficult.

Second, the programs in the different countries were temporally out of phase with one another. In France, developments from 1958 on were affected by pressures to shift more responsibility for nuclear affairs from government to industry. In Germany, pressures acted in the opposite direction to shift more influence from industry to government.

[88]OECD, *Reviews of National Science Policy—Belgium* (Paris: OECD, 1966).

In Italy, programs never evolved much beyond the stage of jurisdictional disputes which France resolved at the outset and Germany disposed of by the early 1960s. In short, each country faced different internal circumstances and preoccupations which shaped its perceptions of international priorities.

CHAPTER 4

COMMUNITY DIMENSIONS OF EUROPEAN REACTOR PROGRAMS

Community efforts to develop nuclear reactors found themselves wedged between Atlantic and national developments outlined in the previous two chapters. This fact ensured that Euratom's origins and evolution would be eminently political, i.e., affected more by relational or contextual considerations than economic or technical factors. As one analyst concludes:[1]

> Looking at the hard economic and technical "facts," one actually finds very little justification whatsoever for the existence of Euratom. . . . Euratom is justified largely by the expedient of political argument, by its role in contributing to a united Europe.

Initially, alliance policies and interests were paramount in the creation and evolution of Euratom. The United States supported Euratom as an aspect of its larger interest in European integration and as a potential instrument for implementing American nonproliferation objectives. As we note below and in chapter 5, American and, to a lesser extent, British policy played a crucial role in the direction and programs undertaken by Euratom. These countries acted in the capacity of "external elites" to promote certain types of nuclear integration favorable to their larger political interests but to limit other types of integration which might threaten Anglo-American monopoly of nuclear weapons policy.[2] Both countries sought to forestall the acquisition of nuclear weapons by France and to influence early Euratom negotiations to preclude military development of atomic energy in Europe. Once this effort failed, as Harold Nieburg observes, "the United States and Britain moved to find a basis for transforming EURATOM into a harmless regional effort to develop nuclear power reactors."[3] If Euratom could not be used to

---

[1] Arnold Kramish, *The Peaceful Atom in Foreign Policy* (New York: Harper and Row, 1963), pp. 233–34.

[2] The concept and role of "external elites" in the process of integration are developed by Amitai Etzioni, *Political Unification* (New York: Holt, Rinehart and Winston, 1965).

[3] Harold L. Nieburg, *Nuclear Secrecy and Foreign Policy* (Washington, D.C.: Public Affairs Press, 1964), p. 143. Nieburg goes on to argue that U.S. support of Euratom may

achieve political aims, i.e., nonproliferation, it had to be limited to technical aims so as not to develop an independent political significance which might threaten the unity of Western policy.[4]

On the European side, Euratom was the expression of quite different political motivations. Jeroslav Polach summarizes these motivations:[5]

> . . . Euratom was looked upon as a policy instrument by means of which the six would establish their political, economic and atomic equality with other atomic powers. Internally, it was to be translated into rising economic welfare for the Community population and greater political unity among the member states. Internationally, Euratom should help restore the influence of the six in the world power politics (*sic*).

For some Europeans, therefore, Euratom's *raison d'être* was to achieve greater equality *vis-à-vis* the United States rather than to strengthen Western defense and unity *vis-à-vis* the Soviet Union.

The tension between these competing aims accounts for a large part of the history of Euratom and for many of the disputes over the use of American versus European technology in the development of nuclear reactors. (See, in particular, chapter 5.) Europe, of course, was less than fully united on aspirations for Euratom. In addition to Atlantic and East-West parameters, national factors affected the attitudes of individual members toward the new community. France, as the country most sensitive to the symbolic importance of nuclear energy, was quick to perceive the possibility that the purpose of Euratom, under American tutelage, was "to prevent any European nation from acquiring an independent nuclear weapons capability and to promote American domination of the European power reactor market."[6] Germany, on the other hand, with an interest in building up the substantive aspects of its program while downplaying the symbolic significance, welcomed American leadership and assistance. Italy and the low countries did likewise. The Euratom Commission stood in the middle of this tug-of-war and could not remain neutral. Attacked initially for its external policies, the Community also contended with the subsequent growth and competition of internal national programs, especially in Germany. The revival of national politics in the mid- and late 1960s (see chapter 2) left Euratom facing a widening assortment of problems with a dwindling arsenal of cash and confidence.

---

not have succeeded as an economic venture on behalf of nuclear power, but "as a diplomatic play designed to undercut a strong threat to the nuclear unity of NATO, it brilliantly succeeded" and "isolated the main French motive, one also shared elsewhere in EURATOM: creation of an independent nuclear technology to enable the continental nations to challenge the US-British strategic nuclear monopoly" (p. 147).

[4]*Ibid.*, p. 130. See also Jeroslav G. Polach, *Euratom: Its Background, Issues and Economic Implications* (Dobbs Ferry: Oceana, 1964), p. 61.

[5]Polach, *Euratom*, p. 61.

[6]Robert Gilpin, *France in the Age of the Scientific State* (Princeton: Princeton University Press, 1968), p. 405.

The expansion of the membership as well as the functional tasks of the Community (now involving general science policy rather than nuclear research alone) may have only added to these difficulties.

In this chapter we will trace the highlights of Euratom's evolution by examining five related themes.[7] First, we will look at how the political origins of Euratom influenced its mission, institutions, and programs. This section highlights the way in which external factors affected technological cooperation in Europe. Second, we will examine the structures of internal decision-making in Euratom, looking at the Commission's struggle to chart a course between the Scylla of competition with national programs ("the seventh power dilemma") and the Charybdis of supranationalism. Third, we will discuss the debate over alternate means of implementing cooperative research (national versus community laboratories). Fourth, we will examine the widening scope of nuclear and other research activities and the problems raised for comprehensive research cooperation in Europe. Finally, we will look at the premises and problems of nuclear and general technological cooperation in the altered circumstances of what we have called national as opposed to Community politics (see chapter 2). This discussion sets the stage for looking at the plight of specific reactor projects, since the probable mode of cooperation in the future will be ad hoc and sectoral rather than institutional.

Consequences of Political Origins of Euratom

The fact that Euratom owed its existence to politics rather than economics or technology had three important consequences for Euratom's development. It meant that the drafting of the Euratom Treaty had to deal with the relationship of peaceful and military uses of atomic energy. The pre-eminence of politics would not allow the *silent* separation of peaceful from military uses. Secondly, it meant that Euratom was charged with industrial aims of much wider political significance than the institutional authority it was given. Finally, it meant that Euratom's initial programs, designed to meet political expectations, vastly inflated the urgency of energy requirements and the prospective role of nuclear power in meeting these requirements. In short, political factors caused

---

[7]Our purpose is not to present a systematic discussion of Euratom's institutions and activities but only to sketch those features of Euratom's history essential to an understanding of the case studies in chaps. 5–8. For more comprehensive treatments of Euratom, see Polach, *Euratom*; and Lawrence Scheinman, "Euratom: Nuclear Integration in Europe," *International Conciliation*, No. 563 (May 1967). On the Euratom Treaty and related commentary, see *Treaty Establishing the European Atomic Energy Community (Euratom)* (1931/5/57/4) (Brussels, March 25, 1957); and J. Errera *et al.*, *Euratom, Analyse et Commentaires du Traité* (Brussels: Bibliothèque de l'Institut Belge de Science Politique, 1958).

Euratom to be established largely on the basis of contextual experiences and developments unrelated to the specific technical and administrative requirements of nuclear research.

The issue of the relationship between peaceful and military uses of atomic energy was a carry-over from earlier attempts to establish a European Defense Community and Political Authority (EDC and EPA).[8] The defeat of the EDC left open the question of nuclear forces in Europe (except for Germany, which renounced nuclear weapons as a precondition for joining NATO in 1955). Jean Monnet and his Action Committee for the United States of Europe hoped to resolve this issue by including in the Euratom Treaty a clause limiting nuclear development in Europe to exclusively peaceful aims.[9] Monnet's Committee recommended that the new Atomic Energy Community possess exclusive rights of ownership of all nuclear fuels to safeguard against diversion to military uses. The Spaak Committee established at the Messina Conference in 1955 supported this proposition but justified controls more in economic than strategic-military terms (as a way of maintaining fair market prices for nuclear fuels, which experts thought would be in short supply in the future, and guaranteeing equal access to U.S. fuels, which might be distributed discriminatorily under bilateral agreements).[10]

The United States and Great Britain tried to win approval of the exclusion clause.[11] At the time the six foreign ministers met in February 1956 and agreed on the basic provisions of the Community's supply policy, it appeared that the prevailing rationale for Community supply responsibilities was to prevent diversion of nuclear fuels to military purposes.[12] The debate over a nuclear weapons policy in France, however, was just reaching its climax. The French government was too weak to assure acceptance of the exclusion clause. In addition, Italy supported France and procrastinated on the question of whether or not Euratom should possess monopoly rights in the supply field.[13] Germany opposed centralized fuel controls for industrial and general ideological reasons (fear of *dirigisme* and interference with private access to lowest-cost

---

[8]See Daniel Lerner and Raymond Aron (eds.), *France Defeats EDC* (New York: Praeger, 1957).

[9]*Keesing's Comtemporary Archives* (hereafter *Keesing's Archives*), 1955/56, X, 15141; see also Lawrence Scheinman, *Atomic Energy Policy in France under the Fourth Republic* (Princeton: Princeton University Press, 1965), p. 136; and Ernst B. Haas, *The Uniting of Europe* (Stanford: Stanford University Press, 1958), pp. 301–4.

[10]Intergovernmental Committee established by the Conference of Messina, *Bericht der Delegationsleiter an die Aussenminister* [MAE 120 d/56 (korr.)] (Brussels, April 21, 1956), pp. 120–24 and 128.

[11]Nieburg, *Nuclear Secrecy*, p. 132. The British Prime Minister went to Washington in January 1956 to try and coordinate Anglo-American interests on this point.

[12]See Scheinman, *Atomic Energy Policy*, pp. 137–42.

[13]F. Roy Willis, *Italy Chooses Europe* (New York: Oxford University Press, 1971), pp. 57–58.

fuels).[14] As a result, the fuel controls eventually incorporated into the Euratom Treaty neither prohibited military uses of nuclear energy nor permitted fuel arrangements to be determined by exclusively economic forces.[15] On the one hand, the Community's Supply Agency could not interfere with fuel purchases or inspect any national facility designated for defense; and, on the other, it could not allow the free interplay of market forces without compromising its authority to intervene in future circumstances when supply conditions might be tight (the expected situation in 1957 which did not materialize). France accepted these results only because they did not exclude a French atomic weapons program and yet guaranteed French access to U.S. fuel supplies (which might have been cut off under a purely bilateral arrangement, particularly after France decided officially to go ahead with its nuclear force program).[16] Germany accepted only because Adenauer refused to sacrifice the goal of European integration to industrial skepticism.

While these decisions glossed over the issue of nuclear forces in Europe, they did define the limits of Euratom's responsibilities in the gray area where civilian nuclear activities shade into military activities.[17] These limits remained clear until the nonproliferation discussions in 1966–67 reopened the question of European nuclear forces and Euratom jurisdiction over nuclear fuel supplies. By this time, France had gone ahead with an independent weapons program. After 1964, when the Treaty (Article 76) called for confirmation or revision of Community authority in the supply field, France no longer recognized Euratom's jurisdiction and concluded agreements for fuel supplies without Community involvement.[18] The proposed nonproliferation treaty would have given

[14]German firms were advocating private ownership of nuclear fuels in the domestic debate over these questions. Duncan Burn, *The Political Economy of Nuclear Energy* (London: Institute of Economic Affairs, 1967), p. 81.

[15]Articles 52, 57, 64, and 86 gave the Community the right of option on all nuclear materials (including the right of ownership of all special fissile material) and the exclusive right of concluding contracts related to nuclear materials coming from within or outside the Community. Articles 52 and 84, however, qualified these rights in the case of nuclear materials designated for the purpose of defense. As it worked out in practice, the Community exercised the purchase option only on materials required for Community (i.e., common) programs and restricted its exclusive right of contracting to approving contracts concluded by the commercial parties themselves, in most cases such approval being automatic. See copy of Supply Agency regulations in *Amtsblatt der Europaeischen Gemeinschaften* (official bulletin of the European Communities, Brussels), May 11, 1960.

[16]De Gaulle is reported to have remarked upon being shown the Euratom Treaty clauses: "Is that all it is?" Related to the author in an interview with a member of the French delegation to the Euratom negotiations, Brussels, January 6, 1970.

[17]One consequence of the early definition of these limits was the relatively successful separation of Euratom activities from military issues prior to 1966. Euratom encountered no serious violations of the security provisions. The Supply Agency, of course, could not inspect any military installations. But as long as France required access to U.S. fuel supplies, it respected Euratom's civilian responsibilities. See Gordon L. Weil, *A Foreign Policy for Europe?* (Bruges: College of Europe, 1970), chap. 13, especially p. 264.

[18]This defiance was made possible, in part, by the availability of fuel from sources other than the U.S., including the Soviet Union. When the French concluded an agree-

official sanction to French exemption from controls by imposing mandatory inspections of the IAEA on the civilian activities of all nonnuclear countries while leaving the placement of controls on nuclear powers open to voluntary choice. As a nuclear power, France, even if it signed the nonproliferation treaty, would not be subject to such controls. Thus, Germany and the low countries rallied to the defense of the Euratom inspection system to prevent potential discrimination within the Common Market. German initiatives in 1967 forced changes in the final draft of the nonproliferation treaty, and negotiations since have essentially assured the continuation of the Euratom system subject to indirect supervision by the IAEA.[19]

The issue demonstrates the ongoing tie between civilian and military uses of nuclear energy. Germany's desire to preserve a nondiscriminatory relationship with France aims at safeguarding industrial interests but also at keeping options open until the issue of a European nuclear force is faced. In the nonproliferation debate, Germany and other European countries explicitly insisted that the Treaty not preclude the eventuality of a unified European deterrent force.

A second consequence of the political origins of Euratom was the gap between aims and authority assigned to Euratom institutions in the Treaty. There was widespread agreement during the Treaty negotiations that Euratom's task should be primarily industrial. The Spaak report stated:[20]

If it were only a question of satisfying energy needs, the required nuclear fuels and equipment might be imported. It concerns a much larger task, however, namely the development in Europe itself of a nuclear industry.

The issue was whether the new Community would be outfitted with the necessary authority to accomplish this task. If the objective was "the creation of conditions necessary for the speedy establishment and growth of nuclear industries," as proposed in Article 1 of the Treaty, the Community had to possess real powers to affect industrial conditions in the nuclear sector. The conduct and promotion of research itself could not serve as the sole instrument of an industrial promotion policy.

---

ment with the Soviet Union in March 1971 for supply of enriched uranium, the Commission learned of this transaction through the press. It asked the French government to comply with Chapter VI of the Treaty and formally report the purchase to the Community. The French government refused, and the Commission filed an appeal to the European Court of Justice for a ruling on the continued applicability of Chapter VI. In November 1971, the Court ruled in favor of the Commission, but France has yet to take note of this ruling. See *Agence Europe*, February 12, 1971; March 15, 1971; October 13, 1971; and November 29, 1971.

[19]See Lawrence Scheinman, "Nuclear Safeguards, the Peaceful Atom, and the IAEA," *International Conciliation*, No. 572 (March 1969), pp. 38–42.

[20]Intergovernmental Committee, *Bericht*, pp. 107–8.

Monnet's proposals for a supranational nuclear community aimed at providing institutional powers to carry out an industrial mandate.[21] Unfortunately, these proposals derived from a Europeanist desire to advance integration, not a careful survey of political willingness among the member states to reach agreement on industrial differences. As a result, the Treaty, while holding to the industrial aim, provided Community institutions with hardly any industrial authority. By default, research became the only effective means by which Community organs could implement the Treaty's objectives.

The ECSC precedent was crucial in determining this outcome. Industrialists in Germany and the low countries singularly opposed the adoption in the nuclear sector of supranational features such as those of the ECSC High Authority.[22] Of particular distaste to these groups were the High Authority's powers to tax production and float bond issues in the coal and steel markets, thereby acquiring an independent source of income which could be distributed as the High Authority saw fit. Also unacceptable was the High Authority's capacity to restrict investments it deemed undesirable by blocking access of firms to necessary financial resources.[23] Rather than the Monnet plan, these groups favored the much looser form of intergovernmental cooperation embodied in the OEEC plan for nuclear integration.[24] For different reasons, French nationalists also opposed putting the new Community into "the Procrustean bed of the E.C.S.C. institutions."[25] The combination of industrialist and nationalist resentment of the ECSC thus sharply reduced the chances of investing the new Atomic Energy Community with significant industrial responsibilities.[26]

The Euratom Treaty, in fact, contained weaker industrial provisions than the EEC Treaty, despite the fact that Euratom was charged with an

---

[21]In addition to ownership rights of all nuclear fuels, Monnet's community was to possess significant powers of intervention and coordination in the nuclear industrial sector. A community of this character effectively excluded Great Britain which opposed such supranationalism. *Keesing's Archives*, 1955/56, X, 15141.

[22]See, e.g., *Deutsche Zeitung*, December 24, 1955; *Frankfurter Allgemeine*, February 11, 1956, and May 8, 1957.

[23]See William Diebold, Jr., *The Schuman Plan* (New York: Praeger, 1959), chap. 13.

[24]The German science minister, Siegfried Balke, came out openly in favor of the OEEC plan which called for a very loose, voluntary nuclear community (including Great Britain) with no supranational powers or common budget. *Rhein Zeitung* (Koblenz), February 26, 1957. Constant tension existed in this period between the German Economic and Science Ministries, which opposed a supranational Euratom, and the Chancellor's Office and Foreign Ministry, which supported meaningful European institutions.

[25]Richard Mayne, *The Community of Europe* (London: Victor Gollancz Ltd., 1962), p. 124.

[26]Conflict between the Monnet and OEEC models of nuclear cooperation led to a fragmentation of nuclear institutions in Western Europe. Opposed to supranationalism on the continent, Great Britain backed in 1957 the establishment of a separate agency within the OEEC, known as ENEA. The latter sponsored several loosely organized nuclear projects such as the Eurochemic reprocessing plant at Mol, Belgium, and the DRAGON and HALDEN reactors. For more on DRAGON, see chap. 7 of this study.

explicitly industrial task.[27] The careful pruning of Euratom's industrial powers left research as the principal means for affecting Community industrial developments. Even here, most of the Commission's authority was hedged in by the requirement of unanimity. The common research program authorized under Article 7 required unanimous approval, though the annual appropriations under this program (which covered a period not to exceed five years) could be decided by majority vote. In addition, while the Commission possessed certain responsibilities under Articles 5 and 6 for the coordination and promotion of nuclear activities outside the common program, the practical chances for Community intervention in these areas were limited by the absence of an independent source of Community revenues. As long as the only funds available to the Commission came from the common program subject to the unanimity rule, the Community had little effective room for independent action.

A final consequence of the pre-eminence of politics in Euratom's creation was the inflation of economic problems to match the magnitude of political aspirations. There were many reasons for the mood of energy crisis in the period from 1956 to 1958. But the dramatization of this crisis, which soon proved to be an illusion, betrayed unmistakable political designs. One indication of this is that agreement was reached on Euratom's institutional powers before serious thought was given to the specific programs Euratom would implement. Treaty negotiations were essentially completed before the foreign ministers, in the wake of the Suez crisis in November 1956, appointed a commission of three men (Louis Armand, Francesco Giordani, and Franz Etzel, who subsequently became known as the three wise men) to report on the practical role Euratom might play in meeting the energy requirements of member-countries. In great haste and with considerable political fanfare, this commission visited the United States, Great Britain, Canada, and individual Euratom countries to ascertain future nuclear energy requirements and the technological facilities needed to meet these require-

---

[27]The EEC Treaty (Articles 85 and 100) sets out guidelines for industrial competition and the harmonization of industrial laws. The Euratom Treaty did not contain even these minimal provisions. In the field of investments, the Euratom Commission was authorized to discuss and communicate its views with regard to proposed investments (Article 43) but was given no recourse to see that these views were followed. While industries were obligated to report investment intentions to the Community within a limited period of time (Articles 41 and 42), they were not obligated to follow the Community's advice or even await the Community's opinion before proceeding with the planned expenditures. The Community's only instrument for guiding investment activities was the periodic publication of target programs indicating long-range production goals for nuclear energy and the various types of investment necessary to achieve these goals (Article 40). The Community could also intervene directly in certain instances by conferring "joint enterprise" status on "undertakings of outstanding importance to the development of nuclear industry in the Community," a status granting certain legal and tax advantages to these undertakings (Article 45). Most of the significant advantages under this arrangement, however, as well as the Community's own financial participation in such ventures, could only result from a unanimous vote of the Euratom Council.

ments. The Commission's report, known as the Three Wise Men Report, dramatized the Community's urgent need for new energy sources and recommended that the Community undertake in cooperation with the United States a sizeable nuclear reactor construction program.[28] These grandiose industrial-scale plans contrasted sharply with the meager powers of the new Atomic Energy Community. Reflecting the divorce between institutions and programs, the report was not even submitted to the foreign ministers until two months after the Euratom Treaty had been signed in March 1957.

An interim committee was established to monitor Community nuclear developments until the Euratom Treaty came into effect on January 1, 1958. While plans for cooperation with the United States fermented during the period, the interim committee took no action to coordinate nuclear activities within the Community. As our discussion in chapter 3 indicated, this was a period of great activity in national nuclear programs, including the widespread construction of nuclear research facilities in individual Euratom countries.[29] In face of this activity, the Community lost the initiative even before its official inauguration. When Euratom formally came into being, it was only marginally related to the practical realities of nuclear activities in the Community.

Decision-Making Structures in Euratom

The circumstances of Euratom's founding were not auspicious for the work of the Euratom Commission. Amidst the swirl of political events in the nuclear field, including the second U.N. Conference on the Peaceful Uses of Atomic Energy in 1958, the Commission faced a choice between politically visible actions, which would establish its profile in a rapidly developing field, and quiet technical consultations, which would improve the substantive basis of Euratom's interventions. As a practical matter, this choice was never explicit, and circumstances were more significant than design in determining the eventual outcome. The outcome, however, was to place the Commission immediately in a politically charged arena. In its early activities, the Commission dealt largely with politically sensitive external agreements which antagonized the Community's leading nuclear member, France. The resulting delay in establishing internal programs disappointed other members, including Germany and Italy. Dissatisfaction contributed to the perception of Community programs as competing rather than complementary actions. The Commission was pinned with the label of a "seventh power." In

[28]Louis Armand, Franz Etzel, and Francesco Giordani, *A Target for Euratom*, A report prepared at the request of the governments of Belgium, France, German Federal Republic, Italy, Luxembourg and the Netherlands (May 1957).

[29]From 1956–58, new research centers sprang up at Grenoble (France), Juelich and Karlsruhe (Germany), Ispra (Italy), and Petten (Holland). The CEN establishment in Belgium was also reorganized and expanded.

some measure, as we note below, this was inevitable given the wide divergence of interests and programs among the individual members. Without agreement on specific common interests, the establishment of common institutions was bound to create the appearance, if not the reality, of just another group representing partisan interests.

The Euratom Treaty provided for a range of Commission actions in research:

(1) Coordination (*coordonner*) of research undertaken by member-states (Article 5).
(2) Promotion (*promouvoir*) of research programs in member-states (Article 6).
(3) Completion (*compléter*) of member-state programs through a Community program (Article 7) carried out in Community facilities (Article 8) or contracted out to persons or enterprises in member-states or third countries (Article 10).

A low-profile approach would have called for the Community to concentrate on the coordination of member programs. Article 5 anticipated a survey of national programs. Completed in 1959, this survey disclosed that dispersion and duplication in the nuclear sector were already rampant.[30] Apparently, each member-state wished to establish programs and facilities before the Community took effect and could intervene in these activities. This process of "planting the flag," as it was called by one Community official, made even the collection of information difficult for Community officials. Without adequate information, the Community could do little to coordinate programs, let alone undertake its second function of promoting member-state research. Attempts to contribute to member programs may have only added to the existing dispersion. Thus, by default, the Commission took recourse to establishing its own programs, a step bound to create impressions of competition with national programs. The only way to avoid this impression was to initiate programs that were remote enough to be neutral (and probably also irrelevant) or large enough to go beyond the objectives of individual national programs. The two projects of the latter kind comtemplated during the Treaty negotiations—an enrichment plant and a reprocessing facility—did not materialize or were undertaken in another context (see chapter 5 and note 26 below). Thus, the Commission was left with a choice between irrelevance and competition. In point of fact, it was simply impossible to design *common* Community activities to complement *diverging* national activites.

Internal fragmentation also made it more convenient to initiate Community programs through foreign agreements rather than through the

[30]Euratom, Directorate-General for Research and Education, *Première tentative de bilan des recherches nucléaires en cours dans la communauté à la date du 1er janvier 1958* (EUR/C/229/59/1) (Brussels: Euratom, April 8, 1959).

JNRC, the Community's own laboratory facilities authorized under Article 8. Nuclear energy in this period was the center of considerable international appeal. The U.S. Atoms for Peace Plan in 1954, the First U.N. Geneva Conference on the Peaceful Uses of Nuclear Energy in 1955, and the Second U.N. Conference scheduled for September 1958 bathed the peaceful nuclear sector in a spirit of international cooperation and good will. The United States was also eager to conclude a joint nuclear power agreement with Euratom. The Commission welcomed this interest, seeing the advantage of getting a piece of the action before proliferation of bilateral agreements with third countries pre-empted Community responsibilities in external relations.[31] The first president of Euratom, Louis Armand, understood the importance of public visibility and promotion (witness his chairmanship of the Three Wise Men Commission). He recognized that a quick start was achieved better by joining existing programs outside Europe than starting from scratch independent programs inside Europe.

Thus, the Commission devoted the greater parts of its energy in 1958 to the negotiation of international agreements with the United States (light water reactor agreement—chapter 5), with Great Britain (DRAGON agreement—chapter 7), Canada (heavy water reactors—chapter 6), and with Norway (HALDEN project—chapter 6). This dependence on outside technology, especially the purchase of U.S.-type light water reactors under the Euratom-U.S. joint agreement, aroused opposition in some member-countries, particularly in France, which was eager to sell its own gas graphite reactors.[32] In accepting the creation of Euratom, French nationalists, who came to power under de Gaulle in May 1958, expected this organization to provide a technical supplement to the French civilian program without interfering with the political prerogatives of national agencies.[33] Above all, Euratom was to strengthen Europe's independence in the fields of energy supply and industrial capability. Since external agreements not only compromised Europe's independence but also infringed on national sovereignty, France soon voiced displeasure over the Community's activity in this area. In 1960 France excluded the Commission from negotiations leading to the French-Rus-

---

[31]During this period, the Euratom countries were busily concluding bilateral agreements with the USAEC and other foreign groups. In most cases, these agreements dealt with the purchase of research reactors and the delivery of enriched fuel. At the time, the U.S. did not regard these bilateral contracts as being in conflict with U.S. support for Euratom. However, these agreements, especially regarding fuel deliveries, served to undercut the will of the Euratom countries to build their own enrichment plant (which the U.S. opposed—see subsequent discussion in text) and provided a means for the liberal industrial countries in Euratom to circumvent total dependence on the centralized supply system of the new Community. Bilateral agreements were eventually "folded in" with U.S. agreements with Euratom (except for one with Italy which does not expire until 1978).

[32]For more details, see chap. 5.

[33]Scheinman, *Atomic Energy Policy,* p. 201.

sian Accord in nuclear energy.[34] Sensitivity in this area was not limited only to France. After 1959, the Commission encountered difficulties with other Community countries in the implementation of Chapter X of the Treaty, which called for the eventual transfer of authority for external relations to the Community.[35]

Because the Commission was preoccupied with external affairs, the proposals for the establishment of the JNRC were not dealt with until 1959. Given the dispersion of national facilities by this time, the Commission abandoned the original idea of constructing a separate JNRC uniquely suited to Community needs and proposed instead to take over an existing national center. France, consistent with its view that the Community should add to, but not interfere with, national programs, rejected the Commission's first proposal, which was to take over the Grenoble center.[36] Belgium likewise declined to shelter the Community center, fearing that the other members would object to the location of both the JNRC and Euratom headquarters on Belgian soil (the latter to be located in Brussels). The next choice fell to the Karlsruhe center in Germany, but German officals quietly explained that they were having enough difficulty "Germanizing" this center (in face of local and industrial resistance to federal intervention), let alone "Europeanizing" it.

By progressive default, interest eventually centered on the Ispra center in northern Italy. In July 1959 Italy concluded an agreement with Euratom, leasing Ispra to the Community for ninety-nine years at the nominal fee of $1 per year. Italian domestic opposition to this arrangement delayed ratification of the Ispra agreement for one year (see previous chapter). Not until the end of 1960, therefore, was the Community able to move into its new home and begin work on its own reactor project, ORGEL. Even then the Ispra center consisted of nothing more than one small research reactor and a few related facilities. In the uncertainty

[34]The Accord concluded between the CEA and Glavatom, the Russian nuclear agency, called for exchange of non-secret information and scientific personnel. See *The Economist*, April 23, 1960. France based its case for excluding the Commission on Article 29 of the Euratom Treaty, which required Commission involvement only if the agreement "requires on either part the signature of a state exercising its sovereignty." France argued that the CEA was not an organ of state sovereignty but an independent, technical agency.

[35]See Euratom, *Second General Report*, pp. 69–70; *Fourth General Report*, p. 117; *Seventh General Report*, pp. 79–80; and *Eighth General Report*, p. 9. Article 106 of Chapter X called for the Community to assume gradually the rights and obligations of bilateral treaties concluded before the date of entry into force of the Euratom Treaty. Member-states remained free to conclude new bilateral agreements (Article 103) but had to submit the agreements for Commission review and satisfy any objections the Commission might raise. Despite the important role which these provisions gave the Community, other articles in the Treaty (Articles 29, 64) provided loopholes permitting states to circumvent Commission review. For a typical, limited view of Community responsibility in this field, see comments of one German official who became a member of the Euratom Research Directorate, Hans-Hilger Haunschild, "Die Bilateralen Abkommen nach dem Euratom-Vertrag," *Atomwirtschaft*, IV (February 1959), pp. 58–62.

[36]Scheinman, "Euratom," p. 36.

surrounding the delay of the Ispra transfer, the Community acquired three other facilities as part of the JNRC—the Measurements Bureau at Geel, Belgium, the Transuranium Institute at Karlsruhe, and the Petten center in Holland.[37] The establishment of another common facility, a European University, called for in Article 9 of the Treaty, never materialized, though discussions on this matter continue to the present day.[38]

It is doubtful that these early activities of the Commission were the sole factors determining subsequent national attitudes toward Euratom. National attitudes were already partly fixed before Euratom was established, and they shaped the circumstances governing the Commission's options. The French, while critical of Euratom's external policies, were paradoxically the principal supporters and beneficiaries of early Commission programs.[39] As the Community member most advanced in nuclear technology, France hoped to determine unilaterally the political objectives of Euratom while encouraging the multilateral integration of technical resources to implement these objectives. CEA officials saw their own organization as the principal administrative anchor of European nuclear programs. Through early cooperation with the Commission, they hoped to "nip in the bud" any nascent pretensions that Euratom might become the European equivalent of the CEA. While France sought to avoid dependence on Euratom as much as dependence on the United States, it supported cooperation through Euratom as long as such cooperation supplemented French resources and did not become the basis of independent Community programs.

Belgium, for other reasons, also emphasized the technical aspects of Community cooperation. Seeking to downplay the political implications of reliance on foreign technology, Belgium argued that European unity and external dependence were not incompatible, since development of the most efficient technology maximized European potential. Not surprisingly, given the technical interest and competence of Belgium and France, these two countries received the greatest share of initial Euratom contracts.[40]

---

[37]Though Article 8 of the Treaty permitted geographic separation of JNRC establishments, the principal factor causing this was national pressures for *juste retour*. Acquisition of these facilities and recruitment to staff them inevitably raised issues of competition between Community and national laboratories.

[38]The university question was of special interest to President Hirsch and consumed a good part of the Commission's energies until Hirsch's dismissal in 1961. In 1969–70, on an Italian initiative, the issue became once again a topic of discussion in the Community.

[39]For example, during the period 1956–58 when Euratom discussions largely glossed over technical issues, France initiated the only contacts with Germany's nuclear program. (See chap. 3, note 22.) Between 1958 and 1961, France also proposed a number of common projects with Germany (enrichment uranium plant, EdF participation in a German nuclear plant, and cooperation with German industry on the ORGEL project—see chap. 6, note 20), enthusiastically attended nuclear trade fairs in member-countries, and invited German utilities to common meetings (which the latter did not attend). See *Deutsche Zeitung*, March 3, 1960, and January 28, 1961.

[40]This result was helped by the fact that Frenchmen and, to a lesser extent, Belgians played a prominent role in the early administration of Euratom. There is no reason to

In contrast to France, Germany supported Euratom's policy of external cooperation while resisting significant attempts at internal cooperation. Cooperation with the United States and Great Britain in civilian nuclear programs was a natural complement to Germany's dependence on these countries in strategic nuclear areas. Cooperation internally, however, especially with France, risked a permanent institutionalization of Germany's backwardness. Thus, Germany recognized early, as expressed by a high-level German official, that "the common research center of Euratom was not the place for closing the gap with France."[41] This would have to be done in Germany's own laboratories. A rule of thumb (*Faustregel*) was adopted which stipulated that "whatever one did internationally, one must do at home on at least twice that scale."[42] By the mid-1960s, this relationship had become more like four to one in favor of home programs. Germany's technical interest, therefore, focused on its own national programs; Euratom programs were supported for political, not technical, reasons.

Italy took the view that Euratom programs should not aim at technical efficiency for the sake of technical efficiency (since this approach was bound to favor more advanced members) but should develop programs in less advanced states. Euratom's purpose, in other words, was not to close the nuclear gap with external powers but to close the gap internally between Italy, France, and Germany.[43] Italy for domestic political reasons was unable, like Germany, to develop a consistent national program, so it came to depend increasingly on Euratom support of national projects.[44] This was also true for the Netherlands, which lacked the necessary resources for a home-based enterprise. Accordingly, Italy and Holland protested the award of early contracts to France and Belgium and supported a German proposal in late 1960 which led to the establishment of the CCNR, an expert committee of *national* representatives to look after the Commission in the drafting and implementation of Community research programs.[45]

----

imply that these officials were consciously implementing national biases in contract awards. They simply knew more about the state of research and industrial interests and capabilities in their home countries.

[41] See J. Pretsch, "Europaeische Zusammenarbeit in der Kernforschung," *Atomwirtschaft*, XI (August/September, 1966), p. 420.

[42] *Ibid.* This German position was also the result of early industrial unwillingness to rely on Euratom contracts which entailed bureaucratic supervision from Brussels and called for public dissemination of information. Industrial attitudes softened somewhat after 1962. (See chap. 5.) See "Euratom im Sog der Politik," *Atomwirtschaft*, XIX (February 1964), pp. 69–82.

[43] Scheinman, "Euratom," pp. 32–33.

[44] The dependence was so pervasive that "international rules [were] incorporated in the municipal law in default of any domestic legislation to cover the subject." See John E. Hodgetts, *Administering the Atom for Peace* (New York: Atherton Press, 1964), p. 21.

[45] *Agence Europe*, November 5, 1960. The Euratom Treaty (Article 134) provided for a Scientific and Technical Committee to advise the Commission on common programs and

Implementation of Common Research

When members do not agree on the ends of common research, the means of common research become the target of considerable contest. *Where* research is performed may determine *what* research is performed or toward what ends it is performed. This is the essence of the *juste retour* problem in which each state tries to recapture a portion of Community contracts approximately equal to its Community contributions.

The contest for control of the means of research manifested itself in the drafting of Euratom's second five-year plan and the two revision debates that followed (1962–67). The issues concerned the time span of the research to be carried out in common programs and whether this research should be conducted in Community or national laboratories. France and Germany favored Community concentration on a few major medium- and long-term reactor projects (in the case of France, heavy water, fast, and nuclear fusion reactors; in the case of Germany, high temperature, fast, and nuclear fusion reactors). Given the adequacy of their own resources for immediate objectives, these countries wanted Euratom to specialize and remain remote from existing industrial activities in the nuclear sector. Italy and the Netherlands, on the other hand, supported programs with more immediate and varied objectives such as the light water and ship propulsion programs.[46] These countries required Euratom contributions to stimulate and sustain immediate programs. Belgium fell somewhere between these two positions.

On the issue of where common research should be conducted, Italy and the Netherlands pushed JNRC activities (not a surprising position since two of the JNRC establishments were located in these countries). Belgium, fearing interference with industrial research, wanted to limit JNRC programs; while France, to reduce the Commission's political clout, and Germany, for industrial reasons, advocated an outright reduction of these activities. These countries favored the alternative of association contracts which would locate Community research projects in national laboratories.

The second five-year program embodied these cross-cutting objectives.[47] The Commission's request for $480 million for the program was cut to $425 million. This was still almost twice the size of the first program and appeared, on first glance, to represent a significant upgrading of the Community's role. A closer look, however, revealed just the op-

---

facilities. But this body was composed of technical experts "appointed in their personal capacity." The sponsors of CCNR wanted a body of representatives more responsive to national requirements.

[46]The ship propulsion program, approved in 1961, amounted to a series of Euratom contracts with national ship propulsion centers in Germany, Italy, and Holland.

[47]For a selective chronological account of the second five-year budget discussions, see *Agence Europe*, January 20, 1962; January 26, 1962; February 23, 1962; March 12, 1962; March 28, 1962; April 12, 1962; May 12, 1962; and June 14, 1962.

posite. In contrast to the first five-year plan in which only 22 percent of total expenditures went to association contracts, the second plan called for 41 percent of total research to be carried out by this means. This amounted to a relative downgrading of the JNRC and a risky gamble that programs carried out in national laboratories would somehow be as "common" as those carried out in Community facilities. Moreover, all future programs would be implemented through association contracts (fast reactors, high temperature reactors, nuclear fusion, and the biology program). By contrast, Community projects, ORGEL and other JNRC activities, had been cut back from original requests by $10 million and $13 million respectively.[48]

The program sought to satisfy everyone, but succeeded in satisfying no one, paying least attention, in the process, to Community requirements. The Commission hoped to reconsider the budget after the expected expansion of the Community to include Great Britain.[49] But de Gaulle's veto of British membership in 1963 precluded this possibility, and budget squeezes provided the occasion for reopening debate. The cuts made in 1962 in ORGEL and JNRC programs combined with rising research costs to create a financial crisis at Ispra. In October 1963 France voted against the 1964 budget, arguing that the crisis was owing to Commission overspending and must be managed by consolidating existing programs rather than raising expenditures.[50] The Commission, nevertheless, requested in early 1964 an increase of second five-year appropriations totaling $48 million. France responded to this request by submitting a memorandum to the Council outlining French grievances against Euratom.[51] The other members responded in kind.[52] The positions taken in these memoranda made clear that the Euratom crisis was less a financial matter than a political controversy going to the *raison d'être* of the Atomic Energy Community.

The French memorandum brought together a range of French positions taken in earlier controversies, but which had not been presented systematically prior to 1962, the year de Gaulle shed his Algerian albatross and shifted attention to Community politics. In sum, France sought to strip Euratom of all political significance, reducing it, according to one official, to the status of a "philanthropic organization" (*oeuvre de*

---

[48]ORGEL was the Community's primary reactor project (heavy water, organic cooled), involving the construction and use of a critical assembly (ECO) and test reactor (ESSOR) at the Ispra center. This project is the main focus of our case study in chap. 6.

[49]On discussions between Euratom and British officials, see *Agence Europe*, November 15, 1962; November 29, 1962; and December 14, 1962.

[50]Approval of annual budgets, as we noted earlier, does not require unanimity.

[51]For a summary of the French memorandum, see *Agence Europe*, May 8, 1964.

[52]For a summary of the German memorandum, see *Agence Europe*, May 30, 1964; for English translations of the Italian and Belgian memoranda, see *Agence Europe* (*Europe Documents* No. 270) July 3, 1964. The Dutch did not table a memorandum; for their views, see *Agence Europe*, June 24, 1964.

bienfaisance).[53] Consistent with its desire to dominate unilaterally the political orientation of Community reactor policies, France reiterated attacks against Community reliance on foreign (especially American) technology and the dispersion of internal resources to develop technically unsound projects in backward member-countries. Instead, France felt Euratom had to come to grips with the broader implications of nuclear research, which included the control of American nuclear industries in Europe (in line with France's position on American investments generally—see chapter 2) and the conscious development of European technologies, in particular gas graphite and heavy water reactor systems.

The German memorandum rejected proposals for a protectionist external policy and centrally directed European reactor projects (expressing reservations about the one existing project of this type, ORGEL). Germany agreed that Euratom should stress technical rather than developmental aims but did not want the technical weight of common programs to become great enough to advance French political designs for the Community. Belgium proposed a way to achieve greater technical coordination without enhancing the status of Community laboratories. It called for fixing minimum amounts to be spent by individual members in national programs which would then be coordinated closely through the establishment of liaison bodies. Not surprisingly, Italy and Holland rejected this proposal. While criticizing French political designs, they also attacked German and Belgian emphasis on narrow research objectives. Holland wanted the Petten center to be treated according to its status of "center of general competence" on the same footing as Ispra, and Italy wanted to coordinate industrial as well as research activities.[54]

An active Commission role in this period possibly would have facilitated compromise. As it was, the Commission suffered from a growing cancer of indecision. This was due, in part, to the expectation that Euratom would shortly merge with other Community bodies (EEC and ECSC) to form a single Community executive.[55] More importantly, however, the indecision was a result of sharp divisions within the Commis-

---

[53]See the articles by *Le Monde's* science writer, Nicolas Vichney, *Le Monde*, March 7, 1964, and March 9, 1964.

[54]As an Italian member of the European Parliament put it in the fall of 1964: ". . . Euratom must not be an institution merely aiming at the progress of research, as some seem to wish; it should rather assume a political function of economic progress in the energy and production sector, creating infrastructures and favoring the promotion of a European nuclear industry." *Atomo e Industria*, October 1, 1964.

[55]A meeting of the EEC and Euratom Councils in February 1964 reportedly agreed on a unification of Community executives effective January 1, 1965. Euratom's *Seventh General Report* released in May 1964 assumed that this would be the last report of the separate Euratom Commission. These plans were torpedoed, however, by the subsequent Common Market crisis of 1965. Talks were not resumed until early 1966, and unification did not ensue until July 1, 1967.

sion itself. After the removal of President Hirsch, whose continuation in office was opposed in 1961 by France, the Commission became a feeble and fragmented spokesman for Community interests. (See chapter 5.)

Pierre Chatenet, a former Gaullist minister, succeeded Hirsch. Chatenet possessed neither the promotional flair of Euratom's first president, Armand, nor the administrative enthusiasm of Hirsch.[56] Intimidated or, perhaps, inspired by French policy, Chatenet harbored Gaullist sympathies both for the requirement of European nuclear independence and for the preferability of natural (the French technique) over enriched uranium reactors (the American technique).[57] He had the dubious distinction, as a Community official, of being the first to introduce the concept of "additional programs" (also called special, complementary, or supplementary programs), a formula which France subsequently used to undermine Euratom's common program. In a series of newspaper articles in 1966, Chatenet contended that future Euratom programs must differ in both style and structure from previous ones.[58] He added:

. . . it is necessary, as Louis Armand has said, to construct Europe "à la carte." If fast reactors interest France, Germany and Great Britain, then it is among these countries that an agreement should be negotiated. On other topics it will be necessary to find other formulas, different scales of participation with Euratom acting at the same time as a central planning agency and as an investment bank. The Treaty is flexible and permits this.

Chatenet, in effect, called for the abandonment of the requirement of unanimity for Euratom programs, letting member-states choose, on the basis of interest, which programs they wanted to participate in and what financial contribution they wanted to make. The idea of a more flexible scheme of cooperation was not itself a bad one. What was unfortunate was the manner and timing of the proposal and the implications given to the additional-programs concept by Chatenet's further comments concerning Euratom's industrial responsibilities.[59]

. . . Euratom does not have to promote a nuclear industry. It is an international organization for studying cooperatively common problems. The industries of the Community will construct the nuclear power stations. Euratom is in no way an organization of production or distribution. . . . What then might the Community do? Its task is essentially to centralize information, bringing to bear in this process its intelligence, expertise and relations with third countries.

---

[56]Hans A. Schmitt, "French Politicians and the European Communities: the Record of the 1950's," in Sydney Nettleton Fisher (ed.), *France and the European Community* (Columbus: Ohio State University Press, 1964), p. 68.

[57]Pierre Chatenet, "Aspects Nucléaires de le Politique Européenne," *Chronique de Politique Étrangère*, XVII (March 1964), pp. 134–54.

[58]*Le Figaro*, April 28, 1966; see also *Côte Desfossis*, March 17, 1966.

[59]*Les Echos*, October 20, 1966.

Chatenet appeared to be redefining Euratom's aim as set out in Article 1 of the Treaty. If Euratom had no responsibilities to promote development in the industrial field and if research was better organized through scattered rather than common programs, Euratom would become little more than a service organization. Rather than being raised to meet the problems of industrial cooperation, Euratom was being lowered to avoid these problems.

Chatenet's comments provoked consternation and criticism from both the European Parliament and fellow commissioners.[60] There was less disagreement about the idea of additional programs than the relationship between these programs and common programs. Concerned about the fate of scientific personnel at JNRC establishments, Chatenet's critics argued that Article 6, while permitting cooperation outside the common budget, intended for this cooperation to be an extension of, not a substitute for, the common program under Article 7. Unless additional programs were accompanied by common objectives and improved coordination of national activities, these programs, the critics argued, went contrary to the letter and spirit of Chapter 1 of the Treaty.

These critics rightly perceived the shift in Community developments from institutional to more informal modes of research cooperation. Though financial "band-aids" were found to keep the second five-year plan going,[61] the trend after 1964 involved more and more bilateral and multilateral projects outside Euratom. Under the framework of the 1963 Franco-German Treaty of Cooperation, France and Germany began talks to build a joint high flux reactor at Grenoble (a project the Commission originally proposed within the Euratom budget), as well as a joint commercial reactor at Fessenheim on the Franco-German border. Somewhat later, Germany, Holland, and Great Britain initiated the centrifuge enrichment project. (See chapter 5.) Apparently, after 1965, the member-states lost faith in Euratom (that is, as much or as little as they had at the beginning). The feeling existed that the easiest way to complicate cooperation was to let the Euratom Commission get involved.[62]

---

[60]*Agence Europe*, May 26, 1966, and comments of Belgian Commissioner, *Volksgazet*, May 6, 1966, and Dutch Commissioner, *Elseviers Weekblad*, May 14, 1966. Chatenet's views may have been the cause of earlier conflicts with other commissioners. Enrico Medi, the Italian commissioner, resigned in December 1964, allegedly over opposition to Chatenet's support of programs carried out in national as opposed to Community laboratories. *Agence Europe*, January 21, 1965. Krekeler, the first German commissioner, complained, when he resigned in 1964, that the Gaullist concept of a "Europe of States" was gaining favor in the Community (*Die Welt*, February 18, 1964); and his successor, Margulies, noted that German officials in the Commission were at a disadvantage because Bonn, unlike Paris, did not give them a consistent policy to push in Brussels (the implication being that Chatenet was pushing Gaullist policy). *Bremer Nachrichten*, August 6, 1965.

[61]A first budget revision in 1965 added $5 million to the five-year plan and redistributed other funds. The second revision in 1967 merely shifted funds.

[62]The author heard this view expressed repeatedly in interviews with national officials in all member-countries.

Scope of Common Research

The early decisions associated with the establishment of Euratom permitted, for a time, the separation of research from industrial and larger political issues. Not only was much nuclear research still in a pre-industrial phase but agreement on the importance of European unity overrode instances when industrial differences intruded (as for example, when Adenauer refused to bow to German industrial skeptics). By 1964–65, however, reactor developments (at least, first-generation reactors) were entering the industrial stage. More importantly, a change in European political circumstances was taking place. As we outlined in chapter 2, European countries were becoming more conscious of the national significance of R&D activities. The technology gap issue in 1966 fixed the relationship between research and international commercial competition. The nonproliferation discussions fixed the link between commercial and strategic interests. In short, the context of the mid-1960s facilitated the recognition of a wide variety of problems and consequences associated with advanced technological research. Whereas Common Market activities sharply overshadowed Euratom activities in the late 1950s, R&D emerged in the mid- and late 1960s as the linchpin of a whole set of economic and strategic processes central to the life of individual countries as well as European unity.

The industrialization and, in some instances, "nationalization" of R&D contributed to the erosion of Community influence and forced the Commission increasingly toward a role of coordination rather than centralization of nuclear programs. *The Seventh General Report* of the Commission in 1964 recognized the emerging industrial scope of research issues, noting that, despite the elimination of tariff and quota restrictions in the nuclear sector (completed in 1959), a common market in nuclear goods still did not exist. Industrial structures and procurement patterns remained largely national. Preparation of Euratom's first target program to estimate nuclear needs and resources (see note 27) provided the occasion to discuss these problems with industrial and utility groups concerned with nuclear power (UNICE and UNIPEDE).[63]

The Commission presented its target program to these groups in Venice in April 1965.[64] The focus of discussion was Community industrial policy in the nuclear sector. France, along with the Commission, took the most expansive view of the requirements of a common indus-

[63] This initiative issued from the adoption by the Six in April 1964 of the Protocol on Energy Problems, which represented the first firm step toward a common energy policy. Under this Protocol, Euratom issued its first target program, the High Authority launched an emergency program for coal (to improve the competitive position of Community coal *vis-à-vis* imports), and the EEC Commission formulated an initial position on Community policy for oil and natural gas. ECSC High Authority and European Community Information Service, *Europe and Energy* (Luxembourg, 1967), pp. 53–61.

[64] Euratom, *First Target Programme for the European Atomic Energy Community* (EUR 2773. e) (Brussels: Euratom, March 1966).

trial policy. Both sought a Community program for prototype construction and the setting up of a restricted number of European industrial groups capable of meeting international competition.[65] France, expectedly, pushed gas graphite and heavy water technologies as the basis of such a program. Italy agreed with these proposals in principle but rejected the specific emphasis on gas graphite and heavy water technologies. Germany and the Benelux countries recoiled from the very notion of a common policy or "target goals." Germany, in particular, objected to anything more than a Community role in supplying information about the nuclear market and opposed Community action in the prototype field as well as any attempt to "cartelize" nuclear industries through the use of industrial promotion funds, such as the Commission recommended in the draft target plan.[66]

Discussion of the industrial problems connected with research thus resulted in a widening of the scope of disagreement among Euratom members. Agreement on a third five-year program now depended critically on leadership initiatives to bring together the disparate aspects of common research and to provide a political rationale for Community cooperation. Whatever the criticism of its initial programs, the Commission prior to 1962 provided decisive leadership. After 1962, demoralized by internal discord, the Commission became immobilized. The new Commission, formed in July 1967 by the long-awaited merger of Community executives, displayed more vitality, but by this time, the stakes of continued cooperation had been increased. The resolution of the Six Science Ministers at Luxembourg in October 1967 to expand cooperation to other technological areas (see chapter 2) widened the context of nuclear discussions. In addition to industrial issues, nuclear research now faced competition with other research priorities. The Euratom debate took on new significance, since the forms of cooperation adopted for Euratom might also be applied to other areas.

Recognizing this possibility, the new Commission struck back hard against the concept of additional programs. In proposals tabled in March 1968, the Commission called these programs detrimental to the Community spirit.[67] A subsequent communiqué in May emphasized that, while nuclear programs in the past suffered from obvious mistakes and inadequacies, this was no justification for abandonment of common programs in nuclear or other fields.[68] The point was made most emphatically in the Commission's "white paper" on nuclear policy issued in 1969.[69] Common efforts were necessary now more than ever, the white

[65] Agence Europe, February 11, 1965.

[66] See various articles in Atomwirtschaft, X (September 1965); XI (August/September 1966); and XII (March 1967).

[67] See Agence Europe, March 8, 1968; March 13, 1968; and March 18, 1968.

[68] Agence Europe, May 22, 1968.

[69] See Commission of the European Communities, "Survey of the Nuclear Policy of

paper said. After ten years, Euratom was still far from reaching the objective of creating favorable conditions for the growth of a powerful nuclear industry. The reason had nothing to do with the size of the Community effort in the nuclear sector. As the paper noted, "the effort of the Six, on both the national and Community levels, as regards public spending on civilian research, has been only marginally lower than in the USA, which means that it has been higher in proportion to the gross national product." Yet the industrial and commercial returns in Europe were vastly inferior. Whereas four or five contracting firms were building or planning to build eighty-seven nuclear power plants in the United States, twelve firms were building only sixteen plants in Europe. The cause of Europe's inferiority, the report concluded, lay in the "fragmentation of the [European] effort, the bulk of which has been pursued at the national level and with national objectives in view." The report continued:

. . . Member countries have reserved appropriations and public contracts for their own domestic industries, and orders placed by the electricity utilities have been awarded solely to domestic contractors. . . . The weakness of industrial structures within the Community is in fact the result as much as the cause of this lack of co-ordination of officially sponsored projects.

The white paper urged a comprehensive approach: The member-states must map out jointly "a grand strategy" for nuclear development, including common policies in energy supply, reactor development, uranium enrichment, basic research, and procurement policies. As specific Commission proposals in June 1969 suggested, this strategy did not require Community facilities as such, though the Commission continued to worry about the conversion of the Ispra center and the future of its 2,000 employees.[70] Instead, the Commission emphasized coordination of national efforts through a series of technical advisory committees in various fields. The emphasis registered a long-term shift in Community focus from its own programs (Article 7) to the function of coordination (Article 5). It was also an attempt to halt the drift toward additional programs under Article 6.[71]

---

the European Communities," *Bulletin of the European Communities,* Supplement (September/October 1968).

[70]These proposals, for example, downplayed specific Community projects such as ORGEL and recommended instead that JNRC facilities be used for infrastructure activities, including public service functions in safety and health areas and the performance of toll work for outside contractors. See Commission of the European Communities, "Euratom's Future Activities," *Bulletin of the European Communities,* Supplement (June 1969).

[71]As we noted above, some members argued that Article 6 was unrelated to Article 7 and that programs undertaken under Article 6 did not require Community distribution of information as called for under the common program. The Commission rejected this interpretation. After 1969, member-states began to refer to additional programs as "special" programs to emphasize this difference with the Commission.

Commission efforts took account of the disillusionment with JNRC programs without sacrificing the principle of Community responsibility. The revival of national politics in Europe, however, was rapidly diminishing the opportunity for effective Community leadership. Initiative was passing to national governments. Germany was primarily responsible for the compromise in December 1967 to continue Euratom activities on a transitional year-to-year basis until agreement could be reached on a new multiple-year plan.[72] German support was based on the desire to keep Euratom going in the midst of the nonproliferation and technology gap disputes. Technical interest in Euratom programs, however,' remained low. In 1969 the common budget was reduced still further to $24 million, and for the first time, additional programs (another $24 million) were officially included in the Euratom budget. Throughout 1968, national conflicts over the admission of Great Britain also halted discussions to expand cooperation to nonnuclear fields (Maréchal group).[73]

The New Milieu of Common Research

The EEC summit conferences of December 1969 (Hague) and October 1972 (Paris) symbolized the new character of European politics in the field of science and technology. Nuclear as well as general technological cooperation became the subject of discussion and bargaining at the highest levels. Great Britain, in particular, exploited the subject of technology to enhance its bargaining leverage in seeking Common Market membership. From 1967 on, Britain promoted the idea of a European Technological Community in which British technology would play a prominent role.[74] The prospect of a Technological Community boosted but also complicated efforts to sustain nuclear cooperation. The new Technological Community could build on the experiences of Euratom and the JNRC, or it could serve to undercut the principle of Community programs in favor of a loose collection of specific projects funded independently by interested parties. The choice, in other words, was between the Community principle of centralized leadership for common programs (à la Euratom) and the ad hoc, informal principle of national interaction for specific and uncoordinated purposes. Summit diplomacy

[72]The decision approved a budget of $40 million for 1968 (a considerable reduction from the $90 million requested) but stipulated that a new multiple-year plan make maximum use of JNRC facilities for nonnuclear as well as nuclear activities. *Agence Europe*, December 11, 1967.

[73]The Netherlands boycotted these discussions in retaliation for France's second veto of British Common Market membership.

[74]The proposal was first made by Prime Minister Wilson in late 1966. *The Economist*, November 19, 1966.

made clear that, whatever the choice, national governments would call the tune. In the new milieu, science and technology were too important to leave to Community bureaucrats.

The principle of Community leadership hinged on the fate of the JNRC, which, in the broadened context of nonnuclear research, dropped the specific nuclear label and became known as the JRC. The plight of the JRC reflected a number of factors. Disappointment with the nuclear (and space) experience sapped enthusiasm to sustain an unsuccessful form of cooperation. Second, as nuclear power reached the industrial stage, nuclear centers everywhere, not just at the Community level, faced the need to convert to other types of research. This process, necessitating manpower shifts and the molding of a new consensus on research priorities, was difficult enough at the national, let alone the Community, level. Third, the reintegration of scientific and technological activities with national policy-making (e.g., in the development of national science policies) placed science activities in the context of other, higher priority domestic concerns. In the general economic slowdown of 1969–70, European countries cut back science expenditures at home. For example, between 1968 and 1972, France reduced R&D expenditures by 6 percent (increase of 19.2 percent offset by an inflation of research costs around 25 percent).[75] Not surprisingly, France demanded similar cuts in Community expenditures.

The real dispute over JRC, however, was the issue of Community leadership. If the JRC were phased out, the Community's one foothold in the R&D field would be lost. The EEC Treaty provided no specific authority for science activities except in the vague context of economic policy (the Maréchal group, it will be recalled, was a working group of the EEC Committee on Medium-Term Economic Policy). At the practical level, therefore, the Commission sought to keep the JRC going, while at the political level, it sought a new mandate to extend the principle of Community responsibility to new fields of technology.

At the Hague summit in 1969, members agreed "to continue and intensify Community efforts to coordinate and foster research and industrial development in the leading growth sectors" and ". . . to make further efforts to formulate . . . in the near future a research programme geared to the requirements of modern industrial management and enabling the most efficient use to be made of the Joint Research Centre."[76] In connection with the latter aim, Germany, always critical of the centralized and industrial orientation of the JRC, presented new proposals to decentralize JRC controls and restrict JRC activities to long-term

[75] *Agence Europe*, December 1, 1972.
[76] For relevant portions of the Hague communiqué, see *Research and Technology* (bulletin published by the Press and Information Services of the Commission of the European Communities, Brussels) No. 36 (December 8, 1969).

and fundamental research as well as public service functions.[77] Long discussions eventually led in 1973 to a reorganization of Community offices dealing with research. JRC activities were placed under the control of a special office located at Ispra which answered directly to the Commission.[78]

The restriction of JRC activities to remote research and infrastructure programs was the only way to preserve continued support for the operation of Community laboratories. Germany and Belgium strongly opposed industrially related projects at the JRC. The concept of specific projects (or additional programs as they were known in the Euratom context) had become the preferred mode of operation in industrially related enterprises. This concept was the basis of a set of forty-seven proposals worked out by the Maréchal group (also called the Aigrain group after Pierre Aigrain assumed the chairmanship in 1969, and more recently, referred to as the PREST Committee). In the context of British membership negotiations, these proposals were circulated to non-Community countries; and, in November 1971, science ministers from nineteen countries met and approved seven of these projects at a total cost of $21 million.[79] Known as COST, this program paralleled negotiations among Community countries on some twenty other projects at a cost of $30 million (known as the PREST program).[80]

As before, France was the principal advocate of the project mode of cooperation. It objected to the extension of Community responsibility to general science and technology and viewed the ad hoc process of ministerial agreement on specific projects as the only means of Community cooperation consistent with intergovernmental responsibility and national sovereignty. Even for JRC activities, it insisted that expenditures be grouped around specific programs rather than general overhead requirements.[81]

---

[77]These proposals were in large measure the work of the state secretary of the German Science Ministry, Klaus von Dohnanyi, and were known unofficially as the Dohnanyi proposals. See *Neue Zuercher Zeitung*, December 5, 1969.

[78]In this reorganization, Directorate XII, formerly General Research and Technology, was renamed Research, Science and Education; Directorate III. Industry, became Industrial and Technological Affairs; and the Joint Research Centre, formerly Directorate XV, was given autonomous status at Ispra directly under the Commission.

[79]The countries included, besides the Six, Austria, Denmark, Ireland, Norway, Portugal, Spain, Sweden, Switzerland, U.K., Finland, Greece, Yugoslavia, and Turkey. The projects concerned the creation of a pilot European data transmission network, a study of the propagation of radio waves, two projects in the field of metallurgy (materials for gas turbines and desalination plants), and three projects in the field of pollution. In May 1973, these countries minus Norway approved an additional project, a European Medium-Range Weather Forecasting Center at a total cost of $22 million. See *Industry, Research and Technology*, No. 120 (November 16, 1971); No. 122 (December 2, 1971); and No. 190 (May 22, 1973).

[80]The PREST program is thus far a major disappointment compared to the original $150–500 million envisioned for this effort. The principal project, the construction of a giant computer of revolutionary design, could not be agreed upon. See "PREST Depressed," *Nature*, CCXXX (March 26, 1971), p. 200.

[81]*Agence Europe*, December 3, 1971, and December 6, 1971.

With the issue of British membership solved in 1971, the Commission looked to the Paris summit of October 1972 to supply new impetus in the quest for a Community policy in R&D. In a general statement on the "objectives and instruments of a common policy for scientific research and technological development" submitted to the Council in July 1972, the Commission argued that large-scale programs must be a part of a "global strategy" and that, "however or wherever they may be implemented it is the task of the Community to propose methods of cooperation and to act as a catalyst for new projects adopted in or by the Community."[82] Once again, the Paris summit, like the previous one at The Hague, gave rhetorical support to these objectives. The communiqué set a deadline of January 1, 1974, for adopting a common R&D policy.[83]

By mid-1973, however, the realities of implementation continued to diverge from the rhetoric. At the practical level, the Community achieved a significant victory in February 1973 when the Council agreed to a new four-year research and training program for the JRC, the first multiple-year plan since 1967. Calling for total expenditures of $157 million and no reduction of staff from the latest level of approximately 1550, this program included both nuclear and nonnuclear projects (the latter totaling only $19.5 million, however).[84] Given French and British objections as late as January 1973, the agreement indicated some rapid and complex bargaining, the exact nature of which remains speculative. The practical outcome, in any case, was to preserve the institutional basis for a continued discussion of Community responsibilities in the field of R&D. Unfortunately, this willingness to keep the debate alive has not been followed by more general political agreement.[85]

The biggest disappointment in achieving a political consensus, at least from the Commission point of view, has been the attitude of the British. After championing the cause of a Technological Community to enhance British credentials for Common Market membership, British officials have suddenly cooled to the idea of a common R&D program.[86]

[82]For a copy of this statement, see Commission of the European Communities, *Bulletin of the European Communities*, Supplement (June 1972).

[83]See *Industry, Research and Technology*, No. 162 (October 24, 1972).

[84]The program contained three additional programs totaling $37 million or a little over 20 percent of the total (Italy did not participate in part of the transplutonium work at the Karlsruhe center; France opted out of the program for control and management of fissile materials; and France, Great Britain, Italy, Ireland, Denmark, and Luxembourg refused support of the Petten center in Holland). See press release of the Council of the European Communities, General Secretariat, 262e/73 (Presse 18), Brussels, February 6, 1973.

[85]As a former Community official writes in assessing the significance of the February 1973 decisions: "Euratom survives, but it is still not revived." Jules Guéron, "Qu'en est-il d'Euratom?" *L'Europe en formation* (May 1973), p. 20.

[86]As two British commentators remarked: "Now that we are in the Common Market, the government's desire for conspicuous goodness seems to have lessened." See Michael Kenward and Martin Sherwood, "Research and development: the European options," *New Scientist*, LVIII (April 12, 1973), p. 105.

Together with the French, they argue that existing organizations, including national academies, such as the Royal Society and the Max Planck Society, offer a better forum for collaboration than a new or strengthened Community agency. Both countries have reacted icily to Commission proposals to establish new top-level Community policy and programmatic organs in the field of R&D.[87] The British, in particular, are convinced that, given the problems of industrial collaboration, European cooperation in science and technology can develop only slowly and in connection with specific, well-defined projects.

Whatever the outcome of this debate, the new milieu of national politics reflects a shift from integrative to intergovernmental diplomacy in European technological affairs. This shift need not imply stalemate or disintegration in future European technological endeavors. What we may be observing is the preliminary consolidation of national science policies and priorities prior to a comprehensive agreement on European science policies and priorities.[88] The clear indication is, however, that national governments, not the Community, will be the key actors in negotiations to fashion common programs from a set of internally integrated national programs.

*   *   *

The desire to unravel the characteristics of national policies and leadership in specific project areas influenced the decision to organize the case studies of our investigation into European reactor cooperation around specific reactor sectors. In the next four chapters, we will focus more on the interaction of individual groups and programs in reactor areas than the dynamics of Community processes per se. The case studies employ a common, project-based development sequence as the comparative basis of analysis. Each chapter traces relevant projects

---

[87]In its general statement of July 1972, the Commission recommended a new high-level policy committee (CERD—European Research and Development Committee) to evaluate national R & D programs and advise the Commission on the objectives and priorities of Community R & D programs. This committee, purely an internal advisory organ, began work in April 1973. The Commission also recommended two new implementing agencies—a European Science Foundation to promote fundamental research and a European Research and Development Agency (ERDA) to administer Community cooperation in technological areas. See *Bulletin of the European Communities,* Supplement (June 1972); and Martin Sherwood, "An umbrella for European science," *New Scientist,* LV (July 6, 1972), pp. 19–20.

[88]One may argue, conversely, that the stalemate over European science policies follows from a rejection of the concept of a national science policy. Liberal industrial countries such as Great Britain may be unwilling and/or unable to coordinate domestic scientific and industrial activities toward consistent national ends. This argument may be less applicable in the case of continental countries, however. Even in the case of Great Britain, it tends to obscure the enormous attention and importance assigned today by governments to domestic developments in technology.

through successive stages of program definition, R&D, prototype development (known as the demonstration reactor phase in the case of proven reactors), and commercial production. The reader should be aware that these stages inevitably overlap, and the breakdown is more a matter of analytical convenience than descriptive accuracy.

PART III
THE LOW ROAD

CHAPTER 5

THE DEVELOPMENT OF PROVEN
REACTORS: EUROPEAN VERSUS
AMERICAN TECHNOLOGY

Euratom cut its teeth on the development of proven reactors, chiefly light water and gas graphite systems. This development focused primarily on the American light water reactor system and took place in cooperation with the United States under the terms of the Euratom-U.S. joint agreement signed shortly after the Euratom Treaty went into effect.

The decision to develop a foreign reactor design was a crucial one. The Euratom Commission made the choice but was not solely responsible for it. When France refused to share its gas graphite technology with Community partners, the Commission had no choice but to turn to outside assistance. Economically, the situation seemed too urgent to await European development of more advanced reactor techniques. And technically, assistance from the United States offered greater chances of success than association with more limited French and British gas graphite programs. Nevertheless, reliance on foreign technology created a delicate political problem which revealed itself only in the course of the program.

The problem was twofold. First, by relying on foreign assistance, the Community inevitably sacrificed some control over determination of its own priorities. As we will show in this chapter, the Euratom-U.S. joint program was primarily the brain child of U.S. participants and reflected American interests and requirements more than European ones. Strategically, as pointed out in the previous chapter, the United States sought cooperation as a way of containing Euratom's potential for independent political expression. Commercially, U.S. industries stood to gain most from the early exploitation of nuclear power. The joint program imposed these expectations on Europe and may have been responsible for locking Euratom prematurely into the single-minded construction of nuclear power plants. Under less frantic circumstances, Euratom may have invested its resources more widely and in less advanced, indigenous reactor *research* rather than more advanced, foreign reactor *construction*. Instead, once the initial energy crisis abated, Euratom was left saddled with a reactor construction program which it could abandon only at the risk of failing in its first and major programmatic initiative.

One theme of this chapter, therefore, deals with how political aims may give rise to technological programs which poorly match economic and technical circumstances yet must be sustained to preserve political appearances. The chief danger of dependence on external technology is that the external donor may commit the recipient to a course of action (with political implications) which the recipient develops a vested interest in sustaining, even if both the donor and the recipient change their original political justifications for cooperation. The joint program reflected American expectations that Euratom would be the principal agent of Western plans for European integration. When the Common Market assumed this role, U.S. interest in Euratom and the joint program waned. Euratom, on the other hand, expected U.S. assistance to yield immediate benefits in terms of political recognition and visibility. When the energy situation flip-flopped, Euratom suffered from this high public profile. For research purposes, it may have been better off working quietly and without prior commitments to coordinate member-state activities. Research is a more self-contained enterprise than industrial-scale projects. Yet Euratom could not scuttle the joint power program without compromising its credibility in research undertakings.

A second part of the political problem of relying on U.S. technology was the effect on member-state relations (as contrasted with the effect on Community actors). Easy access to outside technology under programs sanctioned by the Community exacerbated the difficulties of co-ordinating internal objectives among Euratom countries. Rather than being forced to rely upon one another, these countries could circumvent internal rivalries by turning to outside parties and doing so with the blessings of the Community. This was the course Germany took to avoid dependence on France. France accused the Community of encouraging such maneuvers and made the issue of foreign technology the spearpoint of its attack against other Euratom programs. Thus, instead of building Community programs around the strength of the leading nuclear country in Europe, the policy of dependence on external technology alienated the Community's strongest internal ally, increasing still further Europe's requirement for external allies and resources.

All of this is not to say that the development of American technology was a mistake. As one analyst concludes, "the vitality imparted by the Joint Program after the Treaty of Rome did much to sustain and strengthen Euratom."[1] The proven reactor program was probably Euratom's chief success, and the long-term economic benefits of an early reactor construction program as well as the technical wisdom of

---

[1] Arnold Kramish, *The Peaceful Atom in Foreign Policy* (New York: Harper and Row, 1963), p. 164.

choosing light water (American) over gas graphite (French) technology were subsequently confirmed by the large-scale introduction of nuclear power plants and the clear-cut superiority of American light water systems. Nevertheless, the joint program entailed political costs which have not always been recognized. The following case study deliberately spotlights these costs and their consequences while also considering the economic and technical requirements of proven reactor development.

The Program Definition Phase

The Euratom-U.S. joint agreement was not a program designed in response to a well-defined need; the agreement itself helped to define this need. The idea of cooperation with the United States was originally proposed in the preparation of the report of the three wise men. This idea inspired, in part, the inflation of energy requirements contained in that report.[2] The report projected a need for 15,000 MWe of installed nuclear power by 1967, an amount nearly ten times the capacity of installed nuclear power planned by Euratom's two principal members, France and Germany.[3] If this estimate had been reached in collaboration with Community members, one wonders how Community needs could have exceeded the combined needs of individual members (after all, the Community in this case was only the sum of its members). The figures, in fact, did not reflect Community needs but an American projection of what would be required to maximize commercial and technical interdependence among Western countries (in support of common goals of over-all Western defense). In initiating programs of international collaboration in technology, much depends on who defines the need for cooperation. As we noted in chapter 3, technological problems, no less than security ones, may be perceived and defined differently by individual countries. The country that exercises primary influence in setting the terms of a problem necessarily places itself in a good position to dominate the cooperative resolution of the problem. In the case of the joint program, the United States aided in defining Euratom's task so as to maximize the integration of Western resources and, in particular, the potential American input to European programs. The fact that the United States played this role as an external partner had particular implications for the emerging atomic community since, as one observer notes, "external relations may be regarded as one of the most sensitive areas politically in the integration process."[4]

[2]Louis Armand, Franz Etzel, and Francesco Giordani, *A Target for Euratom*, A report prepared at the request of the governments of Belgium, France, German Federal Republic, Italy, Luxembourg, and the Netherlands (May 1957).

[3]As noted in chap. 3, French plans announced in 1955 called for the installation of 800 MWe of nuclear power by 1965, while the German Eltville program foresaw a maximum construction of 500 MWe with no specific time limit.

[4]See Frans A. M. Alting von Geusau, *Beyond the European Community* (Leyden: Sijthoff, 1969), p. 67.

Open versus Closed Community

The three wise men were Monnet Europeanists who adhered firmly to the view of an open European Community.[5] This view was dominant in the European *relance* of the mid-1950s. It was a reflection of physical realities as well as psychological predispositions. Europe in this period was still strongly dependent on the United States for both strategic and economic support. In addition, Europe was psychologically weak. Euratom countries were still distrustful of one another and more inclined to look to the United States for leadership than to themselves. The Three Wise Men Report saw no contradiction between this need for outside cooperation and European independence:[6]

. . . strong cooperative ties with other countries . . . must be the foundation of Europe's atomic progress. Far from undermining our independence, it is the only way we can gain our place as equals in the field. The road to dependence would be the opposite one, to confirm our backwardness by resorting to the illusion of self-sufficiency. Cooperation with others will not limit our opportunities, but create new ones, so that our industries can acquire their own distinct nuclear personality.

Article 2 of the Euratom Treaty also urged Community officials to "establish with other countries and with international organisations any contacts likely to promote progress in the peaceful uses of nuclear energy."

This concept of an open community rested on two assumptions. First, it assumed that Europe's backwardness in the atomic field was largely a matter of inadequate resources. Once these resources were obtained through external assistance programs, it was believed that Europe would be able to take its place as an equal in the nuclear field. Thus, the fastest road to independence required initial dependence. Second, it assumed that this initial dependence would not affect the political and psychological will for independence. The feeling was that the latter was already strong enough to channel the inflow of foreign technology to the internal requirements of European sovereignty.

Disagreement with these assumptions was the basis of Gaullist objections to external cooperation, which were raised in the course of the proven reactor program. Proponents of independence regarded development more as a psychological than a physical process. Their analysis indicated that Europe had the resources for independence but lacked the will. Without firm agreement on the priority and purpose of European

---

[5]Franz Etzel was senior vice-president of the High Authority of the ECSC. Armand was a man of impeccable Europeanist credentials, and Francesco Giordani was the principal advocate in Italy of alignment with U.S. technology, opposing CISE scientists who favored a more independent approach. See Mario Silvestri, *Il costo della menzogna: Italia nucleare 1945–1968* (Torino: Giulio Einaudi, 1968), chap. 3.

[6]Armand, Etzel, and Giordani, *A Target for Euratom*, p. 28.

independence, external cooperation risked allowing local resources to be drawn off to implement non-European objectives. At issue was not merely a matter of material or quantitative growth—"raising of the standard of living," as the Treaty expressed it. Europe's nuclear development was also a matter of preserving the quality of industrial life, and the quality of European industrial life depended upon the exercise of political control and choice by European representatives. Already in 1958, Michel Debré, who became de Gaulle's minister keeper of seals, articulated the potential threat which external cooperation posed to European nuclear and scientific autonomy. "It is to be feared," Debré warned, "that if the [Euratom] Commission fails to base its first effort on a scientific, intellectual and industrial competition with the US, the dependence of the European nations will only increase at the great expense of the political independence of the science and future of the West."[7]

Euratom-U.S. Negotiations: Interests and Benefits

While the Euratom-U.S. agreement was being negotiated, however, Gaullist voices were a minority.[8] Aside from some skepticism among utilities about the projections of installed nuclear power,[9] the Three Wise Men Report was well received. The report encouraged cooperation with the United States in two ways. First, despite the general impression in this period that the British and French gas graphite technique was the most developed of the proven reactor designs, the report rated the American light water design of equivalent standing.[10] Second, the report discouraged the construction of Europe's own uranium enrichment plant, a facility required to produce enriched fuel for the

[7]*Agence Europe*, May 20, 1958. Gaullist emphasis on the quality rather than mere quantity of nuclear industrial development reflected a certain prescience of European attitudes today which, in pronouncements such as the Paris summit communiqué of October 1972, place great stress on the intangible social and cultural consequences of European economic and technological growth.

[8]Formal negotiations did not begin until February 1958, but contacts existed from the time of the visit of the three wise men. For example, in July 1957, a group of industrial and government officials from Euratom countries visited the U.S. and received firsthand tours and briefings on U.S. reactor technology. See *Science*, July 26, 1957, p. 158.

[9]German and French utilities were particularly skeptical. *Westdeutsche Allgemeine* (Essen), August 28, 1957; *Die Zeit*, November 21, 1957; *Der Spiegel*, January 1, 1958; interview with EdF official, Paris, April 1, 1970.

[10]Armand, Etzel, and Giordani, *A Target for Euratom*, p. 28. The *actual* competitive relationship between these techniques was disputed. But in the public eye, the gas graphite system held the lead, primarily on the strength of the Calder Hall reactor in England which went into operation in October 1956 and was the first nuclear station in the world to produce electrical power. By contrast, the first U.S. station, known as Shippingport, was still under construction and fell short of economic expectations when it went into operation in 1958. In 1957 the German science minister, Siegried Balke, explicitly acknowledged the lead of gas graphite systems. See *Frankfurter Neue Presse*, April 11, 1957, and *Frankfurter Allgemeine*, April 10, 1957.

American reactor.[11] Foregoing a European facility of this type meant reliance on the United States for enriched uranium supplies. The report contained assurances that the United States was ready to offer these supplies.

The liberal industrial countries in Europe favored cooperation with the United States. As we noted in chapter 3, many industries in these countries already had ties with American partners. Even companies in France had contacts with American enterprises (Framatome with Westinghouse and Alsthom with GE). The extension of these ties to cover nuclear development seemed both natural and expedient. Germany and the Benelux countries also endorsed reliance on American fuel imports. A European enrichment plant, if it employed the American gaseous diffusion technique, would not be able to compete with U.S. fuel prices; and the Germans and Dutch decided after 1958 to invest in the development of more advanced enrichment techniques (gas centrifuge and jet nozzle methods) to equip a truly independent European plant at some later date.[12] Gaullists were not satisfied with this long-run objective. They interpreted the emphasis on economic factors as a lack of political determination to pursue a European policy. As it turned out, Euratom's failure to promote an independent isotope separation plant, at the same time the Community adopted American reactor techniques, rankled Gaullists more than any other aspect of early Community policy.[13]

While the idea of cooperation with the United States was well received, it is doubtful that Europe would have initiated this idea on its own. The decisive impetus came from the United States. As Warren Walsh records, "four nuclear experts from the AEC served as technical advisers to the group which drafted the final version of *A Target for Euratom*."[14] The influence of these experts was extensive.[15] They supplied the technical data for energy projections and assured the three

[11]Armand, Etzel, and Giordani, *A Target for Euratom*, pp. 30–33. The idea of a European enrichment plant had been discussed since March 1956 by a study group set up during the Euratom negotiations. As Polach observes, "the outlook for such a plant was bright, at least up to January 1957 . . . ," the date of the three wise men visit to the U.S. After that, Armand, spokesman for the three wise men, opposed the idea as an immediate objective of Euratom. Jeroslav G. Polach, *Euratom: Its Background, Issues and Economic Implications* (Dobbs Ferry: Oceana, 1964), pp. 62–63.

[12]Worried about this development of alternative enrichment technologies, the U.S. asked Germany in 1960 to classify the centrifuge technology. Kramish, *The Peaceful Atom*, pp. 15–16. Germany had already begun work on centrifuge techniques during World War II. See David Irving, *The Virus House: The German Atomic Bomb Project* (New York: Simon and Schuster, 1968), pp. 127–31 and 229–31.

[13]For the view of a prominent Gaullist figure in these early deliberations, see Polach, *Euratom*, p. 28, note 11.

[14]Warren B. Walsh, *Science and International Public Affairs: Six Recent Experiments in International Scientific Cooperation* (Syracuse: Maxwell School of Syracuse University, International Relations Program, 1967), p. 85. The assistance of these experts is acknowledged in the letter of submittal accompanying the Three Wise Men Report. See Armand, Etzel, and Giordani, *A Target for Euratom*, p. 9.

[15]Kramish, *The Peaceful Atom*, p. 155.

wise men of full U.S. support in meeting nuclear construction goals. They made rosy forecasts of the economic performance of U.S. light water reactors, which were still under construction (see note 10). Most importantly, with firm U.S. government support, they argued against an independent European enrichment facility, emphasizing the proliferation risks of such an undertaking and promising abundant American exports of enriched uranium.[16]

The weight of U.S. technical assistance was overwhelming and illustrates one of the hazards of cooperation between an incipient technical community and a more advanced external partner. Not yet in existence, Euratom had no technical staff or independent data with which to challenge American estimates. Moreover, U.S. industries were in constant contact with AEC advisers, exchanging information and suggestions regarding details of proposed cooperation.[17] American industrialists were eager to find foreign markets to test U.S. reactor techniques. At the time, conventional power was more expensive in Europe, and it was thought that European utilities would purchase nuclear plants before American utilities. By contrast, Euratom had no established policy of contact with European industry. European firms associated individually and bilaterally with stronger American partners. In most instances (e.g., German industries), contacts with American partners were far more intimate than contacts with European firms or Euratom. This situation created subsequent dissatisfaction among some European industrialists. They viewed the joint program as a means not only of selling American reactors in Europe but also of introducing American industrial contract procedures into Europe.[18]

There is little that Euratom could have done to offset these inequities.[19] American technical and industrial superiority were built into

[16]See Lawrence Scheinman, "Security and a Transnational System: The Case of Nuclear Energy," in Robert O. Keohane and Joseph S. Nye, Jr. (eds.), *Transnational Relations and World Politics* (Cambridge: Harvard University Press, 1972), p. 292. Also see Lawrence Scheinman, *Atomic Energy Policy in France under the Fourth Republic* (Princeton: Princeton University Press, 1965), p. 177.

[17]U.S., Congress, Joint Committee on Atomic Energy, *Hearings, Proposed Euratom Agreements and Legislation*, 85th Cong., 2d Sess., July 22, 23, 25, 29, and 30, 1958 (Washington, D.C.: Government Printing Office, 1958), p. 90.

[18]As a French industrialist pointed out, one consequence of the active participation of U.S. industry in AEC negotiations was the inclusion in the joint agreement of a whole hodgepodge of procedures familiar to American firms but unknown in Europe. These procedures included patent regulations as well as practices governing the distribution of nonpatentable information. See *Nucleonics*, May 1959, p. 28; and Jules Guéron, *The US-Euratom Joint Research and Development Programme* (Munich: Karl Thiemig KG, 1966), pp. 32–36. The Community eventually drafted its own patent policy in 1961, which was more liberal than U.S. procedures and dispelled somewhat industrial discontent with American practices, especially in Germany. See various discussions in *Atomwirtschaft*, VIII (December 1963), pp.657 ff; IX (January 1964), pp. 13 ff; and IX (February 1964), p. 79. For the Community patent law, see *Amtsblatt der Europaeischen Gemeinschaften* (official bulletin of the European Communities, Brussels), October 26, 1963, p. 2569.

[19]For example, Euratom did have several representatives who had just joined its staff from industry participate in the negotiations of spring 1958. These representatives were

the structure of nuclear relations at the time. The political consequences of this situation cannot be ignored, however. As one analyst observed when American assistance was first discussed, U.S. aid constituted "a lever of great power in the region's nuclear development and in building a more satisfactory partnership with [Euratom] countries."[20]

Euratom-U.S. Joint Agreement

The agreement concluded in May and signed in November of 1958 gave testimony to the weight of U.S. influence.[21] The mere size of the program betrayed American designs. Called by one source "the most ambitious atomic program since the atomic and hydrogen bomb projects,"[22] the joint program consisted of two parts: a reactor program calling for construction in Europe by 1965 of nuclear stations with a total capacity of 1000 MWe, approximately six reactors of 150 MWe each; and a research program of potentially $200 million—$100 million for the first five years, both Euratom and the United States committing $50 million each, and funds for the second five years of "the same order of magnitude." The reactor program was estimated to cost $350 million, making a grand total for both programs of over a half-billion dollars. The agreement established two joint boards with equal U.S. and Euratom voting rights to supervise implementation of the research and reactor programs.

The United States made some notable concessions in the negotiations. The joint agreement gave Euratom primary inspection authority (subject to American review of inspection data) over nuclear materials transferred from the United States to the Community. In all previous bilateral agreements, the United States had retained direct authority for inspections. The Department of Defense and AEC wanted to retain this authority in the case of Euratom as well, but the White House and State Department prevailed on Congress to approve this provision as a practical expression of U.S. support for European unity.[23]

In addition, the United States agreed to a common research program, which was not a part of the original recommendations of the three wise men.[24] The Euratom Commission insisted on this program to avoid the

isolated figures, however. Unlike AEC representatives, they had no established precedents or existing programs to collaborate with local industry.

[20] Klaus E. Knorr, *Nuclear Energy in Western Europe and United States Policy* (Memorandum No. 9; Princeton: Princeton University, Center of International Studies, September 10, 1956), p. 28.

[21] For a copy of the agreement, see U.S., Congress, Joint Committee on Atomic Energy, *Hearings, Agreement for Cooperation with Euratom*, 86th Cong., 1st Sess., January 21 and 22, 1959 (Washington, D.C.: Government Printing Office, 1959), p. 3.

[22] *Nucleonics*, August 1958, p. 20.

[23] Harold L. Nieburg, *Nuclear Secrecy and Foreign Policy* (Washington, D.C.: Public Affairs Press, 1964), p. 143.

[24] Warren H. Donnelly, *Commercial Nuclear Power in Europe: The Interaction of American Diplomacy with a New Technology*, prepared for the U.S., Congress, House,

impression that the joint agreement was merely a scheme for the import of American reactors.[25] After the early projections of the economic feasibility of nuclear power proved excessive (which became apparent already in 1958), the research program acquired added significance as a means of improving existing reactor designs. The United States, however, wanted greater emphasis on the power program. In the American view, research should be closely tied to the sale and installation of U.S. reactors under the power program. This tie was essential in securing congressional support of the joint agreement.[26] Euratom officials, on the other hand, attached independent significance to research, both because it represented the first sizeable investment of Community research funds and because it held out the prospect that Europe might be able to improve on American technology.

The over-all program, however, contained major advantages for American participants. The reactor program offered generous loan and fuel guarantee provisions which facilitated the sale of American reactors to prospective European customers.[27] These provisions applied only to reactor varieties tested in the United States, which meant at the time chiefly American light water reactors. Moreover, the way the research program was set up, every dollar spent by the United States was matched by a dollar spent by Euratom (the parties agreeing that they would place contracts only on respective sides of the Atlantic). This arrangement, of course, benefited both sides. But because the technology being used was further advanced in the United States than in Europe, the United States obtained through the program a doubling of

---

Subcommittee on National Security Policy and Scientific Developments of the Committee of Foreign Affairs (Washington, D.C.: Government Printing Office, December 1972), p. 96.

[25]Interview with member of Euratom negotiating team, Paris, December 2, 1969.

[26]The congressional debate on the joint agreement took place in the context of Republican-Democratic differences over the issue of public versus private power. Democrats were seeking to stimulate domestic development of nuclear power and charged "that the administration opposed government programs in the United States but favored government programs in Europe." Nieburg, *Nuclear Secrecy*, p. 135. The only way to convince Democrats of the wisdom of the program was to stress the commercial gains expected by U.S. industry. See U.S., Congress, *Hearings, Proposed Euratom Agreements*; and Harold P. Green and Alan Rosenthal, *Government of the Atom* (New York: Atherton Press, 1963), chap. 1.

[27]The U.S. provided $135 million in loans from the Export-Import Bank (repayable at 4.5 percent interest over a period of fifteen years beginning one year after completion of construction). European governments offered additional loans of $65 million, and private utilities were expected to put up the remaining $150 million of the total $350 million program. The most important incentive of the program was a supplementary fuel agreement. The USAEC agreed to supply an initial quantity of 30,000 kgs. of enriched uranium with a guarantee to cover further requirements for a period of twenty years. In addition, the USAEC guaranteed the quality of the fuel elements (a major incentive at the time) and agreed to buy back plutonium and reprocess irradiated fuel from the installed reactors. All fuel charges could be deferred for fifteen years at an interest rate of 4 percent per year.

its resources applied to light water research. All information would be exchanged under the program, and patentable inventions would become co-property of the USAEC and Euratom. The Euratom Commission, recognizing the importance of obtaining information on the spot, secured a clause allowing the two parties to station staff with contracting firms of the other party. Effective use of this clause would have represented a considerable advantage for Euratom; but owing to misunderstandings and insufficient personnel, the clause was seldom invoked.[28]

Given the circumstances, was the conclusion of so large a program with a dominant outside power, focusing primarily on reactor construction, a wise step for the fledgling Atomic Energy Community? The answer is probably yes, but only because there was no alternative. The possibility of cooperating with Great Britain or France on the development of gas graphite reactors was ruled out by the attitudes of these two countries. Great Britain at this time was hostile to the idea of supranational unity in Europe and was in no position to extend the generous terms of cooperation offered by the United States.[29] France, following its basic view that Euratom should supplement, not substitute for, national programs, never offered its gas graphite system as the basis of a Community program. The Commission never asked for it. Since gas graphite systems were already being studied in France, the Commission thought it best to focus on another technology not then the subject of extensive research in Europe.

The French point of view clearly reflected the advanced state of French civilian nuclear technology at the time. In a cooperative program, France had everything to give and little to receive. Moreover, France wanted to tie Euratom programs to French aims rather than put important French programs in the service of Euratom aims. This point of view, of course, underestimated the advantages of leadership and

---

[28]See Guéron, *The US-Euratom Joint Research and Development Programme*, pp. 10–11. According to Guéron, member-states failed to staff Euratom sufficiently to implement this clause. It is also likely, however, that differences between government agencies and private industries complicated use of the provision. For an illustration of such differences in the case of the Euratom-U.S. fast reactor agreement, see chap. 8 and the discussion of the project SEFOR.

[29]The three wise men also visited Great Britain (as well as Canada) but received nothing like the reception they did in the U.S. Initially, Britain tried to circumvent Euratom, supplying fuel to Euratom countries on a bilateral basis. When this tactic aroused Commission ire, Britain finally signed a framework agreement with Euratom. (*The Economist*, May 24, 1958, p. 688.) This agreement offered no specific incentives for the sale of British reactors, however. British industries in this period took a supercilious view of European events, a tactic which may have cost them a share of the European reactor market. When the German utility, RWE, purchased a small U.S. reactor in 1957, spokesmen suggested that this choice was less the result of a careful economic comparison of gas graphite and light water reactors than a lack of British enthusiasm in supplying data on the economic performance of gas graphite systems. *Sunday Times* (London), May 18, 1958; also *The Economist*, July 19, 1958.

disproportionate influence which could accrue to France by seizing the initiative in Euratom and making Euratom programs dependent on French technology. For the moment, these advantages passed to the United States.

The R&D Phase

If the Commission had little choice in concluding the joint program, it bears more responsibility for the manner in which this program was implemented. In late 1958, the energy picture shifted, drastically altering the economic conditions underlying Euratom goals. The European market was suddenly flooded with coal and oil supplies. Overnight, Europe had an energy glut instead of a gap. The coal surplus stemmed, in part, from measures taken after Suez to rationalize coal production and arrange long-term contracts for import of American coal. Oil deliveries increased due to the presence of new suppliers in the world market (such as the Soviet Union) and the diversion of imports from the United States to Europe following imposition of U.S. oil import quotas.[30]

In the face of this altered consumer market for energy, the Community might have done well to reconsider the emphasis on immediate reactor construction.[31] European industrial and power groups pointed out that, in the new market circumstances, joint program incentives were not sufficient to stimulate plant construction. If Euratom forced construction, they argued, Europe risked becoming a "test laboratory" for American techniques.[32] Greater attention, they felt, should be directed to research activities. Instead of installing U.S. reactor plants now, Europe had at least five years to develop its own, more advanced reactor techniques.[33]

The Power Program Stalls

Still caught in the political updraft of its origins, the Commission paid no heed to these dissenting murmurs. Its prestige at stake, the Community could not afford to fail in its first significant endeavor. In December 1958, Louis Armand, the promoter of the joint program from his days on the Three Wise Men Commission, stepped down as Euratom's first president. He was replaced by Étienne Hirsch, former head of the French Economic Plan and another firm Monnet Europeanist.

[30]ECSC High Authority and European Community Information Service, *Europe and Energy* (Luxembourg, 1967), pp. 21–23.

[31]To be installed by 1965, the six reactors foreseen under the agreement had to be started no later than 1960, approximately five years being required for full construction.

[32]*Handelsblatt*, July 18, 1958; *Industriekurier*, January 1, 1959; and *Agence Europe*, June 19, 1958.

[33]*Nucleonics*, June 1959, p. 32. See also OEEC, *Proceedings of OEEC Third Industrial Conference* (Stresa, Italy, May 19–25, 1959).

An adept administrator, Hirsch put himself to the task of making the joint program a success, whatever the prevailing energy picture.

The invitation for proposals under the first phase of the joint power program, which involved the construction of four reactors by the end of 1963, was issued in April 1959.[34] Five power groups indicated a preliminary interest. Only one of these groups finalized its proposals before the deadline (originally set for September but extended one month in hope that other project proposals would materialize). This was the SENN project in Garigliano, Italy. Begun with World Bank support in 1955, this project would have been carried out anyway, even if the joint program had not existed.[35] The decision to construct the reactor had been taken already in September 1958. At that time, SENN announced that GE, in a narrowly decided verdict, had won the international competition for· construction of this reactor (principal competition being British firms). It is possible that this decision in favor of light water (American) over gas graphite (British) reactors was influenced by anticipated participation in the joint power program with its attractive fuel guarantees. But this is unlikely.[36] Choice of the American design, nevertheless, did much to overcome the impression that gas graphite systems were more advanced (see note 10). According to one informed source, the GE contract "lifted the enriched-uranium reactors of the U.S. program to a level of at least equal prominence with Britain's natural-uranium, gas-cooled designs and the outcome may have put enriched reactors in the lead."[37]

With the four other groups expressing preliminary interest, the Commission made valiant attempts to secure decisions. In terms of the requirements of nuclear power development, the Commission was on

[34]The phasing was introduced (four reactors by 1963, two by 1965) on the urging of Congress in the hope that organic reactors, which were not as advanced as light water systems, might qualify for the second phase. See U.S., Congress, Joint Committee on Atomic Energy, *Hearings, Agreement for Cooperation with Euratom*, p. 11.

[35]International Bank for Reconstruction and Development, *Summary Report of the International Panel* (Washington, D.C.: World Bank, March 1959).

[36]More likely was the fact that American reactors entailed lower initial investment costs. Fuel costs were higher but future design improvements promised to lower these costs (see Appendix). In any event, the SENN decision was a close one, as may be inferred from comments in October 1958 by Felice Ippolito, a participant in the SENN project who later became secretary-general of CNEN:

"On the basis of the [SENN] tenders, the costs of power produced in enriched uranium reactors and the costs of power produced in natural uranium reactors are comparable. . . . It appears from the above that the selection of one or another type of plant is based only on the specific terms of tenders. If SENN . . . chose the International General Electric plant, under slightly different conditions, another type of plant or another solution might have prevailed."

Atomo e Industria, December 1, 1958.

[37]*Nucleonics*, October 1958, p. 25. And as another source noted "the hardest hit was probably the British which had seen in SENN an opportunity to strengthen its attempted nuclear beachhead in Europe," Kramish, *The Peaceful Atom*, p. 159.

solid ground by urging participation. Again and again, the Commission warned that a construction program was part and parcel of an effective research program, since actual power reactors alone could supply the necessary data to judge economic performance.[38] Hence, the temporary energy glut was no cause to relax. But Euratom had a weak Industrial Directorate and few effective programs to stimulate initiatives among European industries.

Unfortunately, the Commission's efforts in a time of relaxed energy conditions created adverse impressions. By forcing the joint program, Commission officials gave the impression of lobbying harder for the products of foreign industries than for those of its own.[39] Individuals were hardly to blame for this situation, though tensions existed between the Industrial and Research Directorates of Euratom.[40] The real problem, as we noted in chapter 4, was the Euratom Treaty. With little authority in the industrial field, Euratom could not succeed in putting over an industrial-scale program. As happened in other sectors, the Commission had to fall back on its research program.

The Joint Research Program

Response to the research program of the joint agreement was more enthusiastic. But a potentially adverse consequence of relying on foreign support now came home to roost. U.S. participants, disappointed by the results of the first phase of the power program, showed less than all-out support for a vigorous research effort. After all, as we noted above, the power program was the real pay-off for American participants. Research, being less sophisticated in Europe than the United States, offered fewer dividends. Political developments in the United States reinforced this lack of interest in the joint research program. As the 1960 presidential campaign approached, Democrats, who dominated

[38]See Euratom, *Fourth General Report*, p. 69. The USAEC had followed the same strategy in pushing the joint agreement to enable U.S. industries to construct demonstration-size reactors in Europe.

[39]In the case of a proposed Dutch project (SEP), the Commission was accused of "highwayman tactics" in allegedly threatening to withhold future fuel supplies if SEP did not proceed immediately with construction plans. *Nucleonics*, November 1959, p. 21. A more important case was the German AKS project. Hirsch went personally to Bonn to secure Adenauer's approval of this project. The project was opposed by the German Science Ministry and prominent German industrial participants. Despite Adenauer's efforts, these opponents prevailed. Hirsch's intervention did nothing to lessen German resentment and suspicion of the Euratom bureaucracy in Brussels. See *Industriekurier*, January 30, 1960; and Deutscher Forschungsdienst (the German research service), *Sonderbericht Kernenergie*, April 26, 1960.

[40]The Industrial Directorate was jealous of the role of the Research Directorate and in 1960, along with industrial groups in Holland, Germany, and Italy, set up the ship propulsion program to enhance its bureaucratic weight *vis-à-vis* the Research Directorate. Walsh, *Science and International Public Affairs*, p. 96. The existence of rivalry between these offices and the motivation of the ship program were learned by the author in interviews with former staff members of the directorates.

the Joint Committee on Atomic Energy, launched a vigorous attack against the Eisenhower Atoms for Peace Program. A report prepared for the Committee concluded that "the joint United States-Euratom program for civilian atomic power is not now likely to proceed at a pace which, in relation to our own time scale, will pay material dividends to American technology."[41] Rather than await indirect benefits of programs sponsored in Europe, the Committee wished to increase direct benefits by expanding government programs at home.

The competition between domestic and international programs reflected a potential problem underlying U.S.-Euratom cooperation from the outset. Countries support international cooperation in technology only when the technology involved has a relatively low priority at home. Once domestic interest in the technology increases, international programs may suffer. For Euratom, this situation meant that a critical variable affecting the progress of its first major research undertaking was American domestic politics, a variable completely outside the control and influence of Euratom members.

A lame-duck Republican administration could not resist congressional pressures. AEC officials insisted on an explicit link between the research and power programs. For the time being, research under the joint agreement was restricted to the one reactor concept approved under the power program (SENN boiling water type).[42] Euratom officials favored research on all reactors types "eligible" under the power program (i.e., boiling water, pressurized water, and organic). In addition, they requested permission to transfer some fuel from the joint program to Community projects outside the joint program.[43]

A compromise was eventually worked out,[44] but this early incident symbolized the subsequent plight of the joint research program. Despite the receipt of over 375 proposals and letters of intent by the end of 1959, only 68 contracts had been awarded by mid-1962.[45] U.S. and Euratom spending under the program never exceeded $26 million each

[41]Robert McKinney, *Review of the International Atomic Policies and Programs of the United States*, A report to U.S., Congress, Joint Committee on Atomic Energy, 86th Cong., 2d Sess., October 1960 (Washington, D.C.: Government Printing Office, 1960), p. 1251. This report was prepared in an atmosphere of opposition to Euratom, which was identified with U.S. Atoms for Peace policies. McKinney convened a conference with nuclear officials in Europe but did not invite Euratom representatives. As it turned out, the report was not unnecessarily critical of Euratom, except to suggest that its objectives should be broadened to include more basic research activities, both nuclear and nonnuclear, and de-emphasize power plant construction. *Nucleonics*, June 1960, pp. 20–21.

[42]McKinney, *Review*, p. 816.

[43]*Agence Europe*, March 11, 1960, and April 6, 1960.

[44]The U.S. agreed to permit research on problems common to all eligible reactor types, meaning that research exclusively dealing with reactor types other than SENN was still prohibited. The U.S. also released some fuel for use outside the joint program. *Nucleonics*, April 1960, pp. 24–25.

[45]*Agence Europe*, May 23, 1962.

(of a potential $100 million each).[46] After 1966 the AEC asked for no further congressional appropriations, and the last three years of the ten-year program were spent winding up existing programs. From 1964 on, Euratom's budget crisis restricted European spending. Moreover, by this time, industrial issues affected research activities.

Could Euratom have achieved greater success in this period by working more independently with European industries on European research projects, thus avoiding dependence on U.S. financial and industrial support? The answer is probably no. Research is an ineffective tool unless it is integrated with industrial programs. In this respect, the link between the research and power programs of the joint agreement was not inappropriate. It was unfortunate, however, that this link created the impression of advancing American instead of European industrial technology. Had Euratom dropped the joint agreement altogether and concentrated on European research alone, it would have faced inevitable problems of industrial competition within Europe itself, if not ultimately with the United States. But it may have defined sooner the European issues that had to be faced in this area. As it was, the Commission sought to encourage transnational industrial ties within Europe without acknowledging the complications that continued dependence on U.S. industrial support raised for this objective.[47]

The Demonstration Reactor Phase

If the primary reasons for Euratom's woes before 1960 were economic and external, i.e., declining support in the United States, the obstacles after 1960 became increasingly political and internal. The period from 1960–65 witnessed the full flowering of the Gaullist challenge to the European Communities.[48] The challenge was rooted in France's perception of Europe's external role which required independence in military as well as advanced civilian technologies. The "bitter" of French policy was aimed at the United States, while the "sweet" was directed toward Germany. France courted Germany in the stra-

[46]U.S., Congress, House, Subcommittee on International Cooperation in Science and Space of the Committee on Science and Astronautics, *Hearings, A General Review of International Cooperation in Science and Space*, 92d Cong., 1st Sess., May 18, 19, and 20, 1971 (Washington, D.C.: Government Printing Office, 1972), p. 339.

[47]For example, one of the significant achievements of the Commission was to encourage cooperation under the joint research program between the German firm, AEG, and the French firm, SNECMA. The Commission hoped that this research cooperation would develop into an industrial relationship. In 1964, however, GE signed a formal license agreement with AEG, seriously reducing the chances of further collaboration between AEG and SNECMA. This development provoked the Commission to recognize, for the first time, the potential incompatibility of U.S. and intra-European industrial associations. *Agence Europe*, March 9, 1964.

[48]On the background and events of this period, see John Newhouse, *Collision in Brussels* (New York: Norton, 1967).

tegic field (Franco-German Treaty of Cooperation in 1963),[49] and this courtship extended to civilian nuclear developments as well. France invested all of its resources to win the Community and especially Germany to a policy of development of French gas graphite reactors. Sadly, the courtship came too late. Having lost the initiative to the United States in 1958, France could not recapture it five years later. In trying, it provoked a reactor war. And, in 1969, France had to concede defeat, abandoning development of the gas graphite technology in favor of American light water reactors.

The Participation Program

The opening shots of what became the reactor war (*la guerre des filières*) were fired in 1961. The Commission was in search of new incentives to promote reactor construction. In discussions of the 1961 budget, Italy, with a stake in plant construction (besides SENN, two other plants were underway—see below and chapter 3), suggested that unspent research funds be used to "encourage nuclear industry" or, more specifically, to alleviate directly industrial costs involved in nuclear production.[50] Article 6 of the Treaty prohibited outright subsidies, but Annex V of the Treaty authorized participation in high-power reactors by other means, for example, "supplying fuel and moderators." This assistance would be available for all reactor types, including gas graphite systems ineligible under the joint program. Recipients would be obligated to release data on the design, construction, start-up, and operation of the plant and permit the stationing of Commission staff or seconded staff at the plant site.

France opposed this idea of a participation program. By now, French civilian plants (there were three under construction—EdF-1, EdF-2, and EdF-3) were producing plutonium for the nuclear weapons program. Allowing these plants to participate in the proposed program may have compromised data on the fuel cycle, especially the amounts of plutonium on hand. In any event, gearing up for a major strategic initiative, France was unwilling to permit access to these plants. With French reactors excluded, assistance would go once again primarily to American reactor designs. France thus attacked the program as a sell-out of European in favor of American reactor techniques.

The French also emphasized a commercial disadvantage of EdF participation. Patent structures in France and the other countries differed widely. In France, the CEA held most nuclear patents; in the

---

[49]See Wilfrid L. Kohl, *French Nuclear Diplomacy* (Princeton: Princeton University Press, 1971), especially chap. 7. As Kohl writes, the purpose of this courtship was to suggest "that West Germany should forgo the MLF and accept instead the concept of a more independent European defense organized around the emerging French *force de frappe*" (p. 242).

[50]*Agence Europe*, October 15, 1960.

other countries, private industries did, usually under license from American partners. The participation program called for exchange of information on patents taken out under the program and any other patents related to program activities (so-called basic patents). As a public authority, the CEA feared that private industries would be in a better position to withhold basic patent information. These industries could always claim that such information was restricted under commercial license agreements. German firms, in fact, insisted on explicit recognition of this claim. Before assenting to the program, they demanded that participation contracts include a clause relieving participants from disclosing information falling under commercial license pacts. The German government, concerned over a sputtering domestic program and eager to convince German industry that working with public authorities was not that unpleasant, backed this demand.[51] The clause was included and did much to substantiate French fears.[52]

While somewhat disingenuous (since France did not expect to participate anyway for strategic reasons), the argument suggested a more fundamental commercial obstacle blocking cooperation. The countries more advanced in common technological programs are reluctant to release technical information without immediate compensation or the expectation of eventual commercial benefits. Thus, in the joint program, the United States pushed the power program as fair compensation for U.S. research assistance. Now, in the participation program, France sought commercial gains as reasonable compensation for French gas graphite information. If France granted access to gas graphite technology, the Community would have to promote the sale and installation of French reactors in other countries. Only then would the program offer attractive prospects for French participation. The Community did not accept this proposal, and France launched a vigorous campaign to export gas graphite reactors on its own (see subsequent section on Fessenheim proposals).[53]

The participation program was not, as France charged, a sell-out of European technology. The program made Community assistance contingent on the manufacture of fuel elements and individual reactor

[51]German authorities hoped to soften industrial resistance to national government assistance by having industry participate in international programs, where local political strings were not so obvious.

[52]The clause is found in Article 4 of the standard participation contract. See, for example, Euratom, *Contrat pour la participation à la Centrale Nucléaire des Ardennes* (SENA) (EUR/C/3016/5/61f) (Brussels, n.d.).

[53]While no French plant took part in the participation program, France went on to contribute more than 50 percent of the total non-Commission personnel seconded to installations participating in the program in other countries (fifty-six of eighty-one people). This practical interest in the information-gathering opportunities offered by the participation program belied French arguments that patent regulations would restrict significant information exchanges.

components by European firms.[54] Moreover, the program applied to gas graphite reactors as well as American techniques and ultimately included one gas graphite plant (the SIMEA plant in Latina, Italy). Overall, the program was good for the economic development of nuclear power in Europe. But, alas, it took its toll in political costs. Passed over strenuous French objections in July 1961, the program made President Hirsch *persona non grata* with the French government. In December, the French government refused to renew Hirsch's term in office. The Community lost its last aggressive leader. As we saw in chapter 4, Hirsch's successor, Chatenet, was, if anything, the political antithesis of Monnet Europeanists like Armand and Hirsch.

The Gundremmingen Plant

The participation program, Euratom's first use in 1961 of the joint enterprise provision of the Treaty (see note 27 of chapter 4), and new incentives in the joint power program raised prospects for additional plant constructions under the second phase of the Euratom-U.S. joint program.[55] Two plants eventually were approved. The SENA plant, constructed by France and Belgium at Chooz, France, was a repeat applicant from the first phase and would have probably employed a light water reactor even without the additional incentives of the joint program. The same may have also been true for the second plant approved, the KRB plant in Gundremmingen, Germany. But the German choice was a more significant one, having consequences which marked a turning point in German reactor developments. It deserves a closer look.

By 1961 Germany still lacked a demonstration-size reactor of the type being built by Italy (SENN), Belgium (SENA), and the EdF (SENA and EdF-1, -2, and -3). German authorities were determined to see that the proposed Gundremmingen plant (joint project of RWE and Bayern Atomkraft) materialized. The bidding came down to a contest between GE/AEG for a boiling light water reactor (250 MWe) and English Electric/Siemens for a gas graphite plant (340 MWe). Only the light water reactor was eligible for assistance under the joint program. The contract went to GE/AEG. In a specific sense, the joint program

---

[54]European firms accounted for an increasing share of the construction and fuel costs of plants taking part in the participation program. Except for the SENN and SIMEA plants, they manufactured all but minor percentages of the important nuclear components of these plants. Unfortunately, however, their increasing independence of outside industrial sponsors was not matched by a growth of transnational industrial cooperation within Europe. In most instances, firms from the country in which the plant was located carried out the major share of construction. See Euratom, *Activités dans le domaine de la participation de l'Euratom aux réacteurs de puissance* (EUR/C/3542/66f) (Brussels, n.d.), p. 3.

[55]In the fall of 1961, the U.S., relieved of election pressures, offered to lease rather than sell fuel for reactors constructed under the program. This provision was formalized in June 1962 in a second amendment to the 1958 agreement.

was probably not a decisive factor in this decision. As early as 1960, RWE had become convinced that the American reactor was more economical.[56] Nevertheless, in a more general sense, the influence of the joint program was considerable. The existence of this program altered expectations in favor of American reactors from 1958 on. Europeans were assured of a hand in research results in the United States, and U.S. guarantees of enriched uranium supplies removed a primary obstacle to light water developments in Europe. Without these provisions, European authorities would possibly have had to invest more attention and resources in gas graphite reactors. And with enough investment, these reactors may have reached an economical stage by the time of the Gundremmingen bidding equivalent to that of light water systems.

The point is worth making because the Gundremmingen decision caused Siemens to switch priority development lines from natural uranium to enriched uranium systems.[57] After 1962, Siemens moved its considerable resources into the development of light water and, secondarily, heavy water systems. It lost interest altogether in the natural uranium, gas graphite line. This switch came at the same moment that France and Germany began discussions on joint construction of a commercial-size gas graphite plant (500 MWe) at Fessenheim on the upper Rhine.[58] Siemens represented Germany in these talks, and its loss of interest in gas graphite systems did not improve the prospects of cooperation with France. The ordering of two additional light water plants in Germany in 1964 (Obrigheim and Lingen) destroyed these prospects altogether. (See subsequent section.)

While the joint program may not have been primarily responsible for this triumph of American technology in Germany, it was certainly easy for that impression to arise. No doubt this impression contributed to the new vehemence with which France attacked the Euratom light water program after 1962.

Fessenheim Proposals

The proposal for Franco-German cooperation at Fessenheim was part of the CEA's general offensive to export gas graphite reactors.[59] At a joint meeting of the French and German Atomic Forums in Decem-

[56] *Frankfurter Allgemeine*, October 25, 1960. This conviction was a common one in Germany at the time and was based chiefly on the lower initial investment costs of light water reactors. For example, the light water plant proposed by GE for Gundremmingen involved capital outlays of only $88 million compared to $133 million for the gas graphite plant proposed by English Electric. *Nucleonics Week*, May 24, 1962, p. 5.

[57] Interview with Siemens official, Erlangen, July 7, 1970.

[58] *Le Monde*, September 14, 1962.

[59] This offensive also included talks with Spain, which, after protracted bargaining, eventually culminated in a reactor sale in 1966. As the price for this sale, France agreed to represent Spanish interests in the Common Market and to extend loans covering 90 percent of the reactor costs. *Nucleonics Week*, October 20, 1966, p. 2.

ber 1962, EdF sounded out utilities (principally RWE) on this project.[60] Neither EdF nor RWE was particularly enthusiastic. Fresh off the Gundremmingen decision, RWE was looking toward light water systems and did not relish the thought of cooperating with a state-owned body like EdF. For its part, EdF entertained growing doubts about the gas graphite system, particularly after it had difficulties with EdF-1 and EdF-2.[61] Throughout 1962, however, political pressures existed to foster Franco-German cooperation.[62] In this context, CEA and Siemens representatives sat down to investigate the possibilities of a common plant.

The discussions culminated in June 1964 with two studies of gas graphite and heavy water systems, prepared jointly by Siemens and the CEA.[63] The gas graphite study concluded that this type of plant would produce electricity more cheaply than either conventional or light water plants.[64] This estimate scarcely concealed French political aims, since light water technology had just achieved a dramatic breakthrough in the United States in June 1964.[65] Nevertheless, France pushed hard to win German agreement, consenting to drop its opposition to joint enterprise status for two German plants (Obrigheim and Lingen) if Germany moved forward on the Fessenheim proposal.[66] In December it appeared that this compromise had been accepted. The German minister of science, Lenz, told the German Bundestag that the French and

---

[60] *Neue Rhein Zeitung* (Cologne), December 21, 1962.

[61] The problems involved the steel pressure vessel which cracked on EdF-1 in early 1959 and caused the CEA to shift to concrete vessels starting with EdF-3 in 1961. See Bertrand Goldschmidt, "Les principales options techniques du programme français de production d'énergie nucléaire," *Revue Française de l'Énergie*, Numéro spécial (October 1969), p. 89.

[62] These pressures climaxed in January 1963 with the signing of the Franco-German Treaty of Cooperation. The Treaty established a formal mechanism for consultation between the two countries and called for cooperation in defense and foreign policy as well as general economic and industrial areas. One of the reasons for French interest in civilian nuclear cooperation in this period may have been the desire to free French resources for nuclear arms projects by enlisting German technology and resources in the French civilian effort. See Kohl, *French Nuclear Diplomacy*, pp. 276–81.

[63] For the gas graphite study, see CEA/Siemens, *Perspectives techniques et économiques des centrales électronucléaires à uranium naturel, première partie—réacteurs modérés au graphite* (Paris: CEA, June 1964). For the heavy water study, see chap. 6 of this study.

[64] *Ibid.*, p. 38.

[65] In the first purely commercial competition for a power plant (no significant public support), U.S. utilities selected a boiling light water reactor for a plant at Oyster Creek, New Jersey. This development sparked a major review of the British gas graphite program and was the first of a sequence of market developments establishing the eventual superiority of enriched uranium reactors. See Duncan Burn, *The Political Economy of Nuclear Energy* (London: Institute of Economic Affairs, 1967).

[66] France opposed this status because neither plant represented an "undertaking of outstanding importance" to the Community. They were exclusively national plants and did not have the transnational character of the joint French-Belgian project, SENA, the first recipient of joint enterprise privileges.

German governments would examine the Fessenheim project "with all good will" (*wohlwollend*) and initiate preliminary steps.[67]

Despite extended discussions, the project never materialized.[68] Though the primary obstacle was disinterest in the economic sector, the German government also established a limit on support for this project. Federal aid was set at the same level as that offered for the much smaller Gundremmingen plant. Whether additional assistance would have saved the project is beside the point, since any project becomes economical at some level of support. But the German decision not to pay a higher price for cooperation with France was as much a political choice as the decision to pay this price would have been. In debates going on in Euratom at the time, German officials frequently took refuge in the argument that economic factors should determine the level of industrial cooperation in the Community.[69] This was an admirably dispassionate point of view; but, given German economic strength, it was also a political argument and entailed important consequences for Franco-German nuclear cooperation. Had the German government decided to press agreement on the Fessenheim proposals, a pattern of industrial cooperation may have been set in motion between the power and nuclear construction sectors of the two countries. If it was in the cards that gas graphite systems would prove inferior, this cooperation may have resulted in an earlier French decision to drop the gas graphite design.[70] Moreover, cooperation in 1963 would have insured a more balanced development between French and German industrial capacities in the proven reactor sector. As it turned out, French and German capacities grew more unequal; and when France finally turned in 1969 to light water systems, French industry was not strong enough to risk cooperation with powerful German counterparts.

Germany also had important strategic reasons for not boosting Franco-German civilian nuclear cooperation in this period. In Washington the Franco-German Treaty of January 1963 had aroused suspicions of impending nuclear cooperation between Bonn and Paris.[71] German enthusiasm for civilian cooperation may have been interpreted as an initial step toward Franco-German strategic cooperation.

[67]Federal Republic of Germany, Bundestag, *Parliamentary Debates*, 4th election period, Vol. 56 (1964), p. 7620.

[68]Discussions continued for three years; but after Bonn rejected in summer 1965 a French proposal to jointly subsidize the project, the project effectively died. In March 1967, German Science Minister Stoltenberg, who replaced Lenz, announced that the project had been dropped. Federal Republic of Germany, Bundestag, *Parliamentary Debates*, 5th election period, Vol. 63 (1966/67), pp. 4655–56.

[69]Lawrence Scheinman, "Euratom: Nuclear Integration in Europe," *International Conciliation*, No. 563 (May 1967), p. 47.

[70]For example, the support RWE could have provided EdF, an early critic of the gas graphite line, may have facilitated this outcome.

[71]Kohl, *French Nuclear Diplomacy*, p. 280.

After Adenauer recognized continued differences between himself and de Gaulle, Germany sought to prevent appearances of Franco-German rapprochement from substituting for realities of German-American dependence. Thus, "the year 1963 saw the Bonn government renewing its transatlantic loyalties."[72] New agreements with the United States provided for cooperation in defense technology and set the context for strengthening ties in civilian technology.[73]

These strategic developments, of course, were not direct considerations in the decisions made by German nuclear groups in the period from 1962 to 1964. Nevertheless, the choice of American light water over French gas graphite technology and the extension of industrial ties with U.S. firms (e.g., renewal and broadening of Siemens license ties with Westinghouse in 1962 and a license agreement between AEG and GE in 1964) coincided with policy preferences at higher strategic levels. There was no reason for Bonn to intervene in these choices and offer larger subsidies for the Fessenheim project. Civilian industries, in these instances, are not consciously implementing government directives; they are operating within a context in which they rely heavily on government R&D support and nuclear safeguard regulations. They inevitably take note of general political orientations. What is even more important, their decisions entail political consequences. The penetration of American nuclear industries abroad, for example, may foreclose national options for foreign governments.[74] They may also create "the possibility that the United States government might eventually use these actors . . . to manipulate or at least to exert influence over the nuclear programs of a number of advanced industrial states."[75] This point has to be recognized without minimizing the basic economic character of these transactions. Franco-German nuclear cooperation failed in 1963–64 as much because strategic conditions were unfavorable as because economic incentives were lacking.

The Reactor War

The reactor war, the popular label given to the Euratom revision debate of 1964–65, reflected French concern over the political implications of U.S. industrial penetration in the nuclear sector. Recognizing the costs of sacrificing early leadership in Community programs to the United States, France now offered its gas graphite program as the basis of an intensive Community effort to develop natural uranium systems (gas graphite and, secondarily, heavy water). France clearly sought a

---

[72]*Ibid.*

[73]For example, in the summer of 1963, Germany decided to cooperate with the U.S. instead of France on the development of a new heavy tank. *Ibid.*, p. 282.

[74]Lawrence Scheinman observes how this may have occurred in the case of U.S. nuclear industries in Sweden. See "Security," pp. 284–85.

[75]*Ibid.*, p. 292.

political decision to reverse the commercial drift toward American enriched uranium reactors. Germany suspected as much and responded by arguing that it was too late to establish new programs.[76] "The development of proven reactors," the Germans argued, "had progressed so far that further development could be left to the industries engaged in the construction of these reactors or the respective national programs." Euratom's intervention was unnecessary, as suggested by the AEC decision in 1965 to terminate federal subsidies for U.S. proven reactor research. Moreover, "in the present situation," as German spokesmen concluded, "the American light water reactors enjoyed a considerable competitive advantage over all other reactor types." Italy agreed with this estimate but sought Community support for industrial-scale projects in Italy (particularly EUREX, a plant for reprocessing enriched uranium fuel). Thus Italy supported France in the sense that it desired to see decisions taken "at the collective Community level" rather than in the private sector.

The French and Italian positions reflected a policy characteristic of industrially weaker states. These states seek to compensate for industrial disadvantages by urging political intervention. If events are left to private forces, they fear, cumulative inequities may result. Politics is thus a means of arresting unfavorable economic trends.

The prospect of Community intervention was ruled out by Commission weakness and indecision.[77] By this time, however, it was impossible for the Community to appear neutral on the reactor issue. Intentionally or not, Euratom's policy had provided significant inducements for the development of light water reactors in Europe. The joint power program produced three water stations; four of the five reactors in the participation program were water types; and all four of the nuclear plants receiving joint enterprise status employed water reactors. The Commission did not err in providing this support but in failing to recognize that, without common industrial objectives, Community support of American industrial technology could adversely affect the prospects of transnational groupings within Europe.[78]

[76]For German and also Italian reactions, see memoranda referenced in notes 51 and 52, chap. 4.

[77]The Commission waffled, for example, on the issue of reactor competitiveness: "The positon today, in fact, seems to be that in the Community as a whole no decisive advantage can be reasonably attributed to either of the two proven reactor types. . . ." Euratom, Directorate-General for Industry and Economy, *First Target Programme for the European Atomic Energy Community* (EUR 2773e) (Brussels, March 1966), p. 22.

[78]For example, all of the reactors constructed under Community programs were built through bilateral arrangements with American or British firms. The only project which brought together firms from more than one European country was SENA, and the industrial group building this plant (Framatome/ACEC) operated under a Westinghouse license. The consequences of U.S. industrial arrangements for European mergers are noted by Scheinman. "While relatively little information about these arrangements is available," Scheinman writes, "it does appear that some licensing has been done on the

One wonders what Euratom's industrial effect would have been had the Community begun already in 1957 a careful and publicized program of industrial promotion and cooperation. Perhaps the obstacles were too great, even then. After all, the primary issues obstructing industrial cooperation, namely the questions of Europe's external policy (open versus competitive) and internal administration (centralized versus decentralized), were present already at Euratom's founding. Moreover, as David Coombes argues in the case of the EEC Commission, direct Community relations with industry and interest groups are affected by the fact that these groups continue to maintain close liaison with national government departments and tend to share the same position with these departments.[79] What can make Community efforts more successful is not more intimate contact with industrial parties (*engrenage*) but decisive Community formulation of the larger problems of industrial cooperation and effective Community lobbying at political levels to solve these problems. In the case of Euratom, the political requirements of industrial cooperation were overlooked in too much optimism and good feeling that Europe could be built by the inexorable march of technical and economic forces alone.

The Commercial Phase

Commercialization of nuclear power precipitated two types of development—industrial consolidation to finance the manufacture and sale of nuclear reactors and renewed interest in the construction of fuel facilities to supply these reactors. Both of these developments occurred at levels which further weakened Community institutions (though not necessarily European competitive interests *vis-à-vis* the United States). Industrial consolidation took place predominantly within national boundaries and, in continuation of an earlier trend, bilaterally with American industries rather than multilaterally within Europe. This time, however, Germany emerged as the principal proponent of European competitiveness *vis-à-vis* the United States, while France reversed a two-decade policy of independence and concluded new license agreements with American partners. Deliberations to construct enlarged fuel facilities, in particular, an enriched uranium plant,[80] proceeded at intergovernmental levels. These deliberations raised old issues of competition with the United States and new prospects of cooperation between France and Germany. A European enrichment plant may precipitate

basis of exclusive dealer contracts in which, in the name of antitrust provisions, licensees in different countries have been precluded from merging." See "Security," p. 289.

[79]David L. Coombes, *Politics and Bureaucracy in the European Community* (Beverly Hills: Sage Publications, 1970), pp. 189–91.

[80]This was the urgent issue in the fuel field, though the last few years have witnessed a range of other developments to improve mining, fuel fabrication, and reprocessing facilities in Europe.

an exclusive alignment of European countries against American competitors (especially if the technology utilized is the centrifuge rather than gaseous diffusion process). This alignment will reflect contemporary patterns of intergovernmental cooperation in Europe (along the lines of specific projects—see chapter 4), however, rather than earlier patterns of Community leadership.

Industrial Nationalism

In the summer of 1967, German utilities placed commercial orders for two light water reactors at Wuergassen and Stade (600–650 MWe). These orders, one to AEG and one to Siemens, prompted AEG and Siemens to begin discussions in the fall of 1967 to consolidate their nuclear activities.[81] In April 1969, the two companies announced the creation of a joint subsidiary, KWU.[82] A month later, Siemens acquired the outstanding shares of Interatom held by the American firm, North American Aviation.[83] These actions constituted a major *démarche* to establish German independence in the nuclear sector. Siemens did not renew its license agreements with Westinghouse when these expired in June 1970. AEG license ties with GE expired in 1973. Today, KWU rivals former American partners, offering light water reactors on a fully competitive turnkey basis (meaning ready to operate). The power of this new grouping is already evident in the string of orders KWU has received, including one for a power station in Holland (400 MWe).[84] In Germany itself, only one order has gone to a domestic rival, a joint subsidiary of Deutsche Babcock and Wilcox and BBC (holding a license from the U.S. parent firm, Babcock and Wilcox). In European reactor circles, it is generally believed that this order placed by RWE was mainly intended to keep KWU honest.[85]

While this consolidation took place in Germany, France continued to agonize over the future of its gas graphite program. A breakdown of EdF-3 in 1966 led EdF officials to begin talks with Belgian and Swiss groups on joint construction of water reactors.[86] These talks culminated in December 1967 with a decision to construct a second joint Franco-

---

[81] *Industriekurier*, October 31, 1967. Merger was favored by the German government, after Bonn terminated support in 1968 for AEG's fast reactor activities. See chap. 8.

[82] *Die Zeit*, September 5, 1969.

[83] *Die Welt*, May 19, 1969. Outstanding shares totaled 60 percent, half of which Siemens planned to transfer to AEG once U.S. license agreements expired.

[84] The Dutch contract was the first awarded in one Euratom country to a principal contractor in another Euratom country. To win this contract, however, KWU had to agree to subcontract 75 percent of the construction to Dutch firms. *Industriekurier*, April 2, 1969.

[85] This view was conveyed to the author in personal correspondence with a top executive officer of a leading European nuclear firm.

[86] The EdF-3 incident delayed start-up of new construction under the Fifth Plan (1965–70) which called for a total of 2500 MWe of new gas graphite stations. See PEON Commission, *Rapport sur les perspectives de développement des centrales nucléaires en France* (report obtained from the French CEA, Paris).

Belgian water reactor at Tihange, Belgium (a sequel to the SENA plant at Chooz, France).[87] The bidding on this reactor offered a small chance for Franco-German industrial cooperation. AEG and SNECMA, the two firms brought together by Euratom under the joint research program (see note 47), submitted a joint proposal for Tihange. For a time, Siemens considered a joint bid with ACEC. ACEC's ties with Westinghouse were too close to suit Siemens, however, and domestic pressures in Belgium built up to award the contract to a Belgian firm. Thus, despite a slight price advantage in favor of the AEG/SNECMA offer, the contract went to Framatome/ACEC (the same consortium that constructed SENA).[88] Had this contract, placed in December 1967, gone to AEG/ SNECMA or a Siemens/ACEC/Framatome consortium, it is conceivable that the domestic consolidation of AEG and Siemens in 1969 may have been forestalled. Once this consolidation took place, the German company, KWU, was too awesome a power to attract European partners.

This fact became clear in 1969. After the fall of the de Gaulle government in June 1969, France finally made the overdue decision to abandon the gas graphite system. The Sixth Modernization Plan (1970–75) called for construction of one or more light water reactors and a continued search for an intermediate reactor system (either heavy water or high temperature gas reactors) to fill the gap until fast reactors reached the market. In fast reactors, France held a technical lead; and if these reactors reached the market soon enough, France might avoid undue dependence on light water systems and, in particular, the enriched fuel these systems required.

The question now was where France would acquire the light water technology. French decisions in 1969 coincided with Westinghouse efforts to take over a string of European licensees in the nuclear field, including the Jeumont Schneider group in France.[89] The French government had to decide whether to permit this takeover or arrange other assistance for Schneider, either from German firms or through reorganization of French industries. Germany offered the possibility of cooperation through an unprecedented offer by the Siemens company to sell French industry a one-third interest in KWU.[90] Closely coordinated between the French and German governments, this offer entailed a trade-off of German light water technology for French fast reactor technology. In the summer of 1970, France rejected the idea. Fearing commercial disadvantages, French officials considered local industries

---

[87]Other decisions at the same time called for continued construction of gas graphite plants, but these plans were never implemented. *Le Monde*, December 9, 1967.

[88]*Le Monde*, January 28–29, 1968.

[89]*Le Monde*, November 16–17, 1969.

[90]*Agence Europe*, November 17, 1969, and November 27, 1969. The Siemens plan was very ambitious, involving negotiations with Belgian and Italian as well as French partners.

too weak to work with powerful German partners. For the time being, France also rejected Westinghouse plans to take over Jeumont Schneider.

Instead, the French government used the occasion of bidding for France's first light water plant to encourage industrial reorganization. Two groups emerged, Framatome/SFAC (the latter a member of the Schneider group) and SOGERCA (CGE, Alsthom, and GAAA). After difficult negotiations to renew its license agreement with Westinghouse, Framatome got the contract.[91] In 1971, Framatome received three additional contracts for light water reactors.

Financially, however, Framatome was still too weak, and in 1972 the French government reversed itself to permit Westinghouse participation in French industry. A new company was established, known as Compagnie Nucléaire Française (CNF), in which French firms controlled 51 percent of the shares and Westinghouse 45 percent.[92] This company, with contracts for five nuclear plants (four national ones and one joint plant with Belgium at Tihange), faces domestic competition from SOGERCA, which in June 1973 received its first contracts from EdF for two boiling light water plants to be built under license from GE. The CEA still has to negotiate "agreements of cooperation" with GE, and SOGERCA is reportedly looking for European partners.[93] The search for partners may be complicated by new ties with U.S. firms, however.

Industrial alignments in 1971 revealed the consequences of new associations with American partners for European cooperation. In July of that year, a nuclear group including KWU, Belgonucléaire, Interatom, and Agip Nucleare signed a series of reactor and fuel agreements with the British nuclear firm, TNPG (covering all reactor types, principally light water and fast reactors, being developed by KWU and TNPG). The Framatome group was conspicuous in these agreements by its absence. The explanation was that recent French license arrangements with U.S. firms were incompatible with the new consortium's desire for independence *vis-à-vis* U.S. competitors.[94]

A European Enrichment Plant

For a time, France also appeared to be the odd man out on alignments to build a European enrichment plant. The need for such a plant derived from projections that by 1978 the United States would no longer be

[91]Westinghouse was less than eager to renegotiate license agreements following its rebuff in the attempted takeover of Schneider. The details of these industrial arrangements were learned by the author in correspondence with knowledgeable sources.

[92]*Nuclear Industry*, October 1972, pp. 39–41. The company merges the nuclear shops of Framatome and Creusot-Loire. The remaining 4 percent of CNF will be owned by other investors.

[93]*Nuclear Industry*, June 1973, p. 38.

[94]*Agence Europe*, July 14, 1971, and July 19, 1971.

able to meet European enrichment requirements. Alternate supplies were available from the Soviet Union, but most European countries, including France, which purchased Soviet uranium in March 1971 for its first light water plant, were unwilling to rely on Soviet sources over the long run. The same held with respect to U.S. sources, even if the United States expanded domestic enrichment facilities. Congressional legislation passed in 1964 authorized private ownership of fissionable materials in the United States. European customers feared that, even if the United States expanded enrichment capacity, American firms might exploit competitive advantages *vis-à-vis* European nuclear manufacturers, since these firms would now control the fuel as well as the reactors in future international bidding.[95] Moreover, the price of American fuel was going up, in anticipation of conversion to private control of enrichment activities.

The maneuvering to determine when, where, and how a European plant might be constructed began in 1968. German, Dutch, and British representatives opened talks to explore the joint construction of an enrichment plant using the gas centrifuge technique.[96] After lengthy negotiations involving three-tier contacts between governments, utilities, and industries, these countries signed a tripartite agreement in March 1970.[97] The agreement called for the construction and operation of separate pilot plants (three in all—one at Capenhurst and two at Almelo in Holland) and the formation of a joint company, URENCO, which has plans to construct a larger production facility for operation by 1976. On the basis of these plans, British and Dutch spokesmen have become firm advocates of the centrifuge process for a European plant. German spokesmen are more ambivalent. They favor the centrifuge because of Germany's large investments in this technique, but they are also determined, under pressure from German utilities, to see that economic considerations dictate this choice. They prefer to wait as long as possible before committing themselves.[98]

France is more impatient. To offset the 1970 tripartite agreement, the CEA launched a vigorous campaign to convince Community partners of the virtues of the competing gaseous diffusion technique. At first, this

---

[95]In heightened commercial competition for reactor contracts, nuclear firms may offer guaranteed fuel supplies and, in some instances, even enrichment technology to improve the terms of their bids. See *Nuclear Industry*, February 1973, p. 52.

[96]Germans and Dutch had been doing research on this technique since 1958. The advantages of centrifuge over gaseous diffusion (the process employed by all U.S. plants as well as the British Capenhurst and French Pierrelatte plants) include a less expensive operating cycle and much smaller plant size, reducing capital costs. The disadvantages have to do primarily with the fact that the technique is unproven and may not be as economical as gaseous diffusion plants, at least until 1980 or so. *Nuclear Industry*, October 1972, p. 10.

[97]*Financial Times*, March 6, 1970, and March 23, 1970.

[98]*Nuclear Industry*, September 1971, pp. 4–6.

campaign drew no response. But after U.S. proposals in October 1971 failed to stimulate European interest in sharing U.S. diffusion technology, interest appeared to grow in sharing French technology. In March 1972, the CEA succeeded in organizing a multinational study group (EURODIF) to assess the economics of a full-scale diffusion plant.[99] The group included private and governmental organizations from Belgium, Britain, Germany, Italy, and the Netherlands. German participation represented the first bridge between German and French plans and indicated that Germany might be willing to see a first plant employ the gaseous diffusion process while development of the centrifuge process continued and made this technique the likely choice of subsequent plants.

These indications were apparently misleading, however. The present situation suggests that intra-European differences continue on the issue of what kind of enrichment plant should be built and when. France argues that, to have sufficient capacity by 1980, a decision on the European plant must be made by the end of 1973.[100] Germany is in no such hurry and continues to oppose the construction of a common plant (of whatever technology) in France. Germany is also indifferent to the idea that the next plant must be built in Europe. These differences may have contributed to the decision of the tripartite countries (Germany, Great Britain, and the Netherlands) in May 1973 to withdraw from EURODIF.[101] To explore the possibility of locating a common plant outside Europe, these countries are continuing discussions with other countries, in particular Canada and Australia. Australia is regarded as an ideal location for capturing the Japanese market for enriched uranium.

Despite continuing differences, enrichment diplomacy contains the seeds of a potential European decision to establish independence of superpower technology. U.S. proposals in 1971 to share American technology aimed at perpetuating superpower controls. The United States hoped that the offer would stimulate foreign countries to band together and construct a single, large diffusion facility which could be easily monitored for nonproliferation purposes.[102] Europeans read the offer as an attempt to maintain the plethora of conditions under which American technology and resources have been supplied in the past. Since the end of 1971, developments in the United States have increased the desire to attach conditions to the American offer. Protectionist groups see the offer as an untimely "give-away" of American technology, potentially diminishing America's future share of the multibillion dollar uranium

[99] *Nuclear Industry*, March 1972, pp. 21–22.

[100] *Nuclear Industry*, November-December 1972, p. 9.

[101] *Agence Europe*, May 7–8, 1973, and May 12, 1973.

[102] USAEC, *U.S. Claims Capability to Meet Growing Demands for Uranium Enrichment Services*, AEC Press Release No. 0–152, September 8, 1972, p. 2.

market. Acknowledging this point of view, the AEC ruled in 1972 that no American firm may participate in any foreign enrichment project without prior AEC approval.[103]

The future of a European plant still hinges critically on U.S. plans. The price European utilities will pay for future independence will depend on the terms and security of their relationship with U.S. suppliers. Currently, the United States is upgrading facilities at its three enrichment plants. Forecasts now estimate that these improvements will allow U.S. plants to supply expected demand until 1982.[104] These projections continue to hold interest for economic-minded groups in Europe. Should American industries commit themselves to the construction of a fourth plant (or more), European groups may decide that their interest in dependable supplies has been met.

At some point, however, Europe will probably build its own plant.[105] U.S. proposals may delay this enterprise—which was the effect of U.S. proposals in 1957—but they cannot substitute for it. Strategically, the United States is better off accepting a European plant than discouraging such a plant at the risk of encouraging national plants—such as Pierrelatte, which France decided to build in July 1957 about the same time that Euratom, under pressure from the United States, decided not to build a European plant. Industrially and technologically, the United States is simply not that important any longer to European needs. The years between American intervention in the joint program and U.S. proposals to share diffusion technology testify to Europe's enhanced capacity to develop alternatives to American assistance. This development may have been predictable from the outset. As the American analyst who called U.S. aid under the joint program "a lever of great power" foresaw, "it is a lever . . . whose effectiveness is likely to diminish in time as Western Europe's nuclear development progresses."[106]

---

[103] *Nuclear Industry*, May 1972, p. 17, and February 1973, p. 51. Also U.S., Congress, Joint Committee on Atomic Energy, *Hearings, AEC Authorizing Legislation Fiscal Year 1973*, 92d Cong., 2d Sess., March 7, 8, 9, 1972 (Washington, D.C.: Government Printing Office, 1972), pp. 2338 and 2315.

[104] U.S., Congress, Joint Committee on Atomic Energy, *Hearings, AEC Authorizing Legislation*, p. 2316.

[105] As one AEC official stated: "There is no doubt today that enriched uranium production capabilities on a commercial scale will come into being outside the United States." U.S., Congress, House, Subcommittee on International Cooperation in Science and Space of the Committee on Science and Astronautics, *Hearings, A General Review of International Cooperation in Science and Space*, p. 336.

[106] Knorr, *Nuclear Energy*, p. 28.

CHAPTER 6

THE DEVELOPMENT OF HEAVY WATER REACTORS: THE ROLE OF COMMUNITY LABORATORIES

The development of heavy water reactors in Europe highlights the problems of institutionalized cooperation in advanced technology. These problems result chiefly from differing perceptions of the role Community leaders and laboratories should play in the conduct of industrially related research. From the outset, the Euratom Commission took a supranational view of this role. Brussels, it felt, was responsible not only for specific programs contained in the Community budget but for all programs. National and Community programs constituted a single effort, and Community leaders were charged to insure the unity and balance of this effort. Under this conception, Community laboratories acquired a central significance. The JNRC installations were not merely additions to existing technical facilities in the Community; they were weights or centers of gravity for attracting, orienting, and ultimately integrating national facilities and programs. This was the purpose, as the Commission saw it, of the Community's Ispra center in Italy and the ORGEL heavy water reactor project carried out at Ispra.

The member-countries had somewhat different views. France, as we have noted, felt that the Community's role should be more complementary than comprehensive and regarded ORGEL as a back-up rather than a bulwark of national programs. Germany thought this role should be more symbolic than substantive, particularly in industrial areas, and supported ORGEL for political reasons while opposing it on technical and economic grounds. Italy favored a developmental role for the Community and backed Ispra and ORGEL largely for what they could offer to Italy's national programs. Finally, the Benelux countries sided with the Commission's view in principle but took different views in practice depending on the specific issue. Belgium agreed with France on certain issues of specialization and with Germany on matters of industrial freedom. The Netherlands supported Germany on industrial questions but took Italy's point of view on policies of balanced Community development (especially concerning Petten and JNRC appropriations).

The ORGEL story, therefore, exposes the problems of internal co-operation in a technological community much as the proven reactor story exposes the problems of external cooperation. The key issue in the latter case, as we saw in the previous chapter, is the extent to which the community pursues cooperative or competitive policies toward third countries. The key issue in the former case is whether the community exercises central leadership or takes a public service role, deferring to member-country initiatives.

The internal issue is not necessarily unique to international organization. The role of public authorities and institutions has often been a subject of dispute in domestic organization of R&D. Over the past decade, national as well as international laboratories have confronted the limitations of "forced development" through large, publicly financed projects. Criticism of past programs in atomic energy and space fields has prompted a reassessment of government responsibilities in domestic R&D.[1] The shift from centralized (i.e., institutional) to decentralized (i.e., ad hoc and informal) practices of developing advanced technology, which we described in chapter 4, may be a national as well as international trend and a widespread rather than uniquely European phenomenon.

Nevertheless, in the European integration process, the role of joint public institutions, such as Ispra, was unique. The creation of common laboratories to develop large-scale technology (and not just basic research) was a novel undertaking, and the attitudes and expectations associated with Ispra and ORGEL were necessarily more primitive and volatile than those associated with public institutions at the national level. Not surprisingly, therefore, the difficulties encountered by Ispra and ORGEL contributed to a gradual disenchantment with the concept of centralized facilities and programs. Even the most European-minded officials closest to ORGEL were forced to conclude, after the program was halted in 1969, "that the procedure laid down in Article 7 of the Euratom Treaty, which has governed the Euratom programmes, including ORGEL, up to now, is not ideally suitable for the carrying out of a large-scale project, where time and efficiency are all-important. . . ."[2]

ORGEL and Ispra were the centerpieces of larger issues, in particular the issue of what type of research and industrial community Europe would build. Such issues are never decided on the basis of technology and economics alone. Economic factors were important in the evolution of ORGEL—in particular because this and other heavy water reactor

[1]See, for example, George Eads and Richard R. Nelson, "Governmental Support of Advanced Civilian Technology: Power Reactors and the Supersonic Transport," *Public Policy*, XIX (Summer 1971), pp. 405–27.

[2]See the study by the ORGEL project leader and his associate, J. C. Leny and S. Orlowski, *The ORGEL Project 1959–1969* (EUR 4505f, e) (Brussels: Commission of the European Communities, 1971), p. 43.

types were intermediate-generation systems designed to fill a gap between the development of light water and fast reactors and thus dependent on how rapidly these other two systems developed. But economic decisions and especially economic evidence on which these decisions are based are often directly or indirectly linked to earlier investment and developmental choices, taken at a time when political preferences and personal prejudices may have been more significant than technical data. The following case study illustrates the extent to which political choices (i.e., partisan choices reflecting group biases) determine the kinds of economic and technical data that are accumulated and thus influence ultimate choices taken on the basis of these data.

The Program Definition Phase

The draft outline of Euratom's first five-year program (Annex V of the Treaty) authorized the development of reactor prototypes in Community laboratories and set aside more than one-quarter of the first five-year budget for this purpose ($60 million from a total of $215 million). The outline also called for the establishment of an expert group to select the technology for this project. Before this group actually met, Euratom's *First General Report* (issued in September) indicated that a Community project should focus on heavy water, natural uranium systems.[3] This choice seemed obvious for several reasons: a natural uranium string was consistent with Europe's long-term objective of independence; other reactor strings (light water, gas graphite, and high temperature gas) were already the subject of various external and internal programs; and heavy water systems were potential but not immediate items of commercial interest. The choice also demonstrated, however, some initial constraints on Community development of industrially relevant technologies. Proven reactors were too close to commercial exploitation to justify a Community prototype program; fast reactors were too significant as a major source of future energy to permit Community intervention; and high temperature gas reactors were not significant enough to enjoy Community-wide appeal (the only country with any program at the time was Germany—see chapter 7). Heavy water reactors, by contrast, were neither too significant nor too unappealing. If they should become either too significant or too unappealing, the implication was a direct Community role might be less justified.

ORGEL Is Conceived

The choice of heavy water reactors having been decided, the expert group which met for the first time in October 1958 had only to decide on

[3]Euratom, *First General Report*, p. 45.

the particular variant or type of cooling system to be developed. Four cooling techniques were being studied at the time—pressurized heavy water, gas (usually carbon dioxide), organic liquids, and boiling light water. Heavy water cooling was the subject of experimental work in Canada and preliminary studies by Siemens in Germany. Gas cooling was the basis of France's high-priority gas graphite program and the preferred cooling system for a back-up program in heavy water reactors. Organic cooling was being studied in Canada, France (preliminarily), and, in connection with an all organic reactor (both organic moderation and cooling), in several Community industries (for example, Interatom in Germany and Montecatini in Italy). Boiling light water was the cooling system of the HALDEN reactor in Norway and a small design project in Italy (Ansaldo and CISE). Of these techniques, most was known about heavy water and gas cooling; least was known about boiling light water cooling. None of the techniques was so advanced as to be conspicuously superior.

Thus, the discussions of the expert group became a debate over the relative merits of each technique.[4] At this early stage of development, such debate is neither surprising nor undesirable. Technical choices are seldom black and white, and decision-making requires competitive engagement among professionals to sort out the alternatives and minimize the uncertainties. Yet the lines drawn in this debate suggest that political as well as technical factors informed the debate. CEA representatives supported their own gas cooling technique as the basis of a Community program. Siemens officials supported their own heavy water technique. In addition, French spokesmen wanted the Community project to use pressure tubes to contain the coolant, the system employed in French graphite reactors. German spokesmen, on the other hand, wanted the Community to develop a unique pressure vessel concept, the basis of the Siemens reactor project known as MZFR (Mehrzweckforschungsreaktor). Finally, German representatives made clear that, whatever role the Community assumed, it must not get involved in industrial-scale activities. If the Community project should include prototype development, as the Treaty clearly intended, this work should be contracted out to industry, not conducted in Community laboratories.[5]

This type of professional nationalism precluded agreement on a single set of reactor characteristics for a unified project. What was at stake was the technical and administrative features of a common program. Each national group hoped to get the Community to focus on its technology, thereby multiplying the resources that could be devoted to

---

[4]This group met three times—October 1958, January 1959, and April 1959. The information above was taken from the minutes of these meetings, which are not available for public citation.

[5]J. C. Leny, "Le projet Orgel: 1959–1969," *Énergie Nucléaire* (October 1970), p. 406.

this technology.[6] In addition, each group sought to influence the administrative structure of research. As we noted in chapter 3, scientists, too, are affected by their respective national traditions and institutions in the field of research. For German scientists, working with industry was natural and stimulating; for French scientists, at least those in government laboratories, it was unprofessional and distracting. Each group sought a common program that would accommodate its particular traditions.

Amidst such disagreement, the Community might have confined its role to coordination of national heavy water projects. The Commission believed, however, that its effectiveness as a coordinator depended critically on technical competence which could only be developed through concrete projects in JNRC facilities. To have influence, the Commission had to control resources and not merely shuffle papers. If successful, a Community heavy water project, even as only one fish in the pond, might still serve as catalyst for ultimately rationalizing programs in the heavy water field. Without a Community project, national projects would only grow farther apart.

With gas and heavy water cooling pre-empted by France and Germany, the Commission decided to investigate organic cooling (the project getting its name ORGEL from the French *ORGanique Eau Lourde*).[7] Francis Perrin, the CEA scientific administrator, was a personal advocate of organic cooling and persuaded Euratom's Scientific and Technical Committee in April 1959 to approve the Commission's choice. Perrin's support contributed to the later impression that ORGEL was a French-inspired concept.[8] This was hardly true given the then modest interest of the CEA in this variant. But the relative absence of government interest in ORGEL in either Germany or Italy, coupled with German industry's general suspicion of industrial-scale Community projects, gave the impression that France was the only country with a real stake in the ORGEL project.

The R&D Phase

Conceived in disunity, ORGEL was locked, to a certain extent, in unavoidable competition with national programs.[9] This impression was

[6]We saw in the case study of proven reactors how the U.S. was able effectively to double its outlays on light water research by making this American technology the focus of U.S.-Euratom cooperation.

[7]As some Community officials expressed it in interviews with the author, "ORGEL was the crumb thrown to the Community after the cookie had been consumed by national programs." The Commission also participated in studies of light water cooling through an agreement with the HALDEN project and obtained information on heavy water and organic cooling through the agreement signed with Canada in 1959.

[8]See, for example, the reference of the Italian government to ORGEL as "a natural uranium reactor project of French design." *Atomo e Industria*, March 1, 1967.

[9]In this respect, ORGEL illustrates the general dilemma faced by Community programs which, in the absence of common objectives, had to compete with national programs. See discussion of this point in chap. 4.

heightened when the expert group creating ORGEL disbanded in 1959. Though information was exchanged in the Community through a multitude of other committees, this group might have served as a special medium for coordinating heavy water objectives. Instead, ORGEL became identified with Community programs in general and suffered increasing isolation as the Community itself came under attack.

Nevertheless, in 1959, ORGEL still had a fighting chance. The organic cooling technique held out enough promise to warrant optimism.[10] The Commission simply had to move fast. Not only were the other programs somewhat more advanced, but national groups were naturally more attached to their own programs than to the Community effort. ORGEL would have to turn out to be clearly superior to convince them to abandon their pet projects.

The Conditions of Birth

Unfortunately, ORGEL's start was impeded by two factors. First, this project was to be the *épine dorsale* of the Community JNRC which, in the spring of 1959, did not yet exist. At the Ispra center in Italy, which the Commission expected to take over in July 1959, none of the scientific laboratories (chemistry, physics, metallurgy, etc.) or technical services (equipment shop, maintenance, etc.) existed to support a major reactor development program. Staff also had to be recruited, a situation which inevitably put the Community in competition with national centers for qualified personnel. To attract good people, the Community initially offered higher salaries and appointed new employees to the position of "officials for life" (*Beamten auf Lebenzeit*). The latter provision, especially when applied to scientists and engineers working in rapidly changing technological areas, built a certain inflexibility into the Ispra program, which greatly complicated life when Ispra later tried to convert to other activities.[11]

This situation alone did not make the ORGEL experience unique. Many national projects were begun in this period where research facilities and staff had first to be assembled. But the delay of one year by the Italian Parliament in ratifying the Ispra agreement made ORGEL's birth a particularly painful and protracted one. To be sure, a few preliminary ORGEL contracts were awarded to private industries as early as September 1959, but the installation of major equipment at Ispra could not begin until the fall of 1960. Altogether, ORGEL was over a year old before it could take up residence in its new home.

---

[10] For example, at one of the expert group meetings, Canadian visitors rated both organic and boiling light water cooling higher in the long run than gas cooling.

[11] Commission personnel practices drew early criticism from German sources, which warned against the inflexibility of these practices and resented the detailed management of personnel activities from Brussels. See *Atomwirtschaft*, VII (August/September 1962), p. 384; and IX (February 1964), p. 411.

A second factor added to ORGEL's troubled start. Not only was the JNRC not constructed; the JNRC itself was a new type of institution. True, the CERN international laboratory had existed since 1954 near Geneva; but this laboratory was dedicated to "research of a pure scientific and fundamental character relating to high energy particles" and derived its international significance from the need to finance a major piece of scientific equipment, the nuclear particle accelerator.[12] By contrast, the Euratom Ispra center was dedicated to "the creation of conditions necessary for the speedy establishment and growth of nuclear industries" and was authorized to undertake major programs of developmental, as well as basic, research. The industrially related character of this mission raised some complex and unprecedented issues about the organization and administration of international research.

The contest to resolve these issues began already in 1959. Gerhard Ritter, the German engineer selected to head the new Ispra establishment, requested at the time of his appointment that the director of the Ispra center be placed under the direct authority of the Euratom Commission rather than the Research Directorate of the Commission's staff. The Commission per se was a body of five commissioners of different nationalities (Luxembourg not being represented because it had no nuclear program) selected, according to the Treaty (Article 126), "for their general competence in regard to the special purposes of this Treaty." In fact, however, the commissioners were chosen on the basis of political interests and compromise rather than scientific or technological expertise;[13] and, though pledged to "perform their duties in the general interest of the Community with complete independence," they constituted a more "political" body than the Commission's staff.

Thus, a German director of the Ispra center, who anticipated difficulties with Commission staff personnel, might feel more confident if he could appeal his views directly to the Commission than if he were totally dependent on a subordinate chief of the Commission's staff. A Frenchman, Jules Guéron, was head of the Euratom Research Directorate. Ritter feared that, under the stewardship of Guéron, or any Frenchman for that matter, the Brussels bureaucracy might practice *dirigisme* and unduly restrict the freedom and authority of Ispra officials. In any event, a Frenchman would have little sympathy for German conceptions of the autonomous nature of research institutions, which in Germany are frequently the exclusive empires of individual professors. (See chapter 3.)

With the support of the German commissioner, Heinz Krekeler, Ritter's request was granted. This administrative arrangement placing

---

[12]For details on the activities and administration of CERN, see OECD, *International Scientific Organizations* (Paris: OECD, 1965), pp. 123–31.

[13]Lawrence Scheinman, "Euratom: Nuclear Integration in Europe," *International Conciliation*, No. 563 (May 1967), p. 22.

the Ispra director outside the jurisdiction of the Euratom Research Directorate produced adverse consequences for ORGEL. The ORGEL project, though being carried out at Ispra, remained a responsibility of the Research Directorate in Brussels under its general obligation to administer the common research program. Until 1963, the ORGEL project team headed by Jean-Claude Leny, another Frenchman, worked out of Brussels in close association with Guéron. At the same time, other activities at Ispra, being more specialized and short-term in nature, were determined largely by Ritter, who answered not to Guéron but to the more diffuse and politically oriented body of Euratom commissioners. This situation bred a division between ORGEL and other activities at Ispra, which was exacerbated by professional and personal differences between Ritter and Guéron. Jealous of his authority, Ritter developed a certain resentment toward ORGEL, which was the activity at Ispra least subject to his control. On the other hand, Guéron saw ORGEL as the primary instrument at his disposal for giving Ispra a general purpose and insuring the compliance of Ispra's activities with the over-all goals of the common research program.

On top of this, there was a difference of professional opinion between the two men concerning the proper mix of project-oriented and general research in a modern technological center. Guéron, based on his experience during the war with the allied bomb project and after the war with the French CEA, was a champion of the project-oriented or "horizontal" approach for organizing research facilities.[14] The separate, "vertical" departments of the research center (chemistry, physics, etc.) had to be tied together through major technological projects which would cut across specialized departments and would relate the activities of these departments to specific goals with specific time parameters. Ritter, on the other hand, was an advocate of a looser form of organization in which as much freedom as possible was given to the individual departments, permitting them to select their own topics and focus on more basic, spontaneous research objectives.[15] In Guéron's view, therefore, ORGEL was a vital project to the effective operation of Ispra as a whole; while, in Ritter's view, it was, at best, a distraction and, at worst, an annoying intervention from an overzealous bureaucracy in Brussels.[16]

[14]Jules Guéron, "Euratom and Nuclear Research," *Euratom Bulletin*, I (September 1962), pp. 2–10.

[15]G. Ritter, "Errichtung und Zielsetzung des Gemeinsamen Euratom-Zentrums Ispra," *Atomwirtschaft*, VI (March 1961), pp. 129–42. Ritter's views may have been one reason why he left (or was asked to leave) the Karlsruhe center where he was director before going to Ispra. Through the fast reactor program, Karlsruhe was trying to break away from the traditional model of decentralized research departments. See chaps. 3 and 8 of this study.

[16]Relations between Guéron and Ritter also suffered from personality contrasts. Guéron, a scientist and nuclear chemist, had an insatiable appetite for technical details

Infancy—the First Steps

As defined at the outset, the ORGEL project consisted of "all studies preliminary to the construction of a prototype reactor moderated by heavy water and cooled by organic liquids." Construction of a prototype was not excluded but would be decided on the basis of preliminary studies. These studies required several major pieces of equipment: in particular, a critical assembly and a low-power, high-flux experimental reactor. To secure Community resources to build this equipment, the ORGEL team, organized in the spring of 1960, opened immediate contacts with Community industries.

It was not originally intended to build another heavy water critical assembly, since such facilities were already available in France and, outside the Community, in Canada, Sweden, and the United States. But pressures from Ispra to equip the Community center with the facilities befitting a major establishment led to the decision to design and construct the critical experiment, ECO (*Expérience Critique ORGEL*). Similar pressures resulted in the construction of hot laboratories at Ispra.[17]

The construction of a low-power experimental reactor, on the other hand, was foreseen from the beginning. ORGEL directors decided that facilities of this type abroad (such as the NRX reactor at Chalk River in Canada) were not large enough for Community purposes and that the two high-flux reactors under construction in the Community (BR-2 in Belgium and the Petten high-flux reactor in Holland) did not offer the necessary technical features. Thus, in September 1960, ORGEL specialists drew up the initial specifications for a Community test reactor, ESSOR (*ESSai ORGEL*), and requested that interested industries submit tentative proposals for construction of this reactor.[18]

The industries contacted broke down into two groups, companies interested in doing ORGEL work on their own and groups of companies willing to put their resources together and form industrial teams. ORGEL directors preferred that all companies join a group, especially groups comprising firms from different countries. But at this stage, Euratom's Industrial Directorate was able to provide little direction; and *juste retour* pressures favored national industries over Community groupings. The result, therefore, was a compromise. The ECO contract

---

and little time or patience for public relations. Ritter, a chemical engineer and product of the more deferential German research community, knew less about the specific nuclear field but was more sensitive about rank and issues of public relations. In the subsequent conduct of Brussels-Ispra relations, Guéron's curiosity about the technical details of Ispra programs often irritated Ritter's sensibilities, while Ritter's flair for public relations struck Guéron as a disguise for scientific incompetence.

[17] By 1963 hot laboratories in the Community were in oversupply, suggesting the duplication involved in equipping Ispra. *Atomo e Industria*, May 1, 1962.

[18] Leny and Orlowski, *The ORGEL Project 1959–1969*, pp. 16–17.

went to a single company, the Dutch firm Neratoom (on a turnkey basis);[19] while preliminary design contracts for ESSOR went to two international groupings, one consisting of the firms GAAA (France) and Interatom (Germany) and the other bringing together Belgo-nucléaire (Belgium), Indatom (France), and Siemens (Germany).[20] These two groups submitted proposals in May 1961. The Commission staff compared the proposals, and, after extensive appraisal, chose the GAAA/Interatom design for the ESSOR construction.

Thus, in summer 1961, ORGEL appeared to be getting on its feet. Laboratories were under construction at Ispra, the ECO contract had been awarded, and the Commission was about to order the start of construction on ESSOR. Unexpectedly, however, new political difficulties intervened, and a final decision on ESSOR was delayed for still another year.

Solomon's Dilemma—ESSOR versus BR-2

While ORGEL studies were moving ahead, the Commission concluded agreements with Belgium and Holland for participation in the BR-2 and Petten reactors.[21] During discussions of Euratom's second five-year plan in 1961, Belgium and Holland requested additional Community funds for these reactors. Because funds for ESSOR were still uncommitted, they suggested that the Petten and BR-2 reactors substitute for ESSOR. Organic loops installed in these reactors would permit the same irradiation tests as ESSOR, and use of existing facilities would be less expensive and more expeditious than the construction of a new facility. In effect, Belgium and Holland were asking the Commission to carve up the ORGEL infant and abandon original intentions to carry out this project in one piece at the Ispra center.

The Commission may have possessed the wisdom of Solomon, but it did not have the authority. Consequently, under pressure from Belgium and Holland, the Commission postponed the ESSOR decision until a comparative survey could be made of the alternative facilities.[22]

Besides Petten and BR-2, there was a third possibility which figured into Community calculations at this point. As Annex V of the Treaty indicated, the Community originally contemplated the construction of

[19]Neratoom was ill-equipped to do this job alone and ultimately had to deliver the reactor to the Commission unfinished and considerably behind schedule. *Ibid.*, p. 26.

[20]The initiative in forming these groups came largely from the French side under prompting from Euratom research personnel. GAAA and Interatom were licensees of the same American firm, Atomics International. Interview with Interatom official, Bernberg/Cologne, July 13, 1970.

[21]The Petten agreement established Petten as a branch of the JNRC.

[22]This survey quickly established that only a central loop in BR-2 could provide the conditions necessary to test ORGEL-type fuel. The Commission requested SERAI, a Belgian firm, to study this alternative in more detail. The survey was an internal Commission document and is not available for public citation.

low-power prototypes in connection with the JNRC program. A low-power prototype (or reactor experiment) differed from a test reactor like ESSOR in that its characteristics more closely approximated a full-scale ORGEL power station. The prototype could employ only one cooling technique—in this case, organic cooling—while the test reactor could be used for experiments involving a variety of cooling techniques. Thus the prototype was less flexible, but this disadvantage was offset by the more precise information it could yield about the eventual economic performance of a full-scale plant. To be sure, the small prototype, as a more advanced test facility, was also more risky. Yet some Euratom officials felt the risk was worth taking, especially if the gain to be realized was the early acquisition of precise information about ORGEL's prospects, a factor which would be of great value to ORGEL in competition against the other heavy water variants.[23]

Two factors, nevertheless, discouraged the construction of a small prototype. At the time, Canada planned a facility of this type; and Euratom officials wished to avoid duplication.[24] More important, however, German groups opposed anything that smacked of a Euratom prototype role. They preferred the test reactor because it could be used by other projects in the Community investigating different cooling techniques (like the German MZFR and AKB projects—on the latter, see note 65 and accompanying text). In this respect, they had the support of Italy which, from 1961 on, showed more interest in an all organic reactor and thereafter boiling light water cooling than the ORGEL program. (See subsequent discussion.)

The option of a small prototype, therefore, did not materialize. According to some observers, this decision may have made the difference in the ultimate outcome of the ORGEL project.[25] Both the French and German heavy water programs (EL-4 and MZFR) began with small prototypes (see subsequent discussion), which were in operation by 1966. By comparison, ESSOR did not diverge until 1967, and the information it provided as a test reactor was less advanced and hence less convincing than that provided by the national prototype reactors. This evaluation is subject to dispute,[26] but it does illustrate the constraints under which the Community program operated. These early decisions, made more on political than economic grounds, had a considerable effect on the type and quality of economic data which subsequently determined the outcome of the ORGEL project.

<hr/>

[23]For a general discussion of the prototype/test reactor options, see J. C. Leny and S. Orlowski, "The Orgel Project," in *Euratom: Scientific and Technical Activities* (EUR 1850) (Brussels: Euratom, 1964), chap. 3.

[24]The Canadians later changed their minds and also built a test reactor, WR-1.

[25]Opinions expressed to the author in interviews with French and Community officials.

[26]For example, the Canadians took the test reactor route with no more or less success than the German and French programs. But the Canadians did not face the immediate competition or time limitations affecting ORGEL.

In the bargaining package associated with the passage of the second five-year plan, the BR-2 and Petten alternatives were also dropped.[27] Thus, in October 1962, the Commission ordered that construction begin on ESSOR. Another full year had been lost; and even then, it was April 1963, three years after the organization of the ORGEL team, before the ground for ESSOR was officially broken.

With construction taking place in Italy, the Commission urged the ESSOR consortium (GAAA/Interatom) to seek out an Italian partner. Montecatini was invited to participate.[28] To this enlarged group with GAAA acting as *chef de file*, the Commission assigned the task of industrial architect (i.e., responsibility for design work but not over-all management). Aside from the predilection of Guéron and Leny to utilize familiar French procedures, the "industrial architect" formula was chosen to maximize the integration of ORGEL research with the construction of ESSOR. This way the Commission retained responsibility for all contract placements, rather than the consortium dispensing contracts for ESSOR and the Community supervising more general ORGEL activities. The Commission also hoped to shield the industrial group from *juste retour* pressures which could affect the distribution of contracts. The Commission considered itself better equipped to deal with these pressures. This assumption may have been too optimistic, as ESSOR did experience a number of contract delays caused by the requirement to insure a balanced placement of contracts. Nevertheless, the fact that the Commission retained over-all control of the project probably did account, in large part, for the completion of ESSOR within scheduled time-limits.[29]

Where the architect engineer formula may have been deficient was in failing to accord sufficient responsibility to industry. This might have provoked the latter to invest resources in the commercialization of ORGEL-type reactors. As we shall see below, none of the firms involved in the ESSOR consortium developed a strong interest in the organic, heavy water reactor, despite their participation in ESSOR.

Generation Squeeze—ORGEL Competes with Light Water and Fast Reactors

Just as ORGEL seemed to be gathering momentum inside the Community, developments outside the Community dealt the organic-cooled

---

[27]Belgium and Holland had bargained well, however. The Council decision of June 1962 raised Euratom's participation in BR-2 from $5 million in the first plan to $12 million in the second and increased appropriations for Petten from $4 million to $19 million, giving this center a designation of "center of general competence" on the same basis as Ispra. By contrast, initial Commission requests for ORGEL and Ispra were slashed by $10 million ($67 million to $57 million) and $18 million ($93 million to $75 million) respectively.

[28]Like GAAA and Interatom, Montecatini was a licensee of the American company, Atomics International.

[29]Leny and Orlowski, *The ORGEL Project*, pp. 20–24.

variant a technical and psychological setback. Canada was proceeding with the construction of a test reactor similar to ESSOR (the first Whiteshell reactor or WR-1). Through contracts placed with Atomics International, the USAEC was also investigating an all organic reactor (OMRE). Under the 1959 agreement with Canada, Euratom exchanged full information with the WR-1 project. Formal ties did not exist with the American program, but some studies on organic coolants were being carried out under the Euratom-U.S. light water reactor agreement. In June 1962, these formal and informal contacts led to a tripartite meeting of Euratom, USAEC, and AECL (Atomic Energy of Canada Limited) representatives in Los Angeles. ORGEL derived considerable support from these international ties, both in terms of direct assistance received (Canadian experts, for example, advised the Commission on the ESSOR contract award) and in terms of indirect psychological support for the organic cooling technique.

Suddenly in December 1962 this supportive framework collapsed. The USAEC announced a cutback and review of the OMRE program in light of growing technical difficulties.[30] Six months later, the USAEC discontinued this program altogether. Canada, under urging from the United States (which sought to keep the organic option alive in case the technical problems were overcome), continued its program but stepped up studies of alternative coolants.[31] Without the flexibility to pursue other options, Euratom had to stay with the organic system. As it happened, the decision turned out to be a good one. But for two years (1962–64) during the critical early life of ORGEL, the U.S. announcement cast a cloud of skepticism over the economic prospects of organic-cooled heavy water reactors and correspondingly reduced interest in ORGEL. The incident illustrated the extent to which European efforts in this period were dependent on events in the United States, whether or not formal links existed between the two programs (such as they did in the joint program on light water reactors).

The U.S. decision coincided with, and was in part the result of, accelerated progress in the development of first- and second-generation reactors. As light water and fast reactors advanced, intermediate systems such as heavy water reactors got caught in a "generation squeeze."[32] These systems retained a function as converters (i.e., to produce plutonium for second-generation reactors—see Appendix). But

---

[30]See the USAEC's report to the President, *Civilian Nuclear Power* (Washington, D.C.: Government Printing Office, 1962). The difficulties stemmed primarily from the decomposition of organic liquids under irradiation and the subsequent "fouling" of the various reactor parts.

[31]From 1963 on Canada took an increasing interest in the use of boiling light water cooling (GENTILLY project). Great Britain also announced in 1962 that it was investigating a light water-cooled, heavy water reactor known as SGHWR.

[32]The OMRE program was terminated, in part, to make more funds available for fast reactors.

their economic future depended on costs of producing power. Calculations at the time suggested that the greatest success would be had with heavy water reactors which utilized heavy water cooling (owing to the Canadian program) or boiling light water cooling (owing to the similar cooling in light water reactors). Organic cooling and ORGEL were given lower probabilities of success.[33]

While in a number of respects these forecasts were premature,[34] the USAEC's termination of the OMRE program and the emerging generation squeeze triggered a series of decisions in industrial and national programs in' Europe, which adversely affected ORGEL's long-term prospects. Once taken, these decisions could not be easily reversed, even after the technical evaluations of organic systems improved.

Sibling Rivalry—ORGEL Competes with National Projects

In 1962 both Interatom and Siemens took investment decisions which sharply affected their future interest in organic systems. Interatom dropped its development of organic reactors for nuclear marine propulsion, switching to light water ship reactors.[35] Work on organic cooling continued under the ESSOR contract, but this work was undertaken originally as a complement to the ship program. Now that the latter focused on light water systems, the ESSOR work became little more than a practical way for Interatom to amortize its investments in the organic field.

Siemens made the decision in 1962 to switch from heavy water to light water reactors as a priority *filière*. Work on heavy water systems continued but only as an export commodity.[36] Siemens officials assumed that the heavy water reactors, which burn natural uranium, would retain their attraction for third world countries possessing large domestic supplies of uranium or desiring to be independent of U.S. enriched fuel deliveries. But inside Europe, heavy water systems, even with more advanced heavy water or gas cooling, faced stiff competition from light water reactors.[37] Organic cooling, which Siemens monitored up to 1962 through its participation in the ESSOR competition, was felt to have no chance at all.

[33]The greater interest in light water cooling was reflected in Canadian and British programs. See note 31 above.

[34]A point which Euratom officials argued, in particular, noting that the difficulties in the U.S. program were due to a failure to purify adequately the coolant. Leny, "Le projet Orgel," p. 407.

[35]Interview with Interatom official, Bernberg/Cologne, July 13, 1970.

[36]Interview with Siemens officials, Erlangen, July 7, 1970.

[37]Siemens' own projects, which employed both heavy water (MZFR) and gas (AKB) cooling, illustrated these difficulties. The MZFR faced size limitations imposed by the pressure vessel concept. No one expected this design to serve for units larger than 300 MWe. The AKB project encountered problems in the development of an economic fuel-cladding material, which could withstand decomposition at high temperatures. To gain assistance on the latter problem, Siemens concluded the agreement in September 1963 with the French CEA. See chap. 5.

Decisions in Italy also affected ORGEL's prospects. Studies by Montecatini and the CNRN on all organic reactors culminated in 1960 in the establishment of the PRO program. PRO was heavily inspired by the U.S. OMRE program and experienced a setback when the United States terminated OMRE.[38] Nevertheless, Italian officials pressed for Euratom contracts, eventually winning funds for PRO which would have otherwise gone to ORGEL.[39] In addition, Italy became more interested in the CISE heavy water reactor employing boiling light water cooling. From 1961 on, Italy received limited funds for this project under the Euratom-U.S. joint research program. In 1964 Italy and Euratom concluded a new set of contracts, expanding research in preparation for the construction of a prototype reactor known as CIRENE.[40] Thus, as a curious consequence of *juste retour* pressures, Euratom found itself financing and encouraging direct competitors of the ORGEL project.

Ironically, developments in France in this period increased interest in heavy water reactors, but with gas, not organic, cooling. France began construction in 1961 of an 80 MWe gas-cooled, heavy water prototype reactor (EL-4). This commitment suggested that France was seriously interested in heavy water systems but considered organic cooling and ORGEL, at best, as a back-up system to the EL-4 variant. Indeed, only after EL-4 ran into difficulties in 1964–65, did France take a serious interest in ORGEL.

Even as ORGEL's star dimmed, prospects of Community cooperation seemed to brighten with the agreement in 1963 between the CEA and Siemens to conduct a joint study of heavy water sytems.[41] In the case of France, however, this agreement was nothing more than bait to attract Germany to buy its gas graphite technology. And in the case of Siemens, the agreement reflected, in part, the decline of interest in heavy water reactors. Now that these reactors were no longer a priority line, Siemens found it economical and consistent with commercial competition to share further development costs with outside collaborators. Also, aside from political pressures forcing this collaboration, Siemens and the CEA had a common message to pass on to the Community. The joint study concluded that the requirement to develop European reactors

[38]*Atomo e Industria*, January 15, 1960. PRO was based on an American experimental concept which, in 1957, was acclaimed by American representatives as holding great promise for the future. After this kind of build-up, Italy was unable to understand the 1962 decision to terminate the U.S. program, or subsequent U.S. pressure to get Italy to maintain PRO in case the U.S. decision proved to be wrong (same tactic U.S. pursued with Canada). See Mario Silvestri, *Il costo della menzogna: Italia nucleare 1945–1968* (Torino: Giulio Einaudi, 1968), p. 250.

[39]*Atomo e Industria*, August 1, 1964. Italy had suggested already in 1962 that PRO substitute for ESSOR in the ORGEL program. *Agence Europe*, June 15, 1962.

[40]Italy, National Committee for Nuclear Energy, *Programs and Activities* (Rome: National Committee for Nuclear Energy, 1970), p. 94.

[41]*Le Monde*, September 9, 1963. The agreement also included a study of gas graphite systems, which we discussed in chap. 5.

(meaning natural uranium reactors), "together with the fact that two of the principal partners of the Community have decided to invest sizeable sums in the gas-cooled, heavy-water variant, should move Euratom to consider this variant as one of the major objectives of the Community and to take the most serious account of this fact in the partition of its efforts."[42] In short, Euratom was being asked to shift its support from organic- to gas-cooled reactors. Siemens and the CEA were collaborating less to improve the chances of ORGEL than to compete against this Community project by taking a united stand in favor of the gas-cooled variant.

A Black Eye

In 1963–64, rising costs and the consequences of the short-sighted cuts made in Ispra and ORGEL appropriations in 1962 (see note 27) added internal difficulties to ORGEL's troubled existence. In an attempt to minimize these difficulties, Euratom officials gave ORGEL top priority in the distribution of funds at Ispra. This generated immediate resentment among those laboratories and personnel doing non-ORGEL work or desiring to do such work. In some instances, these laboratories accepted ORGEL funds but diverted the money for use on their own projects. To control this fudging, Brussels officials exercised closer supervision of ORGEL assignments and placed more contracts with private and public institutions outside Ispra. These measures succeeded only in further alienating Ispra officials, particularly the director and his supporters, who resented the ORGEL project already because of Brussels management.

Tension peaked in the spring and summer of 1963 with a spate of newspaper articles, primarily in the German press,[43] attacking the ORGEL and Ispra policies of the Euratom administration in Brussels. Triggered by the release of several Ispra scientists,[44] these articles aired, above all, the long-percolating resentment of Brussels and ORGEL in the German scientific and industrial communities. German scientists

[42]CEA/Siemens, *Perspective techniques et économiques des centrales électronucléaires à uranium naturel, deuxième partie—réacteurs modérés à l'eau lourde* (Paris: CEA, June 1964), p. 63.

[43]For a representative sample of these articles, see *Koelner Stadt-Anzeiger*, April 6, 1963; *Frankfurter Allgemeine*, May 2, 1963; *Die Zeit*, June 14, 1963; *Hannoversche Allgemeine Zeitung*, June 29, 1963; *Der Spiegel*, July 10, 1963; and *Der Volkswirt*, August 9, 1963.

[44]Four scientists—three German and one Dutch—were dismissed for reasons which most observers, including Ritter, appeared to accept as legitimate. The dismissals were obviously the occasion rather than the cause of discontent. In fact, there is some evidence to suggest that disgruntled German employees at Ispra exploited, if not engineered, the press criticism by inviting journalists to Ispra to record their grievances. See, in particular, *Koelner Stadt-Anzeiger*, April 6, 1963, and January 28, 1964.

disliked the monopoly exercised by ORGEL activities at Ispra[45] and regretted, in particular, the failure to establish a low-temperature laboratory under the direction of the German Nobel winner, Rudolf Moessbauer.[46] German industrial leaders objected to the continuing focus on what they considered to be an uneconomical reactor type. They welcomed the press attacks as a way of acquainting the public with the poor prospects ORGEL faced at the commercial stage.

The German government viewed all this with mixed feelings. On the one hand, it did not like to see Euratom, a Community institution, vilified. On the other, German authorities recognized that they could support specific Euratom projects, like ORGEL, only to the extent that German industry was willing to participate in them. With German industrial support declining, the German government drew some advantage from the press criticism as a way of pointing out to France, ORGEL's most ardent supporter, that there was a limit to official German support for this project.

The public controversy prompted some changes in the administrative and budgetary organization of Ispra and ORGEL. In September 1963, the ORGEL project team, up till then operating from Brussels, moved to Ispra. This move followed, in part, from the desire to supervise more closely the work on ESSOR which had begun in April. It also reflected, however, the desire to defuse complaints about excessive centralization of ORGEL management. In a second step to improve over-all Brussels-Ispra relations, a new technical director, the Dutch professor Kramers, was appointed at Ispra. Kramers was charged with responsibility for the scientific side of Ispra's relations with Brussels, an arrangement which eased some of the problems of communication between the scientist, Guéron, and the engineer, Ritter. Third, in the 1964 Euratom budget discussions, the member-states insisted on a limitation of the amount of money ORGEL directors could spend outside Ispra. This step sharply reduced the flexibility of ORGEL as well as the opportunity to use outside contracts to attract industrial interest in ORGEL. After 1964 the

[45]ORGEL was predominant at Ispra. As Guéron remarked in 1962, "the main departments in Ispra (reactor physics, materials, engineering) are for the time being mainly or wholly engaged in ORGEL problems." See "Euratom and Nuclear Research," p. 4.

[46]The initiative for this proposal came from German scientists at Ispra and in Germany. The Commission supported the proposal as a way of enhancing the significance of the JNRC but suspected German motives in pushing basic research projects to dilute the importance of ORGEL. France rejected the project out of hand as an unnecessary dispersion of Community resources. Domestic groups in Germany pressed the government to keep trying in the effort to convert Ispra from industrially related to basic research activities. *Stuttgarter Zeitung*, November 18, 1963. This pressure affected German policy in the 1964 Euratom budget discussions when German representatives supported the proposal to limit Commission authority to distribute contracts outside Ispra. (See further discussion.) It also contributed to the strong emphasis contained in the German memorandum of 1964 concerning the need to strengthen long-term, basic research activities at Ispra.

percentage of non-Ispra contracts dropped rapidly, reaching negligible levels by 1967.[47]

While the press outburst in 1963 reflected some legitimate issues in the conduct of international scientific cooperation, the incident gave ORGEL a public black eye before the project had a chance to produce economic data to defend itself.[48] The bad publicity also had wider implications for Euratom, since prior to 1963 relatively little had been reported about JNRC activities. Now, suddenly, the Community's major research center and top priority reactor project were cast in a highly disparaging public light.

The Prototype Phase

ORGEL's struggle toward maturity ensued at three different levels, with varying degrees of success (or failure). At the technical level, the project progressed on schedule. After painful beginnings, this feat alone was worthy of praise. At the political level, ORGEL's fortunes became entwined with those of Euratom. The project attracted flak for its own and its parent's sins, and the barrage never allowed the project to establish an independent identity. As the Community went down, so did ORGEL. Finally, at the economic level, ORGEL failed to survive the test of natural selection. The generation squeeze reduced ORGEL's prospects, no less than that of other heavy water projects. In ORGEL's case, however, economics was helped along by politics. Commercial competition is serious business; and no one was prepared to alter, for the sake of Community spirit, the conditions of competition established by earlier commitments.

A Friend Returns and Deserts

Despite the drift toward first- and second-generation reactors, the USAEC announced at the Third U.N. Conference on Peaceful Uses of Nuclear Energy in September 1964 that it was reactivating its organic cooling program, this time in connection with heavy water moderation and desalinization rather than power applications. In Brussels the United States followed this announcement with a request to conclude an agreement of information exchange with ORGEL. ORGEL officials responded enthusiastically. Here was proof that they had been right to stick with ORGEL in 1962 when others deserted the organic concept. What is more, after two years, Euratom was now ahead of the United States and could bargain with American officials from the unfamiliar

[47]Leny and Orlowski, *The ORGEL Project 1959–1969*, pp. 10 and 99.

[48]Even a newsletter in Germany reflecting views of the German scientific community admitted that the attacks on ORGEL were premature and urged that the project be continued until definitive data could be obtained. See Deutscher Forschungsdienst (the German Research Service), *Sonderbericht Kernenergie*, November 28, 1963.

position of strength. This twist of circumstances, Commission officials hoped, should be enough to convince skeptics of the value of ORGEL and provoke an expanded Community effort to keep ahead of unfolding American plans.[49]

By 1964, however, the Commission had exhausted its credit in the field of external relations. The U.S. proposal for heavy water reactor co-operation came close on the heels of the Euratom-U.S. fast reactor negotiations. In these negotiations, France had declared its distrust of the Commission as a vigorous defender of European interests (see chapter 8). Weak and often politically divided, the Commission, France felt, was no match for the confident and aggressive Americans. This fact had been demonstrated repeatedly in the light water reactor sector. Now, in the organic, heavy water field where Euratom was avowedly ahead, France saw no need to risk Europe's advance in negotiations with a partner which had little to offer but much to gain.

With less interest in ORGEL to begin with, the other member-states followed the French lead on this issue. The result was an interminable series of delays. Despite repeated appeals by the Commission, the Council failed to act on either the principle or the substance of an agreement with the United States.[50] After three years, the matter finally died. In March 1967, the USAEC terminated its organic work for the second time. To say the least, this vacillation of U.S. intentions did not help ORGEL and confirmed the dependence of Community programs on U.S. technology, whether or not formal exchange agreements existed. By 1967, however, ORGEL was dying of internal causes. The desertion once again of a friend had less effect than it did in 1962.

The Crisis of Adolescence

The denouement of the ORGEL drama came in 1965. The year began well enough when in May the Council approved budget increases of $7 million and $8 million respectively for ORGEL and Ispra activities. These appropriations relieved the immediate financial squeeze. As part of the revision package of Euratom's second five-year plan, however, the decision reflected the declining support for ORGEL. France supported ORGEL for technical reasons, particularly as problems with a fuel-

---

[49]The U.S. program called for a vigorous start-up involving expenditures of $20 million in the first year. To save time, the U.S. rented test facilities in Canada. On these developments as perceived in Europe, see Leny and Orlowski, *The ORGEL Project 1959-1969*, pp. 30-31.

[50]In the meantime, soundings by technical personnel revealed that the principal issues in an agreement with the U.S. were the application of exchange agreements to prototype projects and the supply of heavy water required for the ORGEL project. U.S. negotiators made the lease of heavy water for ORGEL dependent on the conclusion of a satisfactory exchange agreement. *Nucleonics Week*, November 24, 1966. On the other side, France demanded that the U.S. pay a cash price before Europe would even consider exchanging its more advanced information.

cladding material slowed progress on EL-4; but CEA officials maintained strong reservations against the Community project because of de Gaulle's political challenge of Community institutions.[51] Italy approved the increases only after obtaining expanded Community support of CIRENE, including agreement to order a light water cooling loop for ESSOR. Germany remained a sympathetic political ally of Brussels but warned that ORGEL was nearing the end of its Community phase and must be transferred shortly to industry.[52]

Nevertheless, the Commission, buoyed by the revival of interest in organic cooling techniques in the United States and by ORGEL's technical progress, pushed ahead with proposals for a Community prototype project. At the conference convened in Venice in April to discuss Euratom's first target program, the Commission reaffirmed the need for intermediate-generation systems and suggested that Euratom participate in prototype development of these systems at the same time it put together an industrial promotion program for first-generation reactors. Identification of an ORGEL prototype project with the emotionally charged issues of industrial policy was unfortunate, though perhaps unavoidable. By tying intermediate-generation reactor programs to first- and second-generation reactor developments, the Commission hoped to demonstrate the indispensability of the former. It succeeded, however, only in identifying intermediate-generation prototype proposals with the growing controversy over the Community's role in industrial promotion programs. The matter got worse in the summer of 1965 when the Commission specifically proposed direct Euratom involvement in the management as well as capital outlays of an ORGEL prototype reactor.[53] The Commission conceded that it could not undertake this project alone; it lacked both funds and authority for industrial-scale activities. But the Commission insisted that the Community supply the leadership in this endeavor and take the responsibility for finding appropriate industrial partners.

The search for industrial partners was the theme of an ORGEL symposium convened at Ispra in October.[54] Two circumstances—one political, the other economic—governed the outcome of this symposium. By now, the Euratom Commission was no longer a unified body. The commissioners as well as the Commission's staff were divided by the controversies of the larger Euratom debate (see chapter 4). In particular, the Research Directorate stood alone in its attempt to win industrial support for ORGEL. Always weak, the Industrial Directorate was never very

[51]Le Monde, October 10–11, 1965.

[52]See Agence Europe, May 30, 1964.

[53]Euratom, Note au sujet du prototype ORGEL (EUR/C/3214/1/65f) (Brussels, July 6, 1965).

[54]For a complete record of this symposium, see Euratom, Proceedings of the ORGEL Symposium, meeting held at the C.C.R. Ispra, October 1965 (Brussels: Euratom, 1965).

enthusiastic about this project. For some time, the task of exciting industrial interest had devolved upon Guéron and the ORGEL research team. Not surprisingly, these research leaders defined their responsibilities in narrow technical terms, disdaining the task of proselytizing industry to adopt this reactor.[55] They disregarded the fact that an ORGEL prototype had to be not only technically feasible but also economically desirable.

This was especially true in the face of a second circumstance prevailing at the conference. Industrial participants did not come to the symposium with completely open minds. Investment decisions taken years before had reduced their flexibility and made them increasingly reluctant to revise existing plans.[56] If ORGEL really expected to find industrial advocates, the time for doing so may have already passed—unless ORGEL spokesmen could convincingly demonstrate that their reactor was *economically* superior.

Commission personnel themselves recognized that ORGEL's economics were not that good.[57] Thus, Commission representatives marshalled two arguments to get around the economic issue. Stressing ORGEL's technical success,[58] they argued initially that it was too early to make a definite economic judgment and that a prototype should be constructed to answer this very question. The argument was valid as far as it went, but industries would undertake a commitment of $100 million or more (the cost of a medium-scale prototype, 100 MWe) only on the basis of sound existing prospects. If the Community had concentrated on a small prototype rather than a test reactor, the economic evidence may have been more convincing. In any case, with ESSOR still not in operation (the reactor did not diverge until March 1967 and reach full power until December 1968), the risk was too great.

[55]As Guéron told the delegates at the symposium, "we are not telling you to buy an ORGEL reactor rather than another type; that is not our job. . . . our task is completed the moment we provide you with solutions and the possibility of working out their cost. After that it is a problem of general economics. . . . All that is beyond us." While Guéron's remarks ring true from a technician's point of view, they understate the responsibilities of Euratom in promoting industrial advancement. *Ibid.*, chap. 11, p. 68.

[56]The point was well put by a German representative at the symposium: ". . . The important question which arises for firms which supply nuclear power plants on a turn-key basis is whether they should use more of their capacity, which is, as in the case of all firms, limited, for an additional type of reactor, namely ORGEL, possibly to the detriment of other equally promising projects. What important reasons can the representatives of the Euratom Commission give which would assist a company in arriving at a genuine business-like decision to include the ORGEL series in its program now?" *Ibid.*, chap. 11, p. 26.

[57]In cost comparisons with other nuclear and conventional reactors, the original ORGEL design utilizing natural uranium came out with a slight competitive edge. These comparisons, however, were subject to considerable criticism, especially concerning the justification for comparing already mature reactor-types, like light water systems, with types still in early development stages, like ORGEL. *Ibid.*, chap. 9.

[58]The major technical problem of "fouling" causing the setback to organic prospects in 1962 had been solved.

The Community's second line of attack anticipated the charge of insufficient economic justification to proceed with an ORGEL prototype. Euratom spokesmen presented data on an ORGEL design utilizing enriched uranium. This design considerably improved the economic prospects.[59] But as the ORGEL project head, Leny, noted, enrichment was "an alternative which [could] not be treated only in technical and economic terms."[60] Indeed, the suggestion of enrichment provoked the sharpest controversy of the entire symposium. French representatives, though conspicuously silent during the discussions (no doubt as part of the French boycott of Community institutions), pointed out that enrichment undermined the political justification of ORGEL as a reactor line promising independence of foreign fuel supplies.[61] German participants were more blunt. If ORGEL were enriched, then other variants must also be enriched before fair comparisons could be drawn. Moreover, enrichment eliminated the advantage of heavy water reactors as export items to third world countries.

To be sure, the opposition to enrichment was inconsistent, if not disingenuous. Both France and Germany were entertaining the possibility at this time of turning to enriched fuels in their own heavy water programs. (See subsequent discussion.) But the controversy revealed something unique about Community as opposed to national policies. Euratom, as a Community institution, could less afford the appearance of abandoning the goal of European independence than the member-states. Euratom, in short, had to be more European than Europe.

On the whole, the ORGEL symposium passed on a positive note. The technical achievements of the project were unquestioned, especially in view of the consensus in 1958 that the organic concept was a long shot with little chance for technical, let alone economic, success. But, in the quest for industrial partners, the symposium was much less encouraging. It was too late for this quest. Industries have to acquire an early stake in technological developments. The Commission, by holding back larger responsibilities from industry, discouraged initial commitments to ORGEL. More important, the Commission never had the authority or the enthusiasm to stimulate industrial cooperation.

The Commission's dilemma may reflect a larger European one. As one commentator notes, European countries tend to practice a linear approach to innovation in which each phase of the technological process (discovery, applied research, prototype development, and eventually

---

[59]Enrichment improved the neutron quality of the reactor fuel, and ORGEL's fuel (uranium carbide) responded better to enrichment than the fuel (uranium oxide) of competing types.

[60]Euratom, *Proceedings of the ORGEL Symposium*, chap. 10, p. 2.

[61]France had opposed earlier suggestions that ORGEL switch to enriched uranium. It also opposed Euratom support for the Italian PRO and CIRENE projects which employed enriched uranium.

marketing) is pursued independently and sequentially.[62] When one phase is completed, only then is the next phase begun. The alternative to this approach is an integrated method, practiced most extensively in the United States. The idea behind this method is to cultivate industrial prototype support in the initial research phase and to map out marketing strategies during the prototype construction phase.[63] In Europe, the roadblock to this alternative is not only conceptual but structural. Universities are isolated from industry; government laboratories function apart from corporate laboratories; and financial institutions are closer in ideology and business practice to traditional sectors of the economy than to innovative sectors. That a Community institution, conspicuously devoid of industrial powers, was unable to surmount these obstacles is less surprising than symptomatic.

ORGEL Is Orphaned

After 1965, ORGEL's rivals absorbed whatever interest remained in Europe in heavy water reactors. Despite the generation squeeze, political support operated to keep these rivals alive.

In Germany, the MZFR reactor went critical in September 1965. This variant achieved some degree of commercial success when, in 1968, a government-utility group in Atucha, Argentina, ordered from Siemens a 300 MWe heavy water plant (the maximum size considered feasible for the pressure vessel variant). This sale was not concluded, however, without generous government financing and balance-of-payments considerations.[64] The AKB project in Germany (pressure tubes and gas cooling) also survived for political reasons.[65] Experiencing problems with the fuel-cladding materials, this project, by all technical estimates, should have been dropped. But too much government money had already been invested. Thus, with government backing, Siemens ordered in 1966 the beginning of construction of a small prototype reactor, KKN. To reduce costs and risks, Siemens sought cooperation with foreign partners.[66]

[62]Jacques Defay, "Technological Collaboration in Europe," in *European Technological Collaboration*, A report of a conference sponsored by the Federal Trust in London, September 16–17, 1969 (London: Federal Trust, 1969).

[63]A good example of how this is done is given by the German fast reactor program. See chap. 8 of this study.

[64]*Industriekurier*, March 21, 1968. Moreover, despite the emphasis on the independence of this reactor variant, Siemens had to acquire the heavy water for the Atucha plant from the U.S. Further commercial exploitation of heavy water systems would require Europe's own heavy water plant. *Nucleonics Week*, May 2, 1968.

[65]This project was initiated by Siemens in March 1959 as a back-up program to the pressure vessel, MZFR reactor.

[66]These discussions involved the French consortium, SOCIA, and the Swiss firm, Sulzer, on heavy water cooling and the Swedish company, ASEA, on boiling light water cooling.

In France, EL-4 came on line in December 1966, but only after the first fuel core had been slightly enriched. The need for enrichment sharply reduced the advantages of heavy water reactors compared to light water systems. To study alternatives to enrichment, therefore, France looked for outside assistance. Talks with Germany culminated in a joint bid for the construction of an MZFR-type reactor in Rumania,[67] but political considerations prevented France from adopting the German variant in its own program. Discussions with Canada led to an agreement in October 1968 calling for an eighteen-month study of the economic prospects of the main Canadian heavy water variant (heavy water–cooled with pressure tubes).[68] Still, the chances of actually constructing a first commercial-size heavy water reactor in France depended on French policy toward light water reactors.[69] When France decided in 1970 to build light water plants, heavy water plans were once again put on the back burner.

Italy's heavy water program also limped along. CNEN and ENEL reached agreement in July 1967 to construct a small CIRENE prototype (35 MWe), but administrative and technical difficulties delayed start-up of this project for several years.

A Tidy Burial

As time went on, advances in light water and fast reactors progressively reduced the chances that heavy water systems might reach the market stage. In these circumstances, ORGEL could expect little more than a tidy burial. By the end of 1966, ORGEL's directors had recognized this fact. Backing down from schemes to involve Euratom directly in a prototype project, they proposed to transfer ORGEL's technical results to industry to allow the preparation of a prototype design under realistic commercial conditions. If several industrial groups responded, a competition might be stimulated, with a cash prize awarded the group with the best design.

It is doubtful that this proposal was meant to catalyze an industrial commitment to prototype construction. The design competition meant another year of preliminary studies, and this delay was hardly justified in view of already lagging information on the economic performance of ORGEL. Moreover, without a commitment to construct a prototype at the prices quoted (which the competition did not require), industries

---

[67]Under Russian pressure, Rumania could not accept the Franco-German bid. Siemens-SOCIA ties ended subsequently when Babcock, the firm that handled heavy water activities for SOCIA, merged with Atlantique and became a part of the rival consortium, GAAA.

[68]Le Monde, October 17, 1968. The French-Canadian agreement was concluded without consultation with the Commission, following France's policy after 1964 to ignore Euratom's authority in the field of external relations.

[69]Le Monde, May 7, 1968.

were not likely to submit realistic estimates. Instead, Commission personnel were looking for some way to keep ORGEL alive until the new multiple-year plan began in 1968.[70] Morale among Euratom scientists at Ispra was dangerously low, and Commission directors sought to prevent a cutback until a formal, political decision was taken with regard to Euratom. So tense was the situation in Brussels that the Council would have probably vetoed the industrial design competition, if the Commission had not salvaged funds for this proposal from the 1966 budget and avoided the need to request new funds.[71]

Only one industrial group responded to the design competition, the same consortium that constructed ESSOR (GAAA/Interatom/Montedison, the latter formed by merger of Montecatini and Edison in 1964). This group was apparently motivated by the desire to tidy up work on ESSOR and bring the ORGEL experiment to an acceptable scientific conclusion. None of these firms exerted any pressure on national governments to continue support of ORGEL. After 1965 Interatom and GAAA were fully absorbed in fast reactor development.[72]

The Legacy of ORGEL

With ORGEL dead except for the final rites, questions remained concerning future use of ORGEL facilities, in particular, the reactor ESSOR. The process of bringing this reactor to full power began in 1967, but by now, the difficulties of recruiting staff and shifting people within the JNRC were so great that almost two years were required to complete this job, which normally takes only one year. The budget approved in December 1968 did not even make provision for the commissioning and operation of the organic loop in ESSOR. ESSOR reached full power in 1969 with only a boiling light water loop constructed for the CIRENE program.[73]

The future of ESSOR was tied to the larger issue of what would happen to the Ispra center and the JNRC in general (in this period, renamed JRC). In June 1969 the Council formally terminated the ORGEL project. This decision marked the passing of the original concept of the JNRC, which saw these laboratories as major centers for the cooperative development of big technologies. Events since 1969 have witnessed the progressive conversion of Ispra and JRC activities to small-scale, basic

---

[70]Leny, "Le projet Orgel," p. 411.

[71]Belgium, in particular, had become an adamant opponent of any continuation of ORGEL, as much from anger over French policy during the Common Market crisis as from a greater interest in high temperature than heavy water reactors. *Agence Europe*, May 21, 1968.

[72]The ESSOR experience was not entirely lost, however. GAAA and Interatom continued their association and went on to win the contract for the Franco-German high flux reactor constructed at Grenoble.

[73]Leny and Orlowski, *The ORGEL Project 1959–1969*, pp. 23–24.

research projects, public service studies, and actions assisting the Commission in the performance of Community functions. The largest items in the new multiple-year program (four years) approved for the JRC in February 1973 included reactor safety studies, nuclear measurement programs, environmental studies, and management of Euratom controls on fissile materials. The same agreement provided for Italy to take over the ESSOR reactor and Belgium to assume responsibility for the operation of the BR-2 reactor at Mol.[74]

These decisions completed the withdrawal of Community laboratories from direct reactor programs. In the future, as a statement in 1973 by Mr. Dahrendorf, the new commissioner in charge of research, suggests, the JRC must confine its field of action to "high risk research still far remote from any industrial exploitation."[75] Even in these areas, it is unlikely that direct actions will increase (i.e., actions performed within Community laboratories). The expansion of Community activities will lead in the first instance to indirect actions, involving placement of contracts outside the JRC. As we discover in the next two chapters, effective use of this method of cooperation, especially through association contracts, presupposes close coordination of industrial policies and programs. Until the Community makes greater progress toward the formulation of a common industrial policy, indirect actions may only contribute to a further aggravation of technological nationalism.

For the moment, the JRC has been isolated, as the only way of insuring its continued survival.[76] What comes after is still uncertain. The Community concept today is dormant. ORGEL's plight symbolizes the loss in Europe of "a profound common motivation to forge ahead."[77] An institutional legacy remains, both at Ispra and in Brussels; but this

[74]Press release of the Council of the European Communities, General Secretariat, 262e/73 (Presse 18), Brussels, February 6, 1973. Before acquiring ESSOR, Italian participation at Ispra increased substantially. Beginning in 1966–67 with the difficulties the Commission encountered in finding qualified personnel to operate ESSOR, Italian employees filled the gap left by the departure of Ispra staff. Industrial engineers withdrew from Ispra with the completion of ESSOR. Frenchmen left Ispra to find a new home in national programs. Germans resisted assignment to the often criticized Community center. Italians, anticipating acquisition of ORGEL facilities, were the only interested recruits. By 1969, Italian personnel constituted over 60 percent of all Ispra employees.

[75]Commission of the European Communities, *Working Program in the Field of Research, Science and Education*, A personal statement by Mr. Dahrendorf (SEC 73 2000/2) (Brussels, May 23, 1973), p. 20.

[76]The decision (noted in chap. 4) to give the JRC greater autonomy by locating the general director at Ispra and having him answer directly to the Commission was more a step to insulate Ispra from Community warfare in Brussels than to upgrade the JRC. This decision, it should be noted, confirmed the arrangement requested by Ritter in 1959 to make Ispra more independent of the Brussels bureaucracy and reflected, in particular, the German desire to see that the JRC not be used to support centralized policies in Brussels.

[77]Leny and Orlowski, *The ORGEL Project 1959–1969*, p. 44.

legacy alone will not sustain the Community. The element of pride and self-purpose is missing. Leaving Ispra in May 1970, this writer was struck by the overgrown and unkempt condition of the roads and landscape. In comparison to the manicured lawns of the numerous national centers he had visited, this seemed a fitting reminder of the gap between the visions and vicissitudes of research cooperation in Western Europe.

CHAPTER 7

THE DEVELOPMENT OF HIGH TEMPERATURE GAS REACTORS: COOPERATION WITH GREAT BRITAIN

One of the two legs of the Euratom high temperature gas reactor program was the DRAGON project, carried out jointly with Great Britain (and several minor partners) under the auspices of the ENEA.[1] At the inauguration of the DRAGON reactor in 1964, the Secretary-General of OECD described this project in glowing terms. "I see in the success of DRAGON," he said, "an augury which points to international co-operation as a realistic and feasible method for carrying out technological developments."[2] Some years later, a long-time student of European technological affairs called DRAGON "one of the few bright stars in the sombre European nuclear sky."[3] These appraisals suggest that the development of high temperature reactors experienced a somewhat happier history than other Euratom programs. If true, this history may reveal the ingredients of successful international cooperation; it may also provide insights into the future of European technological relations now that Great Britain is a full member of the European Community.

Before beginning, however, it is fair to note two unique features of DRAGON and high temperature reactor development. First, DRAGON was blessed by being implemented outside the Community in Winfrith, England, and by being comfortably remote from commercial applications. The first circumstance shielded DRAGON, to some extent, from the crush and caprice of internal Community politics; and the second gave it a low enough profile to avoid the polemics of British membership negotiations. DRAGON had neither the internal significance of ORGEL nor the external significance of the Euratom-U.S. joint program. Second, DRAGON benefited from more favorable technical and economic prospects than ORGEL. Whereas ORGEL was adversely affected by circumstances in the U.S. program, DRAGON received support at a critical moment from technical developments in the United

---

[1]The other leg was the German AVR/THTR project. See further discussion.
[2]See *AWRE News*, December 1964, p. 22.
[3]Christopher Layton, *European Advanced Technology* (London: George Allen and Unwin, 1969), p. 122.

States. High temperature reactors also have a better chance for commercial success, benefiting from the earlier requirement for nuclear power caused by the energy crisis. Though being intermediate reactors like heavy water systems, they attract wider interest because their higher temperatures permit the production of process heat for industrial use as well as electricity generation. High outlet temperatures also permit the eventual use of a direct cycle, helium turbine system which dispenses with heat exchange equipment (used in normal gas-cooled high temperature systems which transfer heat to a secondary steam cycle) and vastly reduces capital costs of high temperature plants. High temperature systems have the additional advantage of minimizing undesirable environmental effects.

DRAGON's success may also reflect an ironic political characteristic of effective international cooperation. The project was strongly dominated by British manpower as well as British technology. A dominant partner facilitates control and continuity in cooperative undertakings. The United States played this role in the joint program, which achieved technical and commercial success even in the face of political controversy. No one was able to play this role in the heavy water and fast reactor programs, which may explain, in part, the greater difficulties of cooperation in these programs.

The role of a dominant participant may also prove critical in commercial areas. Dominant industries, such as American firms in the light water sector, supply the incentive and institutional basis of cooperation. A dominant industrial partner, therefore, may be required to push high temperature reactors into the commercial phase. Recent developments described at the end of this chapter find the American firm, Gulf General Atomic, assuming a commanding role in the consolidation of European industries to manufacture and sell these reactors.

The Program Definition Phase

DRAGON was originally a British undertaking. In one respect, the internationalization of this project resembled that of the U.S. light water program under the Euratom-U.S. joint agreement. In the mid-1950s, the domestic development of civilian nuclear power in the United States was a low priority program. In 1958, the development of high temperature gas reactors in the United Kingdom was also a low priority program. (See below.) In both cases, this fact contributed to the willingness of the two countries to internationalize these programs. In another respect, the incentives for internationalizing the two programs were profoundly different. The United States sought to affirm the concept of nuclear unity in Europe, albeit in a form that would emphasize the technical rather than political potential of Euratom. Great Britain hoped to dilute this concept by supporting a looser nuclear grouping under the auspices of the OEEC.[4] Known as ENEA, this grouping included other European countries and challenged the political exclusiveness of Euratom's "little six." Through British initiatives, DRAGON became the top priority project of ENEA.

Wedded to both integration and openness, the Euratom Commission welcomed both opportunities of cooperation. In time, however, the Community's support of external programs acquired internal critics: France, because of its interest in gas graphite systems, eventually opposed the joint program, which emphasized light water reactors; and Germany, which developed its own unique pebble-bed high temperature gas reactor fuel design, eventually opposed DRAGON, which employed a competing prismatic fuel design.

Origins of DRAGON

It was not surprising that the high temperature concept should appear first in Great Britain, the country with the most ambitious gas graphite program. This concept offered several important advantages over first-generation, gas graphite reactors, as well as a number of unique problems.[5] To explore some of these problems, the UKAEA assembled in 1956 a small team of scientists at the Harwell research center. Within several months, this team submitted proposals for construction of a reactor experiment known as DRAGON. The proposals were interesting but ran into stiff competition for funds with other reactor concepts being pursued by the UKAEA (advanced gas reactors,

[4]Harold L. Nieburg, *Nuclear Secrecy and Foreign Policy* (Washington, D.C.: Public Affairs Press, 1964), p. 130; Jeroslav G. Polach, *Euratom: Its Background, Issues and Economic Implications* (Dobbs Ferry: Oceana, 1964), pp. 130–31; Klaus E. Knorr, *Nuclear Energy in Western Europe and United States Policy* (Memorandum No. 9; Princeton: Princeton University, Center of International Studies, September 10, 1956), pp. 11–12. British support, even for this loose grouping, was never wholehearted.

[5]With high temperature reactors, one can achieve an outlet temperature more than twice as high as that of proven reactors, including light water reactors (approximately 800–850 degrees centigrade compared to 300 degrees centigrade). The higher temperature vastly improves the efficiency of power production. Beyond a certain point, however, these temperatures become superfluous for power production and create the possibility of using excess heat for industrial purposes (process steam or vaporization of brown coal, etc.). The only way to exploit the full power potential of temperatures projected as high as 1300 degrees centigrade is to convert to direct turbine drive. This possiblity has given rise to recent experiments with single-cycle helium turbine systems. (See subsequent discussion in text of Geesthacht reactor concept developed by German firm, GHH.)

A second advantage is that high temperature reactors, because of their greater efficiency, permit a considerable reduction in core size, which, in turn, lowers initial investment costs. Higher capital costs of gas graphite systems constituted a primary disadvantage of these systems compared to light water reactors. (See chap. 5, notes 36 and 56.)

Higher temperatures also create several problems, however. The high temperatures melt any metallic substance in the reactor core. Hence, a nonmetallic cladding material has to be found to contain errant fission products from the fuel elements. Or a dynamic flow process must be designed to remove these fission products continuously from the reactive zone. Finally, a cooling gas has to be found which remains inert at high operating temperatures. For more on these technical matters, see the Appendix.

fast reactors, and other systems).[6] In face of this competition, DRAGON plans were postponed, though some research work continued. For a time, interest dropped so low that the project was referred to as "DRAG-ON." Several members of the Harwell team, including the director, emigrated to the United States to join the high temperature program of General Atomic, a division of General Dynamics Corporation.[7]

Great Britain may have had plans to revive the national program once commitments to other reactor systems were satisfied. On the other hand, the initial lack of government support may have been intentional. High temperature reactors utilized enriched uranium, and the British program at the time stressed independent, natural uranium concepts. In either case, as it was carefully expressed later on, "the idea gained ground that the high temperature gas-cooled reactor might be an important subject for a collaborative programme within the then O.E.E.C. framework."[8] Cooperation reduced individual costs and risks to the British program and still allowed significant work to be done on the DRAGON concept.[9] In addition, given British attitudes toward the continent, there were political as well as technical benefits to be derived from cooperation.

DRAGON Is Internationalized

As Miriam Camps points out, Great Britain declined to participate in nuclear integration on the continent.[10] Because the British program was clearly more advanced than those of the Euratom countries, cooperation with Europe seemed to entail few advantages while risking the potential disadvantage of encouraging British competitors. Like so many French calculations, of course, this British assessment overlooked the value of exploiting a technological lead by making potential competitors dependent on one's own technology. Both Great Britain and France lost this opportunity to the United States.

---

[6]See remarks of the British official who became chief executive of the DRAGON project, L. R. Shepherd, "The Ten Years of DRAGON," *Atom*, No. 154 (August 1969), p. 223.

[7]Ten years later, the chief executive of DRAGON was asked if the departure of these scientists had been one of the more costly features of Britain's brain drain. The British émigrés contributed significantly to the similar and rival program the U.S. developed in high temperature systems. See *Financial Times*, June 25, 1969.

[8]Shepherd, "The Ten Years of DRAGON," p. 223.

[9]For example, after DRAGON was internationalized, the UKAEA cut back the proportion of its staff engaged in high temperature work from 18 to 12 percent while maintaining the proportion involved in fast reactor work at 36–38 percent. See Kenneth Green, "The DRAGON Project—a Case Study of International Cooperation in Science" (unpublished manuscript obtained from the DRAGON Project), June 1970, p. 17.

[10]Miriam Camps, *Britain and the European Community, 1955–1963* (Princeton: Princeton University Press, 1964), pp. 48–49.

To insure that nuclear unity on the continent did not work to Britain's disadvantage, the United Kingdom proposed the establishment of a rival organization under the auspices of the OEEC and initiated discussions to carry out joint construction of experimental reactors within this organization.[11] In 1957 the ENEA was established; and, in March 1958, the UKAEA recommended to this agency that the DRAGON project become a joint European undertaking to be located at the Winfrith center in England.[12]

The Euratom Commission, representing the Euratom countries in ENEA, saw both political and technical merits in this proposal. On the political side, the Commission did not perceive the ENEA as a rival to Euratom. In fact, the Commission welcomed this institution as a means of keeping communications with Great Britain open. Perhaps, in time, Great Britain would accept and even affirm nuclear cooperation on the continent. Furthermore, just as cooperation with the United States enhanced the political image of the new Commission, cooperation with Great Britain, the only other Western nuclear power at the time, also added to the Community's prestige. On the technical side, certain Commission officials, including Jules Guéron, Euratom's research director, had close personal contact with the British program. They appreciated the technical advantages of the high temperature concept and would have considered it unfortunate if Great Britain had been forced to drop this program.

The Italian commissioner of Euratom voiced some reservations.[13] He felt that Community funds might be better spent organizing and building up the Community's own research centers. Aside from national self-interests (the Community center at Ispra was being negotiated at the same time), the Italian commissioner may have also been responding to the fact that Euratom research officials seemed to have greater interest and knowledge of American and British programs in this period than the incipient programs of some Community countries, especially Germany and Italy. As we noted in chapter 4, the charge was not totally unfounded. Yet Italy had as much to gain from contacts with advanced partners as other Euratom countries (and more to gain in a technical sense, given its weaker position). What Italy wanted was a limitation on

---

[11]*Ibid.*, pp. 50–51 and 93–94; also Nieburg, *Nuclear Secrecy and Foreign Policy*, p. 136. The rival character of ENEA was accented by remarks of Pierre Huet, director of the group that organized ENEA. The purpose of ENEA, as Huet put it, was "to inject some realism . . . and to get away from continental Europe's frenzied determination for total self-sufficiency in [reactor] design construction and fuel fabrication." See Warren B. Walsh, *Science and International Public Affairs: Six Recent Experiments in International Scientific Cooperation* (Syracuse: Maxwell School of Syracuse University, International Relations Program, 1967), p. 39.

[12]DRAGON High Temperature Reactor Project, *First Annual Report: 1959–60*, pp. 12–13.

[13]Interview with member of Euratom negotiating team, Paris, March 17, 1970.

outside spending. In the DRAGON negotiations, Italy forced a ceiling on Euratom contributions. Under Commission urging, France and Germany agreed to pay any cost overruns.[14]

None of the other Euratom countries expressed particular enthusiasm or opposition toward the DRAGON project, a fact which considerably eased the task of the Commission in concluding this agreement. For these countries, high temperature systems were interesting only in the long-run; and, even then, unlike fast reactors, there was no assurance that intermediate reactors would be needed at all, since the generation squeeze might eliminate the requirement for them. Only France and Germany had the resources to take these long-run possibilities into account and include high temperature reactors in early planning.

France, like Great Britain, followed high temperature studies as a long-term sequel to gas graphite reactors. But, also like Great Britain, France disliked the enrichment feature except for possible use in ship propulsion reactors.[15] French interest, therefore, was remote enough, yet reasonable enough, to support an international program. Moreover, France may have had political reasons for backing cooperation with Great Britain. With a nascent atomic weapons program, France might benefit from association with the only other Western country, besides the United States, with nuclear capabilities.

Germany was the only Community country with concrete ambitions in the high temperature field. Under the first German nuclear program in 1957, the federal government granted support to a group of fifteen small utilities in the area of Duesseldorf to build a test reactor, AVR. Searching for a reactor design suitable to the needs of small utilities, AVR directors came into contact with Rudolf Schulten, a young physicist working for BBK (the joint subsidiary of BBC and Krupp established in 1958). Schulten had just designed a high temperature reactor employing a unique pebble-bed fuel concept. Otherwise similar to DRAGON, Schulten's reactor used spherical bullet-type fuel elements instead of conventional fuel rods (the DRAGON fuel design being referred to as the prismatic concept). This feature permitted the continuous loading and unloading of fuel while the reactor remained in operation. Costly and time-consuming shutdowns were thereby avoided. AVR was negotiating a contract with BBK when Euratom proposed participation in the DRAGON project.

The AVR design bore the earmarks of a future competitor to DRAGON. Considerations of competition and, to some extent, national

---

[14]Interview with Euratom official, Brussels, September 15, 1970. This issue was the cause of the delay in DRAGON negotiations in December 1958. See *Agence Europe*, December 6, 1958.

[15]CEA, *Rapport Annuel: 1957*, p. 11. This report discussed the possibility of a reactor experiment, BRENDA, to test the high temperature design for marine propulsion. Temperatures envisioned, however, were lower than those anticipated in DRAGON.

chauvinism were not absent from its original conception.[16] Still, in 1958, Germany had more to gain from cooperation than competition with DRAGON. The larger and politically more significant ENEA project provided useful psychological and technical justification for the AVR program, which still needed to win wider domestic support. In addition, many groups in Germany (especially the Economic and Atomic Ministries) had supported, along with Great Britain, the OEEC proposals for a more decentralized approach to nuclear cooperation in Europe. For these groups, association with DRAGON offered political advantages. A joint effort with Great Britain could serve to check centralizing tendencies in Euratom, even though the latter was a weak version of the tightly integrated community originally proposed by Monnet supranationalists.

The DRAGON Agreement

Thus, the low priority of high temperature studies, the relatively free hand the Commission exercised in this early stage, and differing but converging political interests in France and Germany combined to bring about speedy negotiation of the DRAGON agreement. Signed in March 1959 by Euratom, Great Britain, and five other countries (Norway, Sweden, Denmark, Austria, and Switzerland), the agreement covered a five-year period and called for programs of research and construction of a high temperature reactor experiment known as DRAGON (20 MWth). A total of $38 million was appropriated, with the United Kingdom and Euratom contributing equal amounts (43.4 percent) to the first $28 million and the United Kingdom covering the last $10 million. The latter provision took account of the fact that the reactor and other equipment constructed under the program would revert to British ownership at the end of the five-year agreement. The agreement also set up a Board of Management to supervise the program. Voting was apportioned according to financial contributions, with decisions requiring a two-thirds majority. This gave the two principal participants, Great Britain and Euratom, an effective veto.[17]

---

[16]AVR was a part of the emphasis in Germany's first nuclear plan on unique German concepts. In 1959, Professor Schulten observed that "the idea of the pebble-bed high temperature gas reactor was born in Germany and Germany must do all in its power to preserve the present advantage it has achieved in this field." Then, as well as later, the German press frequently referred to the Schulten reactor as the "only pure German development in the nuclear reactor field." *Westdeutsche Allgemeine*, June 28, 1968.

[17]Euratom could seat three representatives on the Board of Management. These representatives usually included a Commission staff member and one official each from France and Germany, the two countries which had agreed to cover cost overruns of the Community's share in DRAGON. For a copy of the DRAGON agreement, see DRAGON, *First Annual Report: 1959–60*, Appendix I.

The R&D Phase

The developmental stage of the DRAGON program benefited from association with a dominant partner (Great Britain) without falling victim to the close tie between research and nuclear power construction which plagued the Euratom-U.S. joint program. As in the case of the joint program, relying on a dominant partner insured the rapid take-off of research and avoided the delays encountered in ORGEL where the institutions and procedures of research had to be established from scratch. Moreover, the basically experimental character of DRAGON, compared to the quasi-commercial character of the joint program, enabled it to survive the sudden loss of interest in commercial nuclear power after 1958. DRAGON did have to compete with other research priorities, especially in Britain, and toward the end of the initial five-year program, DRAGON also encountered growing competition from the German AVR project for scarce funds. Within Euratom, German officials sought the same treatment for internal projects as that being accorded foreign projects (much as French officials sought the same treatment for local gas graphite systems as that received by foreign light water technology in the proven reactor sector). Nevertheless, minor adjustments in 1962 permitted the expansion and extension of DRAGON. Even the arrangement in 1964 for a Euratom association with the German program did not seem to affect support for DRAGON. In fact, the incorporation of the German project into the Community program established, for a time, effective liaison between DRAGON and German investigators. As industrial issues began to intervene, however, competition between the two programs intensified. To some extent, this competition was the outgrowth of commitments already undertaken at the national level during the R&D phase.

Ingredients of Success

While some time was lost in starting up the DRAGON program, "none of the delay," as the DRAGON research director noted, "could be attributed directly to problems arising from multi-national participation."[18] The smoothness of transition from a British to an international project, as well as the coherent development of DRAGON throughout the R&D phase, was owing, in large part, to two important factors: (1) the predominant role of British manpower and institutions, particularly industry, in the execution of DRAGON and (2) the advantages of the legal and personnel statutes under which DRAGON operated.

British authorities exercised a formal role in DRAGON through the same institutions (e.g., the Board of Management and the General Pur-

[18]See Shepherd, "The Ten Years of DRAGON," p. 224. Shepherd became chief executive of DRAGON in 1968.

pose Committee, a group of senior technical specialists from each member-country assisting the Board on technical and administrative matters) as other participants. At the highest levels, therefore, the international character of the project was preserved. At the administrative level, however, British participants dominated. The chief executive appointed by the Board to supervise daily activities was British; seven of fourteen top staff personnel were British.[19] British participants were even more numerous at the middle-level and junior positions. U.K. employees never totaled less than 70 percent of all DRAGON personnel and in certain departments, such as administration, averaged as high as 90 percent.[20] Familiar with UKAEA procedures under which DRAGON operated, these personnel added coherence and confidence to DRAGON's development. In contrast to ORGEL, no time was lost developing new contract and patent procedures.

One consequence of this predominance was the disproportionate distribution of contracts to British industries. Excluding contracts for services and civil construction (which are always let to local firms), Britain's share of total contracts by value through 1969 equaled 60 percent, compared to 21 percent for Euratom countries.[21] There was nothing illicit about this imbalance, though some German circles insinuated as much from time to time.[22] The imbalance was a simple consequence of the British origins and basis of DRAGON. Administratively, it was also DRAGON's greatest asset. The use of British industries and procedures made it easier for DRAGON to monitor contract proposals and implementation and to insure that this work related directly to DRAGON and not peripheral scientific activities. The problems ORGEL directors faced in accomplishing this same task at Ispra are well known from the previous chapter.

In contrast to ORGEL, which was carried out in Community laboratories by permanent Community officials, DRAGON operated more like an association contract (which the Commission used to participate in the AVR program—see subsequent discussion—and the fast reactor

[19]See article by DRAGON's first chief executive, C. A. Rennie, "O.E.E.C. High Temperature Reactor Project (DRAGON)," *Nuclear Engineering* (July 1960), p. 199.

[20]See, for example, DRAGON, *Second Annual Report: 1960–61*, p. 79; *Eighth Annual Report: 1966–67*, p. 131; and *Thirteenth Annual Report: 1971–72*, p. 125.

[21]Green, "The DRAGON Project," p. 29.

[22]For example, the publication of the German Research Service (Deutscher Forschungsdienst) complained about the low share of Euratom contracts in the DRAGON program and, in particular, the low proportion of this share coming to Germany. By the end of 1961 only one contract of thirty in Euratom had been received by German industry, this one albeit a significant one for the DRAGON reactor pressure vessel. By 1964, Germany had received only 15 percent of the Euratom share of research contracts and only 24 percent of the reactor construction contracts. By contrast, France got 40 and 45 percent respectively of the Euratom share. These percentages, however, were more the result of a preoccupation in Germany with its own high temperature project, AVR, than a deliberate political partiality on the part of DRAGON or Euratom officials. See *Sonderbericht Kernenergie*, November 30, 1961, and October 8, 1964.

programs—see chapter 8). Research was done in national (in this case, British) laboratories where existing equipment and expertise facilitated continuity. In addition, personnel with the DRAGON project remained employees of their parent organizations.[23] They were assigned to DRAGON on a temporary basis either as representatives of the signatory parties (e.g., the Euratom Commission) or as representatives of private parties seconded by the signatory parties (e.g., an employee of BBK seconded by the Commission). This arrangement immensely facilitated the free flow of personnel to and from DRAGON. After assignments with DRAGON, individuals returned to former jobs without loss of pay or status. Moreover, they often returned to original employers as advocates of or, at least, knowledgeable spokesmen for the DRAGON concept, a circumstance which was likely someday to ease the transition of DRAGON to the commercial stage. The setup had obvious advantages over the Ispra and ORGEL programs, where Euratom had to institute a permanent employment status for Community personnel. This system was highly inflexible (as ORGEL officials discovered, for example, in trying to find qualified people to operate ESSOR) and imposed costly pension and career programs on the Community.[24]

Implementation of the DRAGON agreement differed from the association contracts in two respects. First, it was decided not to create a new legal personality for DRAGON. All legal responsibilities were vested in the UKAEA, whereas Euratom and national nuclear agencies shared these responsibilities in the case of association contracts. This arrangement simplified the formal procedures connected with DRAGON, especially in the area of contracts.[25] Second, and more important, the Euratom countries utilized the flexible provisions for personnel assignments to DRAGON, while these provisions were all but ignored in the case of the association contracts (see chapter 8, note 27). Of the individuals seconded to DRAGON by Euratom, one-half came from organizations (industries, national research centers, etc.) other than the Commission.[26] The spirited participation of these groups reflected, in part, the relatively remote industrial character of DRAGON

[23]The parent organizations continued to pay their salaries but were reimbursed by DRAGON according to an agreed salary schedule. In this way, individuals retained superannuation rights and long-term career opportunities with original employers.

[24]At one point in 1969 when the dismissal of large numbers of Ispra personnel was being discussed, the Commission estimated that it would cost the Community almost $100 million in employee compensations just to close down the Ispra center.

[25]The legal nature of DRAGON was not unique. Euratom participated in the HALDEN project, whose legal personality was exercised by the Norwegian Institute of Atomic Energy. On the other hand, Eurochemic, another ENEA project, was established with a separate legal personality in the form of a joint company owned by thirteen separate participants.

[26]Interview with Euratom official, Brussels, September 15, 1970. The numbers cannot be verified exactly from DRAGON Annual Reports because these reports do not distinguish, except in later years (when Community industrial participants outnumbered Commission personnel), between Commission and non-Commission personnel.

research. Participants were less conscious of commercial obstacles to the exchange of ideas and information. In addition, except for Germany (and its program was relatively small until 1964–65), member-states had no significant programs of their own in the high temperature field.

Beyond this, however, there is a political explanation for Community cooperation in DRAGON. The only other Euratom program to experience a fruitful exchange of personnel was the participation program.[27] Ironically, this program (except for one gas graphite reactor, which did not attract many outside participants) and DRAGON both focused on foreign technologies. Pressures toward commercial competition are apparently felt more strongly between countries within the Community than with countries outside the Community. When their own technologies are involved (as in the case of fast or heavy water reactors), the member-states behave with greater reserve toward one another. The pattern suggests a situation that has plagued industrial cooperation in Europe from the beginning of the nuclear (and Common Market, for that matter) experiment: economic rivalries are more intense inside Europe than between Europe and outside countries.

Expansion and Extension of DRAGON

DRAGON not only benefited from a strong administration but also from important technical advances. As luck or fate determines, these advances came from the United States, where technical setbacks in the case of organic reactors had such deleterious effects on ORGEL. The USAEC high temperature program, under the guidance of emigrated British scientists, involved the construction of a reactor experiment (40 MWth) at Peach Bottom, Pennsylvania. In 1960 DRAGON officials concluded an agreement of exchange of information and personnel with the U.S. program.[28] This agreement soon returned significant dividends.

In 1959 several American companies intensified work on a new concept of coated fuel particles for high temperature reactors. The original DRAGON design dealt with the problem of errant fission products through a continuous process of bleeding and purifying the coolant. This process was clumsy and expensive. The new concept proposed to contain fission products by sheathing the fuel element with layers of carbon. The trick was to find a coating process that was effective yet did not reduce the neutron economy of the fuel. Because of the agreement with the United States, work on this problem came to the attention of

---

[27]As we noted in chap. 5, even the French, who strongly opposed this program, participated enthusiastically in the information exchange.

[28]DRAGON, *Second Annual Report: 1960–61*, pp. 60–61. The Peach Bottom reactor was being built by General Atomic for the Philadelphia Electric Company. The design used the same type of fuel (i.e., prismatic) as DRAGON.

DRAGON scientists in 1960.[29] DRAGON immediately set up its own research project on coated particles. By 1962 this research had achieved sufficient results to justify an official change in the DRAGON design.[30]

These developments forced a reassessment of the time schedule of DRAGON. Expected to diverge in 1963, the reactor would now become operational only in 1965. Desiring to experiment in the DRAGON reactor, and not just participate in its construction, the signatory parties favored an extension of the five-year agreement. In May 1961, the Board of Management proposed a three-year continuation through 1967.

The key issue in the extension proposal concerned allocation of financial shares.[31] Great Britain was eager to reduce its share. For several years, the British gas graphite program (Magnox) had progressed very slowly. The UKAEA was eager to step up domestic research on the advanced gas reactor (AGR), an intermediate design more sophisticated than the gas graphite system but less advanced than high temperature reactors.[32] Cutting back international obligations might release funds to revitalize domestic programs. Thus, in the DRAGON negotiations, British officials advocated a reduction of the cooperative research program and a concentration of expenditures on the operation of DRAGON.[33] This attitude was consistent with the United Kingdom's advanced technological position in high temperature reactors and reflected motivations similar to those which caused the United States to tie research to reactor construction in the joint program and France to seek commercial compensation for gas graphite exchanges in the participation program. The most advanced country in a research alignment has a principal interest in specific programs related immediately to commercial exploitation of technology. Less advanced partners prefer a broader-based research effort intended to circumvent and eventually surmount existing commercial imbalances. In this case, Britain wanted to get the most out of short-term experiments with DRAGON, while Britain's partners wanted to continue research on potential improvements of DRAGON as well as on preliminary design of longer-range power reactor concepts. At the same time, these partners were willing to accept some reduction of Britain's financial share, especially in view of the fact that, under the extension, ownership of the reactor would not revert to Britain at the end of 1964 as originally scheduled.

The revised agreement was signed in November 1962, extending cooperation through March 1967. The agreement raised total expenditures to $70 million, but Euratom now contributed 46 percent, while the

[29]*Ibid.*, p. 61.
[30]DRAGON, *Fourth Annual Report: 1962–63*, p. 30.
[31]*Agence Europe*, July 13, 1962, and September 28, 1962.
[32]*The Economist*, July 7, 1972; also *Nucleonics Week*, May 17, 1962.
[33]Euratom, *Report on the DRAGON Project* (EUR/C/745/62e) (Brussels: Euratom, n.d.).

British share dropped to 41 percent. The new program continued a significant research effort and included funds for the drafting of preliminary reference designs of large-scale power plants.[34]

The German Association—THTR

Extension of DRAGON was discussed during the preparation of Euratom's second five-year plan. In these discussions, Community members issued, for the first time, a potential challenge to Euratom's exclusive focus on non-Community technology in the high temperature field. France appeared, for a while, to seek Community support for a new high performance gas reactor (operating at intermediate rather than high temperatures).[35] Strapped by other priorities, however, France never pressed this demand. The important challenge came from Germany.

With federal support, the Duesseldorf utilities and BBK concluded a contract in August 1959 for construction of a 15 MWe high temperature reactor. To be located at the new research center at Juelich (known as KFA), this reactor employed the Schulten pebble-bed fuel concept. Schulten and his associates had been asked by Euratom officials in 1958 to join the Euratom team and work on Community high temperature projects. The German group, however, was committed to the national project.[36] Schulten and his associates were not unaware of the Science Ministry's *Faustregel* that favored national over international programs (see chapter 4, text and note 42). Since no one anticipated unmanageable costs at this point, the fledgling pebble-bed concept was thought to have a better chance to succeed as one of a few unique German designs than one of many Community projects. Also, in 1958, estimates gave the German concept a nine-month edge over British and American high temperature programs.[37]

The development of coated particles changed these estimates and forced the German project out of isolation. By 1960, AVR could no longer compare with DRAGON and Peach Bottom.[38] The collaborative agreement between the latter two projects threatened to add to Germany's disadvantage. Also, by 1961, Germany's advanced reactor programs needed Euratom funds, both to supplement immediate resources and to guarantee financial support over a longer time period (five years) than federal grants, which were limited to annual appropriations.[39] This

[34]For a copy of this agreement, see DRAGON, *Fourth Annual Report: 1962–63*, Appendix 4.

[35]*Agence Europe*, May 23, 1961.

[36]Interview with German official, Juelich, September 24, 1970; interview with Euratom official, Paris, March 17, 1970.

[37]See estimates reported by *Nucleonics*, August 1958, p. 24.

[38]Deutscher Forschungsdienst, *Sonderbericht Kernenergie*, September 27, 1960.

[39]The KFA center at Juelich was in particular financial straits by virtue of the diversion of state (*Land*) funds to other priorities and the still minor role of federal grants in the over-all budget. See *Mannheimer Morgen*, March 17, 1962; and *Main-Post* (Wuerzburg), May 17, 1962.

requirement coincided with the German government's desire to redress the low percentage of Euratom contracts placed in Germany. Taken together, these factors prompted German officials to request in 1962 an association agreement with Euratom. The contents of the proposed program were vague, but German delegates left no doubt that the scale of this program must be large, around $16 million, with Euratom's share equaling 40 percent.[40]

At the time, the Commission envisioned a total program closer to $10 million (Euratom contribution $3 to 4 million) and hoped to avoid a drastic dispersion of resources between DRAGON and the German association. German pressure, however, was not to be denied. The second five-year budget set aside $25 million of Euratom funds for high temperature studies, $10 million of which was intended for the German program.

Though approved in 1962, these funds were not incorporated into a formal association contract until May 1964. The negotiations which took place between these dates were difficult and complex.[41] German policies in these negotiations paralleled policies pursued simultaneously in fast reactor negotiations (see chapter 8). Government negotiators deferred to the influence of private German groups, especially industry; government and industrial parties dealt bilaterally with the USAEC as well as U.S. industry as a means of exerting leverage on Euratom; and German industries carefully safeguarded potentially valuable commercial information. The purpose of these policies, as in the fast reactor and participation program negotiations, was to secure Euratom funds without compromising industrial freedom or becoming too dependent on what was perceived as a French-dominated Brussels bureaucracy.

The negotiations took place in two phases. During the first phase, BBK, the private utilities purchasing AVR, and the German Science Ministry negotiated with the USAEC for delivery of coated fuel particles. Once again, the USAEC found itself in an enviable negotiating position. It agreed to provide the first fuel core for AVR on condition that U.S.-manufactured fuel be given priority rights to irradiation tests in the AVR reactor for the equivalent of two full power years.[42] These tests would have monopolized the AVR reactor until the end of 1967. Euratom officials found such conditions unacceptable, since one of the purposes of the German association, from the Community's point of view, was to develop and test coated particles manufactured in Europe.

Disagreement on this issue led to a change in focus of the cooperative program. AVR dropped out of the discussions, and KFA directors proposed a new program of research and fuel studies aimed at a prototype

---

[40] *Agence Europe*, March 12, 1962.

[41] The details of these negotiations were obtained by the author in interviews with various Euratom and German officials, including subsequent correspondence with some of these individuals.

[42] *Nucleonics Week*, April 30, 1964.

reference design of a high temperature reactor operating on a thorium-uranium fuel cycle, THTR.[43] Euratom and KFA reached agreement on a total sum of $25 million for this program; but in early 1964, AVR requested additional funds to cover construction difficulties encountered with heat exchangers. Euratom did not want to contribute to the capital costs of AVR. Hence, Germany took $5 million from its commitment to THTR and gave it to AVR, leaving Euratom and Germany contributing equal shares to the association program of $10 million each.

After the agreement was signed, arrangements still had to be worked out with AVR and the USAEC. The THTR program required use of the AVR reactor and, in early 1965, THTR officials succeeded in working out a contract with the private utilities for operational use of AVR. A subsequent agreement with the USAEC also modified earlier American proposals, permitting fuel not manufactured in the United States to be tested in AVR intermittently with U.S. fuel.[44]

As a result of these complications, Euratom contributed a larger proportional share to the THTR association (50 percent) than other associations (35 percent in the case of fast reactors). The point is not significant except that Community benefits from THTR may have been less than those from other association contracts. Pressures from BBK resulted in the inclusion of clauses in the THTR association contract which limited information exchanges more explicitly than in other associations.[45] The influence of BBK also restricted the placement of contracts under THTR. By the time the association was signed, all contracts for AVR had been let. Thereafter, no THTR contracts of any importance were awarded outside Germany.[46]

[43]The thorium-uranium cycle was another means of minimizing enriched uranium requirements. With a small amount of uranium 235, thorium 232 was converted under bombardment to uranium 233, a fissile fuel. This uranium 233 might then be consumed in the same reactor to produce further power or be extracted for use in other systems, notably fast reactors.

[44]*Industriekurier*, May 20, 1964. This agreement also provided for exchange of information and personnel. Because of resistance to the Commission's authority in the external field (which prevented conclusion of the ORGEL agreement with the USAEC—see chap. 6), the agreement was formalized through an exchange of letters rather than an official accord. For various discussions of U.S.-AVR negotiations, see *Nucleonics Week*, February 6, 1964; April 30, 1964; and June 4, 1964.

[45]Whereas the partners in the fast reactor associations were obligated to exchange with one another *all* information bearing on the cooperative research program, the THTR association obligated partners to do this only "to the extent that they disposed of such information" (leaving BBK with an out by arguing that its Swiss partner, BBC, actually controlled the information). The provision was similar to the one German industry included in participation contracts. (See chap. 5.) Also, in contrast to other associations, property rights under THTR went exclusively to KFA and BBK, rather than to Euratom and national partners as co-patent holders.

[46]The distribution of these contracts was managed by a Comité de Gestion consisting of three Commission representatives, two KFA employees, and one BBK official. This committee took decisions by a majority vote (provided at least one member of the German and Euratom representations was included—in effect a veto system for each party) and was responsible for all aspects of the common program. Daily supervision, however,

Cooperation between DRAGON and THTR

The THTR association brought all significant work on high temperature reactors under the wing of Euratom. In July 1965, a formal agreement of cooperation was signed between DRAGON and THTR, completing the network of relationships between these projects, Euratom, and the USAEC.[47] This agreement set up a liaison group to exchange information and arrange common use of facilities between the two programs. Cooperation was particularly close on fuel developments. NUKEM, charged with the manufacture of fuel elements for THTR, sent personnel to DRAGON; and test elements produced by NUKEM were irradiated in DRAGON's first charge, which went critical in August 1964 and reached full power in May 1966. The two legs of Euratom's high temperature program seemed to be moving in unexpected harmony.

The Prototype Phase

The first commercial consideration of high temperature reactors fractured this harmony and precipitated industrial alignments which created open wounds between the DRAGON and German programs. The successful establishment of an industrial consortium (known as Inter Nuclear) to prepare for the commercial sale of DRAGON-type reactors stirred up latent resentment in Germany and triggered a government-sponsored attempt to consolidate German industrial efforts in the high temperature field. German industry was caught between nationalist pressures to maintain the pebble-bed reactor program and competitive pressures to join international alignments preparing to market prismatic fuel, DRAGON reactors. Political pressures proved strong enough to inaugurate a German pebble-bed prototype project, but industrial interest increasingly shifted to DRAGON-type reactors which, on the basis of developments in the United States, clearly began to outdistance the pebble-bed design in terms of economic promise.

Avoiding the Generation Squeeze

During the mid-1960s, high temperature systems, like heavy water reactors, felt the pinch of developments in light water and fast reactors.

---

was left to the project head, Rudolf Schulten, who was also head of the German program. Schulten could award contracts of $25,000 or less without approval of the Comité. Commission staff and parties seconded by the Commission could participate in the research work at Juelich; but throughout the association, these individuals numbered ten or less and included only Commission staff personnel. For a copy of the association agreement, see Euratom, *Assoziationsvertrag zwischen der Europaeischen Gemeinschaft, der Brown Boveri/Krupp Reaktorbau-Gmbh und der Kernforschungsanlage Juelich* (EUR/C/2867/5/63d) (Brussels, n.d.). The author was allowed access to the minutes of the meetings of the Comité de Gestion, but these documents are not available for public citation.

[47]DRAGON, *Seventh Annual Report: 1965–66*, p. 84.

The drama unfolded in England where three different models of gas reactors were being developed.[48] In addition to the original Calder Hall gas graphite reactor, Great Britain pursued studies of advanced gas and high temperature gas reactors. Under pressure from light water advances, the UKAEA initiated a review of these programs. The question was whether Great Britain should stay with the Calder Hall model until high temperature systems reached maturity (with perhaps one or two light water reactors constructed in between) or go into commercial-scale production of advanced gas reactor plants, a less sophisticated system than the high temperature design. If the second solution were chosen, it would mean a cutback in the significance and support of DRAGON.

The issue focused on the award of a reactor contract for the Dungeness-B power station planned for construction in 1965. After receiving bids for light water and advanced gas reactors, the CEGB, Britain's state-owned utility, chose the advanced gas design. The result was a temporary setback for DRAGON. One side effect, however, was the establishment of industrial contacts which later worked to DRAGON's advantage. British firms launched an extensive campaign to export advanced gas reactors to the continent. TNPG, one of three British nuclear consortia at the time, established marketing contacts with Belgonucléaire in Belgium, SNAM-Progetti in Italy, GHH in Germany, and GAAA in France. APC, a second British consortium, negotiated sales agreements with BBC in Switzerland and BBC Mannheim in Germany. (BBC's interest in the advanced gas reactor, despite the work of its joint subsidiary, BBK, on high temperature systems, suggests the relative decline of interest in this period in high temperature systems.) These groupings subsequently became the basis for tentative arrangements to manufacture and sell high temperature reactors.

Meanwhile, DRAGON scored a public relations advance over the German pebble-bed design. Before 1966 it was thought that at least part of the DRAGON fuel core would have to be strongly enriched (93 percent). Coupled with the generation squeeze, this feature reduced DRAGON's attractiveness. At a DRAGON symposium convened in May 1966, officials announced that the DRAGON reactor could also operate on a low enrichment fuel cycle (3–5 percent).[49] At about the same time, Germany experienced some problems with the THTR design (having to do with the ingress of control rods into the reactor core). Taken together, these two events created the impression that the pebble-bed concept was falling behind. The impression was partly the fault of BBK. Whereas DRAGON promoted a wide and relatively free distribution of information, BBK kept the lid on information outputs. Moreover,

[48]For a critical view of these events, see Duncan Burn, *The Political Economy of Nuclear Energy* (London: Institute of Economic Affairs, 1967).

[49]For a complete record of this symposium, see special issue of the *Journal of the British Nuclear Energy Society*, V (July 1966).

despite British predominance, some 30 percent of all DRAGON contracts went to non-British industries. Only a small fraction of THTR contracts went to non-German industries. The result was that more was known about DRAGON developments, and in this sense the DRAGON design attracted greater interest.[50] Even BBC, a joint industrial sponsor of the THTR project, requested in 1966 an official exchange agreement with DRAGON.[51]

If the generation squeeze forced a consolidation of effort in high temperature systems, DRAGON was in good position to become the unity candidate. Euratom officials apparently favored this course. DRAGON was an older project more closely identified with Community aspirations; the German program, by contrast, had muscled its way into the Community program through long and difficult negotiations. The fact that Euratom officials had close relations with British institutions while the German program developed in greater isolation magnified this preference for DRAGON. During the difficult years toward the end of Euratom's second five-year program, Euratom officials lobbied enthusiastically in support of DRAGON and succeeded in securing extensions of the DRAGON agreement.[52] At the same time, the THTR association became entangled in the general Community stalemate and was effectively terminated, though Commission personnel remained on at Juelich pending eventual agreement on a third multiple-year program.

Establishment of Inter Nuclear

Enthusiasm for DRAGON among Community officials also contributed to the establishment of an initial industrial base for the DRAGON reactor type. Through behind-the-scenes initiatives, Euratom representatives succeeded in bringing together an industrial consortium to plan the eventual manufacture and sale of DRAGON plants. This initiative generated considerable controversy in Germany, where, by now, the THTR program had advanced far enough to be viewed by some German groups as a direct competitor to DRAGON. The initiative unquestionably reflected a desire among officials engaged in Community high

[50]For example, on the basis of DRAGON contracts placed with Belgonucléaire, Belgium developed an interest in high temperature reactors, incorporating them in the national five-year program in 1968. At the same time, Belgium lost interest in heavy water reactors, in part owing to the monopoly of ORGEL contracts exercised by Ispra. The wide placement of contracts is an essential aspect of good public, especially industrial, relations in big technology projects.

[51]Interviews by the author at BBK, Cologne, August 18, 1970, disclosed that disagreement existed between BBC and Krupp concerning the prospects of THTR reactors. BBC had less faith in the German pebble-bed concept than Krupp.

[52]Two extensions in April 1967 until the end of the second five-year plan and in June 1968 until June 1970 added an additional $16 million to DRAGON expenditures, bringing the total since 1959 to approximately $94 million.

temperature programs to consolidate future efforts on the DRAGON rather than on the pebble-bed reactor type. The initiative further reflected an awareness on the part of these officials of the need to encourage industrial participation through informal soundings and suggestions rather than the open-air type of confrontation used by Community officials at the ORGEL symposium in 1965. Finally, the initiative provided an illuminating illustration of one way international organizations may exploit domestic divisions to advance the cause of transnational industrial alignments.

In May 1967, Euratom convened a joint DRAGON-THTR symposium in Brussels.[53] As in the case of the ORGEL symposium in 1965, this gathering examined critically the economic prospects of high temperature systems. The outcome of the gathering was fairly positive.[54] Buoyed by this result, Euratom officials sought an immediate industrial follow-up. Their thinking was revealed in a later article.[55] At this point, they noted, DRAGON and THTR compared favorably with the American program. The American program, however, was moving forward with an industrial-scale program, the construction of a 300 MWe prototype at Fort St. Vrain (near Denver). Thus, the Community, "although ahead in the purely technological field, [was] lagging behind as regards the commercial development of this hardware." "In view of the challenge presented by American decisions," Euratom directors concluded, "the commercialization of high temperature reactors only has a chance within the framework of an international consortium, where every member is free to develop fully its individual abilities beyond the frontiers of its own country."[56]

Events in England in 1967 offered the opportunity to establish such a consortium. The Select Committee on Science and Technology of the British House of Commons had just proposed that Britain's three nuclear industrial groups (TNPG, APC, and NDC) be combined into one to improve the sagging prospects of British reactor exports.[57] British firms responded to this proposal with expected reserve. Hoping to avoid consolidation, they were open to alternatives which would demon-

[53]For a report on this symposium, see *Neue Zuercher Zeitung*, August 24, 1967.

[54]Assisting in this outcome was a series of technical and economic improvements in high temperature reactors. Design studies revealed that DRAGON as well as THTR could operate on the thorium fuel cycle and that performance might be improved still further by the use of direct-drive turbines (see discussion above on GHH's Geesthacht reactor). It was also shown that high temperature reactors might be needed alongside fast reactors, rather than being cut out by the generation squeeze. The flexibility of high temperature systems made them more suitable than fast reactors for non-base power loads. See Pietro Caprioglio and Mario de Bacci, "Long Life for Converters," *Euratom Bulletin*, VI (March 1967), pp. 2–5.

[55]Mario de Bacci and Pierre Marien, "The moment of truth for high temperature reactors," *Euratom Bulletin*, VIII (June 1968), pp. 42–45.

[56]*Ibid.*, p. 44.

[57]See discussion of Select Committee's report in *Financial Times*, October 10, 1969.

strate their continued vitality as separate organizations. Knowing this, Euratom officials met informally with TNPG directors and suggested that the establishment of new international ties might counteract the impression of lagging interest in British designs and effectively undercut the parliamentary proposal. TNPG was involved at the time in discussions with Belgonucléaire concerning expanded collaboration in gas reactors. Under urging from Euratom friends, TNPG delayed these discussions until partners from other countries could be found. TNPG's earlier contacts on advanced gas reactors now paid off. GHH, SNAM-Progetti, and GAAA joined the discussions. In January 1968, these companies announced plans to establish a joint company to promote the development of DRAGON reactors.[58] In the course of further negotiations, GAAA dropped out, largely under pressure from the CEA, which had not yet abandoned the search for acceptable natural uranium alternatives. The others, however, concluded in October 1968 a formal agreement creating the company, Inter Nuclear.[59] Shares were divided equally among TNPG, GHH, and SNAM-Progetti (30 percent each), with Belgonucléaire assuming a smaller share (10 percent). For the time being, the company remained a paper organization, mostly interested in coordinating promotion and design activities. The conversion to a full manufacturing operation would have to await the first commercial order from electrical utilities. But the establishment of Inter Nuclear brightened DRAGON's public image and forestalled a potential consolidation of British industry, which may have worked against future attempts to find foreign industrial partners for DRAGON (just as consolidation of Siemens and AEG in Germany worked against subsequent cooperation with French firms).[60]

THTR Seeks To Avoid Isolation

Though an unofficial initiative on the part of Euratom officials, the creation of Inter Nuclear invited sharp criticism from THTR directors. The latter interpreted the initiative (correctly, one might add) as an attempt to isolate the THTR program and force consolidation on DRAGON. The fact that a German firm was included in Inter Nuclear sharpened rather than dulled domestic displeasure. Public groups criticized GHH for joining a foreign consortium competing against the "only pure German development" in the nuclear power field. The criticism was based on one of the key arguments standing in the way of significant

[58] Nucleonics Week, January 25, 1968, p. 7.

[59] For a copy of the agreement establishing Inter Nuclear, see Annexe au Moniteur Belge (official register of the Belgian government, Brussels), August 22, 1968, pp. 19529–33.

[60] British industries did reorganize in 1969 with APC combining with NDC to form the grouping BNDC. Merger into a single domestic industry finally occurred in 1973. See further discussion in text.

transnational mergers among European firms in the nuclear sector (or any other sector, for that matter). As it was put by one German publication:[61]

It is perfectly reasonable to allow individual firms in Germany to decide for themselves whether and with which other firms they wish to cooperate. In the case, however, in which a project has been financed with large public funds, the state has not only a right but indeed an obligation to its taxpayers to see that these firms coordinate their intentions and come to some sort of cooperation.

As the publication continued on a later occasion:[62]

Although Gutehoffnungshuette may have many reasons to join Inter Nuclear, which from the point of view of the individual firm certainly have their justification, we would have welcomed it more if beforehand GHH had come to an arrangement with BBK concerning cooperation on the development and construction of a German prototype reactor.

The criticism pointed to the nationally based financial roots of big technology projects and faulted both GHH for failing to invest in German-financed high temperature designs and, more importantly, the German government for failing to encourage such investment. The criticism, it should be noted, is not an argument against international cooperation per se but for national cooperation prior to international involvements. The effect of prior national cooperation, of course, may be to complicate subsequent transnational alignments, as we saw in the case of KWU cooperation with French partners.

There had been attempts to coordinate GHH and BBK activities as far back as 1966. The problems encountered had to do with conflicting license ties with the United States and top management personality conflicts. In 1960 GHH, specializing in turbine construction and pressure vessels, signed a license agreement with General Atomic covering the reactor types being developed by this American firm.[63] These types included the Peach Bottom reactor, which employed the prismatic or DRAGON-type fuel design (rather than the German pebble-bed concept). In 1964, before GHH went into its own design program on high temperature systems, the management of General Atomic visited Juelich and discussed with BBK the merits of the competing fuel concepts.[64] BBK urged a switch to the German concept (which would have brought GHH into the fold), but General Atomic was already committed to the prismatic design and decided to work with GHH as subcontractor for the development of this design in Germany.[65] In 1966

---

[61] Deutscher Forschungsdienst, *Sonderbericht Kernenergie*, May 2, 1968.

[62] *Ibid.*, October 24, 1968.

[63] *Industriekurier*, April 20, 1960.

[64] See reference to this visit in *Ruhr-Nachrichten*, July 3, 1968.

[65] The U.S. never had a serious program to study the pebble-bed concept. The AEC awarded an initial study contract in 1957 to Sanderson and Porter but discontinued this program in December 1962.

BBK initiated direct but unofficial contacts with GHH to involve the latter in the pebble-bed program. By this time, GHH was preoccupied with a reactor program of its own, featuring a direct cycle, helium turbine drive. In addition, personality differences between top management at BBK and GHH limited effective action to coordinate objectives.[66]

The criticism generated by GHH participation in Inter Nuclear created a government interest in trying to coordinate industrial efforts in the high temperature field. During the planning of Germany's third five-year nuclear plan (1968–72), German officials stressed the importance of beginning the design and construction of a prototype reactor (300 MWe to be located at Schmehausen), utilizing the thorium, pebble-bed fuel concepts. The third plan approved funds for this purpose, as well as the development of a 25 MWe direct drive, helium turbine reactor to be constructed by GHH at Geesthacht.[67] The government plan also called for preliminary work on the design of a commercial-scale, 600 MWe direct drive THTR reactor. This latter proposal was deliberately designed to encourage convergence of BBK and GHH activities.[68] Initial specifications left open the choice of fuel concept (i.e., either BBK pebble-bed or GHH prismatic design), hoping that preliminary collaboration would lead to a joint decision on this matter.

Pressure from Juelich officials was clearly behind these government plans. Not only was the German high temperature program threatened with isolation, but Juelich itself was lagging badly in comparison with Karlsruhe, where major efforts were being made to establish this center and the fast reactor program as the priority focus of German nuclear plans.[69] The federal government responded by assuming a larger proportion of Juelich expenditures under the third five-year plan[70] and by pressing, simultaneously with efforts to encourage industrial consolidation in the fast reactor field (see chapter 8), the merger of BBK/GHH (along with a third firm, MAN) activities in the high temperature field.[71]

---

[66]Interview with BBK official, Cologne, August 18, 1970. The management of GHH was more contemporary in style and outlook, whereas the management of Krupp was more traditional and conservative. Too little is known about the influence of such individual as well as corporate styles of management on relationships among national and international corporations. Economic studies tend to ignore these factors altogether.

[67]Germany, Federal Ministry for Scientific Research, *3. Atomprogramm der Bundesrepublik Deutschland* (Bonn: Federal Ministry for Scientific Research, n.d.), p. 27.

[68]*Industriekurier*, October 12, 1968.

[69]For example, in early 1966, Schulten and other officials at Juelich complained to federal officials that KFA was a victim of discrimination in favor of federal support of Karlsruhe (GfK). At this point, Bonn financed over 75 percent of GfK expenditures, while Juelich still recovered only a small proportion of its total expenditures (though the sums themselves were substantial) through federal support of THTR studies. *Handelsblatt*, January 1, 1966.

[70]Bonn assumed 50 percent of total expenditures at Juelich, and this proportion increased steadily thereafter in line with federal support of Karlsruhe (by 1970, around 90 percent).

[71]*Die Welt*, October 4, 1968.

The effort to avoid isolation on the international front took the form of German representations in Brussels to continue the Euratom THTR association at the research level and to initiate the formation of a German-led industrial group at the commercial level. A German memorandum to the Council in May 1968 explicitly proposed an international industrial group.[72] Recognizing the public trend in favor of DRAGON-type reactors, the memo made clear that participation of other industries in the German project would require putting aside activities on other high temperature reactor concepts (i.e., prismatic fuel designs).[73] Germany was less anxious to obtain for financial reasons the support of outside firms than to relieve the impression of isolation of the German program. In all likelihood, BBK was prepared to consider only minor participation by foreign firms (much as German firms in fast reactors accepted only minor participation of Belgian and Dutch partners in the SNR consortium—see next chapter). International partners, however, could enhance the German program's external image and alleviate German concern at this point about potential effects of the proposed nonproliferation treaty on exclusively national industrial alignments. (See discussion on this point in chapters 2, 3, 4, and 8.)

The German counteroffensive did not immediately affect support of DRAGON. While there was some hint in early 1968 that German officials sought to tie continued support of DRAGON with an extension of the THTR association,[74] Germany recognized the benefits of continued participation in DRAGON as long as German plans left open the eventual choice of fuel design for reactors beyond the prototype stage. The long-term threat to DRAGON was German industrial activities. If BBK and GHH succeeded in coordinating programs, a German consortium might rival the international grouping of Inter Nuclear. Fragmentation caused by competing industrial efforts might then leave Europe vulnerable once again to penetration by U.S. industries. This was particularly true in an intermediate reactor sector such as high temperature systems where it was doubtful that Europe could sustain two full-scale industrial programs against American competition (this factor was less true in the fast reactor sector, where European programs benefited from higher priority national efforts).

The requirement to select the most competitive design placed German industries in a difficult bind. On the one hand, they were faced with nationalist urgings, evident in the case of KWU, to compete inde-

---

[72]*Die Entwicklung von gasgekuehlten Hochtemperaturreaktoren in der Bundesrepublik Deutschland,* A memorandum of the German government to the Euratom Council, May 27, 1968 (obtained from the German Science Ministry).

[73]As the German memorandum expressed it: "Partners of German institutes and firms would have to participate in the development and construction of prototypes to the extent that further national efforts by these partners outside the project would be unnecessary." *Ibid.,* p. 5.

[74]*Agence Europe,* May 21, 1968.

pendently against foreign rivals. On the other hand, they became increasingly pessimistic that the prognosis for pebble-bed technology was indeed sufficient to undergird such competitive aims.

The Commercial Phase

The commercial breakthrough of high temperature reactors was expected to take place in Great Britain. Instead the breakthrough came in the United States and occasioned a new offensive by American industries to exploit industrial divisions and weakness in Europe. Gulf General Atomic, in particular, played a significant role in the internal debate in Germany over future choices in the high temperature field. The ambitious plans of this firm met considerable skepticism in German government circles, much as Westinghouse plans encountered opposition in French circles in the light water sector. (See chapter 5.) In the high temperature sector, however, the stakes were not quite as high as in light water and fast reactor sectors (since unexpected developments in the latter sectors could always squeeze the market for high temperature reactors). Consequently, an American-dominated consortium may emerge as the primary agent of commercialization of high temperature systems in Europe. A TNPG/KWU alignment could add some balance to this outcome, but neither TNPG or KWU has done extensive work on high temperature systems comparable to BBC construction of the Schmehausen prototype in Germany or Gulf General Atomic's prototype in the United States.[75]

British Indecision

The initiative taken by TNPG to establish Inter Nuclear was followed by initiatives on the part of APC (the second British nuclear group which merged with NDC in 1969 to form BNDC) to bring together a rival DRAGON-type consortium on the continent. APC opened discussions in 1968 with BBC in Switzerland, BBC affiliates in France (particularly CEM), and BBC subsidiaries in Germany (BBC Mannheim and BBK).[76] After the decision in 1969 to abandon gas graphite reactors, France demonstrated a growing interest in high temperature reactors. Under CEA urging, CEM teamed up in 1970 with several other French firms to form the Groupement Industriel pour les réacteurs à Haute Température (GIHTR).[77] Cooperation with German firms under the auspices

[75]This alignment, it will be recalled from chap. 5, involved TNPG, KWU, Interatom, Belgonucléaire, and Agip Nucleare and constituted a series of agreements (not necessarily involving all participants—for example, Agip Nucleare was not included in fast reactor agreements) covering all types of reactors being developed by TNPG and KWU.

[76]*Nucleonics Week*, June 30, 1968, p. 8. These firms, as we noted earlier, were already collaborating on the sale of advanced gas reactors.

[77]*La Vie Française*, June 12, 1970.

of BNDC (formerly APC) now ran into obstacles, however. The French rejection of Siemens' proposal in 1970 to cooperate through KWU in the manufacture and sale of all reactor types (fast, light water, and high temperature) prevented strengthening associations. Instead, GIHTR and BBC turned increasingly toward bilateral associations with American partners to obtain the necessary technology.

This shift of interest from British to American firms was accelerated by the delay of commercial orders for high temperature reactors in Britain. In fall 1970, the British state electricity board, CEGB, seemed on the verge of placing a first commercial order for a high temperature plant. Several weeks later, however, British officials announced that further studies were necessary to improve the DRAGON fuel design.[78] The desire to conduct these studies contributed to another extension of the DRAGON agreement, this time for three years, through June 1973. But industrial attention in Europe now swung increasingly toward rapidly developing events in the United States.

American Breakthrough

In the United States, the Peach Bottom reactor outside Philadelphia had been operational since 1967. In that same year, Gulf Oil Company bought out General Atomic, formerly a division of the General Dynamics Corporation. New to the atomic power field, Gulf launched a vigorous effort to catch up with the American nuclear giants, Westinghouse and GE. Construction began in 1968 on the 300 MWe high temperature prototype at Fort St. Vrain, Colorado. This facility went operational in 1973. In the meantime, Gulf had already received a number of contracts for commercial plants. Influenced in large measure by the debate on the environmental impact of nuclear power reactors and the advantages offered by gas-cooled over water-cooled (light water) reactors,[79] Philadelphia Electric, operator of Peach Bottom, ordered in August 1971 two 1160 MWe high temperature stations. By the end of 1972, Gulf had secured additional orders for a total of six high temperature reactors, approximately 5500 MWe installed power.[80]

Gulf's successes in the United States prompted it to make immediate efforts to break into the European market. In 1972 Gulf concluded a license agreement with the CEA and the French high temperature consortium, GIHTR.[81] On both the light water and high temperature fronts,

---

[78] *Financial Times*, November 17, 1970.

[79] The principal advantages include the smaller core size of gas-cooled reactors (owing to greater efficiency of operation at higher temperatures), which permits the construction of containment vessels with higher radiation resistance, and the fact that gas-cooled systems avoid the discharge of contaminated water necessary in water reactors.

[80] USAEC, *Annual Report to Congress—1972*, Senate Document No. 93-2, Pt. 1, 93rd Cong., 1st Sess., p. 18.

[81] *Nuclear Industry*, October 1972, p. 39.

France now enjoyed U.S. support in potential competition with Anglo-German industries (TNPG/KWU). Gulf also initiated discussions with the British group, BNDC. These discussions were complicated, however, by a British government announcement in March 1973 that the long-contemplated merger of British nuclear firms into a single company would take place with TNPG and BNDC combining to form a new consortium headed by British General Electric Company.[82]

Gulf's offensive entailed particular consequences for high temperature developments in Germany.[83] As we noted earlier in this chapter, BBC, principal partner with Krupp in BBK, had been interested for some time in the DRAGON-type reactor design, obtaining in 1966 an official exchange agreement with the DRAGON project. Influenced by U.S. advances in this design, BBC was looking for some way to dilute its commitment to the German pebble-bed design. A debate within BBK, with Krupp apparently siding with domestic groups supporting the pebble-bed design, delayed the start-up of construction on the pebble-bed prototype at Schmehausen. Finally, in summer 1971, Krupp withdrew from BBK, selling its 50 percent share to BBC (40 percent) and Hochtemperatur-Kernkraftwerk GmbH (10 percent), the contracting group for Schmehausen. Krupp's decision reflected a pessimistic assessment that the pebble-bed design could overcome growing commercial skepticism, even if the Schmehausen prototype were constructed. Indeed, BBC went ahead with the construction of Schmehausen (primarily owing to domestic political pressures), but as subsequent negotiations revealed, BBC's interest was now clearly directed toward DRAGON system developments.

The departure of Krupp created an opening for direct ties with foreign, in particular American, partners developing the prismatic or DRAGON-type design. According to the terms of its withdrawal, Krupp had the option of reselling its share to another buyer at a higher price than that received from BBC. Prospective buyers included potential European partners; but, despite initial interest of various groups, including Inter Nuclear, no purchasers could be found. It seems safe to conclude that during these negotiations, BBC, with its eyes on American partners, was not particularly disappointed when the negotiations failed.

The opening of direct negotiations between BBC and Gulf intensified the domestic debate. Government officials raised the concern that association with Gulf would soon lead to majority control by the American firm, a situation which could result in the neglect of certain goals of primary interest to Germany but not to a foreign company (meaning, most

[82]*Nuclear Industry*, May 1973, pp. 38–39; September 1972, p. 34. What the British merger means in terms of former commitments of TNPG and BNDC, in particular TNPG agreements with KWU, is as yet unclear.

[83]The events described in this paragraph were reported to the author in correspondence with officials of participating firms.

likely, continued development of the pebble-bed design). BBC, on the other hand, maintained resolutely that only an association with Gulf could broaden and enrich the technical basis of German programs. "All other firms in Europe which have been suggested as partners," a BBC position paper declared, "would be unable to contribute anything to the expansion of present knowledge at Hochtemperatur-Reaktorbau" (the new name given to BBC's German operation after the withdrawal of Krupp).[84] Given the need to catch up and compete with more advanced proven reactor systems, BBC felt that Germany should ride on the strongest horse, namely the American one.

In 1972, the debate was temporarily resolved by a Gulf-BBC license agreement giving Gulf 45 percent participation in Hochtemperatur-Reaktorbau.[85] This group hopes to offer a bid on and secure its first order for the Gulf high temperature reactor system in 1974. While the pebble-bed design is no longer in competition for immediate commercial sales, Gulf and BBC have agreed to continue the Schmehausen project in the expectation that this reactor type may have future applications in the production of process heat for industrial purposes. This commitment may only be a temporary concession to domestic advocates of the German program, however. It seems unlikely that the pebble-bed design, which attracts no industrial interest outside Germany, will find the necessary market support to warrant commercial-scale production.

Europe's Dilemma

Gulf's role in engineering the commercial breakthrough of high temperature systems and in gearing-up European industries for the commercial production of these systems suggests a number of continuing limitations on European independence in the nuclear power field. Commercial successes in the United States remain the primary signal for developments in Europe (as they did, for example, in the case of light water reactors in 1964). It took Gulf's comercial sales in 1971 to bring European utilities together to study the economic prospects of high temperature reactors. In December 1971, CEGB, RWE, EdF, ENEL, and VEW (operator of the German Schmehausen reactor) set up a joint company known as Euro-HKG. Had this group existed earlier (for example, in 1970, when the CEGB was considering a commercial order for high temperature systems), it may have encouraged European industry to regroup to prepare for commercial orders. Instead, European firms re-

[84]See report by Hochtemperatur Reaktorbau GmbH, "Zur HTR-Politik in der BRD" (Bericht Nr. 72/10) (Cologne, October 6, 1972) (obtained from Hochtemperatur Reaktorbau GmbH).

[85]*Nuclear Industry*, January 1973, p. 36; and July 1972, p. 20. Gulf also established a joint subsidiary with the German firm, NUKEM, to manufacture fuel for HTR systems. Known as HOBEG, Gulf holds an option of 49 percent control, with NUKEM retaining 51 percent.

mained fragmented and awaited the initiative of a dominant industrial partner from abroad, i.e., Gulf General Atomic.

The point may be, of course, that Europe simply does not possess the technology or is unable to develop this technology as rapidly as U.S. competitors. This seems particularly true in back-up sectors, as the high temperature sector was originally perceived to be. For example, KWU only belatedly showed an interest in high temperature systems. The TNPG/KWU alignment may still result in a European-based development of these systems.[86] As we see in the next chapter, this alignment offers Europe a fully competitive alternative in higher priority sectors, namely fast reactors and proven reactors. (See chapter 5.) Nevertheless, the continued fragmentation of European markets and industrial structures will probably offer for some time to come an ongoing opportunity for American firms to penetrate and, in some instances, dominate European developments. This is particularly likely in face of the more fluid, less constrained (especially in a strategic sense) internal circumstances characterizing European alignments. The next chapter illustrates how internal European rivalries continue to complicate efforts to consolidate European resources in competition with the United States.

---

[86]These firms continue to benefit from extension of the DRAGON accord, now effective through March 1976. *Agence Europe*, December 20, 1972.

CHAPTER 8

THE DEVELOPMENT OF FAST REACTORS: FRANCO-GERMAN RIVALRY

Franco-German cooperation is still the linchpin on which European cooperation will succeed or fail. The development of fast reactors best illustrates the deep-seated difficulties of this cooperation. The development of proven reactors also involved Franco-German differences, but this development was complicated by the issue of foreign technology. By contrast, fast reactors did not raise the problem of Community dependence on outside technology. From the outset, European expertise in this field was as advanced as, if not more advanced than, that of the United States. Moreover, unlike the case of heavy water and high temperature gas reactors, fast reactors enjoyed priority status in national plans. The future of these reactors did not depend, as did that of intermediate-generation reactors, on the relative technical and economic success of first-generation reactors. It was known from the outset that fast neutron systems would play a major role in future energy production. Thus, the development of these systems offered a prime opportunity for exclusive and priority action on the part of the Euratom countries.

The development of fast reactors was also unencumbered by the requirement to build cooperation around commonly owned Community facilities. Unlike the ORGEL program, fast reactor programs were carried out primarily in national laboratories with Community participation taking place through association contracts. Thus, the fast reactor story illustrates the internal problems of *decentralized* cooperation, much as the ORGEL story illustrates the internal problems of *centralized* cooperation. Given the shift of interest during Euratom's evolution from centralized, institutional cooperation to decentralized, intergovernmental coordination, the fast reactor story also provides some unique insights into the dynamics of future Community cooperation, which will probably center around specific projects (additional programs). Though constituting a single Community program in the technical sense of Article 7, the fast reactor associations operated much like independent national projects, with important aspects of coordination among these projects depending largely on member-government rather than Community initiatives.

As this chapter reveals, the primary obstacle to effective Community action under these circumstances is political and commercial rivalry within Europe. The chief rivalry is that between France and Germany. If Franco-German conflict in proven reactor development may be explained primarily in terms of different responses to the penetration of foreign technology, this conflict in the case of fast reactors itself facilitated the penetration of outside interests. Germany was determined to establish parity with France in civilian nuclear power, and this objective precluded reliance on central Community institutions (as we noted in chapters 4 and 6) as well as reliance on French institutions (as we note in this chapter). Instead, Germany looked to the United States for principal guidance.

A secondary rivalry within Europe is that between Italy, on the one side, and France and Germany, on the other. Generally weaker and a less interesting partner for American industry, Italy looked primarily to France and Germany for fast reactor support. Such support was not enthusiastically forthcoming, because France and Germany felt Italian demands would divert resources from more pressing objectives of competition with one another and with non-Community rivals. Accordingly, Italy, while participating in Community programs during the R&D stage, was consistently excluded from industrial alignments in the fast reactor field. In 1971, Italian utilities (i.e., ENEL) reached cooperative study agreements with French and German counterparts concerning fast reactor projects, but these agreements do not deal with Italian demands for industrial participation.

The entry of Great Britain into the European Community adds a further dimension to European rivalries. After Germany failed in 1970 to achieve cooperation with French industrial partners in the fast reactor field (Siemens' offer of French participation in KWU), German firms concluded a series of agreements with British partners covering fast reactors (the TNPG/KWU alignment in July 1971). These developments indicated one type of role British organizations might play in future Community politics as alternative partners for France or Germany in attempts by these two countries to outmaneuver one another. France is aware of being closed out by British-German alignments (also evident in the uranium enrichment field) and, at least in the light water field, has sought American support to balance off this threat. In fast reactors, France is unwilling to see British partners (CEGB) participate in a cooperative grouping of Franco-German-Italian utilities for fear that these utilities might then select Anglo-German instead of French industrial suppliers. While France is ahead of Germany in fast reactors, Britain may be ahead of France. Thus, fast reactor politics offers tantalizing insights into some of the new patterns of polycentric, multi-tiered relationships in Europe, which are rapidly replacing the integrative, unifocal relationships of the past.[1]

The Program Definition Phase

The fast reactor story in Europe begins before the establishment of Euratom. In 1955 France initiated some preliminary investigations of sodium cooling techniques, particularly useful in fast neutron systems; and Belgonucléaire, the nuclear design group in Belgium, dispatched a number of engineers to the United States to participate in the construction of the Enrico Fermi fast reactor near Detroit, a part of the USAEC's program in fast reactors.[2]

A First Proposal for Unity

In 1959 the Euratom Commission proposed that these activities be coordinated and accelerated within the framework of a Community program centered at Cadarache in southern France.[3] Cadarache was the site of French fast reactor investigations and the tentative location of a fast neutron reactor experiment, RAPSODIE, which France decided upon in 1957.[4]

For both technical and political reasons, France opposed the Commission proposal. Technically, French plans for RAPSODIE were still incomplete. Though a preliminary decision to begin construction had been taken by the end of 1959, certain technical features of the reactor remained undefined and were the subject of continued debate in the French program. Until these features were determined, French scientists were reluctant to relinquish any part of national control of RAPSODIE. Moreover, at this point, French specialists could not see any advantage in a Community program. Euratom itself was a relatively new body with no proven expertise, and Belgonucléaire, with a relatively modest fast reactor program, was the only other organization in the Community that could contribute anything to cooperation.

On the political side, CEA administrators recognized the future importance of fast reactor systems and were unwilling to share France's advanced knowledge without appropriate compensation. Working on the assumption that French technology would call the shots in future Community developments, France saw fast reactors as another source of leverage over its Euratom partners (not unlike the attitude France adopted with respect to gas graphite reactors—see chapter 5).

---

[1]The case study that follows is a slightly revised version of an article by the author, "The Practice of Interdependence in the Research and Development Sector: Fast Reactor Cooperation in Western Europe," *International Organization*, XXVI (Summer 1972), pp. 499–526.

[2]See *Science*, August 24, 1956, p. 358.

[3]For a reference to this early proposal, see Euratom, *Fifth General Report*, p. 34.

[4]CEA, *Rapport Annuel: 1957*, p. 11.

In these considerations, France probably underestimated the advantages of having the Cadarache program form the nucleus of a Community-wide program. In 1959, neither Germany nor Italy was pursuing activities in this field. While a Euratom association may have restricted somewhat the CEA's freedom of action, it would have also meant French leadership in this important sector. By the end of 1961, when France attempted to assert this leadership, interim developments in Germany had markedly reduced the chances of a single Community effort based exclusively on French facilities at Cadarache.

A Brief Interlude, 1959–61

Discussions on fast reactors at the U.N. Geneva Conference in September 1958 prompted German scientists to take a closer look at this reactor concept.[5] In 1959 a group of scientists at Goettingen, who had been responsible for the conception and design of Germany's first research reactor, FR-2, dispatched one of its members—Wolf Haefele, who later became head of the German fast reactor program—to the USAEC center in Oak Ridge, Tennessee. His mission was to gather information and experience on U.S. fast reactors (and U.S. nuclear research in general). The decision to seek American as opposed to French or British assistance followed the general inclination in Germany to avoid the military overtones of French and British programs. In addition, German scientists rated the potential of U.S. assistance higher than that of France, displayed a greater affinity for American industrial and scientific ideas, and were determined to avoid the pattern of centralized nuclear research practiced in France and England. Germany planned to give more responsibility to industry.

As a result of his stay abroad, Haefele became convinced of the advantages of the industrial orientation of American research, as well as the general promise of the fast reactor concept for German development. Upon his return in early 1960, the Goettingen group shifted the locus of its activities to Karlsruhe (GfK) and began preliminary studies of fast reactors. Based on a number of technical ideas being developed in the United States[6] and, above all, on conceptions of industry-research relations in the United States, the GfK program assumed, from the start, different outlines from the French program. Close contacts continued between the German and American programs.

Parallel to these developments in Germany, the Commission initiated studies for the design and construction of a zero-power critical assembly, a smaller facility used to investigate the core characteristics of larger reactors such as RAPSODIE. At this time, neither France nor Germany

[5]An account of the beginnings of the German program appears in W. Haefele, "Das Projekt Schneller Brueter," *Atomwirtschaft*, VIII (April 1963), pp. 206–9.

[6]For example, the German program envisioned use of an oxide fuel being developed by GE in the U.S. in place of the metallic fuel in the French and English programs.

planned such a facility, but both showed an interest in the idea. The Commission exploited this interest to maintain close contacts with Cadarache and Karlsruhe.

A Second Attempt at Unity—Yvon Group

Throughout the period from 1959 to 1961, the Commission advocated a single Community program based on an association agreement.[7] By the fall of 1961, in the context of Euratom's initial discussions on a second five-year plan (1963–67), this idea finally began to attract serious interest, first in France and then in Germany. Several factors accounted for the change in French attitude. First, a program on the scale of RAPSODIE required a sizeable amount of plutonium. While France was building up plutonium stocks for military uses, these were not available for civilian purposes; and plutonium purchases outside France required, under the terms of Article 52 of the Euratom Treaty, the collaboration of the Euratom Commission. Second, France now saw technical benefits in an association with Euratom, particularly in view of the Commission's work on the design of a critical assembly. Third, France had become aware of its isolation within Euratom arising from the passage in July 1961, over French opposition, of the Commission's participation program for proven reactors. Unless France offered to place its fast reactor technology in the framework of a common program, its Euratom partners might turn once again to the United States for assistance and cooperation.

France's concern was focused particularly on Germany. As we noted in chapter 5, France launched in this period a strategic and commercial campaign to wean Germany from dependence on U.S. technology. When France attempted in 1962 to confront Germany with a choice between French gas graphite and American light water reactors (Fessenheim proposals—see chapter 5), it also hoped to sever German-American ties in fast reactors. Up to this point, France did not believe the Germans were serious in the fast reactor field.

Germany, however, was becoming more aggressive in Euratom, as indicated by its initiative in 1960 to establish the CCNR. (See chapter 4.) Germany insisted that fast reactors be one of the fields reviewed by a series of ad hoc groups of the CCNR. The Commission hoped to head off this procedure, seeing the CCNR as a potential threat to its influence. But, France and Germany both sought to curb the Commission's influ-

---

[7]There was never any thought of concentrating fast reactor work at the JNRC facilities. Aside from the strong opposition of France and Germany to this idea, the Commission itself favored an association agreement with national programs as a way of balancing direct (JNRC) and indirect (outside contract) activities in the Euratom program (ORGEL being already slated for the JNRC). The only group to advocate locating fast reactor research at Ispra was the Ispra management, which coveted this project as a way of advancing its own influence.

ence.[8] Accordingly, the CCNR established an ad hoc group under the chairmanship of Jacques Yvon, director of Atomic Piles in the French CEA. This group met three times in the fall of 1961 and reached decisions that had broad consequences for future Community activities in the fast reactor field.[9]

The first proposal considered by the Yvon group was a Dutch recommendation to center the Community program around a single critical assembly and the RAPSODIE reactor located at Cadarache. The Community would exercise a majority participation in both the management and financing of the program. The French had some doubt about the principle of majority Community control, but they supported this proposal along with the Commission. German officials, however, rejected the location of all major facilities on French territory. Since RAPSODIE was already planned for construction at Cadarache, they suggested that the critical assembly be located at Karlsruhe. To upstage the French, they consented to a majority Community participation in the Karlsruhe facility and recommended the appointment of a Frenchman to head the project and insure its Community character.

The German proposal reflected two motivations of German policy. More so than France, Germany was dependent on the establishment of a Community program in the fast reactor field. This was true both because of the need to allay any suspicions which might be aroused by a German program utilizing plutonium, a potential weapons material, and because of the requirement for Euratom technical assistance and research funds. A novice in fast reactors and nuclear research generally, Germany stood to gain from Commission expertise and access to the French program. Moreover, because German federal and state authorities granted funds in this period only on an annual basis, Germany also stood to benefit from Euratom five-year grants, which guaranteed the financial security required for major technological projects.

Second, German policy, no less than French policy, reflected the desire to coordinate participation in Community programs with the establishment of a strong national program.[10] The German program did not include a reactor experiment comparable to RAPSODIE. Hence the construction of a critical assembly in Germany was doubly urgent. Without a military program, German officials felt that only the location of civilian nuclear facilities on German soil would enable German scientists and industrialists to acquire the firsthand knowledge and experience necessary to compete in commercial exploitation of "big science"

[8] *Agence Europe*, November 5, 1960.

[9] The report of the Yvon Group has never been released for public use, but the author was able to read the text and question Community and national officials about its content. For some general reporting on the discussions of this group, see *Agence Europe*, January 20, 1962, and January 26, 1962.

[10] The German formula, as we observed in chap. 4, was to spend twice and later four times as much on national as international programs.

projects.[11] To gain the placement of this facility in Germany was worth the price of sharing control with the Community.

France would not accept the idea of a single critical assembly located on German soil, arguing that the decision to build a critical assembly in France had already been taken in the framework of the national program. Though true, this was a slightly misleading argument, since the idea of a critical assembly was not part of the French program in 1959 and had materialized since then chiefly on the basis of the Commission's initiative. French officials feared that German scientists would monopolize the Community facility, leaving the RAPSODIE project standing on only one leg. There was some technical justification for this concern because the German program envisioned the use of both enriched uranium and plutonium as fuels for fast reactor studies and planned to investigate steam and helium cooling in addition to the sodium cooling being employed in RAPSODIE. But the technical differences in the two programs were not fundamental at this stage. The differences were rooted in future plans, not existing activities. The real source of disagreement was political. France could not count on German support of RAPSODIE, and Germany was not willing to accept a French monopoly.[12]

The result of these discussions was predictable. The Yvon group recommended that the Community support two critical assemblies, one at Cadarache and one at Karlsruhe. The Commission would participate in both programs through association agreements and coordinate them by means of a Groupe de Liaison bringing together the Project personnel for regular exchanges of information and plans.

Except for appearance, this solution all but sanctioned duplicate programs, a fact subsequently borne out by the nearly identical technical characteristics of the Cadarache and Karlsruhe critical assemblies. Some sources (left unnamed but probably the Benelux countries, which had strongly advocated a single program) considered the decision "un-

[11]This point was a critical one in the minds of German fast reactor scientists. It reflected the desire not only to possess modern technologies but to benefit from the social, cultural, political, and educational spin-offs of the development of this technology. In a later paper, German scientists connected with the fast reactor program summarized these profound ramifications of big technology, in particular, the stimulus provided to government policy to consider technology in the context of broad social and political goals. See W. Haefele and J. Seetzen, "Innovationen durch ziviltechnologische Grossprojekte in den siebziger Jahren" (unpublished manuscript obtained from authors), April 1969.

[12]There is some evidence to suggest that Germany proposed a program with technical differences from the French program in order to justify a separate German effort. An indication of the personal and national suspicions dividing German and French officials at this point emerges from a comment made in the newsletter published by the German research service. The newsletter warned that close integration with the more advanced French program would risk turning German scientists into "mere handymen of their French colleagues." Deutscher Forschungsdienst (the German Research Service), Sonderbericht Kernenergie, February 7, 1962.

european."[13] Italy viewed it as an invitation to submit its own fast reactor program for Community participation.[14] As part of its policy in 1962 to increase Euratom contributions to Italian programs, Italy put together a wide-ranging fast reactor project based on a paste fuel reactor known as RAPTUS and a 100 MWe prototype reactor with primary sodium and secondary mercury cooling circuits.[15] This project, drawn up in haste and incorporating advanced ideas (one of which, the paste fuel concept, had already been discarded by the U.S. program because of its infeasibility), was larger than the German effort and equaled the size of the RAPSODIE project. When Italy demanded that Euratom include RAPTUS in the Community program by means of a third association agreement, the Commission's fast reactor proposals had to be drastically revised.

The situation was made to order (or disorder) for the type of cross-program bargaining which wrecked the second five-year budget (see chapter 4). No one was ready to increase total expenditures. Hence funds for the Italian program had to be taken from other Community activities. Under pressure from France and Germany, Ispra programs were cut to make room for fast reactor increases. The final compromise raised the five-year sum for fast reactors from $60 million to $73 million. Italy received $9 million of this amount, with the rest going to French and German programs.[16]

Thus, by the time the Community program was fully defined, it consisted of three associations instead of the originally intended single association. What is more, the three associations did not represent a division of labor based on technical considerations but constituted instead overlapping and competing programs based on political and prestige factors.[17]

[13]See "Euratom und die Atomindustrie," *Atomwirtschaft*, VII (August/September 1962), p. 384.

[14]*Agence Europe*, April 12, 1962, and May 12, 1962.

[15]*Atomo e Industria*, March 15, 1962.

[16]The Commission did convince Italian officials to drop the idea of a sodium-mercury prototype reactor, reducing considerably the scope of Italian ambitions.

[17]The association contracts concluded with France, Germany, and Italy provided for a Community share of 35 percent in the over-all costs of the programs and covered all fast reactor studies leading up to, but not including, the construction of prototypes. The Commission preferred to include prototypes; but the association partners thought it too early to make this decision, and the Netherlands rejected the idea ouright for fear the Community would commit itself to support two prototypes just as it had agreed to finance two critical assemblies. Besides, a prototype commitment seemed unnecessary, since Article 1 of the association agreements specified that signatory parties would not undertake any new activities (prototypes being included) without first presenting proposals to the association for collective action. Only if one party was unable to participate in these new activities for lack of funds (or otherwise) could the other party undertake the activities on its own.

Organizationally each association contract established a Comité de Gestion composed of equal numbers of Commission and national representatives to exercise over-all

The R&D Phase

The R&D phase covered the period of the second five-year plan (1963–67) and revealed two major problems in the coordination of Community research objectives: (1) national differences concerning industrial participation in Community research and (2) political differences with respect to third countries, principally the United States.

Problems of Internal Coordination

The difficulties of reaching agreement on the industrial aspects of Community research are illustrated by the attempts to coordinate the French and German programs and by the inability to find a satisfactory and complementary role for the Italian program.

Subcontracting by the separate associations was to be conducted on the basis of open bidding, with special consideration given to transnational industrial groupings. As it turned out, however, the association partners showed a marked preference for their own national industries. A primary German objective, as we noted, was to obtain outside funds to build up local industrial capabilities. France, on the other hand, resisted placing contracts outside French industry for fear of losing public control over these activities. The result was that little, if any, significant transnational industrial cooperation grew out of the association contracts.[18]

The factors at work contributing to this preference for national industry are well illustrated by two specific incidents.

---

responsibility for performance of the common research program. The Comité took decisions by a majority vote, provided this majority included at least one representative from each signatory—in effect a veto system if the national or Commission representatives voted as a block. Daily supervision of research was entrusted to the project head who turned out, in each case, to be the head of the corresponding national program. Contract conditions permitted the assignment of Commission personnel to the research work teams and the exchange of national staff members among the associations.

The Groupe de Liaison set up to coordinate the separate associations consisted of representatives from the Commission and each of the association partners. This group had no powers of decision or a regular meeting schedule. Its function was exclusively that of review and information exchange.

For copies of the French, German, and Italian association agreements, see, respectively, Euratom, *Contrat d'association entre l'Euratom et le CEA* (EUR/C/1124/6/62f) (Brussels, n.d.); *Contrat entre l'Euratom et la GfK* (EUR/C/2015/5/63f) (Brussels, n.d.); and *Contrat d'association entre l'Euratom et le CNEN* (EUR/C/489/3/63f) (Brussels, n.d.). Much of the information discussed in the rest of this chapter was culled from the minutes of the Comité de Gestion of the individual associations and confirmed in conversations with association officials. The documents themselves are not available for public citation.

[18]Exact percentages of contract funds going to nonnational firms are not available, but conversations with association officials disclosed that, in no case, did any association disperse more than 10 percent of total program expenditures outside the national economy. France, by placing the design contracts for its critical assembly with Belgonucléaire and minor subcontracts for RAPSODIE with the Dutch firm, Neratoom, awarded the highest percentage to outside firms; while Germany awarded scarcely 1 percent of total funds to non-German industries. Italy distributed all of its funds to local industries.

At the time the French and German associations were being concluded, the Commission expressed an interest in using the Euratom Transuranium Institute at Karlsruhe (one of four installations making up the JNRC) to carry out some of the R&D work on the fuel elements destined for the French and German critical assemblies.[19] Operating on assumptions and procedures prevailing in France, where the CEA controls all fuel element activities, Euratom officials (several key ones being Frenchmen themselves) and CEA representatives agreed that the Transuranium Institute would not only perform R&D work but also fabricate the fuel elements. German officials disagreed with this kind of arrangement. Believing that the fabrication of fuels was a task of private industry, not public authorities, these officials helped bring about the establishment of a new company, ALKEM, a joint subsidiary of the German firm, NUKEM, and the American firm, Dow Chemical. ALKEM was then charged with primary responsibility for plutonium fuel development in Germany. When the association management placed the fuel fabrication contracts for the German critical assembly, German representatives insisted that these contracts go to ALKEM despite lower bids in a number of instances from Societé Générale des Minerais in Belgium.[20] As a result, the Euratom Institute at Karlsruhe, while manufacturing the fuel elements for the French critical assembly, played no part in the manufacture of German plutonium fuels.[21]

A second incident involved the declared intention of French and German officials in December 1963 to build a common factory near Karlsruhe for the reprocessing of plutonium fuel from fast reactors.[22] The second five-year plan set aside $5 million for reprocessing activities, and the Commission urged cooperation in this field as a desirable means of conserving Community resources. Though German and French scientists had different ideas about the technical characteristics of a common plant,[23] the failure to realize this common project was

[19]The Commission stated this interest explicitly in a letter drafted at the time of the signing of the German association. See Euratom, *Benutzung des Prototyplabors auf dem Grundstueck des Kernforschungszentrums Karlsruhe* (EUR/C/2549/1/63d) (Brussels, n.d.).

[20]Before receiving the contracts, ALKEM did reduce its bid to that of the Belgian firm. In this limited sense, the purpose of competitive bidding was served. But subsequent cost overruns led to a 75 percent increase in the ALKEM contract, and the entire proceedings did nothing to advance transnational industrial contacts, a principal objective of the common program.

[21]The French position did not necessarily reflect any greater Community spirit, since at the time France's own fuel production facilities were overloaded and France insisted that the Karlsruhe contract match conditions offered to France by a potential American supplier.

[22]*Agence Europe*, December 13, 1963.

[23]The French favored a dry reprocessing technique involving the construction of a separate plant, while the Germans preferred an aqueous technique which would permit expansion of existing facilities used in reprocessing natural and slightly enriched uranium. The French later switched to the aqueous concept.

again owing to differing assumptions about the relation of industry to research. In 1963 the German program had placed a contract with the German firm Leybold, Lurgi and Uhde for design of a reprocessing facility for natural and slightly enriched uranium (known as WAK). This facility, to be located at Karlsruhe, was to be financed by the federal government but operated by a society of four private German firms. Desiring to promote this form of government-industry relations, Karlsruhe directors favored expanding the WAK facility to permit reprocessing of plutonium fuels as well. Talks with France revealed that the CEA preferred to keep reprocessing activities in the hands of public authorities. As a result, after a token offer to Euratom to participate in the construction of two reprocessing plants (one in France and one in Germany), French and German officials decided to construct separate plants. The two parties agreed to continue discussions about a larger facility to handle the fuel of eventual prototype and commercial reactors, but these talks seemed to be nothing more than a *pro forma* concession to the wishes of the Commission.

The national orientation of the French and German associations was perhaps best revealed in discussions to find a Community role for the Italian program. Shortly after its conception, the Italian RAPTUS program came under attack during investigations connected with the Ippolito scandal in CNEN (see chapter 3). A review of this program resulted in the redrawing of Italian plans, calling for work on only limited aspects of fast reactor research rather than a full-scale prototype program.[24] To ascertain prospects of integrating these activities with French and German plans, Italian officials visited Cadarache and Karlsruhe in the summer of 1964.

These visits convinced Italian officials that the French and German programs were not willing to give up essential parts of their industrial activities to permit the meaningful participation of Italian industry. The Germans favored cooperation only at the level of basic research, and France made no secret of the fact that competition with Germany necessitated the promotion of a strong and autonomous French industrial capacity in fast reactors. From this point on, Italy saw little value in continuing its contribution through Euratom to the French and German associations, as long as Italian industry was excluded from the emerging industrial aspects of fast reactor development.

Italy was particularly dissatisfied with the exchange of information under the association agreements. The Groupe de Liaison set up to promote this exchange met officially only once between June 1962 and May 1965 (the first meeting in December 1962 was unofficial since the German and Italian associations were not yet signed). Italy felt that the circulation of technical reports did not compensate for this lack of direct

---

[24] *Atomo e Industria*, March 1, 1964.

exchange. For various reasons, reports were a much less effective means of obtaining information than the stationing of personnel on location where the actual research was being conducted.[25] Yet the exchange of personnel under the associations was also minimal. Commission personnel were assigned to the individual associations; but because of financial limitations, these personnel never numbered more than a few in comparison to the large national staff employed in the association programs.[26] The direct exchange of national staff members between separate associations, for all practical purposes, did not exist.[27]

Italy's dissatisfaction was attributable, in part, to the weakness and disorder of Italy's own program. The French and German programs, with more to offer one another, enjoyed a somewhat more fruitful exchange. Yet there was no doubt that the associations, set up along competitive rather than complementary lines, also operated along competitive lines.[28] After 1965, Italy regarded the associations as little more than Community subsidies to national programs rather than effective instruments for promoting Community cooperation.[29]

Problems of External Relations

Differences among the association partners regarding relations with third countries, especially the United States, compounded the obstacles arising from internal developments. When funds for the second five-year plan were approved, the Commission counted on leasing from the United States the plutonium required for RAPSODIE and the two critical assemblies.[30] In late 1962, however, the United States informed the

[25]The practice developed to classify information into three types of reports—those for internal use only within the separate associations, those for distribution to other associations and interested organizations in the Community, and those for publication in journals or presentation at international congresses. As a Community country, Italy received only the second and third types of reports, the same ones available to the U.S. under the Euratom-U.S. fast reactor agreement concluded in 1964. (See further discussion above.) Not only did this practice fail to offer any special advantages to Community participants, but the whole system of reports generally depended on the willingness of the individual project heads to include significant information in these reports. Under pressure from local industries, the project heads were not likely to divulge commercially relevant findings.

[26]Of 400 persons involved in the French program, about 29 were Commission personnel; of 400 in the German program, 18 were Commission staff. Euratom, *Les moyens d'action utilisés par Euratom: inventaire et analyse* (EUR/C/2064/1/67f) (Brussels, n.d.), p. 30.

[27]Only one CEA scientist was seconded by the Commission to Karlsruhe, and no Germans were officially assigned to Cadarache. Italy had no national representatives stationed at either Karlsruhe or Cadarache.

[28]See comments in Deutscher Forschungsdienst, *Sonderbericht Kernenergie*, May 15, 1963, which urged Karlsruhe to push its program vigorously so as to meet the competition of the French and Italian programs.

[29]*Agence Europe*, March 22, 1965.

[30]This was to be arranged through an extension of the amendment reached in 1962 to the Euratom-U.S. joint agreement permitting the leasing of enriched uranium fuels and small quantities of plutonium for recycling studies. The Community needed around 43 kgs. of plutonium; the joint agreement provided for only 30 kgs.

Community that the provision of larger quantities of plutonium was possible only in the context of a comprehensive agreement for the exchange of information on fast reactors. The USAEC saw a good opportunity to utilize its plutonium supply position as a wedge to gain access to European technology in fast reactors. France became immediately suspicious of the American proposal. Fearing another penetration of U.S. reactor technology into the European market along the lines of the Euratom-U.S. light water agreement (which, it will be recalled, resulted in the sale of three American-type reactors in Europe), France insisted that the association partners participate alongside the Commission in the negotiations with the USAEC.[31]

Germany and Italy went along with this suggestion. Germany did so out of a fear that the Commission might commit the Euratom countries in these negotiations to a long-term agreement with the United States covering prototype development. Since European programs were thought to be more advanced at this point, prototype exchanges might result in Europe giving away more valuable commercial information than it would receive. Furthermore, a long-term agreement with the United States might commit the association partners to an extension of internal cooperation beyond the five-year duration of the existing association contracts. No one wanted to prejudice the option of not renewing these contracts should the cooperative experience prove dissatisfying. When it was clear that France and Germany would participate, Italy also decided to participate, if for no other reason than to protect its interests vis-à-vis France and Germany.

The participation of four members in the negotiations on the Community side inevitably delayed the conclusion of an agreement. During this delay, the United States, for balance-of-payments reasons, withdrew the leasing option and insisted that the plutonium be purchased; simultaneously, the United States raised the price of plutonium. The Commission was now faced with much higher costs than originally anticipated.[32] It appealed to the association partners to advance the additional funds ($2.8 million each) as a prepayment on obligations to be incurred under Euratom's third five-year plan scheduled to commence in 1968. When the Euratom-U.S. fast reactor agreement was finally signed in 1964,[33]

[31] France justified this demand by arguing that the fast reactor associations, unlike the Community light water program, were not exclusively a Commission responsibility but the responsibility of all four partners. This was an interesting distinction between the associations and other Community programs which showed that association contracts always had a somewhat lower Community significance than other activities, at least in the eyes of some member-states.

[32] The Commission initially planned in 1962 to lease plutonium selling in the U.S. for $12–15 per gram. As it turned out, it had to buy this fuel outright at a price of $43 per gram. In addition, because of the delay in the U.S. negotiations, the first core for RAPSODIE had to be purchased from the UKAEA, which charged $112 per gram. *Nucleonics Week*, April 25, 1963.

[33] In exchange for plutonium, the Euratom members agreed to an extensive program of information exchange with the U.S. covering both in-house and private industrial research

the Commission thought it had secured the assent of its partners. Indeed, Germany paid, but France demurred. Dissatisfied with the outcome of the Euratom-U.S. negotiations, France refused to pay until the Commission and its Euratom partners agreed in 1967 to revise the Euratom five-year plan a second time and concentrate additional resources in areas of special interest to France.

A further incident illustrates the different attitude France and Germany took toward relations with the United States and U.S. industries. When the German association was negotiated in 1962, Karlsruhe officials insisted, over French and Commission objections, that the common research program include a venture planned by Karlsruhe in cooperation with GE and a group of private utilities in the southwestern part of the United States (Southwest Atomic Energy Associates). The venture involved the construction of a test reactor (known as SEFOR) to investigate certain safety aspects of the fast reactor.[34] The Commission regarded Euratom participation in this foreign and essentially private undertaking as undesirable,[35] and France saw this participation as nothing less than a direct Community subsidy to an American industrial competitor, GE. As soon as the issue was resolved in favor of the German point of view, however, France decided that it would like to station a scientist with the SEFOR project.

This assignment could be made in two ways. First, because Euratom participated in SEFOR through the German association, Germany, as *porte parole* for the Community, could request approval of the assignment by GE. A second alternative was to station the Frenchman under the terms of the Euratom-U.S. fast reactor agreement which authorized the exchange of personnel (see note 33). German officials, angered by France's initial opposition to SEFOR, were less than enthusiastic about the first alternative. They stalled and then submitted the request to GE in such a way that the latter found it easy to reject.[36] When France

---

contracts. Valid for ten years, the agreement, nevertheless, met European concerns for balance by stipulating that the two programs would remain about the same size from 1963 to 1967 (around $200 million each) and would have to construct prototypes within three years of one another, or the agreement would have to be revised. The parties also agreed to a long-term exchange of personnel. A mixed Euratom-USAEC Committee, meeting twice yearly, was set up to supervise the agreement. For a copy of the agreement, see *Amtsblatt der Europaeischen Gemeinschaften* (official bulletin of the European Communities, Brussels), July 20, 1966; see also *Le Monde*, May 20, 1964.

[34] *Nuclear Industry*, July 1962, p. 18. For a general discussion of the SEFOR project, see W. Schnurr and J. R. Welsh, "The SEFOR reactor—Aspects of International Cooperation," A paper presented at the Third United Nations International Conference on the Peaceful Uses of Atomic Energy, Geneva, September 1964.

[35] The USAEC financed the R&D program connected with SEFOR but did not participate in the capital costs. The Euratom-German share contributed to capital costs. The Community's participation in a private capital venture in which even the USAEC was not involved particularly disturbed the Commission.

[36] German representatives told GE officials that the man was a CEA employee rather than a Euratom representative under the German association. Relations between GE and

pressed the Commission to have the assignment made under the Euratom-U.S. agreement, the Commission was embarrassed to learn that the USAEC had failed to include a clause in the GE contract permitting this exchange. France took the oversight as proof of American bad faith.

The whole incident dragged on for more than three years, fraying tempers between the French, on the one hand, and the Germans and the Commission, on the other.[37] Though the Frenchman was finally assigned to SEFOR in 1967, France concluded from this incident that neither the Commission nor the USAEC could be trusted to meet their obligations in cooperative undertakings with U.S. industry.

The Prototype Phase

The Commission's objective had always been to harmonize the separate association contracts into a single Community program at the prototype stage. With the association contracts due to expire in 1967, Euratom officials urged at a conference called in Venice in 1965 that a single consortium be established to initiate design studies for a common prototype plant.[38] From 1965 on, however, Euratom was in a state of financial crisis and lacked funds to finance Community participation in prototype development. Moreover, the duality of preceding programs (two critical assemblies and two reprocessing plants) reduced chances that the Community could now avoid two prototype plants. This became fully evident as the French and German programs regrouped to take into account the industrial aspects of prototype development.

Franco-Italian Talks

After 1964, the French program was affected by de Gaulle's hostility toward the European Communities. The same Belgian and Dutch firms that carried out a number of R&D contracts for the French program (see note 18 above) made overtures to participate in French prototype plans. But CEA officials opted for a prototype project on an exclusively national basis. In 1965 they determined the principal characteristics of PHENIX, a 250 MWe prototype reactor, to be constructed at Marcoule.[39] In addition to ending ties with Belgian and Dutch partners, France also pressed for a reduction of Euratom's role in the French pro-

---

the CEA were not particularly amicable (a question of personalities), and GE promptly rejected the request.

[37]See, e.g., the comments of the French Project Head, George Vendryès, in *Nucleonics Week*, August 31, 1967.

[38]*Agence Europe*, February 13, 1965; see also the subsequently published report, Euratom, Directorate-General for Industry and Economy, *First Target Programme of the European Atomic Energy Community* (EUR 2773e) (Brussels: Euratom, March 1966).

[39]Bertrand Goldschmidt, "Les principales options techniques du programme français de production d'énergie nucléaire," *Revue Française de l'Énergie*, Numéro spécial (October 1969), p. 92.

gram, arguing that the Commission should cover the extra costs of the plutonium purchase (see above) by reducing its contribution (and hence also its claim on information) to the over-all association program with France.

The French decision to go it alone became clearer in discussions with Italian officials in the fall of 1965.[40] Once the Commission gave up hope for a single prototype, it encouraged cooperation in the south between France and Italy and in the north between Germany and the Benelux countries. The Italian program now centered on the construction of a fuel test reactor known as PEC and the study of sodium cooling components. In conversations with the French, Italy proposed that PEC substitute for PHENIX. The Italians argued that there was no need to build a second prototype identical to the one being planned in Germany (see below), and the French experience with RAPSODIE was sufficient already to permit, on the basis of PEC, a direct jump to commercial-size reactor stations (600–1000 MWe).

Given Gaullist attitudes in this period, France did not take well to these suggestions. PEC was no substitute for PHENIX because PHENIX was necessary to meet the German competition. Moreover, French officials felt RAPSODIE could perform the same functions as PEC, and thus did not regard PEC as a particularly necessary complement to PHENIX. In 1967 France authorized the construction of PHENIX and suggested that PEC be adapted for experimentation in the later commercial phase of development. Italy felt this was but another of a long series of "put-offs," preventing Italian industry from assuming its rightful role in fast reactor industrial development.

Nor was the Commission convinced of the need for PEC. A few German scientists felt this reactor might alleviate the shortage of irradiation facilities in the Community (which compelled Euratom to use British and American facilities) but were unwilling to commit themselves to specific use of PEC. Italy, nonetheless, demanded release of Community funds for the project (only $2.5 million of the original $9 million for the Italian association had been spent) and delayed resolution of the second revision of Euratom's five-year plan until this request was met. The final decision in July 1967 approved PEC; but to attain French and German support, Italy had to agree to shift funds ($7.8 million) from programs it favored (chiefly JNRC activities and proven reactors) to the German and French fast reactor associations.[41]

---

[40]For a description of the context in which these talks occurred, see *Agence Europe*, March 28, 1966. The details of the talks were gained in interviews with association officials.

[41]France and Italy did finally get together in a minor way in April 1970 when the CEA, CNEN, and COREPEC (consortium established by SNAM-Progetti and Italimpianti to supervise construction of PEC) signed a technical assistance agreement concerning PEC. While this agreement was heralded as a first step toward further Franco-Italian cooperation, it was in itself relatively insignificant. *Atomo e Industria*, May 1, 1970.

Cooperation in the north fared somewhat better. The impetus came from the German program. Starting behind and pursuing a broader-based program than France (steam and helium as well as sodium cooling), Germany faced a growing requirement for cooperation as industrial-scale activities approached. Belgium and Holland, after being turned away by France, stood ready to cooperate with Germany. These countries, like Italy, resented their exclusion from evolving industrial activities. Thus, on the initiative of the German project head, Haefele, Karlsruhe worked out a closely coordinated research program with these countries. Euratom gave this cooperation a Community framework by concluding in 1965 new association agreements with Belgium and Holland.[42]

German leaders also took steps to initiate a cooperative framework for a German prototype program. An expansion of the German second five-year nuclear plan in 1965 set aside funds for the construction of two thermal test reactors for investigating the properties of sodium and steam cooling techniques (helium cooling being reevaluated in a somewhat longer-term perspective).[43] Preliminary studies of these reactors were already underway in private industry. To encourage the start-up of construction, Karlsruhe proposed making available to the concerned industries all of the information acquired under the association program, including patents on a royalty-free basis.[44] With this incentive, Interatom undertook the construction of the sodium-cooled KNK reactor at Karlsruhe, and AEG began construction of the steam-cooled HDR reactor at Grosswelzheim. Technically, these were not fast reactors,[45] and they therefore fell outside the purview of the association program. Thus,

---

[42]The Belgian association dealt primarily with physics and design studies for a sodium-cooled commercial-size reactor, together with preliminary studies of a steam-cooled reactor. The Dutch association focused on large-scale conventional reactor components, such as steam generators, heat exchangers, and sodium pumps. For copies of the Belgian and Dutch contracts, see respectively, Euratom, *Convention d'association entre l'Euratom et l'état Belge* (EUR/C/3688/2/65f) (Brussels, n.d.); and *Contrat d'association entre l'Euratom et la TNO-RCN* (EUR/C/3754/7/65f) (Brussels, n.d.).

[43]*Bulletin des Presse- und Informationsamtes der Bundesregierung* (bulletin published by the Press and Information Office of the Federal Republic of Germany, Bonn) December 1, 1965, p. 1524.

[44]Theoretically, any transfer of information outside the association, especially into private hands, was supposed to occur only on the basis of appropriate compensation to the association. This fee, of course, could be set at zero, and this is what happened in the case of the Karlsruhe proposal. Italy regarded these arrangements as proof of the inequities of the association system, since it was unlikely that the German association would agree to make this information available to Italian industries on a royalty-free basis. See inquiry of an Italian representative in European Parliament concerning patent policies under the associations, *Agence Europe*, April 14, 1966.

[45]There was no doubt, however, that they were intended for fast reactor experiments. They were built for subsequent conversion to fast cores. See Germany, Federal Ministry for Scientific Research, *3. Atomprogramm der Bundesrepublik Deutschland 1968-72* (Bonn: Federal Ministry for Scientific Research, n.d.), p. 11. KNK was to receive its fast core in 1973. *Nuclear Industry*, April 1971, p. 30.

the effect of these industrial initiatives was not unlike the effect of France's more open opposition to cooperation, namely a reduction of Euratom's influence over emerging industrial programs.

Unlike France, however, Germany initiated bilateral discussions to establish a transnational industrial framework for prototype development. Under prodding from Karlsruhe, Interatom and Siemens began discussions with Belgonucléaire and Neratoom; at the same time AEG along with GHH and MAN conducted exploratory inquiries with IRI and ENEL in Italy.[46]

An important political factor accounting for this initiative toward industrial transnationalism was Germany's desire to protect the commercial prospects for its fast reactor from potentially adverse effects of the nonproliferation treaty.[47] Within an international consortium, German industry might be less vulnerable to discriminatory applications of this treaty. For this reason and because public financing would be involved, governments also participated in these industrial negotiations. In October 1967 the Belgian, Dutch, and German governments announced that they had reached agreement in principle to construct a common prototype plant of 300 MWe.[48] Following this agreement, a joint industrial consortium, SNR, was established to initiate design studies of the common plant.[49]

The Associations Expire

Thus, by the time the association contracts expired at the end of 1967, the Community fast reactor scene was fragmented into three parts— PHENIX, SNR, and PEC. Each of these projects reflected different technical characteristics, organizational arrangements, and stages of development. The PHENIX project utilized a pool-type core arrangement, while SNR employed a loop-type concept. PHENIX was administered under a contract awarded to a mixed group of experts from EdF, GAAA, and the CEA. This group operated under the direction of the CEA. SNR was organized primarily along industrial lines, with sharp

---

[46]Deutscher Forschungsdienst, *Sonderbericht Kernenergie*, January 12, 1967.

[47]German concern was aroused when the U.S. replied to Euratom requests in 1966 for additional plutonium supplies by making agreement conditional on a tighter inspection system, a further exchange of information, and a higher price for plutonium than the price prevailing on the U.S. private market (where plutonium was now being produced as a by-product of electricity output). Christopher Layton, *European Advanced Technology* (London: George Allen and Unwin, 1969), p. 117. Some sources even reported that the U.S. was making signature of the nonprofileration treaty a condition of further plutonium supplies. *Atomo e Industria*, June 1, 1968.

[48]*Agence Europe*, October 10, 1967.

[49]The shares in this enterprise were divided 70 percent, Germany; 15 percent, Belgium; and 15 percent, Holland. Luxatome, a firm in Luxembourg, joined in 1969 at a small percentage. As potential customers, utilities also participated in these agreements, establishing in 1969 a joint company, Projektgesellschaft Schneller Brueter (PSB). Shareholders in this company included RWE (Germany), SEP (Holland), and SYNATOM (Belgium).

distinctions being drawn between the roles of government, utilities, industries, and research organizations. Italy, after the many stops and starts with PEC, was having trouble even getting industry involved. Lengthy negotiations with the state-controlled industrial groups, ENI and IRI, held up the award of the PEC contract until late 1968.

Council decisions in December 1967 resulted in the suspension of the fast reactor associations (as well as all other associations) until a review by the Committee of Permanent Representatives could determine which associations would be continued as part of the common program and which would be converted into additional or special programs. Commission personnel continued to be stationed with the national programs but joint management through the Comité de Gestion, for all practical purposes, ceased.[50]

The attempt to find a compromise foundered on the industrial issue. In proposals forwarded in March 1968, the new Commission called for a continuation of research under association contracts and the consolidation of industrial projects (PHENIX, SNR, and PEC) under a single joint enterprise company, involving both Euratom and private capital participation.[51] Italy reserved judgment on the association contracts until it was assured a place in the industrial programs. France insisted that the negotiation of a common industrial policy for fast reactors precede the consolidation of industrial projects. In a memorandum to the Council, France made clear that this common policy must discriminate in favor of European companies. France's interpretation of a joint enterprise company was one in which European citizens or governments exercised majority control or the firm's headquarters (i.e., parent organization) was located on European soil.[52] Germany and the Benelux countries could not accept such a limitation of industrial freedom. In their own joint memorandum, these countries proposed very loose forms of cooperation for all activities except research work, which might be continued under association contracts.[53]

Commission proposals in 1968 and 1969 tried to bridge these differences by allowing for flexible cooperative arrangements depending on whether research, semi-industrial, or full-scale commercial activities

[50]After this point, if not before, Euratom influence became negligible. In 1968, France concluded a bilateral agreement with Canada for additional plutonium supplies, excluding the Commission on grounds that Euratom's supply authority was no longer operative. Under Canadian pressure, nevertheless, France did make some adjustments in this agreement. *Agence Europe*, November 4, 1968; and *Le Monde*, October 2, 1968.

[51]*Agence Europe*, May 21, 1968.

[52]Euratom, The Council, Note délégation française, *Cooperation européenne dans le domaine des réacteurs rapides: Problèmes de politique industrielle* [817f/68 (ATO 40) nl] (Brussels, April 1968).

[53]Euratom, The Council, Memorandum der deutschen, der belgischen und der niederlaendischen Regierung, *Moeglichkeiten fuer die Zusammenarbeit auf dem Gebiet der schnellen Reaktoren im Rahmen von Euratom* [919d/68 (ATO 47) mp] (Brussels, May 1968).

were involved.[54] These proposals, however, could not circumvent the different French and German conceptions of what constitutes a research or industrial task. An experimental program classified in France as a research activity and hence an appropriate function of public authorities may be perceived in Germany as a quasi-industrial activity and hence a task for private industry.

To conclude that the conflict was industrial is not to say that it was any less political. From 1965 on, fast reactors were priority aims of national programs and priority recipients of government funds. Governments were very much in a position to affect the prospects of cooperation. But each country sought to exploit its strength rather than confront its weakness. France sought to use its administrative weight (the CEA was always a more formidable negotiating partner than the German Science Ministry) to secure a division of the industrial pie unwarranted by its actual industrial strength. And Germany sought to rely on its industrial capability to offset the more decentralized, less coherent administration of the German program.

The Commercial Phase

With cooperation foreclosed in the prototype phase, attention shifted to the next stage of development, the construction of a first commercial-size or "head of series" fast reactor (600–1000 MWe). In the fall of 1967, the French science minister, Maurice Schumann, had called for joint construction of such a reactor.[55] While this proposal was timed to arouse political support for French concern over "the American challenge" (see chapter 2), it also reflected growing commercial constraints, which were increasing interest in Europe in long-term cooperation.

The Competitive Situation

The consensus in 1968 conceded Europe an advanced position in the competitive development of fast reactors.[56] Though opinions differed, the Soviet Union was judged to have the most advanced program, with a 350 MWe prototype expected to be in operation sometime in 1969. Great Britain followed close behind. The 250 MWe reactor at Dounreay was scheduled for service in 1971. In third place came the French, American, and Japanese programs. Behind them, the German-Benelux effort

---

[54]See the Commission's recommendations in October 1968 and again in April 1969 for a third multiple-year plan: Commission of the European Communities, *Entwurf des Mehrjahresprogramms fuer Forschung und Ausbildung* [KOM (68) 801] (Brussels, October 9, 1968), pp. 15–21; and *Kuenftige Aufgaben fuer Euratom* [KOM (69) 350] (Brussels, April 23, 1969), pp. 50–66.

[55]*Nucleonics Week*, November 6, 1967.

[56]For various views on this subject, see Deutscher Forschungsdienst, *Sonderbericht Kernenergie*, January 29, 1961; *Nucleonics Week*, August 31, 1967; and Layton, *European Advanced Technology*, p. 123.

was closing fast. Thus, at this point, Community programs were still very much in the running. If these programs remained fragmented, however, they stood a good chance of falling behind. U.S. plans announced in 1969 and 1971 called for vast expenditures to accelerate its fast breeder program. Spurred by unexpected energy shortages, the United States was moving to use its superior resources to overtake the foreign competition.[57]

The Commission's "white paper" of October 1968 highlighted these threats to European programs.[58] The report warned bluntly that "if the present situation, characterized by the unco-ordinated development of three projects, should continue, it will be disastrous for the future of the Community's industry in this sector." The Community must "arrive as quickly as possible at the first in a series, which would be a pre-commercial 600–1000 MWe reactor." To this end, the Commission envisioned the establishment of a single joint enterprise based on a unity of technical conception, the dovetailing of research efforts, and an industrial grouping of all interested commercial enterprises. The entry of Great Britain into the European Community was expected to give this venture a much needed lift.

A Multilevel European Response

The white paper proposal ignited a spate of rhetoric urging cooperation in fast reactors. In June 1969, the European organization of electricity producers, UNIPEDE, issued a resolution decrying the waste involved in the duplication of prototype projects and calling for the construction of a *single* commercial fast reactor of the maximum power feasible (around 1000 MWe).[59] Two weeks later, the European organization of industries, UNICE, endorsed this appeal and, on the request of UNIPEDE, undertook a survey of European firms to ascertain concrete prospects for establishing an industrial consortium to build the commercial plant. At the Hague summit conference in December, fast reactors were a specific item of discussion among the heads of government, and the Euratom Council communiqué two days later specified fast reac-

[57] *The Times* (London), December 5, 1969, and *New York Times*, September 27, 1971. At a congress in April 1967 called by Foratom (the organization of nuclear press and information agencies in the Euratom countries), a British industrialist pointed out the consequences of intra-European rivalry in face of American plans: "I believe that the present race between the major European (fast-breeder) programs is one which nobody can win outright but which could be lost eventually to the Americans." *Nucleonics Week*, May 4, 1967.

[58] Commission of the European Communities, "Survey of the Nuclear Policy of the European Communities," *Bulletin of the European Communities*, Supplement (September/October 1968), pp. 18 and 51–52.

[59] *Atomo e Industria*, November 1, 1969.

tors as a field of action requiring the "widest possible cooperation."[60] Indeed, market considerations and the high costs of the advanced stages of development seemed to be encouraging at last the kind of political reasonableness which had been missing from Community activities for so long.

Increasing costs forced a narrowing of technical options in the German program. In February 1969, despite some spirited domestic opposition, the German government terminated the steam-cooled fast reactor program being carried out by AEG.[61] Partly to compensate AEG, federal officials urged cooperation with Siemens on the sodium-cooled fast reactor. When KWU (joint subsidiary of Siemens and AEG) was created in April 1969, the stage was set for the unprecedented offer by German industry to obtain French participation in KWU.

Perhaps a major factor behind French rejection of this offer was the belief that France was comfortably ahead of Germany in the fast reactor field. If fast reactors developed rapidly, as France hoped, dependence on light water plants, where Germany held the lead, might be only temporary. Thus the trade-off of French fast reactor technology for German light water technology did not appear to be a well-balanced one. In addition, PHENIX was already under construction, and though SNR was scheduled to begin construction in 1970, difficulties in what a German scientist subsequently described as "software" areas delayed start-up for two years.[62] Construction would only begin on SNR as PHENIX neared completion (end of 1972). France felt confident cooperation could await a later stage.

The need for cooperation at the commercial stage was most clearly recognized by European utilities. Under urging from UNIPEDE, French (EdF), German (RWE), and Italian (ENEL) utilities signed an agreement in spring 1971 expressing interest in building jointly two 1000 MWe commercial plants, one of the PHENIX design (pool-type) and one of the SNR design (loop-type).[63] Tentative financial arrangements called for EdF to retain the principal share of the PHENIX 1000 MWe project and PSB, the German-Benelux utilities operating SNR, to retain

---

[60] Le Monde, December 3, 1969. For a copy of the Hague communiqué, see Research and Technology (bulletin published by the Press and Information Services of the Commission of the European Communities, Brussels), No. 36 (December 8, 1969), Annex 1.

[61] For a discussion of this decision and the controversy it aroused, see Capital (Cologne), February 1969, pp. 82–84.

[62] See W. Haefele, "Entwicklungstendenzen bei Schnellen Brutreaktoren," A paper presented at Reaktortagung 1972, Hamburg, April 14, 1972 (obtained from author). Software issues (as distinguished from the hardware technical aspects of SNR) concerned the integration of the SNR concept into a long-term industrial framework which would allow commercial reactors to be built on a consumer demand basis. The principal issues in this connection were safety considerations, which eventually forced a change of location site for SNR, and the alteration of core construction to permit subsequent manufacture of larger, commercial-size units.

[63] Nuclear Industry, May 1971, p. 43; and Agence Europe, October 1, 1971.

the principal share of the SNR 1000 MWe plant.[64] Through such cooperation among utilities, French and German industries hoped to obtain data on the performance characteristics of each other's reactor designs. Reportedly, this possibility left Italy somewhat dissatisfied since Italian industries were not included in these industrial alignments. From an Italian point of view, ENEL participation amounted once again to an Italian financial contribution to French and German hardware programs.[65]

Eventual industrial cooperation between France and Germany was complicated by further alignments, however. The agreements signed in July 1971 by TNPG (British) and KWU (Germany) established the basis for Anglo-German cooperation in fast reactors. Present plans call for joint construction of a 1300 MWe fast reactor station in England (a follow-up to the British Dounreay prototype).[66] On the basis of industrial participation in this project, together with information obtained through utility participation in the French PHENIX 1000 MWe project, German planners anticipate going directly from the SNR prototype to the construction of a super-large, 2000 MWe SNR-type reactor. British and German industrial plans, like French plans, do not provide for Italian participation.[67]

The final outlines of European fast reactor cooperation are still unclear. Much depends on technical developments. Recently, interest has grown in a high temperature, gas-cooled fast breeder, which promises the possibility of greater efficiency and several safety advantages over sodium cooling.[68] Should this concept take hold, a second European consortium might emerge bringing together firms active in the high temperature field, such as CEM (France) and BBC Mannheim (both subsidiaries of BBC Switzerland), and firms capable of supplying fast and light water reactors, such as GAAA (France) and Deutsche Babcock

[64]For the PHENIX 1000 MWe plant, the percentages broke down as follows: EdF, 50 percent; PSB, 16 percent; and ENEL, 33 percent. For the SNR 1000 MWe plant, the percentages were PSB, 51 percent; EdF, 16 percent; and ENEL, 33 percent. See Haefele, "Entwicklungstendenzen bei Schnellen Brutreaktoren," p. 5.

[65]Agence Europe, October 1, 1971.

[66]Agence Europe, May 13, 1972. The fact that the British design is the same as the French (i.e., pool type) and differs from the German design (loop type) suggests that technical differences are not significant obstacles to cooperation.

[67]The TNPG/KWU agreements of 1971 included an agreement with Agip Nucleare of Italy only in the areas of proven and high temperature reactors (as well as fuel for these reactors).

[68]In 1969, a number of European firms including TNPG, Belgonucléaire, BBK (Hochtemperatur Reaktorbau), BBC, and Neratoom set up a study group called Gas-Cooled Breeder Reactor Association. This group conducted a two-year study of the economic prospects of gas breeders and reached optimistic conclusions. Agence Europe, June 19-20, 1972. The USAEC and Gulf General Atomic are also pursuing work on this concept. See USAEC, Annual Report to Congress—1972, Senate Document No. 93-2, Pt. 1, 93rd Cong., 1st Sess., p. 18.

and Wilcox. Such a grouping should be able to offer all reactor types in competition with TNPG/KWU.

Utilities, in particular, are interested in such alternative alignments as a way of preventing TNPG/KWU from attaining a monopoly supplier position in the reactor field. This was the principal motivation behind the collaboration of EdF, RWE, and ENEL in spring 1971. Apparently, British utilities (CEGB) have also expressed a desire to join this group, but France does not seem particularly eager to include British partners.[69] In addition, as we have already noted, Italy may force ENEL to withdraw from this set-up, unless Italian industry gets a piece of the action.

France and Italy are both concerned about the consequences of collaboration among utilities for industrial cooperation. Utilities are still subject to political pressures to place new orders for commercial stations with domestic suppliers. If CEGB joins the fast reactor utility group, the preference for Anglo-German industrial suppliers may become overwhelming. If CEGB is excluded, France can be certain of a substantial industrial role, especially in view of the advantage PHENIX presently holds over SNR.

The limits of cooperation among utilities, therefore, seem to be set by the limits of cooperation among industries. This is why some countries, notably Italy and perhaps also France, will probably continue to resist the effort to draw sharp distinctions between alignments in the industrial, utility, and governmental sectors (a favorite formula of German groups). As long as national industrial groups are not participating, government officials will place limits on utility cooperation. A differentiated, multi-tiered approach assumes a relative equality among the participants at each level (i.e., industry, utility, research, etc.). When this equality does not exist, vertical linkages may develop; and relations among industries and utilities may become matters of interest and policy in relations among governments.

[69] *Nuclear Industry*, September 1971, p. 7.

PART IV
THE MAP REDRAWN

CHAPTER 9

THE POLITICS OF
TECHNOLOGICAL COOPERATION

If one conclusion emerges clearly from the preceding analysis, it is the trite but sobering conclusion that actor behavior in technological areas is complex and multipurpose. No one analysis can account for all this complexity. An awareness of this fact led us in chapter 1 to specify the focus of this study. We stated and justified our interest in probing the political motivations behind technological change rather than tracing the political adjustments resulting from technological change. We said we were more interested in learning how states and other international actors "use" scientific and technological processes to implement specific group or national purposes than how scientific and technological processes "force" these actors to formulate common purposes. This was said in full awareness that the political (i.e., partisan) approach deals with only one slice of reality, albeit an important and neglected one. It was also said in the firm conviction that analyses based on this approach serve the long-term interests of peace and harmony in the world no less than analyses focusing on the effects of autonomous technological trends. Until we know the saintly or selfish purposes for which men apply the advances of technology, we cannot know how to promote or parry these purposes in the interest of world peace.

In this chapter, we summarize the tendencies nations and other actors repeatedly display in cooperative technological undertakings. These tendencies are drawn from our detailed case study of nuclear reactor development in Europe but may also be characteristic of international behavior in other sectors of advanced technology. In our discussion, we will note examples from other technological sectors which seem to support trends identified in this study of the nuclear sector. We will also note the relevance of our findings for current attempts to resuscitate and expand European technological cooperation. Finally, in a concluding section, we will relate the general perspective adopted in this study to the continuing evolution and evaluation of technology in international politics. We take particular note of the attitudes and policies of the United States and key Western European countries on the continuously shifting relationship of politics, economics, and technology.

The initial discussion is divided into two parts: (1) political patterns associated with the origins of technological cooperation (roughly, the program definition phase) and (2) political patterns associated with the evolution of technological cooperation (the R&D, prototype, and commercial phases). These patterns are determined by the relationship between the goals and capabilities of individual actors, both as perceived by the actors themselves and as perceived by this investigator. We distinguish between two types of policy goals—goals concerned with internal objectives of cooperation and goals concerned with external objectives of cooperation. And we differentiate among three types of capability—technical (R&D), industrial, and political-strategic.

Politics of Origin of Technological Cooperation

It has been argued that technical activities provide a better basis for interstate cooperation than military and economic activities. This is because technical tasks have a low specific gravity in political terms. They concern problems that are functional in scope and content and hence neutral across political frontiers and traditional political conflicts.[1] Insofar as technological communities do not attract the same political attention or urgency as military and economic alliances, especially at the outset, this argument carries some validity. Our analysis suggests, however, that the initially low political profile of technological cooperation is less a result of the functional or neutral content of technical projects than the political context in which these projects originate. Political factors contribute to a de-emphasis of the broader purposes for which cooperation is pursued. In a curious paradox, politics itself accounts for the apparent absence of politics.

This apparent absence of politics stems, in the first instance, from the fact that technical projects offered as the basis of international collaboration are usually projects of relatively low political value and interest to begin with, especially for those actors originally possessing or being most advanced in this technology. Put another way, government or industrial actors tend to offer projects for international cooperation

---

[1]This was the basis of the original functionalist argument that interstate cooperation could be initiated and carried out more easily in technical areas. See David Mitrany, *A Working Peace System* (Chicago: Quadrangle, 1966), especially pp. 149–66. The argument is also implicit in recent studies of interdependence which contend that the increasing technical and organizational content of modern foreign policies contributes a quality of specificity to contemporary interstate relations which renders these relations less conflictive and more cooperative than traditional interstate relations. See Edward L. Morse, "The Transformation of Foreign Policies," *World Politics*, XXII (April 1970), p. 377.

only after these projects have declined in priority or before they have risen in priority in the independent plans of these actors.[2] If projects are judged to be of large, immediate, or potential significance, parent actors reserve these projects for development in their own programs. This option is usually open during the formative stage, since the resources required to start up a major project are small compared to later development and commercial costs. Moreover, at the outset, actors tend to underestimate the costs of development and overestimate the benefits.[3] On the other hand, if projects are considered to be of relatively low or declining importance, parent actors may recommend international cooperation to conserve internal resources and attract outside collaborators to share further development costs. At the least, internationalizing a project promises a tidy way to phase out a struggling project and may even bring some returns through sale of existing information and technology.[4]

[2]Examples of this tendency from our case studies are numerous: (1) low priority of domestic nuclear power when U.S. proposed joint program with Euratom, (2) low priority of DRAGON project at time of British offer of cooperation through ENEA, (3) low priority of organic-cooled, heavy water studies in Community countries when this project was approved as basis of Community ORGEL program, and (4) low priority of heavy water studies when Siemens after 1962 offered these studies as a basis of cooperative discussions with France, Sweden, and other countries.

Examples also come to mind in other sectors of advanced technology: (1) low priority of Blue Streak missile program when Britain offered this project as basis of ELDO and (2) declining priority of current U.S. space program at time when U.S. seeks space cooperation with European allies (space shuttle) and the Soviet Union (space rendezvous).

These findings are consistent with results of studies that seek to explain actor propensities to organize over-all R&D tasks nationally rather than internationally (in contrast to specific projects as in the examples above). John Gerard Ruggie finds that an inverse relationship holds between the proportion of GNP a country devotes to R&D (a measure of the priority of R&D to that country) and the ratio of international to national task performance in R&D (a measure of the gains to that country from R&D performed in international as compared to national organizations). In other words, the lower the priority of R&D in a particular country (or in a particular sector or project within that country—for example, the reactor projects in this study), the larger the performance gains that country can expect to derive from organizing R&D internationally as opposed to nationally. In addition to such performance gains, there may also be political gains. These we discuss further in the text above. For Ruggie's study, see "Collective Goods and Future International Collaboration," *The American Political Science Review*, LXVI (September 1972), pp. 874–93, especially p. 883.

[3]This was clearly the case, for example, in early attitudes of Euratom members toward heavy water and fast reactor cooperation.

[4]Exceptions to the tendency of international projects to focus on technology of low political priority may apply where access to an important technology is impossible without cooperation, such as uranium enrichment technology. Initiation of cooperation, even in these areas, however, usually requires some lessening of the political interest and priority attached to such technology. For example, as long as enrichment technology was an issue of major political significance in Atlantic relations (as it was in the late 1950s and early 1960s), European cooperation to construct a common enrichment plant was impeded. Only after the strategic significance of this technology lessened somewhat through allied accommodation to the French nuclear force and a nonproliferation agreement to prevent additional nuclear forces in the future did the context evolve in a way favorable to the establishment of cooperation (tripartite pact in 1968 and subsequent discussions on a common diffusion plant). (See chap. 5.)

This tendency to offer projects of low political interest for international collaboration does not mean that the offer may not be coupled with other, more important political objectives unrelated to the specific technology. As we noted, the American offer to Euratom of a joint light water program and the British offer of cooperation in high temperature reactors concealed political objectives of broader significance to these actors (in the American case, affirmation of Euratom and European unity; in the British case, establishment of alternatives to Euratom and European unity). The purpose for which technological cooperation is organized may be highly political. The tendency we have noted suggests only that the particular, technical content of cooperation will initially be of low or declining political interest to the parent actor proposing cooperation.[5]

The consequences of this divorce between the political use of the technology and the political value of the technology itself may be important. If the program serves purposes other than the development of technology, the program is vulnerable to collapse when these purposes no longer apply; on the other hand, when these purposes continue to apply, the program may develop in distorted or costly ways.[6]

The initiation of technological cooperation in cases where no larger political purpose is intended also presents difficulties. These difficulties derive from the fact that technical projects in early stages of development, if uninformed by political objectives, may offer so many alternative options for future development that agreement on specific technical choices is impeded. At the outset, the technical characteristics of common projects are poorly defined, and decision-making depends on the inclusion of as many different ideas and points of view as possible. In these circumstances of relatively open-ended decision-making (which contrasts sharply with the "compelling" circumstances usually associated with the initiation of military cooperation—e.g., the Berlin blockade and NATO), wide participation is desirable. If political criteria are not present to narrow the scope of participation and/or inform the direction of technical choices, high-level government offices will not intervene. Decision-making authority devolves to lower administrative levels (specific ministries or departments of these ministries) and to outside technical and industrial groups (scientists, businessmen, etc.). According

[5]For example, larger political purposes lie behind the recent U.S.-Soviet agreement on space cooperation; but space research itself is a lower political priority in the U.S. today than ever before (perhaps also in the Soviet Union).

[6]The U.S.-Euratom joint program may illustrate both cases. When the Common Market overshadowed Euratom as the primary agent of European unity, U.S. political support of Euratom and the joint program declined. By this time, however, Euratom was committed to the success of the joint program; and cooperation continued on a program whose original political justification no longer existed and whose technical and economic costs may have been too high, at least in the opinion of those who wanted to see these resources applied to other technologies.

to participatory theories of policy-making, this pluralization of the decision-making process should enhance the prospects of agreement (by bringing to bear the more concrete interests and objectives represented by specialized groups). Ironically, however, the absence of political interest at the highest levels may actually contribute to an intensification of political maneuvering among lower echelon groups.

Actors immediately involved in the negotiation of common technological programs tend to infuse alternative technical approaches to joint projects with subjective feelings of personal, professional, industrial, and/or national prowess and pride and to show little interest in compromise on technical choices as long as the specific parameters and conditions of cooperation remain open-ended. Such parochial behavior is often expected of petty-minded bureaucrats and industrially employed participants (if any are around at the earliest stages of technical definition). Scientists and technical personnel, on the other hand, are frequently thought to behave more cooperatively and objectively.[7] Yet our case studies suggest that scientific professionals may be no less partisan-minded than other actors. This should not be that surprising given the fact that scientific actors have a great deal at stake both personally and professionally in common enterprises and in what appear, in the program definition stage of cooperation, to be purely technical choices (as we noted, for example, in Community heavy water discussions concerning characteristics of an Ispra prototype project). These stakes become magnified in a nascent multinational setting where personal status is closely tied to national status and the administrative and interpersonal conditions of cooperation are still to be decided.[8] Indeed, as we saw in our case study of fast reactors, technical alternatives may actually be manipulated to meet the desire of scientific groups to structure cooperation consistent with personal as well as national capabilities and research traditions. The cultural and social milieu of scientists and engineers, no less than other actors, determines how they will approach scientific tasks and the organization of research and industry. Their background influences the procedures they recommend to reach a technical answer, as well as the formulation of the initial question to which they seek an answer.[9]

[7]See, for example, the conclusion that among scientists and engineers, "the ethics and standards of their professions tend to outweigh any political considerations." Eugene B. Skolnikoff, *The International Imperatives of Technology* (Research Series No. 16; Berkeley: University of California, Institute of International Studies, 1972), p. 172.

[8]The close tie between personal and national status in multinational settings has been noted in studies of the effects of transnational experiences on participant attitudes. See Donald P. Warwick, "Transnational Participation and International Peace," in Robert O. Keohane and Joseph S. Nye, Jr. (eds.), *Transnational Relations and World Politics* (Cambridge: Harvard University Press, 1972), pp. 312–13.

[9]Albert H. Teich records an interview with a physicist at the Ispra center which succinctly expresses the influence of national factors on scientific choices. "There is no

244   NATIONAL POLITICS AND INTERNATIONAL TECHNOLOGY

Stressing the professional nationalism of scientific actors may seem to do injustice to the often-recorded idealism of these actors.[10] Analysts, frequently themselves scientifically or professionally trained, exhibit a strong reluctance to challenge the norm of internationalism among scientific investigators. From a sociological point of view, this reluctance is understandable, since the influence of scientists frequently depends on the extent to which they can convince others that their input is non-partisan.[11] Yet in all but remote areas of basic research, scientific internationalism is less a reality than a statement of attitude concerning what scientists believe rather than what they practice. To note this discrepancy is not to deny that scientists' contributions often may be more objective than those of purely political actors. But in studying the impact of science on international activities, more attention should be paid to what scientists actually do in international settings than to what they say they do. Attitudes do not translate automatically into behavior. In researching the case studies of this book, the writer encountered frequent statements among scientists affirming their belief in European unity; their actions, on the other hand, frequently contradicted these statements. Their inconsistency in this regard is no more *or less* than that of other participants in the international arena.

Without political guidance, therefore, there is no reason to assume that scientists and engineers will reach agreement on common technological programs any faster or more smoothly than government officials. In fact, it may require an injection of political considerations to override scientific and technical disagreement (as Adenauer recognized, for example, in the case of German scientific and industrial opposition to Euratom).[12] This is the reverse of traditional functionalist logic whereby

national physics," the physicist noted, but "... the thing that is different is the way different people attack a problem. ... I mean a solution is a solution ... but how you get to the solution, this depends on your background, your cultural and national background." See A. H. Teich, "International Politics and International Science: A Study of Scientists' Attitudes" (summary report of unpublished Ph.D. dissertation, Massachusetts Institute of Technology, 1969), p. 9. For a lucid and enlightening study of the impact of national values and traditions on Western science, see Joseph Ben-David, *The Scientist's Role in Society* (Englewood Cliffs: Prentice-Hall, 1971).

[10]For example, Teich's study, which relied heavily on personal interviews with scientists employed in international laboratories, concluded "that an attitude pattern highly favorable to increased political integration in Europe is practically universal among European scientists of all nationalities in all of the laboratories." "International Politics and International Science," p. 18.

[11]The self-interested character of the scientist's universalistic ethic is noted by two British students of the sociology of science: "While the individual scientist might maintain his universalistic ethic, it has increasingly become a reality for only an elite among scientists. ... Perhaps universalism remains a predominant myth just because it is precisely this group who tends to write about the philosophy and ethics of science as an institution and an activity." See Hilary Rose and Steven Rose, *Science and Society* (London: Allen Lane, 1969), pp. 180-81.

[12]The essential importance of political leadership in the context of technical discussions is also emphasized by Paul-Henri Spaak in his account of the negotiations he headed

scientific cooperation is thought to be easier to initiate and implement and subsequently to spill over into political cooperation. In the case of fast reactor and enrichment uranium technology, political accommodation created the conditions for overcoming scientific and technological differences.[13] A convergence of political interests may be necessary to expedite the resolution of open-ended technical discussions and establish the framework of common or complementary goals of cooperation. To be sure, government actors, no less than scientific or industrial actors, may behave on grounds of immediate, parochial advantage rather than long-term, common interests. Still, governments may also employ a more comprehensive perspective than other actors and be in a better position to assess the over-all benefits and drawbacks of cooperation. This is often the justification for government intervention in domestic technological programs. The justification would seem to apply to government action in international programs as well. Governments have not only the responsibility but also the authority to act on behalf of the common good.

Government authority in setting up the initial framework of cooperation may be necessary for another reason. In areas of new technology, it is frequently assumed that vested interests do not exist either at the technical or industrial levels. This assumption governed, in part, the creation of Euratom.[14] Yet vested interests do exist, both at the technical level where government agencies may already be charged with over-all development of new technologies (the CEA, for example, in the nuclear sector) and at the industrial level where established national industries may acquire an early stake in new technologies (in the nuclear reactor sector, for example, the electrical, mechanical, and chemical industries). Vested interests may also exist at the highest political levels (as in the case of French government leaders seeking to use nuclear technology for military purposes). Without top-level government involvement, these special interests may generate considerable conflict. Even with top-level government involvement, there is no guarantee of agreement. But what-

---

to draft the Common Market and Euratom Treaties. See his *The Continuing Battle: Memoirs of a European 1936-1966*, trans. Henry Fox (Boston: Little, Brown, 1971), pp. 227-31.

[13]Such accommodation was induced in the fast reactor case by France's desire to head off another German-American alignment like the one in proven reactors and Germany's desire to exploit the moral and financial support of the Community in order to compete and eventually establish parity with France. In the case of enrichment technology, accommodation followed from European concern over superpower interference under the provisions of the nonproliferation treaty and Franco-German rapprochement on the need to reduce European dependence on the U.S.

[14]As Miriam Camps writes, "most of the 'Europeans' felt that progress was more probable in the new field of atomic energy, where there were as yet no vested interests . . . ," *Britain and the European Community, 1955-1963* (Princeton: Princeton University Press, 1964), p. 31; see also Lawrence Scheinman, "Euratom: Nuclear Integration in Europe," *International Conciliation*, No. 563 (May 1967), p. 9.

ever decision is made, top-level political intervention may assure that the decision is visible and occurs after the appropriate public discussion and debate (for example, the French parliamentary debate in the summer of 1956 which paved the way for French participation in Euratom). Government participation, in other words, may promote a more democratic airing of the total interests of society in technological cooperation than would be the case if special interest groups (i.e., scientific and industrial groups) acted individually on behalf of society. What is more, government participation may bring to bear the requisite authority to integrate special interests into the matrix of common interests.

These observations are not intended to minimize the fact that vested interests may indeed be less in sectors of new technology (e.g., nuclear power in the mid-1950s or oceans and the environment today) than old technology (e.g., space or nuclear power today). We are simply suggesting that in the start-up of common technological programs policymakers should look for and work with what vested interests already exist rather than assume that these interests do not exist and formulate policy as if cooperation begins in a vacuum.

Political factors may facilitate the initiation of cooperation in two ways. The first is by establishing a context of hegemonial consensus in which the dominant technological or industrial actor perceives the advantages of promoting cooperation. By hegemonial consensus we mean a configuration of political influence and power in which one member of the proposed technological community dominates the setting of cooperation and exercises a generally accepted role of leadership in broader relationships among community members (e.g., U.S. role in strategic relations in the West in the mid-1950s). This is the pattern that characterized the establishment of Euratom. A second pattern, which is more characteristic of European technological relations today, is a configuration of relatively egalitarian relations among community members in which no single country exercises consistent leadership in broad areas of interaction. In this configuration, political forces may facilitate cooperation by raising leadership issues to the level of conscious decision-making where deliberate bargaining and compromise may produce consensus (or disagreement). Needless to say, this configuration offers a more challenging context for the initiation of cooperation, as European countries are currently experiencing.

A hegemonial (hereafter dominant) political member has the greatest incentive to initiate common technological programs.[15] This follows from the fact that this member exercises predominant control over the

---

[15]The U.S. supplied the initiative in the joint program; Britain took the lead in establishing the DRAGON program (here we assume, with some justification it would seem, that Britain in the 1950s was politically more influential than continental countries); and France, the dominant political country within Europe, was the principal early supporter of Euratom programs (see text and chap. 4, note 39).

larger purposes served by technical and industrial cooperation. As we noted in chapter 2, interest in technical and industrial cooperation never evolves exclusively from a concern to increase material outputs or efficiency. The question always remains what broader goals (usually strategic or diplomatic) will be served by expanded cooperation (and expanded production resulting therefrom). In hegemonial circumstances, such goals are frequently implicit (for example, the desire in the mid-1950s to integrate Western economic resources, including economic union in Europe, to advance Western strategic interests). Nevertheless, their existence explains the enthusiasm of a dominant political member for cooperation. At the technical level, as we noted above, this partner has little to gain from technical cooperation.[16] Usually, its development of the specific technology is most advanced. The technology therefore is less important in itself than as a convenient idiom for advancing the dominant member's political aims.[17] Already exercising political leadership, a dominant country wishes to avoid direct challenges to its control of major policy issues. It prefers to keep discussions at the technical and economic levels. The focus on technical issues draws other partners into a discussion of problems of implementation of policy, such as the most efficient division of labor, while distracting these partners from issues of formulation of policy, which the dominant partner settles unilaterally. In this way, the dominant partner harnesses the resources of allied partners to policy goals of its own making and circumvents the risk of having these goals challenged or compromised in public or painful bargaining.

Thus, within a technological community, the dominant partner stresses pragmatic, technical, and administrative issues aimed at establishing an institutional division of responsibility and competence.[18] All the while, however, this partner values cooperation chiefly for

---

[16]It has little to gain in terms of *absolute* increases in over-all task efficiency or performance. Our comments in note 2 of this chapter suggest that it may have more to gain from organizing this project internationally than nationally, but even in this case, the absolute level of returns will remain small. This follows from the fact that other members have little to contribute to the technological dimensions of cooperation.

[17]Amitai Etzioni in his studies of political unification finds similar evidence that elite members promote union more for political than technical or economic reasons. These members do not seek, Etzioni notes, "to acquire more utilitarian assets [i.e., technical and economic benefit] from the union . . . than they invest in it." Instead they wind up, on balance, investing more utilitarian assets than other members. But as Etzioni further notes, they also derive more political benefits from union in the form of "symbolic (identitive) gratification such as that gained from the status of leadership." See *Political Unification* (New York: Holt, Rinehart and Winston, 1965), p. 315.

[18]This explains the American interest within the Atlantic community in seeing that Euratom cooperation focused on specific objectives, such as those contained in the joint program, rather than more nebulous and potentially threatening programs which might challenge U.S. hegemony in Western policy-making. It also accounts for the French interest within Euratom in emphasizing the technical coherence and efficiency of Euratom programs while resisting the political pretensions of the Euratom Commission, especially in the politically charged area of external relations.

political, instrumental purposes connected with larger goals, usually goals directed toward problems and actors outside the immediate community (e.g., U.S. containment policy toward Russia). This type of policy approach plays down the political purposes of cooperation, which the dominant partner seeks to disguise in technical deliberations, and contributes another factor to the relative de-emphasis of politics in the early stages of technological cooperation.

These policies of dominant partners are neither nefarious nor unusual.[19] In all instances, they may not even be conscious.[20] Yet without them, it is impossible to explain the attraction of technological cooperation for dominant members, which are least in need of technological support. Furthermore, without these incentives, cooperation might be more difficult to achieve. The interest of the dominant partner supplies the will for cooperation and does this in such a way that the normal political problems associated with instituting cooperation are minimized. Technical issues may be separated and dealt with through administrative expedients. Political issues, which usually create the most difficult obstacles to agreement, are assumed or taken for granted. The success of this effort presupposes, of course, that weaker partners are not strongly opposed to dominant partner aims and that the technical attractions of cooperation are sufficient to invite the participation of weaker countries.

The dynamics of dominant partner participation may conceal a trap for actors in charge of centralized community institutions, however (hereafter referred to as community actors). This is particularly true if the dominant partner is not a member of the proposed technological community. The dominant partner recommends a program of cooperation consistent with its aspirations for administrative, institutional cohesion. Members of the community may not be willing to support this level of cohesion, especially as it affects their relations with one another. Thus, in organizing to deal with a dominant partner, they equip common organs with less than the requisite institutional powers. Community actors acquire program objectives from outside partners without the internal authority necessary to implement these objectives. In a word, this was the story of Euratom and the industrial-scale joint power program.[21]

---

[19] Robert Gilpin notes, in the passage cited at the beginning of chap. 1, that all hegemonic powers have behaved this way historically.

[20] Here we acknowledge the fact, as explained in chap. 1, that the link between motivation and behavior need not be direct or causal in order for one to infer interests served by particular patterns of behavior. Our discussion in chap. 2 suggested that the American response to the technology gap controversy may not have been conscious or directed at the highest levels; yet this response is subject to interpretation in terms of high-level political interests. Whether actual policy is conscious or not, policy behavior may always be evaluated in terms of logical inferences from the position and preoccupations of individual actors at any given time.

[21] Another study (Ruggie, "Collective Goods," p. 882) has concluded that Euratom's performance was disappointing because "the final organizational arrangement turned out

The problem is not an isolated one but has roots in the structure of interests of dominant and weaker partners. The dominant partner will always tend to set higher political aims for cooperation than weaker partners. The higher the political purpose of cooperation, the stronger the institutions necessary to implement these purposes. As we noted above, the dominant partner tends to push institutional issues,[22] which may result in the erection of general organizations before decisions are taken on specific programs. This happened in the case of U.S. support of Euratom where U.S. political interests concerning nonproliferation of nuclear weapons focused Euratom Treaty negotiations around supply and inspection controls before the specific content of programs was considered.[23] The dominant partner's interest in institutional arrangements, which tie down resources of others into policy programs determined largely by the dominant partner, produces circumstances more conducive to the establishment of new institutions than circumstances that would exist if the partners were relatively equal.

Dominant partner participation, especially that of an outside member, may not be all harmful to the interests of community actors. By giving community actors a broader mandate than community members give themselves, a dominant external elite may enhance the political image and prestige of community institutions. Moreover, community actors also have a stake in strong institutions, since these are the basis of their ultimate influence. Thus, not by accident, community actors often end up as allies of dominant partners, giving rise to the impression, if not the reality, of serving dominant partner interests.[24]

---

to entail dependencies far in excess of the need to become dependent . . . ." This conclusion suggests that central organs were equipped with more authority than was actually required. The point may be valid if one considers only the research powers of the Euratom Commission. As we discussed in chap. 4, however, Euratom's primary task was an industrial one. In this area, the Euratom Commission was given much less authority than the task required. The objectives of the industrial-scale joint power program called for powers to stimulate industrial arrangements which the Commission did not possess. As we noted, it had to fall back on stimulating research arrangements which it could only hope would lead to industrial cooperation. See, for example, chap. 5, note 47.

The interesting point, as we go on to discuss above, is who defined the need for dependence so expansively as to entail industrial objectives yet was unable to insure that the Commission was given the requisite authority to meet these objectives. The role of the United States, an outside dominant partner, is illuminating in this regard.

[22]Evidence of this tendency is also found in relations other than civilian technological ones. For example, the U.S. as dominant member of NATO was always more interested in *institutional* consolidation of military cooperation (integration of command and control forces, MLF, etc.) than weaker partners such as France.

[23]See chap. 4, pp. 98–101 and 103–4. While emphasizing fuel supply and control issues, Euratom Treaty negotiations glossed over specific, technical requirements of internal cooperation among member-countries and did not examine specific aspects of external cooperation until the last stages of the Treaty negotiations (the three wise men group being commissioned in November 1956 and delivering its report in May 1957 after the Treaty had already been signed in March).

[24]This explains, in part, the alliance of the Euratom Commission with the USAEC on the joint program, creating the impression during implementation of the power program that Euratom was more a salesman of American than European technology.

Community actors may find their influence more severely circumscribed in circumstances where no dominant partner exists, as officials of the European Community Commission are experiencing today. A situation of bargaining among relatively equal political and technological partners suffers from the absence of overriding or sublimated political goals. Political conflicts lie on the surface. If untreated, these conflicts filter down into technological and industrial areas. No dominant partner is present to inform technical relations with the required coherence of organization and goals.

Unlike two decades ago, Europe exists today without any clear, overriding political-strategic rationale for unity. The need for Western defense cooperation remains, but in an increasingly evolving context of convergent East-West relations. Whereas the earlier Cold War conflict provided a single framework for strategic, economic, and technological cooperation, current circumstances encourage a divided posture of continued strategic vigilance toward the East and increasing economic and technological competition toward the West (i.e., the United States and, in the sense of postwar political alignments, Japan). This Janus-faced division of European concerns sets firm limits on the prospects of important, new initiatives to revitalize European technological cooperation. "The American Challenge" may be important, but it is not important enough to precipitate significant political action, as did, for example, the Soviet invasion of Czechoslovakia. The latter event, in fact, counteracted European concerns over American technological and industrial penetration and brought about French rapprochement with NATO partners and policies, at least at the informal level. Continued dependence on the United States in strategic areas (which even France now recognizes in opposing the unilateral withdrawal of U.S. forces), accompanied by growing competition with the United States in economic areas, suggests the cross-purposes at which current trends in Europe operate. If, as we discuss below, European integration of civilian technological resources depends on partial harmonization of military and strategic plans, the incongruity of strategic and economic interests toward the United States may sharply limit new programs of technological cooperation in Europe.

Britain's entry into the European Community does not fundamentally alter this prospect. As Etzioni pointed out as early as 1965, British entry may overload the integration process and severely complicate the calculus of bargaining and compromise within the Community.[25] Etzioni finds that "unions that have fewer elite-units will tend to be more successful than unions that have a greater number."[26] British participation adds a

[25]Etzioni, *Political Unification*, p. 284.
[26]*Ibid.*, pp. 68–69. This is because "when there is only one elite-unit, [this unit] provides a clear center of policy formation, direction, and responsibility and a locus at which conflicts can be resolved" (p. 69).

third relatively equal power to the existing stand-off between France and Germany. The presence of this third elite-member places strains on Franco-German cohesion and gives rise to a triangular contest in which each elite-unit plays off one partner against the other.[27] The outlines of this type of bargaining are apparent in the nuclear sector (Anglo-German alignments in light water and fast reactors, as well as enrichment technology; Franco-British alignments on the curtailment of the JRC; etc.). One coalition tends to precipitate another, sometimes drawing in outside partners (Anglo-German agreement—TNPG/KWU—when Franco-German agreement fails; or Franco-American agreement—Framatome/Westinghouse—when Anglo-German cooperation succeeds). The fluidity of coalitions pushes issues to the surface and prevents the orderly separation of technical and political aspects. The expanded and more egalitarian context of European relations is as much responsible for the recent surfacing of high political issues in Common Market negotiations (defense and foreign policy cooperation, monetary union, common industrial policy, etc.) as the oft-heralded spill-over effects of sectoral integration. With alignments unclear and leadership issues open, each country places a new priority on functional activities formerly carried out under administrative or industrial auspices. The politicization of functional issues delays decision-making, while actors reassess the implications of sectoral arrangements for over-all national interests.

Though protracting and, in some ways, complicating the process of decision-making, egalitarian politics may, on the other hand, produce more binding commitments once decisions are reached.[28] Thus, the new circumstances governing European cooperation are not necessarily less favorable to further integration than the circumstances that prevailed fifteen years ago; they are simply different. European discussions must take these differences into account. For example, since 1967, European negotiations to expand technological cooperation (Maréchal and Aigrain groups—now known as PREST group) have taken place in isolation from larger developments in the secluded environs of expert committees. The idea is that these committees are best able to consider technical projects on their own merits and avoid identification with larger political issues.[29] In reality, however, the attempt to avoid politics has produced few results, a situation we might have predicted on the basis of our

[27] *Ibid.*, pp. 237–38.
[28] Etzioni argues, for example, that while egalitarian unions find it more difficult than elitist unions to take decisions, "once a decision is made, the members are more likely to feel committed to it, since they had more time to adjust to it and since it was more fully reviewed than would be the case in unions in which decisions are partially or wholly imposed from above, and at a comparatively rapid pace." *Ibid.*, p. 70.
[29] As Altiero Spinelli points out, Community officials "are inclined to regard as a positive rather than a negative factor the absence of real political activity." See *The Eurocrats* (Baltimore: The Johns Hopkins Press, 1966), p. 72.

analysis of nuclear cooperation. For example, agreement thus far has only been possible on projects of relatively minor technical and industrial priority.[30] Without political guidance, technical discussions have consumed inordinate amounts of time and money.[31] Specialized representatives have proven less capable than high-level political officials of reaching agreement, and political exhortations from the highest levels, the summit conferences at The Hague (1969) and Paris (1972), have been necessary just to keep the technical discussions going.

The point that needs to be learned is that politics cannot be avoided in the new milieu of European technological relations. This milieu encourages the perception of functional activities from a more individualistic, national point of view. Issues of technological and industrial content are the essence of international politics in contemporary relations. This fact, which is often interpreted to mean that a new genre of economic politics is replacing the old genre of national politics, means in fact just the opposite: economic and technical disputes today display more of the characteristics of national politics than they did a decade or two ago. Resolution of these disputes will not be left to the initiative of technical representatives working in the sterilized atmosphere of expert committees. Differences will be isolated or narrowed down only when the definition of principal issues involves the participation of political actors with sufficient authority to make concessions or at least to clarify when such concessions are not possible.[32]

The need for high-level political involvement in the integration of technological efforts weakens the Community's role in promoting cooperation. In the new milieu, Community institutions may not be the agencies best suited to take effective political action.[33] Organizational studies, including a recent one of Community institutions, point out the

[30]As we noted in chap. 4, note 80, the one project that may have had significant consequences for European technical and industrial progress, the construction of a giant computer of revolutionary design, could not be agreed upon.

[31]One Community official noted the absurd fact, for example, that technical discussions to establish a common program sometimes cost more because of their interminable length than the amounts agreed upon for carrying out the program. *Industry, Research and Technology* (bulletin published by the Press and Information Services of the European Communities, Brussels), No. 122 (December 2, 1971).

[32]Mr. Spinelli, the European commissioner in charge of general research in 1971, stressed the need to emphasize rather than de-emphasize politics when he urged that the impending enlargement of the Community be utilized as the moment "when a *political* decision must be made to lay the institutional foundation of a joint scientific and technological policy" (emphasis added). *Industry, Research and Technology*, No. 123 (December 14, 1971).

[33]Community actors do not possess independent resources or represent independent constituencies, both of which may be necessary to take decisive leadership initiatives. The chief asset of Community actors is a set of mechanisms and procedures and, as two long-time students of European integration note, these "mechanisms are not *in themselves* processes or agents of integration or system growth." Such mechanisms have to be activated, and "it is . . . the relative availability of leadership that can serve the function of activator." As to where this leadership might come from, these same students are pessi-

conflict between administrative and innovative functions of bureaucracies.[34] Community organs have become more and more specialized, and the trend, as we observed in the case of Euratom, has been toward more and more expert committees consisting of national as opposed to Community representatives. While it was originally thought that this process would result in the cooptation of national officials into the Community system,[35] it has also had the effect of eroding Community leadership potential, displacing effective influence from an original band of partisan (i.e., in the cause of European unity), Community officials (Monnet Europeanists) to a diffuse set of lower echelon committees in which Community representatives play little more than a secretarial role. In these circumstances, Community initiatives, except of an educational or exhortatory kind, are unlikely unless or until the Community is endowed with a broader mandate and a new sense of mission and purpose.

The impetus for a *relance* of Community purpose will probably have to come from member governments influenced more by the requirements of national policy and larger external events than the exigencies of Community politics.[36] As we noted in chapter 2, the first surge of Community consolidation took place in a context of strategic and diplomatic circumstances favorable to the integration of European resources. In recent times, these circumstances have changed. This change has not erased Community achievements; to the contrary, the Community enjoys an institutional life today which, for all practical purposes, is independent of the past. For this reason, Community actors, no less than others, cannot be ignored. But a significant improvement of Community fortunes is as circumscribed by strategic-diplomatic relationships today as it was in the beginning. This fact is particularly evident in advanced technological areas where, as we have observed throughout this study, civilian and military developments remain closely, if indirectly, related. The interaction of civilian and military developments is particularly significant when one contemplates important new leadership initiatives. Our discussion below of the politics of the evolution of technological cooperation makes clear the broad constraints exercised by larger political issues on technological and industrial advance. It reveals the limitations faced by Community as well as nongovernmental (e.g., multinational corporations) actors as long as the outlines of new defense and foreign policy alignments remain vague and multidirectional.

---

mistic about the future availability of either supranational *or* national leadership. See Leon N. Lindberg and Stuart A. Scheingold, *Europe's Would-Be Polity* (Englewood Cliffs: Prentice-Hall, 1970), pp. 282–85.

[34] See David L. Coombes, *Politics and Bureaucracy in the European Community* (Beverly Hills: Sage Publications, 1970), pp. 96–100 and 239–40.

[35] A process known as *engrenage. Ibid.*, pp. 86–91.

[36] For similar conclusions, see Coombes, *ibid.*, pp. 263–64, and K. Pavitt, "Technology in Europe's future," *Research Policy*, I (1971–72), pp. 210–73, especially p. 249.

Politics of Evolution of Technological Cooperation

If, as we argued above, dominant partners place the larger political aims of technological cooperation above research and industrial gains, weaker partners reverse this order of priority. For them, research and industrial benefits are primary and strategic considerations are secondary.[37] These differing sets of priorities cause dominant and weaker partners to take different positions concerning the external and internal orientations of technological communities.

Dominant partners tend to favor a closed external orientation of technological communities. This permits them to use technical cooperation in the defense of strategic interests *vis-à-vis* third countries while simultaneously perpetuating their internal research and industrial hegemony. Thus, the United States supported American-Euratom cooperation as long as this alignment served the interests of Western unity *vis-à-vis* the Soviet Union. U.S. support waned once France began to circumvent this grouping and establish independent ties with third countries (in the civilian nuclear sector, the French-Russian Accord in 1960; and, in European politics as a whole, the Franco-Russian detente of the early 1960s). Similarly, France supported Franco-Euratom cooperation as long as such cooperation promised to advance French goals of independence *vis-à-vis* the United States. French support declined once Germany (in French eyes, with Euratom support) went outside this association and established bilateral ties with the United States (industrial ties in the light water reactor sector and technical-governmental ties in the fast and high temperature reactor sectors). French support of the European Communities as a whole also waned once Germany aligned with the United States rather than France on broader strategic issues (MLF controversy).[38]

The existence of these patterns of dominant partner behavior in the nuclear sector confirms the close tie between political-strategic and technical-industrial aspects of cooperation. The link is established through the policies of the politically most self-conscious or most ambitious member of the community. In the mid-1950s, for example, American policy consciously perceived the political-strategic advantages of international cooperation in the peaceful uses of nuclear energy (Atoms

[37]This is not to say that strategic considerations are secondary in a general sense (quite the opposite for Germany, for example, during its period of relative civilian nuclear inferiority), but that the strategic benefits derived from *civilian technological cooperation* are secondary. Weaker states usually seek strategic benefits through direct military (as opposed to civilian) cooperation.

[38]British policy toward the continent during Britain's second and third entry applications (1966–71) may provide another example of such behavior outside the specific nuclear energy field. As we noted in chap. 4, Britain tried to exploit its presumed technological leadership *vis-à-vis* the continent by advocating cooperation through a European Technological Community. British purpose, however, was primarily political-diplomatic. Once membership was obtained, British enthusiasm for technological cooperation waned.

for Peace plan) as a way of advancing American nonproliferation aims, as well as modifying the diplomatic image of the United States (until then, colored exclusively by military uses of atomic energy).[39] In 1957 and again in 1962–64, French policy also demonstrated the link between military and civilian purposes of cooperation. In both of these periods, French offers to collaborate with Germany in civilian nuclear projects (enrichment uranium plant in 1957 and Fessenheim proposals in 1962) came in the context of broader French initiatives to strengthen Franco-German defense relations and loosen German strategic dependence on the United States.[40] That these events were directly linked cannot be averred, but that they were merely coincidental is also unlikely. This fact may be further evidenced by evolving French relations with the United States. When French strategic policies diametrically opposed U.S. policies in NATO, France pursued a vigorous policy of independence in the civilian nuclear field (gas graphite offensive against light water developments). After the Czech invasion in 1968, France sharply modified its strategic plans, abandoning the doctrine of defense in all directions (*tous azimuts*) and moving French strategy closer to NATO concepts of graduated flexible response.[41] Only then did France temper its official hostility toward American industrial links and approve in 1970–71 new license ties between French and American nuclear firms.

The tendency of technical-industrial developments to move in the same direction as broad strategic developments may be reflected in two other patterns emerging from our study. At the technical level, military-strategic factors inevitably influence the type of civilian-industrial technology developed. In both France and the United States (as well as Great Britain), initial decisions having more to do with the military than economic development of atomic power determined the characteristics of civilian reactor technology. France chose graphite over heavy water moderation because of its better plutonium producing characteristics. The United States developed expensive enrichment factories because enriched uranium was needed to construct more efficient bombs. Once these facilities were built, it became economical to consider enriched uranium (light water) reactors for civilian purposes. Economic considerations would have never justified the development of this technology for power reactors alone.[42] The vast sums the United States invested for

[39] See Mason Willrich, *Global Politics of Nuclear Energy* (New York: Praeger, 1971), pp. 46–47.

[40] On the relationship of the uranium enrichment proposal to Franco-German strategic discussions in 1957–58, see Wilfrid L. Kohl, *French Nuclear Diplomacy* (Princeton: Princeton University Press, 1971), pp. 54–61. Kohl also deals at length with Franco-German strategic relations in the 1962–64 period, pp. 267–98.

[41] *Ibid.*, pp. 265–66.

[42] Klaus Knorr writes: "If the United States had not built gaseous diffusion plants for its military program, in all probability they would not have been constructed for power reactors." See *Euratom and American Policy*, A report of a conference (Princeton: Princeton University, Center of International Studies, May 16, 1956), p. 10.

chiefly military reasons (including development of light water technology for submarine reactors) undoubtedly contributed to the eventual competitive success of U.S. over European civilian reactors.[43] If gas graphite development had benefited from a parallel, cooperative defense effort in Europe (e.g., Anglo-French strategic cooperation), the reactor war may have had another outcome.

A second pattern in industrial alignments suggests the importance of broader, strategic relations. Historically, the rise of multinational corporations seems to be associated with hegemonial political patterns (e.g., British companies in the nineteenth century, U.S. companies in the middle twentieth century). In the postwar period, U.S. hegemony in Europe was most pronounced. This was also the period of most rapid expansion of American multinational corporations in Europe (as well as in Canada and, to a lesser extent, around the world).

The correlation is only of the most general type, and only by making a series of unverifiable assumptions could one conclude that national policy is a direct cause of multinational industrial phenomena.[44] Yet it is curious that while American multinational companies proliferated in the postwar economic and social circumstances of Europe, European multinational corporations did *not* emerge in significant numbers despite the fact that they confronted these same circumstances. A partial explanation may lie in the fact that the political-strategic dominance of a country gives industrial actors from this country the assurance of stability necessary to undertake long-term industrial commitments in foreign markets. Without clarity of political purpose at higher levels, corporate actors may not have the confidence to act independently and may be inclined to coordinate significant initiatives more closely with government plans. This is the pattern that has apparently prevailed thus far in Europe. In the nuclear sector, at least, industrial initiatives have been carefully integrated with official policies (as, for example, in Siemens' initiative toward France in 1970).[45] Progress under these circumstances depends as much on general governmental relations in Europe as on specific industrial and economic conditions.

[43]Willrich, *Global Politics of Nuclear Energy*, p. 62.

[44]Raymond Vernon expresses the relationship as follows: "If the various links in the causal sequence are valid, then the sharp increase in the reach and involvement of U.S.-controlled multinational enterprise in the postwar period is partly a consequence of U.S. official policy and U.S. public power." See *Sovereignty at Bay* (New York: Basic Books, 1971), p. 96.

[45]Obviously, the extent of government-industry collaboration (and hence the influence of political-diplomatic considerations on industrial alignments) depends on traditional domestic practices in industrial relations as well as the different traditions of individual companies (e.g., the strong nationalist traditions of Siemens and Krupp in Germany). One fallacy in assuming that transnational industrial initiatives are usually arms length transactions independent of government involvement is to superimpose what may be a particular American tradition on traditions of other countries (for example, France and, during the fascist period, Germany, where industrial statism has been a part of the historical experience—see chap. 3).

We began this discussion of relationships between political-strategic and technical-industrial aspects of cooperation by observing that dominant partners, for larger diplomatic reasons, usually prefer a closed external orientation of technological communities in which they participate. Weaker partners prefer just the opposite, namely an open orientation toward outside countries. This follows from their desire to maximize scientific and industrial development (first on their list of priorities) and obtain access to the most advanced technology wherever it may be located. It may also follow from their desire to avoid technical dependence on more advanced partners inside the community. Weaker countries are usually most concerned with their relative positions *vis-à-vis* internal partners. Thus, at the outset, Germany measured its nuclear capabilities largely in terms of French capabilities; Italy measured its capabilities in terms of both France and Germany. The Benelux partners evaluated their quasi-permanent inferiority (due to size) in terms of a homogeneous Community ideal. All of these countries sought nuclear ties with the United States, both to exploit American technical superiority and circumvent French hegemony. As far as these countries were concerned, French plans for strategic use of Euratom (to block out American technology and encourage German dependence on French technology) were not only unacceptable (for reasons we cannot go into here); they were also irrelevant. The first purpose of technical cooperation was civilian nuclear development, not European strategic independence.

As Germany moved from a position of weakness to strength, its policy evolved accordingly, and general competitive concerns toward outside powers acquired new priority. To be sure, the link between political-strategic and industrial-commercial motivations of German policy remained muted (due to the artificial character of Germany's postwar situation). This is one of the conditions generally obscuring relations between military and civilian technologies in Europe. Yet in renouncing nuclear weapons, Germany did not renounce strategic interests; Bonn merely agreed to pursue these interests through other than nuclear means. For the first two decades of Germany's postwar existence, strategic considerations called for the avoidance of excessive reliance on France (carried through in civilian as well as military nuclear areas). Until major issues of German security were resolved, including ultimately the issue of reunification, Germany could not permit Franco-German flirtations to interfere with American-German fidelity. Today, Germany continues to face open-ended security issues (though reunification, except in the long-run through a possible confederation of two German states, is no longer a realistic alternative), but detente has produced sufficient progress to relax German dependence on the United States and reduce German suspicion of France. As a result, German policies in the civilian nuclear field reflect more competitive (though not closed) attitudes toward the United States and more cooperative attitudes toward France. To a lesser extent, these attitudes are mirrored in more general industrial relations between Germany and these two countries.[46]

Two obstacles stand in the way of closer Franco-German cooperation, however. Germany is now the dominant industrial partner.[47] Yet Germany lacks the political-strategic motivation of a dominant partner to push cooperation with France (as the United States did in promoting industrial cooperation with Euratom, and as France tried to do in pushing industrial cooperation with Germany—Fessenheim proposals). At the moment, there is little to be gained from closer industrial ties with France (unlike the strategic benefits Germany derived from earlier industrial cooperation with the United States). To maximize political advantage, Germany may find Great Britain to be a more promising partner.[48] In this relationship, however, Germany does not enjoy the same industrial superiority. Moreover, from a diplomatic point of view, it may be advantageous for Germany to expand technological and industrial cooperation with socialist countries. In short, while remaining Europe's strongest industrial power, Germany is not likely to acquire the necessary incentive to lead a major realignment of Western European industrial and technological relations.

Nor is France, whose objectives have been lowered somewhat in face of industrial superiority across the Rhine, a likely leadership candidate. When the French attempt to recruit Euratom and the European Communities in the service of French strategic interests failed (or succeeded in the sense that Europe has moved toward the original French objective of greater European independence, at least in economic areas), France placed industrial interests above strategic purity and concluded license agreements with American nuclear industries to meet the German challenge. With detente, French access to Soviet resources also improved (e.g., the purchase of enriched uranium from Moscow). Both of these movements distracted from the urgency of internal European consolidation.

[46]A recent European Community study reports that the number of international industrial operations (primarily the establishment of wholly owned subsidiaries) between France and Germany doubled between 1966 and 1970, while U.S. operations in Germany during the same period tailed off considerably. *Industry, Research and Technology*, No. 145 (May 23, 1972).

[47]Germany's superiority *vis-à-vis* France is suggested by the fact that from 1965 to 1970, German annual net investments in France increased from $30.6 million to $86.8 million, while annual French investments in Germany remained about the same at $17 million. *Industry, Research and Technology*, No. 142 (May 2, 1972).

[48]The German-British alignment on uranium enrichment technology and the industrial package concluded between KWU and TNPG in 1971 may be indicators. Both of these represent important agreements, and both exclude France and French industry, at least for the moment.

French policy demonstrates a characteristic of dominant partner behavior whose primary interest in cooperation originates from political-strategic motivations. In the hope of political gains, dominant partners may be willing to pay an industrial price for sustained cooperation.[49] Once the political value of cooperation declines, however, these partners adopt a harder line toward industrial issues. When it became clear that Euratom would not become a front for the French CEA, France opposed industrial-scale cooperation in the participation program. Similarly, as Euratom declined in political value (superceded by the Common Market), the United States stiffened terms in connection with the joint program. And, after ENEA had declined in value as a rival organization to nuclear integration on the continent, Britain sought to reduce commitments to DRAGON.[50] On a larger scale, the shift from strategic to industrial criteria of evaluation may also explain, in part, the hardening U.S. attitude toward industrial developments in the Common Market, as well as the growing French concern over industrial events in Germany.

Present European alignments do not suggest that common strategic incentives will re-emerge to promote new industrial consolidations. In an expanded Community, Great Britain and France will probably compete for strategic influence, while Great Britain and Germany maneuver for maximum industrial influence. Marrying strategic and industrial objectives will not be aided by the impetus of a dominant partner, willing to accept disproportionate economic costs in return for strategic benefits. Weaker partners may also be less likely to accept strategic dependence on fellow European powers. They did so *vis-à-vis* the United States but only at a price of some loss of local political and economic autonomy. It will be more difficult to accept such loss of autonomy *vis-à-vis* contiguous European partners.

Negotiations to expand technological and industrial cooperation, therefore, will depend less on external incentives than internal ones. The internal politics of technological communities concerns chiefly two issues: first, what type of technology should be developed and, second,

---

[49]The role that dominant states play in assuming disproportionate costs of common undertakings is explained, in part, by the theory of collective goods, a subject of considerable interest in recent writings on international organizations. Dominant actors accept this role because the marginal costs to them are smaller (given their greater size and resources) and because they derive private (i.e., partisan or political) benefits from cooperation. See Bruce M. Russett and John D. Sullivan, "Collective Goods and International Organization," *International Organization*, XXV (Autumn 1971), pp. 845–65.

[50]Britain behaved similarly in ELDO, initially sponsoring the establishment of this organization as a way of phasing out its military Blue Streak missile program and posing as a friend of European cooperation, and then threatening to withdraw in 1966 to secure a reduction of British obligations. See Warren B. Walsh, *Science and International Public Affairs: Six Recent Experiments in International Scientific Cooperation* (Syracuse: Maxwell School of Syracuse University, International Relations Program, 1967), p. 137.

what type of industrial policies should be followed to convert this technology into European commercial gains. Dominant and weaker partners disagree on these issues, just as they do on issues of external policy.

Dominant partners tend to favor the development of existing technology, that is, technology in which they have already accumulated some experience and know-how. This permits them to exercise control over the technical evolution of cooperation and pre-empt the interest of other partners in potentially more advanced and competing technologies. Weaker partners tend to advocate development of more innovative techniques. They prefer to avoid an initial disadvantage with respect to dominant partners and believe that their chances of achieving equality are better in fields where everyone starts at the same point, even if dominant partners possess greater resources to exploit newer technologies more rapidly.

Thus, the United States pushed first-generation, light water reactors in Europe; while France and Germany, after 1962, placed their hopes for eventual independence from U.S. technology in more advanced fast reactors. Among Community countries, where France was initially dominant, the CEA promoted existing gas graphite technology; while Germany and Italy sought to develop more advanced variants of light water technology (superheating, etc.). Once Germany achieved dominance in proven reactors, France shifted its interest to intermediate- and second-generation reactors. The pattern also prevailed within specific reactor families. In fast reactors, where France was initially ahead, French programs favored use of sodium coolants; German programs elected to go with more novel steam and helium coolants. In high temperature reactors, Great Britain pushed the prismatic fuel design; while Germany, starting behind, went with the new and untested pebble-bed design. In uranium enrichment technology, the United States and France developed existing gaseous diffusion technology; while Germany and Holland focused on unique centrifuge and jet nozzle techniques. In each instance, the weaker partner tried to upstage the dominant partner by going one step higher up the ladder of technical novelty.

The patterns become confused because of the difficulty in comparing the sophistication of various techniques and the rapid change that such comparisons undergo during development. But the basic tendency for dominant partners to pursue existing technology and weaker partners to pursue more innovative technology can still be distinguished.[51] This

---

[51]For example, the tendency appears in ELDO's experience. During initial negotiations, France and Great Britain advocated exploitation of existing rocket technology, in which they had dominant expertise. Germany and Italy, beginners in rocket technology, wished to tackle more novel techniques. See *A Preliminary Examination of Intergovernmental Co-operation in Science and Technology Affecting Western Europe (Project Perseus)*, A report to the Council of Europe by the Science Policy Research Unit, Univer-

tendency contributes to one of the fundamental difficulties technological communities face, namely the different levels of technical interest and capability dominant and weaker partners bring to collective projects. Weaker partners value these projects chiefly in technical terms (first in their order of priorities) and consequently expect maximum technical progress. Yet these partners are least technically qualified to contribute to such progress and frequently underestimate the difficulties of advanced development (Italy being a good example in Euratom). Dominant partners possess the capabilities for, but also less interest in, specific technical outcomes (cooperating more for the political benefits). Furthermore, they are usually less than generous in turning over more conventional tasks to weaker partners, compelling the latter to conceive more advanced, less practical projects (such as Italy's PEC program). The result is something of a dilemma at the technical level of internal cooperation. Dominant partners do not really depend on the collective project for technical progress, while weaker partners do. Yet weaker partners cannot contribute the resources to the project, while dominant partners have no incentive to do so. Community actors, such as the Commission, are caught in between. They fail to receive the technical backing from dominant partners and also fail to meet the technical expectations of weaker partners. The Community is unable to meet either objective of integrating dominant partner programs or developing weaker partner programs.[52]

At the industrial level, dominant partners tend to stress economy and efficiency; weaker partners emphasize balance and equity. The reasons follow from the association between economic resources and political influence. Dominant partners gain most from vertical growth, that is, maximizing output. They control the administrative, manufacturing, and marketing mechanisms for handling output. They therefore control the patterns of distribution. While growth promises *more* for all, it also promises *most* for them. Disproportionate returns to leading industries are justified on economic grounds. Without these returns, investments lag and growth declines. And, for dominant partners, the requirement for continued growth is self-evident (as well as self-serving). The problem, as they see it, is organizing the most efficient division of labor and

---

sity of Sussex, November 1971, p. 85. See also Walsh, *Science and International Public Affairs*, p. 129.

[52]The Commission, to satisfy requirements of technical efficiency, demanded evidence of competence from weaker partners to carry out proposed Community projects. To produce such evidence, weaker partners either had to develop a national capability (the route Germany selected) or rely on Community assistance (the route Italy chose). Dominant partners, however, objected to Community development of weaker member programs. France repeatedly pressed for elimination of such programs (Italian EUREX, PRO, and PEC projects). It was little wonder, then, that Germany downplayed Community programs and adopted the rule of thumb giving preference to national programs or that Italy experienced repeated frustrations in relying on Community programs.

coordination of output. These are pragmatic issues and can be best resolved by experts and technicians. Private sector or nongovernmental initiatives stand the best chance to succeed. Political solutions can only pervert this process.

Weaker partners gain most from horizontal growth, that is, an evening up of industrial and economic advantages. They lack the capital and the competence to play an influential role in decision-making. To be sure, they benefit from maximizing output; measured against their former position, they may benefit more than dominant partners, since they begin at a more modest level. Yet, absolutely, they pay for these gains in declining influence. As long as distribution patterns remain unchanged, they play a complementary rather than consequential role. The issue for them is "whose growth?" The problem is political, not administrative. And leaving it to the experts and specialists only insures that the broader issues will be ignored. Political action and governmental bargaining are necessary to transcend and counteract industrial and administrative inequities.

The performance of American firms in Europe confirms the tendency of dominant industrial partners to stress the specialized character of industrial alignments and avoid comprehensive scrutiny at a more general political level. Despite the responsibility of the Euratom Commission to review new investments in the nuclear sector, U.S. industries consistently circumvented centralized coordination of licensing and manufacturing agreements with European partners. During the early years of Euratom (and the Common Market), American industries infiltrated and divided up European markets, making it difficult to perceive the consequences for European industrial strength as a whole. Transnational European alignments were almost exclusively limited to consortia led by American licensors (ACEC/Framatome under Westinghouse, GAAA/Interatom/Montecatini under Atomics International, etc.). As the politically most self-conscious Community member, France was the first to recognize these consequences and urge a common policy toward American investments. For France, the problem was not only a question of maximizing growth but also preserving the economic and industrial integrity of Europe. European sovereignty was too important to be left to the ebb and flow of private investments.

After falling behind to German industrial growth, France pursued a similar policy within the Community. Along with Italy, France sought a political, i.e., negotiated, solution to the problems of a common industrial policy. The issues of industrial cooperation with Germany were too important to be decided by private sector events. Now that Germany was dominant, however, German actors resisted centralized approaches. Today, German groups (government and industrial) carefully distinguish between industrial and governmental negotiations at the international level (e.g., in the three-tier negotiations leading to the tripartite agreement on the centrifuge process and the international prototype project in fast reactors—SNR), even though industrial and official policies may be closely coordinated at the national level. Given their present strength, German industries, like American industries before them, may be expected to bargain successfully without government interference. German dislike of centralized solutions was not always so intense. In the past, when German actors sensed industrial weakness, they too favored collective, negotiated solutions (for example, the German initiative in an official memorandum to Euratom to encourage participation in the industrial development of the German high temperature reactor program).[53] A position of industrial inferiority encourages either an attempt to outflank superior community partners (such as the early German end run to the United States in both light water and fast reactors) or an attempt to counterbalance industrial disadvantages with political, administrative tactics (the chief recourse of France in industrial relations with Germany). Both alternatives require government complicity (for example, willingness of German government to defer to private initiatives of German industry during association contract negotiations with the United States in high temperature and fast reactor fields).[54]

These tendencies among industrial actors suggest that they do not behave very differently from governmental actors. In positions of dominance, both actors seek to avoid issues of policy (cooperation for what goals, whose growth, etc.) and concentrate on specialized, technical features of cooperation (most efficient division of labor, specific provisions rather than total effect of license agreements, etc.). In positions of weakness, both seek recourse to political tactics focusing on broad issues of development and socioeconomic equity.[55] In addition, just as dominant governmental actors supply the incentive for technological cooperation, dominant industrial actors may be necessary to initiate industrial cooperation. Curiously, the vast majority of industrial alignments in the nuclear field took the form of a superordinate actor initiating ties with a number of subordinate ones. All of the American-led

[53]An earlier example of this tendency was German industrial support of the Schuman plan (ECSC) as a way of alleviating German bilateral dependence on France. See William Diebold, Jr., *The Schuman Plan* (New York: Praeger, 1959), chap. 5; also Ernst B. Haas, *The Uniting of Europe* (Stanford: Stanford University Press, 1958), pp. 162–64.

[54]The differences in dominant and weaker partner behavior in industrial relations are evident in international airline negotiations. U.S. companies, enjoying a considerable economic advantage, advocate maximum carrier freedom in setting prices as well as schedule frequencies for international traffic. Other companies favor strong governmental controls over these functions. See Robert L. Thornton, "Governments and Airlines," in Robert O. Keohane and Joseph S. Nye, Jr. (eds.), *Transnational Relations and World Politics* (Cambridge: Harvard University Press, 1972), pp. 195–96.

[55]One might speculate that, as American multinationals encounter growing competition in foreign markets (from European and Japanese multinationals), their tendency to seek U.S. government support and assistance may increase, particularly if they feel the U.S. government has political capital in these countries which they can draw upon.

industrial liaisons reflected this pattern (with the possible exception of Siemens, which has a long tradition of independence and balanced association with Westinghouse dating back to 1924). The German-led SNR consortium in fast reactors also took this form. Recent alignments in high temperature reactors provide another example of the catalyzing effect of a dominant industrial actor (in this case, Gulf General Atomic). There are some counterpatterns, for example the alignment of TNPG and KWU (though each of these companies is superior in a particular field—TNPG in fast reactors, KWU in proven reactors). But it seems reasonable to assume that just as agreement at the governmental level is facilitated by the existence of a recognized leader, agreement at the industrial level is also facilitated by a dominant participant.

Actor behavior seems to be more a function of relative power than whether the actor is governmental or nongovernmental. The supposition that nongovernmental actors, in particular multinational corporations, behave in a significantly different way from governmental actors is as yet unsubstantiated. Multinational companies, to be sure, are motivated by profit considerations and stand to gain from the advancement of international economic specialization. They are also motivated, however, by requirements of centralized control and security. The benefits of international specialization cannot be reaped without the ability to direct operations from the center (formally or informally) and to move factors in accordance with changing economic and political circumstances in host countries. This desire to maintain centralized control leads to a search for security. Companies seek to diversify their activities abroad, both in terms of products and location. The requirements of diversification may run counter to the requirements of specialization and comparative advantage. In the last analysis, then, multinational corporations, no less than states, seek control over the environment in which they operate. To the extent that this motivation predominates, these corporations tend to behave more like political than economic organizations.[56]

When multinational companies feel relatively secure in their environment, they emphasize the divorce between economic (profit) motives and political (power) motives. As we know so well from corporate behavior in domestic politics, however, this emphasis is itself political.[57] The focus on profits is used to disguise the acquisition of power. Yet

[56]Cf. discussion in David P. Calleo and Benjamin M. Rowland, *America and the World Political Economy* (Bloomington: Indiana University Press, 1973), pp. 172–75.

[57]Huntington points out that U.S.-based transnational organizations would like, at all costs, to avoid involvement in local political systems. This is probably true, but what better way is there for a transnational organization to exercise a decisive control over resources or manpower in a host country than to avoid any involvement with the only other party capable of challenging the organization's control of these resources, namely the host government. See "Transnational Organizations in World Politics," *World Politics*, XXV (April 1973), pp. 357–58.

profits are power; they continue to be controlled and distributed by particular groups. The great majority of multinational companies are still controlled managerially and financially by home country groups influenced, to a larger extent than is generally recognized, by perspectives, loyalties, and interests that are nationally grounded.[58] The tendency of American multinational companies (and some American analysts of these companies) to minimize this fact is consistent with their interests as dominant multinational actors in the present international setting. They seek to divert attention from *policy-making* levels of corporate behavior (which remain national or unilateral) to *operational* levels (which are multinational). This facilitates the integration of foreign resources into policy decisions and programs decided upon by predominantly home country groups. More focus on corporate policy-making (rather than operation) might disclose that these actors seldom challenge vested national interests or established elites at home and more frequently conflict with national interests and elites in the host country. The net effect on both counts is to reinforce rather than undermine national orientations in present world politics. The tendency to separate industrial from national interests may be more a reflection of superior industrial strength (which puts one in a good position to resolve industrial issues without an appeal to national interests and government interference) than an accurate description of contemporary corporate behavior.

The fact that multinational corporations may act independently of home governments, therefore, is no proof that they pursue significantly different interests from home governments. As analysts of transnational actors themselves point out, these corporations cannot win "direct confrontations" with governments when their interests visibly and directly conflict with those of governments.[59] In these instances, therefore, which may be most significant for international relations (since the issues are of high priority to governments and could call forth decisive action on the part of governments), multinational corporate actors are unlikely to exert an impact on international politics which would call into question the basic nation-state organization of world politics. In other instances, involving the routine interaction of multinational companies and home governments, there is no reason to presume that these companies have an interest in transforming the nation-state system. If, as we noted above, they are as much concerned with power to control their environment as with profits to be extracted from this environment,

---

[58] As Howard V. Perlmutter notes, the basic attitudes or "state of mind" of multinational corporate executives toward foreign people, ideas, and resources remain home country-oriented. See "The Tortuous Evolution of the Multinational Corporation," *Columbia Journal of World Business*, IV (January/February 1969), pp. 9–18.

[59] See conclusions by Keohane and Nye (eds.), *Transnational Relations and World Politics*, pp. 372–73.

they have a stake in any system which facilitates their exercise of influence. Today, multinational companies have considerably more influence
with home governments than they might expect to have in an international system in which multinational corporate activities were regulated by nonnational, global institutions. Is it likely, then, that they have
a genuine interest in working toward the erosion of the nation-state
system? Quite the contrary: as this study shows, multinational industrial activities tend to follow the patterns of influence of home governments abroad, increasing in those areas where home and host government relations are politically friendly, and to fall back upon the
influence of home governments when events abroad threaten political
and economic relations with host countries.

Summary Reflections

In this study, we have argued that an essential part (not the whole)
of understanding the impact of technology on international politics is to
consider the way in which conventional motives of group behavior influence the uses made of technological programs. In this regard,
national politics, as opposed to what has been called world politics,[60]
may remain the most important perspective for analyzing the actions
and plans of global actors. The expanding scale and cost of technological activities have reinforced rather than weakened the significance of
national policies. As one study notes in the case of multinational corporations, which are probably the most important new global actors in
contemporary international relations,[61]

. . . the transnational integration of production does not mean that national
differences have ceased to be important elements in operating decisions and
long-range planning in multinational enterprises, as some commentators have
concluded. Quite the contrary: the reduction or disappearance of tariffs and
other trade barriers *per se* makes differences in national economic conditions
and attitudes and in other government policies relatively more significant.

The removal of traditional economic divisions has heightened the significance of traditional political, social, and cultural divisions. Governments are now required to deal with external problems through internal
means, forcing policy-makers to consolidate domestic activities in
economic and technical areas and manage these activities with broad
foreign policy goals in mind. The specialization and pluralism of international ties have themselves precipitated this response. Contemporary
international politics, therefore, reflects an ongoing tension between

---

[60]See the volume with this title: Keohane and Nye (eds.), *Transnational Relations and
World Politics*, especially pp. 370–84.
[61]Theodore Geiger, *The Fortunes of the West* (Bloomington: Indiana University Press,
1973), pp. 185–86.

national consolidation and international specialization, not a unidimensional trend toward increasing global interdependence. In politics, it would seem, unity is in perpetual conflict with diversity and differentiation.[62]

The tendency to resolve this tension in the direction of specialization and interdependence seems to be a particular characteristic of dominant power policy. In the postwar period, U.S. policies frequently exhibited this tendency. Toward Europe, in particular, American diplomacy sought to downplay political differences and restrict relations to more pragmatic concerns. American-style pragmatism drew a sharp distinction between the ends of policy, which were assumed to be self-evident, and the means of policy, which were assumed to be the only issues in dispute. American concepts of Western European economic and military integration contained little room for alternative concepts of political balance and partnership, such as those advocated by de Gaulle or sought by Western European states today, at least in certain economic areas. At times, tight European integration of the kind advanced by Monnet Europeanists and American supporters of a United States of Europe seemed more in the interest of American objectives and intellectual traditions (in particular, American visions of commercial internationalism) than European preferences. The apparent European shift toward intergovernmentalism suggests that, as European power grows, Europe may pursue solutions to European problems quite different from supranational integration, solutions that more closely coincide with Europe's different intellectual heritage and internal historical divisions.[63]

Europe's adjustment to the recent shift in economic and political influence in the West is still in progress. At the level of trade and monetary relations, Europe seems to be moving toward regionalism. The establishment of a preferential trading and investing area in the Mediterranean and North Africa and the agreement in 1971 to create a common monetary union raise the prospect of growing economic competition with the United States. Economic competition is offset, however, by continued and, after the invasion of Czechoslovakia, perhaps even strengthened political-strategic cooperation with the United States. Except on the issue of unilateral troop withdrawals (which the present American administration also opposes), American and Euro-

---

[62]On this point, see the excellent treatment of the tension between unification and differentiation in decision-making structures in Paul Diesing, *Reason in Society* (Urbana: University of Illinois Press, 1962), chap. 5.

[63]On the differences in American and European intellectual and historical experiences, see Stanley Hoffmann, *Gulliver's Troubles* (New York: McGraw-Hill, 1968). The shift toward intergovernmentalism in Europe is apparent in all sectors, not just technological areas. See Roger D. Hansen, "European Integration: Forward March, Parade Rest or Dismissed," *International Organization*, XXVII (Spring 1973), p. 246.

pean strategists have few disagreements. This relative consensus, which takes into account the effects of detente, is one of the reasons for the low profile of strategic issues in contemporary Atlantic politics.

There are a number of potential countertrends to continued U.S.-European strategic cooperation. SALT and the continuing dynamics of superpower politics may provoke European states into a closer coordination of defense and foreign policy interests at the European level. Since 1969 there has been increasing discussion in Western Europe about the need for a European group, voice, caucus, etc. within NATO.[64] A European group within the Atlantic group might constitute the first signs of an emerging and separate European strategic policy in world affairs. Progress in this direction, however, is highly contingent on circumstances, in particular, the convergence of general foreign policy interests. Though Community countries initiated foreign policy consultations in 1969 (twice annually before the Paris summit and now four times annually), activity along this line has not translated readily into agreement. Without a significant shift in general political circumstances, caused by external or internal events, Europe is not likely to move rapidly toward common strategic-diplomatic goals.

For the moment, U.S. policy seeks to exploit Europe's continuing indecision on strategic issues. To distract attention from sharpening economic and monetary disputes, the United States has called for a new Atlantic charter focusing attention on major issues of strategic policy where the allies continue to enjoy surprising agreement. In a reversal of earlier tactics, indicating the relative shift in power, American policymakers seek to emphasize political issues and relegate increasingly aggravating economic and monetary disputes to the back burner. As part of this tactic, President Nixon tried and failed to arrange a summit conference for fall 1973 where Western allies, in a renewed display of over-all political consensus, could generate the necessary spirit and common purpose to put technical differences in perspective and hasten mutual compromise. Europe, on the other hand, is suspicious of the attempt to link strategic and economic issues and is content to let economic and monetary issues fester while strategic protection continues. Like the United States, Europe is reluctant to recognize the inevitable, long-term strategic consequences of growing commercial competition between the two Atlantic partners.

These patterns emerged with even greater clarity in the recent energy crisis. Once again, the United States seized upon the immediate problems created by the Arab oil embargo and rising oil prices to propose a broad program of cooperation among advanced industrialized states. At the energy conference convened in Washington in February 1974, the United States presented "a comprehensive action program to deal with

[64]See Walter Schuetze, *European Defence Co-operation and NATO* (Atlantic Papers No. 3; Paris: Atlantic Institute, November 1969).

all facets of the world energy situation by cooperative measures," including R&D, monetary, trade, and short-term energy supply cooperation.[65] In what seemed at the time to be a predictable solitary stance, France rejected most of these measures, seeing them as merely another attempt by the United States to refurbish its flagging leadership position in the Western alliance. Several weeks later, however, Common Market countries as a whole initiated a separate, independent dialogue with the Arab countries. The United States reacted with strong criticism of this competitive initiative to U.S. plans. Hoping to capitalize on Europe's continued strategic dependence on the United States, President Nixon warned bluntly that Europe "cannot have the United States participation and cooperation on the security front, and then proceed to have confrontation and even hostility on the economic and political front."[66] Europe remains vulnerable to this tactic of linking economic and strategic issues as long as it avoids the tough problems of strategic unity within Europe. In contrast to the middle 1950s when the United States proposed similar cooperation in the nuclear sector, however, Europe does seem to have become more aware of the broader political significance of technological and economic cooperation with the United States. Indeed, there may be useful lessons to be drawn from Europe's experience with Atlantic R&D cooperation in the nuclear sector, which we have analyzed in considerable detail in this study (see, in particular, chapter 5), for proposed European cooperation with the United States today in energy sectors.

In the near future, strategic dependence in Europe will probably continue to mute the interplay of national politics in Atlantic relations. This allows for some separation of economic and technological issues from larger national security concerns. It should be recognized, however, that the type of economic politics evident in contemporary Atlantic relations is contingent on continuing patterns of strategic bipolarity. If strategic consensus should unravel further, the security implications of economic and technological developments may become fully manifest, for economic interdependence and technological specialization are reflections of political agreement, either explicit or implicit. When this agreement breaks down, economic and technical activities become politicized. Even while agreement prevails, these activities reflect political realities. They impose political constraints on some countries, usually weaker ones as in the case of Europe in the postwar period, but conceal political initiatives of other countries, for example the United States as the leader of commercial and technological internationalism in the West.

---

[65]See text of communiqué issued by the Washington energy parley, *The Washington Post*, February 14, 1974.
[66]*The Washington Post*, March 16, 1974.

Enthusiasm for global cooperation in functional areas must be tempered by an awareness of the political character of international specialization. The United States, in particular, may have to guard against a traditional tendency, reinforced after World War II by unprecedented American power, to project domestic patterns of pluralism and interdependence on global affairs, where diversity continues to be considerably greater than that experienced in American politics. One way of dealing with so-called "global technologies" may be to restrain their development in accordance with consciously limited political objectives. As one writer observes,[67]

. . . a policy of self-restraint, especially if adopted by the United States, might moderate international competition for new technologies. More emphasis on measures of self-control and less on technological prowess or exploitation of foreign markets might lead to safer outcomes for the world community.

This kind of self-restraint has long been recognized in the control of military technologies. It may also have application in contending with new civilian technologies (oceans, environment, etc.).

A political perspective of the type we have discussed in this study aids in isolating the role of self-restraint in the management of new technologies. Instead of emphasizing the new opportunities offered by technology, this kind of analysis points out the dangers in a situation where technology overruns too rapidly the limits of political and human tolerance. It affirms a more positive concept of politics and human action which is not only a response to technological events but an important determinant of these events.

[67]Willrich, *Global Politics of Nuclear Energy*, pp. 183–84.

APPENDIX

TECHNICAL AND ECONOMIC FEATURES OF NUCLEAR REACTOR DEVELOPMENT

The basic principle of producing electricity in nuclear power stations is simple enough. An atomic reactor produces heat through the controlled disintegration of nuclear materials, and this heat is passed on through a coolant or secondary steam circuit to drive turbogenerators. There are many difficulties in actual practice, however, and the variety of designs for nuclear reactors is numerous. The main variables are the type of fuel used, the moderator, and the coolant. After discussing these variables, we will examine a few primary economic features distinguishing the various reactor types.

Nuclear Fuels

Nuclear fuels exist naturally in two forms, uranium and thorium. These substances are radioactive and decay over time, releasing nuclear particles and various forms of energy (heat, light, etc.). Natural uranium is a fissile material. When bombarded by neutrons, the isotope uranium 235 disintegrates into two lighter elements. Natural thorium (uranium 232) is not fissile. The thorium atom must first absorb a neutron before it becomes capable of disintegration. If the right conditions exist, the disintegration of these materials becomes self-sustaining. In a nuclear bomb, this reaction builds up in a matter of milliseconds; in a nuclear reactor, the reaction is controlled over a long period of time, permitting the measured release of heat.

During a sustained nuclear reaction, other events occur besides fission. Uranium 238, the other naturally occurring isotope of uranium (isotopes differ from one another only in terms of the number of neutrons in the nucleus), may be converted into plutonium, an even more fissile material which may also be used as fuel. Similarly, uranium 232 (thorium) may be converted into the more fissile material, uranium 233. Economic considerations require that this plutonium and uranium 233 be recovered and utilized in further nuclear reactions. This is done by chemical reprocessing after the fuel is withdrawn from the reactor or, in the case of breeder reactors, by consuming the converted plutonium or thorium in the same reactive process in which it is produced. The fact that breeder reactors can produce and consume new fuel in the same reaction permits high burn-up rates of the initial fuel core and considerably reduces the costs of handling and reprocessing spent fuels.

Besides plutonium and uranium 233, uranium 235, the other naturally occurring isotope of uranium, is also a highly fissile material. Since this isotope constitutes only 7 parts in 1000 of natural uranium, however, it is often necessary to "enrich" natural uranium to increase the content of uranium 235. Increasing the amount of uranium 235 raises the number of secondary neutrons available in the fuel core. The greater number of neutrons sustains and improves the efficiency of the disintegration process.

Enrichment is carried out in isotope separation plants. Various techniques may be employed, including gaseous diffusion, centrifugation, electromagnetism, or jet nozzle mechanisms. The gaseous diffusion technique is most widely used at present. This technique consumes large quantities of electricity and is quite expensive.

Moderators

Two conditions are required for a controlled nuclear reaction. There must be a critical mass of fissile material with a surface area small enough with respect to the volume to limit the number of secondary neutrons which might escape from the reactive zone and thus be lost as carriers of the chain reaction. Second, a moderating substance (graphite, light water, heavy water, etc.) must be present to slow down the speed of the secondary neutrons. If the secondary neutrons impact into fissile materials at too great a speed, they will be absorbed by these materials without causing the desired disintegration.

The type of moderator used in nuclear reactors, along with the type of fuel (i.e., natural uranium, enriched uranium, or thorium), is a primary designator of particular reactor families (*filières*). Graphite moderators are used in gas graphite and high temperature gas reactors. Light water serves as the moderator in light water reactors. And heavy water moderation characterizes heavy water reactors. In some experimental research piles, zirconium and other materials have been tested as moderators. Fast reactors employ no moderator, deriving their designation from the fact that secondary neutrons are not slowed down in these reactive systems. High neutron speeds in fast reactors produce enormous amounts of heat and would be unmanageable if excess neutrons were not absorbed by a blanket of fertile materials (uranium 238 and uranium 232). Absorption converts these materials to fissile fuels which are then consumed in the continuing reaction.

Moderators may be blended homogeneously with fuel elements in the reactor (so-called homogeneous core) or separated from these elements by means of metally sheathed fuel rods (so-called heterogeneous core). The metal parts of fuel rods or pins must be able to withstand the constant bombardment by nuclear particles without absorbing these particles or disintegrating under impact. Absorption reduces the neutron economy of the system (i.e., number of neutrons to carry on the chain reaction). Disintegration results in the fouling or contamination of the reactor core, releasing fission products into the coolant circuit and creating safety problems. Finding appropriate fuel-cladding materials is a particular problem in natural uranium systems whose neutron economy is not as high as that of enriched uranium systems. In the case of natural uranium, heavy water reactors, this was one factor leading to the slight enrichment of fuel cores. (See chapter 6.) Metal cladding materials have to be eliminated entirely from high temperature gas reactors, since the heat attained in these reactors would melt metal parts. Fuel cladding in these systems is accomplished through carbon coating. (See chapter 7.)

The layout of moderator and fuel elements in the reactor core is one of the principal problems of design of nuclear plants. The spacing and placement of the fuel pins, the even composition of homogeneous cores, the placement and operation of control rods (designed to regulate and shut off the nuclear reaction), and the uniform transfer of heat from the reactor core to coolant circuits are all elements that figure into the technical and economic trade-offs of reactor development.

Coolants

The type of coolant used in a reactor usually designates the particular variant of a reactor family. For example, among light water reactors, two variants exist, one utilizing boiling water which produces steam and the other utilizing heated water under pressure. Fast reactors employ liquid metal coolants (sodium or a sodium/potassium alloy), gas coolants (helium), or steam. Heavy water reactors utilize heavy water under pressure, boiling light water, organic, and gas coolants. Gas graphite reactors work with carbon dioxide cooling, and high temperature systems employ helium cooling.

The coolants may be routed directly to drive the turbogenerators, or they may pass on their heat to secondary steam circuits which drive the turbogenerators. In the boiling light water reactor, the boiling water coolant produces steam which goes directly to the turbines. The direct-drive, high temperature reactor also routes the helium coolant directly to the turbogenerators. Most other systems channel the coolant through heat exchangers where coolant heat is transferred to a secondary steam circuit. Efficiency may be reduced in these systems, since some heat is inevitably lost in the transfer process. But safety risks are lower. Using secondary steam circuits confines the task of designing a leak-proof cooling circuit, which always picks up some radioactive materials in the reactor core, to the heat exchange unit rather than the entire turbomechanism.

Economic Features of Various Reactor Types

Nuclear reactors exhibit a number of different economic characteristics compared to conventional power stations. Over the lifetime of conventional plants, construction costs amount to 30 percent of total costs while fuel costs take up the remaining 70 percent. In the case of nuclear plants, construction costs equal 70 percent and fuel costs 30 percent of total outlays. This contrast means that, in times of financial squeeze, utilities will usually opt for conventional instead of nuclear plants. Immediate investment costs dictate this choice. Over the longer-run, nuclear plants may be preferred, because nuclear plants are more efficient and produce more power per unit total cost.

Nuclear reactors also differ among themselves in terms of investment versus fuel costs. The fuel cycle of light water reactors is more expensive than that of graphite or heavy water reactors. The difference lies in the use of enriched uranium in light water reactors, which is considerably more expensive than natural uranium. On the other hand, the use of enriched uranium increases neutron efficiency and permits a reduction in the size of the reactor core. This, in turn, reduces the initial investment costs of enriched uranium reactors. Thus, in terms of initial outlays, utilities may prefer enriched uranium systems. Over time, utilities may prefer systems which promise lower fuel costs (e.g., fast reactors).

Heavy water reactors exhibit a higher neutron economy than graphite reactors (because heavy water absorbs fewer neutrons than graphite) and thus entail lower initial investment costs. But these systems also require the production of large amounts of heavy water, a costly operation. In addition, the neutron economy is not high enough to allow much latitude in the design of the reactor core. Difficulties in this area have led to the requirement in most heavy water variants of some degree of enrichment of the fuel core.

High temperature reactors achieve an advantage over graphite, light water, and heavy water reactors by producing much higher outlet temperatures than these other reactors. The higher the outlet temperature, the more efficient the heat transfer system. These reactors, therefore, promise reduced power costs per unit investment. When operating on a thorium fuel cycle, these systems also function as breeders, producing new fuel which can be consumed in the same reaction.

Fast reactors are the principal variety of breeder reactors. These systems offer the advantage of vastly reduced fuel costs, resulting from the almost total burn-up rates of initial fuel cores. In natural uranium reactors, burn-up efficiency (amount of heat obtained per unit fuel) is so low that the fuel has to be reprocessed and recycled through the reactor several times before the fuel is economically used up. In fast reactors, a process of breeding permits the attainment of much higher burn-up rates. Fast reactors employ a mixed fuel core of a small amount of highly fissile material (enriched uranium or plutonium) and a large amount of nonfissile material (uranium 238). Through neutron absorption, the latter is converted to fissile material and burned up. By converting nonfissile to fissile fuel for use in the same reaction, fast reactors eliminate the costly requirement of unloading and reprocessing unspent fuel. Through such efficient use of fuel, fast reactors offer the greatest promise for conserving nuclear fuel resources, a factor which has increased interest and investment in these systems as the crisis over energy resource shortages has grown.

One final matter of terminology needs clarification. The reactor families are broken down into generation sequences to denote levels of development as well as differences of function. Proven or first-generation reactors include light water and gas graphite reactors. These are systems having undergone most extensive development to date. While most advanced technically, however, these systems are generally inefficient fuel users. In the recent concern over energy conservation, this fact has contributed to growing criticism of nuclear power development.

Heavy water and high temperature systems classify as intermediate-generation reactors. This designation suggests that these reactors represent intermediate levels of sophistication and perform an intermediate function of power and fuel production between the commercialization of first- and second-generation systems. One of the economic functions of intermediate-generation reactors is to convert nonfissile fuel to plutonium for use in later, second-generation reactors. For this reason, these systems are sometimes called converters. Such systems (for example, high temperature gas reactors) offer improvements in fuel conservation over first-generation systems. By converting nonfissile to fissile fuel, they provide a supply of fissionable material for use in other reactors. Whereas first-generation reactors exhaust the fissile materials in natural fuels, intermediate systems replace these fissile materials with newly converted fuels.

Second-generation reactors, primarily fast reactors, offer still another advantage and thus represent the most advanced stage of fission reactor development. These reactors, as we noted before, not only convert fuel to a fissionable state but use this fuel in the same reaction. Fuels are consumed most efficiently both in terms of cost and conservation. If fast reactors are eventually superseded in terms of level of sophistication, fusion reactors appear to be the next step. These reactors employ the principle of thermonuclear fusion (hydrogen bomb) rather than atomic fission (atomic bomb).

INDEX

ACEC, 89–90, 149n, 152, 262
Action Committee for the United States of Europe, 99
Additional (special) programs, 113–14, 116, 118, 120, 212–13, 230
Adenauer, Konrad, 100, 139n, 148, 244
Advanced societies: parochialism in, 61–62; professional class in, 29–30; role of, 28
AEG: license ties of, with GE, 86n, 144, 148, 151; relations of, with Siemens, 87, 203; relations of, with SNECMA, 141n, 152; role of, in German fast reactor program, 228, 229, 233. *See also* Nuclear industry, in Germany
AGIP-Nucleare, 88, 153, 207n
Aigrain, Pierre, 120. *See also* Maréchal group
AKB project, 167, 170n, 179
AKS project, 139n
Albonetti, Achille, 50n, 56n
ALKEM, 221
Allison, Graham T., 18n
Alsthom, 83, 84, 132, 153
Ansaldo Meccanico Nucleare, 88, 160
APC, 86n, 200, 207
Architecte industriel (industrial architect): use of, in France, 82–83; use of, in ORGEL, 168. *See also* CEA, industrial policies of
Armand, Louis, 103, 106, 130n, 132n, 137
Association contract, 110, 111; comparison of DRAGON agreement with, 192–94; and fast reactor development, 212–35; and German AVR/THTR project, 196–98
Atlantic relations: current characteristics of, 266–70; and European technology, 43–65
Atomic energy. *See* Nuclear energy
Atomics International, 86n, 166n, 168n, 169, 262
Atoms for Peace Plan, 106, 140, 254–55. *See also* United States, motivations of, in cooperation with Euratom
Auger, Pierre, 91

Note: For explanation of acronyms, see List of Abbreviations, p. xv.

Austria, 190
Aviation sector, 35, 48, 63, 64, 263n
AVR/THTR project, 86, 184n, 189–90; association of, with Euratom, 196–98; competition of DRAGON and, 200–207

Babcock and Wilcox (U.S. parent firm), 151; subsidiary of, in France, 180n; subsidiary of, in Germany, 151, 234–35
Balke, Siegfried, 102, 131n
Bayernwerk, 75, 144
BBC: and fast reactors, 234n; and high temperature gas reactors, 189, 200, 201, 207, 208, 209–10 and light water reactors, 151. *See also* BBK
BBK: and fast reactors, 234n; and high temperature gas reactors, 189, 196, 198, 200, 204–5, 206, 207, 209
Belgian CEA, 80. *See also* Belgium
Belgium: economic dimensions of nuclear programs in, 89–90; nuclear relations of, with France, 82, 89, 144, 151–52; nuclear relations of, with Germany, 228–29; policy of, toward Euratom, 107, 108, 110, 112, 120, 157, 166, 168n, 181n, 201n, 228; political dimensions of nuclear programs in, 68, 79–80; scientific dimensions of nuclear programs in, 94; and U.S. investments, 53
Belgonucléaire, 89, 166, 214, 220n, 229; relations of, with TNPG, 153, 200, 203, 207n
Ben-David, Joseph, 91, 244n
Benelux countries, 52, 97, 101, 116, 132, 157, 218, 230, 257. *See also* Belgium; Luxembourg; Netherlands
BNDC, 207, 208, 209
Boretsky, Michael, 59n
BR-2, 165, 182; competition of, with ESSOR, 166–68
Brzezinski, Zbigniew, 9, 11n, 19n, 28n
Burn, Duncan, 100n, 146n, 200n

Calder Hall, 131n, 200
Calleo, David P., 20n, 35n, 264n
Camps, Miriam, 187, 245n
Canada: cooperation of, with Euratom, 106, 162n, 169; cooperation of, with

THE JOHNS HOPKINS UNIVERSITY PRESS

This book was composed in Times Roman text by the Jones Composition Company from a design by Edward Scott. It was printed on S. D. Warren's 60-lb. regular text color paper and bound in Holliston Roxite cloth by The Maple Press Company.

Library of Congress Cataloging in Publication Data

Nau, Henry R   1941–
   National politics and international technology.

   Includes bibliographical references.
   1. Atomic energy industries—Europe. 2. Nuclear reactors. 3. Technology—Europe. I. Title.
HD9698.E82N3   338.4′7′621483094   73-19344
ISBN 0-8018-1506-1